APOSTLE
of the
LAST DAYS

THE LIFE, LETTERS, AND THEOLOGY OF PAUL

APOSTLE
of the
LAST DAYS

THE LIFE, LETTERS AND THEOLOGY OF PAUL

C. MARVIN PATE

Kregel
Academic

Apostle of the Last Days: The Life, Letters and Theology of Paul
© 2013 by C. Marvin Pate

Published by Kregel Publications, a division of Kregel, Inc., P.O. Box 2607, Grand Rapids, MI 49501.

The Greek font GraecaU is available from www.linguistsoftware.com/lgku.htm, +1-425-775-1130.

Library of Congress Cataloging-in-Publication Data
Pate, C. Marvin, 1952-
   Apostle of the last days : the life, letters and theology of Paul / by C. Marvin Pate.
     pages cm
   ISBN 978-0-8254-3892-9

  1. Bible. Epistles of Paul—Criticism, interpretation, etc. I. Title.
  BS2650.52.P345 2013
  227'.06—dc23

                                 2013002401

ISBN 978-0-8254-3892-9

Printed in the United States of America
13 14 15 16 17 / 5 4 3 2 1

A book is a collaborative effort and this one is no exception.

I wish to thank first of all Kregel and its fine staff for guiding me through the process of writing this monograph on Paul.

Next, I continue to deeply appreciate the students, administration, and my colleagues here at Ouachita Baptist University for their support and encouragement to research and write.

Then, I sincerely appreciate my work study, Elisabeth Crecink, for helping to type this manuscript. It was a herculean effort on her part to read my writing but she did so exceedingly well.

Finally, I dedicate this work to my precious, newest grandson, Cole Ramsay. I pray that he and his dear brother Ethan will grow up to be men of God even like the apostle Paul himself!

CONTENTS

Introduction

Next to Jesus Christ, the apostle Paul is the most important figure in the Christian faith. His life, letters and theology indelibly shaped Christianity for centuries to come. Some of the greatest church leaders have accorded an exalted place to the apostle to the Gentiles: Peter honored him (2 Peter 3:15–16); Augustine appealed to him; Luther adored him; Wesley found assurance in him; Barth thundered forth because of him; and Old and New perspectives toward Paul alike extol him as their own.[1]

Paul was a product of three worlds: Greco-Roman, Jewish, and Christian. These influences impacted Paul in increasing significance, like concentric circles. At the periphery of Paul's world was the Greco-Roman sphere of influence. Like most travelers in the Roman Empire in the middle of the first century AD, Paul spoke the trade language bequeathed to the masses of his day—koine (common) Greek. Koine Greek evolved from Classical Greek language and dialects of the conquered peoples in the domain of Alexander the Great (ca. 330 BC). Koine Greek was to its day what English is to our day. The influence of Greek culture on Paul is also evident in the way he drew upon ancient Greek philosophical traditions such as Platonism, Stoicism, and Epicureanism, even if by way of refutation. Paul also utilized Greek rhetoric, like the diatribe, the fool's speech, *peristasis* (afflictions) lists, etc. And, of course, the concept of the *polis* (city) and even democracy had a constant bearing on Paul's day to day experiences. Mighty Rome also obviously cast its long shadow across the

---

1   We will have more to say about some of these individuals and perspectives in chapters below.

then-known world and Paul made much use of its contributions: *pax Romana* (the peace of Rome), brought by Caesar Augustus (31 BC–AD 14) to a world torn by civil war and terrorized by pirates on the sea and robbers on the land; a pervasive and sturdy infrastructure; and a fair-minded jurisprudence system that transcended the petty politics of local towns. Indeed, the last-mentioned amenity ensured Paul an audience with the court of Rome, where the apostle was bound and determined to visit (Acts 25:10–28:31).

But Paul was born and raised a Jew. Though reared in the Gentile city of Tarsus, Paul was probably taken by his parents as a young person to Jerusalem to be trained to be a Pharisee, a rabbi (Acts 22:2–3). There he surpassed his peers in his grasp of the Torah and the oral tradition of the Pharisees, and in his love for the land of Israel. Indeed, Paul was so die-hard Jewish that he devoted himself to stamping out Judaism's newest rival—Christianity. Paul's zeal for Moses, his loathing for Gentiles, and his hatred of Jesus the crucified Messiah, drove him to the point of violence against the church. He relates his passion for Judaism and contempt for the church especially in Galatians 1:11–14; Philippians 3:4–6; and 1 Timothy 1:13; cf. Acts 9:1–2.

However, a "funny" thing happened to Paul the Pharisee on his way to Damascus to persecute Christians—he got saved through an encounter with the risen Christ (Gal. 1:15–16; Phil. 3:7–11; cf. Acts 9:3–18; 22: 2–21; 26:4–23). There Paul surrendered to the crucified Jesus who was none other than the glorious Lord and, in a divine touché, Paul the Gentile-basher was there and then called to be an apostle to the nations. In the flash of an instant, Paul exchanged the law of Moses for faith in Christ, hatred of non-Jews for love of the church, the land of Israel for the kingdom of God, and circumcision and the old covenant for the cross of Calvary. Paul's encounter with the risen Jesus was nothing short of both a conversion and a calling.[2] Indeed, God's setting apart of Paul to preach to the Gentiles the gospel of Jesus Christ was the beginning of the fulfillment of the end-time prophecy of the conversion of the nations predicted by Old Testament prophets like Isaiah, Micah, and others.[3]

With the preceding influences in mind—Greco-Roman, Judaism, and

---

2   We will discuss in chapter one the issue of what one should call the nature of Paul's Damascus experience.

3   See our discussion below also in chapter one.

especially Christianity—we now turn to two major points in introducing Paul: (1) his letters, life and theology and (2) Paul's ministry as involving a conflict in eschatologies.

PAUL'S LETTERS, LIFE, AND THEOLOGY

In this section, we discuss Paul's letters from both the traditional and non-traditional perspectives. Then we enter into a discussion of the importance of the book of Acts for understanding Paul's life, noting the debate such a discussion has generated. Finally we survey the competing schools of thought that have claimed to be the center of Paul's theology.

Paul's Letters

Thirteen letters are attributed to Paul in the New Testament, which have traditionally been grouped into four categories: Paul's early epistles (Galatians, 1 and 2 Thessalonians); Paul's major epistles (Romans, 1 and 2 Corinthians); his prison epistles (Philippians, Ephesians, Colossians, and Philemon); and the pastoral epistles (1 and 2 Timothy and Titus).

The traditional approach to Paul's letters, however, has for the last century or so been vociferously challenged by less conservatively inclined scholars. This group attributes only seven of the so-called Pauline letters to the apostle himself—Galatians, Romans, 1 and 2 Corinthians, 1 Thessalonians, Philippians, and Philemon; the rest they think were written by Paul's students after the apostle's death in about AD 64. Therefore the latter "pseudonymous" writings are not to be given serious attention in crafting Paul's theology. This left wing of Pauline scholarship bases its claim essentially on three arguments. First, the vocabulary of the disputable letters is different from that of the indisputable Pauline letters. Second, the history presumed by the pastoral epistles does not match the events of Paul's letters nor the accounts of Paul's travels as recorded in Acts. Third, the theology of the pseudonymous letters is at odds with the real Pauline epistles.

The traditional responses to the above argument are as follows: First, the differences in vocabulary between the disputable and indisputable letters of Paul can rather easily be accounted for by realizing that Paul used different secretaries in his letters (Romans 16:22 names Tertius as one of them) and that the different circumstances of each church to which Paul wrote called for various vocabulary. Second, there is good reason for postulating the theory that Paul was released from his Roman captivity recorded in Acts 28 (somewhere around AD 62), after which he conducted a mission trip to Spain (see Romans 15) and perhaps elsewhere, but then in ca. AD 64 was rounded up with Peter and other Christians to be tried by Emperor Nero in Rome. There, reliable tradition tells us, Paul and Peter were martyred for their faith in Christ. Indeed, the fact that Luke, Paul's sometime missionary companion and author of Acts, does not record Paul's death in Acts 28 decidedly points toward the theory we have been advancing. Third, the overall theology of the indisputable letters of Paul—the overlapping of the two ages (see below)—is also the driving engine of the disputable Pauline letters, as more than one scholar has noted. And, if that is the case for the major theme of Paul's thought, then why should one doubt that it is the same or similar for Paul's minor themes?[4]

Paul's Life as Documented in Acts

Because there is precious little autobiographical material in Paul's letters (mainly Gal. 1–2; Rom. 1; Phil. 3), one must turn to the book of Acts to compile a summary of the story of his life for therein Luke, Paul's missionary compatriot, records Paul's conversion, three missionary journeys, final trip to Jerusalem, and travel to Rome. In tracking Luke's association with Paul, three points need to be addressed: the biblical data, the liberal challenge, and the conservative response. The biblical picture of the relationship between Luke and Paul is straightforward: Luke was a fellow worker and companion of Paul (Philem. 24) who was dear to the apostle's heart (Col. 4:14). Moreover, if the "we" sections of Acts (16:10–17; 20:5–15; 21:1–18; 27:1–28:16) include Luke as a member of Paul's missionary team (as many think they do), then an intimate working relationship between the two is thereby confirmed.

However, the traditional perspective has not gone uncriticized. During the twentieth century, liberal scholars attempted to drive a wedge between Luke (especially regarding the book of Acts) and Paul, arguing that the former is at odds with the latter. The classic expression of this approach is the article

---

4 For documentation and a bibliography dealing with these three liberal arguments and the traditional counter-arguments, the reader is referred to the Introduction in my *The End of the Age Has Come: The Theology of Paul* (Grand Rapids: Zondervan, 1995).

by Paul Vielhauer.[5] That author popularized four apparent differences, or contradictions, between Luke and Paul. First, comparing Acts 17:22–30 (Luke's presentation of Paul's speech at the Areopagus before the philosophers of Athens) with Romans 1:18–21 (Paul's discussion of natural revelation), Vielhauer claimed that Luke's positive portrayal of Paul's attitude toward natural theology is opposed to Paul's own negative attitude toward the same. Second, Luke provides a positive statement on Paul's view of the law of Moses, whereas the apostle himself reaches the opposite conclusion in his letters. Third, Vielhauer maintained that Acts understands Paul's Christology to be adoptionist in nature (Jesus became deity only at his resurrection) and void of a theology of the cross; teachings at variance with the true message of Paul. Fourth, the Lucan picture of Paul detracts from the centrality of eschatology which is characteristic of Paul's thought. That is to say, the doctrine of the end times, which is such a constituent part of Paul's epistles, finds no place in Acts.

In response to this challenge, evangelicals have demonstrated that the preceding inconsistencies are more imaginary than real. E. Earle Ellis' critique is a good example of this line of argumentation. His reply counters Vielhauer point by point.[6] Concerning the first alleged difference, Ellis observes that Acts 17 does not teach that humankind possesses redemptive life by nature, apart from the gospel, something with which Paul would agree. Second, Luke and Paul are in substantial agreement that salvation does not come from keeping the Law (cf. Acts 15 and Gal. 1–2). Third, Acts 13:33, 37 (cf. 2:31, 36) do not teach that Jesus became the Son of God at the resurrection but, rather, that the resurrection proved that he already was the Son of God. This is fully in line with Romans 1:3–4. Moreover, Luke does indeed have a theology of the cross, as is evident in the mutual fate of Jesus and his followers (Luke 9:23; 22:35; Acts 7:60), including Paul (Acts 21:11; 23–34). Fourth, Ellis joins a chorus of scholars who cogently demonstrate that in the teachings of both Luke and Paul the kingdom of God is present spiritually now, and in the future will be a physical reality; that is, the already/not yet paradigm. Both writers are informed, therefore, by the same eschatological tension that exists between the

---

5   Paul Vielhauer, "On the 'Paulinism' of Acts" in *Studies in Luke-Acts*. Studies in Biblical Theology, ed. Leander E. Keck and J. Louis Martyn (Nashville: Abingdon, 1966), pp.33–50.
6   E. Earle Ellis, *The Gospel of Luke*. New Century Bible (London: Nelson, 1974), pp.46–47.

first and second comings of Christ. In light of this discussion, it seems to us that Luke has indeed provided us with an accurate reading of Paul and, therefore, we very much need to include his data in our treatment of the apostle.

Paul's Theology

Here we briefly survey four approaches to identifying a center in Paul's thought: justification by faith; the Tübingen school; the history of religions approach; and eschatology. The importance of this discussion proceeds from the valid assumption that if one can identify the key to the apostle's thought, then one has found therein a frame of reference for interpreting Paul's letters.

With the Protestant Reformation, justification by faith became the leading contender to be the center of Paul's theology (at least among non-Catholics), especially taking into consideration Galatians, Romans, and Philippians (chapter 3). The thesis of those letters is that the sinner is declared righteous before God through simple faith in Jesus Christ, not by the works of the Torah/ the law of Moses. Now, to be sure, justification by faith is a major player in Paul's theology, as we will see in his letters to the Galatians and Romans. But Pauline scholars of the last century observed that, as important as justification is to Paul, it nevertheless is not pervasive in the rest of Paul's writings. Rather, the doctrine of justification by faith seems to have been a teaching that Paul explained and defended vis-á-vis the Judaizers' influence on some, but not all, of the churches to which he wrote. In other words, Paul's apologetic for justification by faith was a polemic against the false teaching of the Judaizers that salvation is by faith in Christ plus obedience to the Torah. Justification by faith, according to these scholars, most probably is not, then, the overarching theme driving the Pauline corpus. But it should be observed that other scholars like Ernst Käsemann argued that justification by faith, wedded with eschatology (see below), is indeed the substructure of Paul's letters. We tend to agree with this counter claim.

The Tübingen theory is named after said German university and was associated with one of that institution's leading theologian-professors—F.C. Baur. In the mid to late nineteenth century, Baur claimed that the key to understanding Paul and, indeed, the entire New Testament, is to see that a theological civil war runs throughout its pages: Paul's message of justification by faith versus Peter's message of justification by faith plus the works of the Torah (so too the Judaizers). It was left to the anonymous work of Acts in the second century to paint an idyllic portrait of the early church, in which Paul and Peter come across as being the best of buddies.[7] Although the Tübingen perspective enjoyed enormous popularity among New Testament interpreters on the Continent during the nineteenth century and the first part of the twentieth century, its influence all but vanished in the second half of the twentieth century thanks to two developments. First, scholars recognized Baur's theory for what it really was—the foisting upon the New Testament the dialectic philosophy of Hegel: thesis (Paul's message) versus anti-thesis (Peter's message) resulting in a synthesis (Acts' reconciliation of the two). In other words, the theology of Paul, and the New Testament, was distorted by imposing philosophical categories on it. Second, no reputable theologian today doubts that Luke wrote Acts and that he did so in the late first century not the middle to late second century.

In the first half of the twentieth century another hypothesis arose concerning the center of Paul's theology—the history of religions school. Although there were various constructs under the umbrella of this approach, they shared the commonality that Paul gave up his Jewish faith for Hellenistic (Greek) religion, whether that was the Greek mystery religions (so Richard Reitzenstein), Hellenistic mysticism (so Adolf Deissmann), or Platonic Gnosticism (so Rudolph Bultmann).[8] The history of religions approach is still championed today by a few high profile radical scholars (for example, the Jesus Seminar, Elaine Pagels, Bart Ehrman), but most Pauline scholars today rather argue that Paul was true to his Jewish heritage and that therefore Hellenistic influence was at the periphery, not the center, of his theology. This is so even after duly noting

---

7   The key works of Baur are *Paul, the Apostle of Jesus Christ: His Life and Work, His Epistles and His Doctrine* (London: Williams and Norgate, 1873) and *The Church History of the First Three Centuries*, 3rd ed.(London: Williams and Norgate, 1878–79).

8   The reader can pursue these theories in the Introduction to my *The End of the Age Has Come*. The Greek mystery religions were secret religious cults that claimed that rites like baptism and sacred meals unified the worshipper with Isis, Cybele, or other Greek deities. Hellenistic mysticism, whereby the worshipper was thought to be deified, was a more general phenomenon that pervaded Greco-Roman spirituality. Gnosticism was a second to third century aberration of Christianity that, in good Platonic fashion, disparaged the body but extolled the soul. One can see Plato's anthropological dualism in this—matter is evil and spirit/soul alone is good. An incipient form of Gnosticism—Docetism (Christ was divine but only appeared to be human)—is refuted by the epistles of John. It would fall to early Church Fathers like Irenaeus and Tertullian in the second century to refute the full-blown Gnosticism that threatened the church of their day.

the interpenetration of Hellenism and Judaism in the first century.[9] We will see in this work that Hellenistic religion made its most significant impact on some of Paul's churches and opponents.

The fourth contender for the center of Paul's thought is Jewish eschatology, but in revised form. Albert Schweitzer in the early twentieth century convinced most New Testament scholars that the two-age structure of the writings of Second Temple Judaism (the time between the rebuilding of the second temple in Jerusalem in 519 BC until its destruction by the Romans in AD 70) was the key to, not only Jesus' message, but also Paul's theology. Apocalyptic Judaism was a dominant strand of Jewish theology by the time of Jesus, teaching that history divides into two ages: this age of sin and sorrow because of Adam's fall and the age to come/kingdom of God, a period of unprecedented righteousness and peace; and it would be the Messiah who would establish the latter.[10] Most Pauline scholars today believe this is the key to the thought of Jesus, Paul, and indeed the whole of the New Testament.[11] And with this we agree. But there is a significant difference between the ancient Jewish two-age scenario and the New Testament, namely, whereas the former expected that the two ages would be consecutive (when the Messiah comes he will completely replace this age with the age to come), the latter claims that the two ages are simultaneous; that is, they overlap. Thus, with the life, death, and resurrection of Jesus Christ the age to come/kingdom of God broke into this present age but without ending it. This is often labeled "inaugurated eschatology"—with the first coming of Christ the age to come *already* dawned but it is *not yet* complete, awaiting the second coming of Christ for that. Most Pauline scholars take this fourth view to be the key to understanding Paul's theology. The following charts by Gordon Fee nicely expresses this view,[12] first from the Jewish perspective and then from the Christian adaptation of that perspective:

---

9   The classic work on the subject is by Martin Hengel, *Judaism and Hellenism*, 2 vols. (Philadelphia: Fortress Press, 1974).

10 For thorough documentation of this point, see again my work, *The End of the Age Has Come* and the works cited there.

11 The classic defense of this approach is the work by George Ladd and updated by Donald A. Hagner, *A Theology of the New Testament* (Grand Rapids, MI.: Eerdmans, 1993).

12 Gordon D. Fee, *Paul, the Spirit, and the People of God* (Peabody, MA: Hendrickson, 1996), p.50.

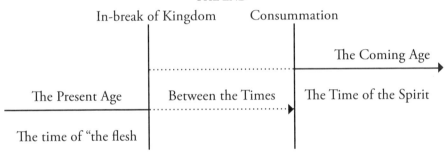

OLD JEWISH VIEW:

The Present Age	The Coming Age
	(or the Kingdom of God)

The Time of Satan	The Time of God
Sin, Sickness, and Death	*Righteousness, Wholeness,*
No Spirit of God	*and Eternal Life*
	God's Holy Spirit

THE CHRISTIAN VIEW:

THE END

In-break of Kingdom   Consummation

The Coming Age

| The Present Age | Between the Times | The Time of the Spirit |

The time of "the flesh"

But we need to nuance the preceding point by noting three eschatological constructs that have been applied to the message of Jesus and by way of application to Paul's apocalypticism: consistent eschatology, inaugurated eschatology, and realized eschatology. "Consistent eschatology" is a label applied by New Testament scholars to the works of Albert Schweitzer, a late nineteenth-century biblical scholar. "Consistent" means futurist, with reference to how Schweitzer interpreted the message of Jesus. As we saw above, Judaism at the time of Christ divided history into two periods: this age of sin, when sin rules; and the age to come, when the Messiah is expected to bring the kingdom of God to earth. Schweitzer concluded that an apocalyptic understanding of the kingdom was not only foundational for Christ's teaching, but also to understanding his life. Thus Schweitzer maintained that Jesus believed it was his vocation to become the coming Son of Man. Initially Jesus revealed this messianic secret only to Peter, James, and John. Later, Peter told it to the rest of the twelve. Judas told the secret to the High Priest who used it as the ground for Jesus' execution (Mark 14:61–64; cf. Dan. 7:13).

According to Schweitzer's interpretation, when Jesus sent out the twelve on a mission to proclaim the coming kingdom of God, he did not expect them to return. The Twelve were the "violent people" (Matt. 11:12) who would provoke the messianic tribulation that would herald the kingdom. Whereas some earlier Jewish theologians believed that one could only wait passively for the kingdom, Schweitzer believed that the mission of Jesus was designed to provoke its coming. When this did not happen, Jesus determined to give his own life as a ransom for many (Mark 10:45) and so cause the kingdom to come.

[handwritten margin note: TRUE BUT I.T. DIDN'T COME AS A SURPRISE TO GOD.]

According to Schweitzer, Jesus took matters into his own hands by precipitating his death, hoping that would be the catalyst for causing God to make the wheel of history turn to its climax—the arrival of the kingdom of God. But, said Schweitzer, Jesus was wrong again, and he died in despair. So, for Schweitzer, Jesus never witnessed the dawning of the age to come; it lay in the distant future, separated from this present age.

[handwritten margin note: GOD DOESN'T "HOPE"]

Evangelical New Testament scholars today generally reject most of Schweitzer's conclusions regarding his "consistent eschatology," especially his disregard for the reliability of the Gospels. On the positive side, he did call attention to the fact that the message of Jesus is rooted in the concept of the kingdom of God, a connection that is still foundational to a proper understanding of biblical prophecy and the Gospels today, even though most current New Testament scholars today interpret that connection quite differently than Schweitzer did.

"Realized Eschatology," in contrast to futurist eschatology where the kingdom of God awaits a final consummation at the end of history, views the kingdom of God as already realized in the person and mission of Jesus. The futurist aspects of Jesus' teaching are reduced to a minimum and his apocalyptic language is viewed as symbolic of theological truths.

The person most responsible for advocating this position was the British scholar C. H. Dodd. In his 1935 book *Parables of the Kingdom*, Dodd focused on Jesus' teachings that announced the arrival of the kingdom with his coming. For instance, in Luke 11:20 Jesus says, "But if I drive out demons by the finger of God, then the kingdom of God has come to you" (cf. Luke 17:21; Matthew

13). Eschatology becomes a matter of the present experience rather than any kind of future event. The kingdom has fully come in the messianic ministry of Jesus.

Most interpreters have criticized Dodd's realized eschatology for ignoring Jesus' teachings that point to a future consummation of the kingdom (e.g., Mark 13; Matthew 24–25). When all of Jesus' teachings are considered, futurist eschatology balances realized eschatology. To be sure, the kingdom arrived with Jesus, but Jesus himself taught that history still awaits a final completion. The kingdom of God is both "already" and "not yet"; which leads us to the third view of the relationship of the kingdom of God to the ministry of Jesus Christ.

"Inaugurated Eschatology" is a concept commonly connected with the twentieth-century Swiss theologian Oscar Cullmann. Like others before him, Cullmann understood that the Jewish notion of the two ages formed an important background for understanding the message of Jesus. According to Judaism, history is divided into two periods: this age of sin and the age to come (i.e. the kingdom of God). For Jews, the advent of the Messiah would affect the shift from the former to the latter. In other words, Judaism viewed the two ages as consecutive. According to Cullmann, Jesus Christ announced that the end of time, the kingdom of God, had arrived *in* history (see Mark 1:15 and parallels; especially Luke 4:43; 6:20; 7:28; 8:1, 10; 9:2, 11, 27, 60, 62; 10:9, 11; 11:20; 13:18, 20; 16:16; 17:20–21; 18:16, 17, 24–25, 29; Acts 28:31). Yet other passages suggest that, although the age to come had *already* dawned, it *was not* yet complete. It awaited the Second Coming for its full realization (Luke 13:28, 29; 14:15; 19:11; 21:31; 22:16, 18; 23:51; Acts 1:6), hence the name "inaugurated" eschatology. Such a view is pervasive in the New Testament besides the Gospels (see, for example: Acts 2:17–21; 3:18, 24; 1 Cor. 15:24; 1 Tim. 4:1; 2 Tim. 3:1; Heb. 1:2; 1 John 2:18). So, for inaugurated eschatology, the two ages are simultaneous: the age to come exists in the midst of this present age. Christians therefore live in between the two ages until the parousia (second coming of Christ). We have argued elsewhere that inaugurated eschatology best describes Paul's apocalypticism.[13] Moreover, we will see in the body of this study that the above three labels—consistent eschatology, inaugurated eschatology,

---

13 See the author's *The End of the Age Has Come.*

and realized eschatology—are at work concerning Paul's opponents, as reflected in his letters and in his missionary endeavors as recorded in Acts.

Paul's Ministry As Conflict in Eschatologies

The book of Acts reinforces the impression one gets from Paul's letters that his ministry was one governed by opposition. Such opposition cannot be explained solely by Paul's forceful personality or his Jewish heritage. Rather, Paul's vigorous debates with and regarding the churches he served centered on the exclusivity of the gospel of Christ that he preached, the non-negotiable apocalypse of Jesus the Messiah. Our work will seek to document this claim. For now, we set the table for that discussion by calling attention to at least six types of eschatology that were current in the first century AD relative to Paul's opposition (including Paul's own teaching of inaugurated eschatology). Those six religious perspectives were: (1) non-*merkabah* (chariot-throne, with reference to the worshipper being caught up to heaven to view the chariot-throne of God; see more on this below) non-Christian Judaism (consistent eschatology), (2) Paul's inaugurated eschatology, (3) non-*merkabah* Judaizers (inaugurated eschatology), (4) the Roman imperial cult, (5) Hellenistic/syncretistic religion, and (6) *merkabah* Judaizers—who we will call "merkabizers" (realized eschatology).

Helmut Koester has identified five components of realized eschatology in the Roman imperial cult.[14] We agree with his five components model and would suggest that the same five components also pertained to all of the above eschatologies in their respective ways except non-*merkabah*, non-Christian Judaism (which espoused consistent eschatology).[15] We now offer the following taxonomy of eschatology regarding the preceding religious perspectives, after which we offer a brief summary of each:

---

14 Helmut Koester, "Jesus the Victim," *Journal of Biblical Literature* 111/1 (1992) pp. 3–15.

15 We will distinguish more explicitly these models of eschatology in the respective chapters to follow. We might mention here that we know from non-Christian Jewish mystic texts that merkabah mysticism abounded in Second Temple Judaism, and apparently came into contact with Paul's churches, or at least a Christian variety of it. We do not include non-Christian Judaism in the chart due to its consistent exchatology stance. But we will incorporate this model in chapter 12.

FIVE COMPONENTS OF ESCHATOLOGY	HELLENISTIC RELIGION (realized eschatology)	ROMAN IMPERIAL CULT (realized eschatology)	MERKABAH JUDAIZERS (realized eschatology)	PAUL (inaugurated eschatology)	NON-MERKABAH JUDAIZERS (inaugurated eschatology)
1) The New Age has dawned	The New Age/Heaven is entered into now through mystical union with the deity	The primordial age is the New Age dawned	The mystic is caught up to heaven in Christ where he/she experiences the age to come in heaven, even before it comes to earth in the form of the kingdom of God	The Age to come/kingdom of Christ and God has dawned and it is received by faith apart from the law of Moses	The Age to come/ kingdom of Christ and God has dawned and with it the power to obey the law of Moses
2) It is cosmic and universal	This mystical union transcends earth by joining the initiate with heaven and the cosmos	It includes the earth and heaven and is universal	The age to come is both cosmic and historical. It is the future age to come (historical) dawning in heaven before it arrives on earth (cosmic)	New Creation	New Creation
3) A Savior inaugurates the New Age	Union with the Deity (Greco-Roman pantheon, Osiris, etc.)	Caesar Augustus	Christ is the heavenly, preexistent Son of Man, the Savior of Israel and of the Jewish mystic	Jesus the Messiah	Jesus the Messiah
4) The New Age/Savior is predicted in sacred writings	Fate and astrology/ and oracles/ sibyls	Priene Inscription and Virgil's *Eclogues*, etc.	Ezekiel 1 and Daniel 7, along with Old Testament prophecies about the coming of the Messiah, essentially equate the Son of Man with the Messiah. These texts (Ezek. 1 and Dan. 7) are interpreted in *Merkabah* Mysticism as prescribing how the believer can be caught up to heaven to experience Christ, the Son of Man/Messiah	OT Messianic prophecies	OT Messianic prophecies
5) The New Age is celebrated through rituals	Sacred meals and rituals celebrate the dawning of the New Age	The Birthday of Caesar and the Caesarean games	Fasting, acts of asceticism, and devotion to the law of Moses are the prerequisite rituals/celebrations for being caught up to the heavenly throne	Baptism and the Lord's Supper	Jewish feasts and Christian baptism and the Lord's Supper

Hellenistic/Syncretistic Religion

Here we follow the remarks of Helmut Koester in his description of the Hellenistic Religion, a syncretistic amalgamation of religious perspectives that coalesced between 300 and ca. 63 BC (from the Hellenization of the world begun by Alexander the Great to Rome's takeover of the world).[16] We suggest the following diagram to account for the various streams of tradition contributing to the mosaic of Hellenistic Religion:

Hellenistic/Syncretistic Religion [ca. 300 BC–AD200]

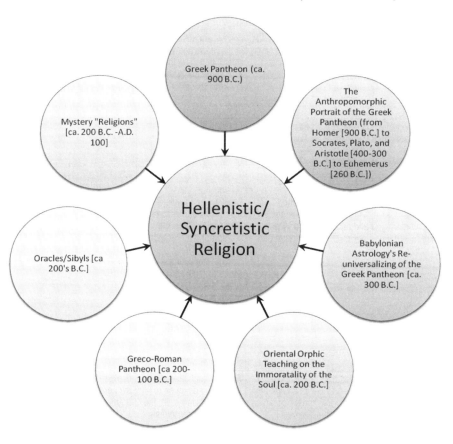

---

16 Helmut Koester, *History, Culture, and Religion of the Hellenistic Age* (Philadelphia: Fortress Press, 1982), pp. 141–204.

The upshot of our diagram is that the Greek pantheon of deities underwent an ebb and flow of development that eventually transformed it into Hellenistic syncretistic religion. Thus the original Greek pantheon attracted to it elements of other religions—Babylonian astrology, oriental Orphic teaching, the Roman pantheon of deities, Greek oracles and sibyls, and the mystery religions.

For our purposes, the five components of eschatology (in this case, realized) noted above can be identified in the Hellenistic Religion:

(1) The New Age, or heaven, can be experienced now through mystical union with the deity (whether the Greco-Roman pantheon of deities; Isis, wife/sister of Osiris; Demeter in Eleusis, or others in the mystery religions). Indeed, Plato's doctrine of illumination (whereby reason perceives the world of the ideas) prepared the way for such an understanding and mystical union with the deity.

(2) Mystical union with the deity transcends earth by joining the soul of the initiate with heaven and the cosmic (astrological) bodies.

(3) The Savior who brings the New Age/heaven is the particular deity with whom the devotee is united.

(4) Fate has determined the destiny of the initiate. Closer to Roman times, the oracles contained sacred predictions regarding those who sought them while the Sibyls recorded the defeat of anti-god forces and the exaltation of the faithful.

(5) Religious rituals such as baptism and sacred meals both united the devotee with the deity as well as celebrated their encounter. The preceding five components are seen in Apuleius' *Metamorphoses XI*, an Isis Aretalogy, a story told to exalt a deity, in this case Isis the Egyptian female deity. Book XI highlights the preceding five components, which I place here in chart form.

The chart summarizes the content of Book XI:

FIVE COMPONENTS OF REALIZED ESCHATOLOGY	REALIZED ESCHATOLOGY OF METAMORPHOSES BOOK XI
1) New Age dawned	Isis—mother of universe—is the first offspring of the ages (XI. 5) who brings salvation (XI. 12) /rebirth in Isis (XI. 25)
2) Cosmic/universal renewal	Through the mystery rites—the initiate joins the gods (XI. 21), is glorious (XI. 10) like the stars (XI. 10), and receives unutterable secrets (XI. 23)
3) Savior	Isis, the savior (XI. 25) who embodies all gods (XI. 5–6) and rules with Osiris (XI. 30)
4) Predicted through the sacred texts	Isis priests give divine promises/dreams/oracles to her followers (XI. 13)
5) New Age celebrated through rituals	Initiates join a processional that makes an offering to Isis (XI. 16), abstains from eating meat for 10 days (XI. 22, 28), participates in a ritual bath (XI. 23), etc.

The Roman Imperial Eschatology

Koester has identified five components of the Roman imperial cult beginning with Caesar Augustus that project the belief that the New Age has been realized (the same five we mentioned above).[17] (1) The primordial age, the New Age is here, (2) which encompasses earth and heaven. (3) This New Age has come because of Caesar Augustus. (4) Augustus' birth marked the beginning of a new day, and his *Pax Romana* has brought that New Age. (4) All of this is foretold by the poets. (5) Augustus' birthday and the Caesarean games celebrate this realized eschatology.

These five components can be found, for example, in Virgil's *Fourth Eclogue* and in the Priene Inscription.

Merkabah Judaizers

Merkabah (throne) mysticism was pervasive in Jewish apocalyptic circles in Second Temple Judaism and even beyond 134–135 AD, the second revolt of the Jews against Rome. *Merkabah* mysticism was based on Ezekiel 1 and

---

17 Helmut Koester, "Jesus the Victim," *Journal of Biblical Literature* 111/1 (1992) pp. 3–15.

Daniel 7 and the descriptions there of the faithful being caught up to heaven to see the throne of God and to commune with the preexistent Son of Man. Enoch's throne vision in *1 Enoch 14* seems to represent the oldest example of *merkabah* mysticism. Four comments about this type of mystic experience need to be made at this juncture. (1) The major texts fitting into this category are: *1 Enoch* 14:2; John; 2 Corinthians 12:1–7; Colossians 2; Revelation; *3 Enoch*; *Hagigah* 11b–16a; *Hekalot Rabbati*; etc. (2) The components of *merkabah* include: (a) rigorous preparation for the heavenly ascent via prayer and fasting; (b) mystic ascent through the seven "houses" or palaces of heaven; (c) negotiations with the angels assigned to each of the palaces by the use of magical formulae, seals, etc.; (d) danger accompanying the ascent; (e) vision of the glorious, divine throne chariot (*merkabah*). (3) Based on Ezekiel 1:15–21 (cf. other biblical throne visions in Ex. 24:10–11; 1 Kings 22:19; Isa. 6; Ezek. 3:22–24; 8:1–18; 10:9–17; 43:1–4; Dan. 7:9–14), one of the purposes of *merkabah* mysticism seems to have been to legitimate sectarian teaching, as is evidenced by Rabbinic attempts to monitor it (*Exod. Rab.* 43:8; m. Hag. 2:1; *b. Hag.* 14a; 15a; *Hek. Rab.* 20:1; *b. Sanh* 38b). (4) It may be that prior to 70 AD *merkabah* mysticism and Jewish apocalypticism were intermingled traditions, which would account for similarities between the two, but with the dashed hopes of Jewish apocalypticism due to the events between 70–135 AD, *merkabah* emerged as an independent movement. As we will document in the respective chapters to follow, one wing of the Judaizing movement embraced *merkabah* mysticism. These folk were professing Christians but whose Jewish roots influenced them to continue to keep the law of Moses. Paul dealt with this aberration of grace in 1 and 2 Corinthians, Philippians, and Colossians.

The five components of (realized) eschatology delineated above can be rather easily identified in the Judaizing *merkabah* mysticism: (1) The age to come is experienced now when the mystic is caught up to heaven. There the believer views the throne of God, communes with Jesus Christ the heavenly, preexistent Son of Man, and is given a vision of the age to come as it has dawned in heaven. (2) Such a vision encompasses both the cosmos and history. (3) The Savior is God but also Christ, the preexistent heavenly Son of Man with whom the mystic communes. Jesus, the Son of Man will soon come to earth to establish the kingdom of God in Israel. (4) Ezekiel 1 and Daniel 7 are viewed as the prophetic texts that invite the believer to mystically experience the throne of God and the Son of Man. These texts predict the coming of the Son of Man to earth, and the mystic's communion with him is a proleptic experience of that event. Jesus, Son of Man is identified with Israel's long-awaited Messiah, predicted in the Old Testament. (5) Fasting, acts of asceticism, and devotion to the law of Moses were the prerequisite rituals that needed to be observed in order for the believer to qualify to be "caught up to heaven."

Paul and the Apocalypse of Christ

We earlier identified inaugurated eschatology to be an important, if not the central, influence on the apostle Paul. That is to say, Paul believed (1) the age to come has dawned on earth (1 Cor. 10:11), which (2) is nothing less than a new creation (2 Cor. 5:17). (3) This is so because Jesus is the Messiah/Christ whose life, death, and resurrection inaugurated the kingdom of God. (4) Jesus is Israel's long-awaited Messiah foretold in the Old Testament. (5) Baptism and the Lord's Supper celebrate entrance into and continuation in the age to come, respectively.

Non-Merkabah Judaizers

This second wing of Judaizing Christians in the early church was not of the *merkabah* variety. This group tracked with Paul's inaugurated eschatology except these Judaizers maintained that salvation was based on faith in Jesus Christ plus obedience to the law of Moses. In their view, the eschatological presence of the Holy Spirit empowers the Christian to obey the Mosaic code: circumcision, dietary laws, Old Testament feasts, and all. But Paul begs to differ with this perspective in Galatians and Romans.

Our thesis for this work flows from the preceding discussion: the conflicts Paul encountered in the cities of the churches he founded and wrote to erupted as he presented his apocalypse of Christ in the face of the various eschatologies delineated above: Hellenistic religion, Roman imperial cult, Judaizing *merkabah* mysticism, Judaizing non-*merkabah* mysticism, and also non-Christian Judaism.

AND 6TH NON-CHRISTIAN JUDAISM (CONSISTENT ESCHATOLOGY)

DEVELOPMENT OF BOOK

Here's how the thesis is developed. Chapter 1 presents the view that Paul's conversion and call were eschatologically driven. This is based on Galatians 1, Romans 1, and Acts. More particularly, the four components comprising Paul's message were eschatological in nature and were rooted in his conversion/call: Jesus is the Messiah; his death and resurrection inaugurated the age to come; this salvation is entered into by faith not by obedience to the law of Moses; and Paul's target audience was Gentiles. Moreover, these four eschatological components of Paul's message would become flash points with the other eschatological constructs highlighted above.

Galatians is perhaps Paul's earliest letter and it sounds a theme dear to his heart: sinners are justified by faith in Christ apart from the law of Moses (Chapter 2). According to the apostle to the Gentiles, being justified by faith in Christ is God's present end-time acquittal of the believer. Indeed, justification before God is a blessing that Judaism relegated to the age to come but which Paul contends is granted in this age to Jews and Gentiles alike. According to Paul, the law of Moses has served its divinely intended purpose and has now run its course in this age. Paul develops this thesis vis-à-vis the non-*merkabah* Judaizers. This reading of Galatians is reinforced by Acts 13:13–15:35, which highlights the showdown between Paul's messianic eschatology and that of the Jewish synagogue. Also to be factored into this discussion is the role the imperial cult played in the crisis in Galatia.

The third chapter sees 1 Thessalonians as patently eschatological in perspective. It equates the sufferings of Jesus, Paul, and the Thessalonians with the messianic woes/great tribulation—those signs of the times that Judaism expected to occur right before the arrival of the Messiah. These afflictions Paul and Christians will continue to experience until the parousia.

Second Thessalonians picks up where 1 Thessalonians leaves off in its discussion of the signs of the end times, except that 2 Thessalonians focuses more on the not-yet aspect of the kingdom of God. This is so because some in the church at Thessalonica, influenced by the Hellenistic syncretistic religion, assumed that the age to come had fully arrived. To counteract such realized eschatology, Paul discusses a number of signs of the end times that were still in progress: the need to endure the messianic woes; the imminent appearance of the man of lawlessness; eschatological apostasy; the removal of the restrainer. In other words, the return of Christ had not yet occurred. This was no time for the Thessalonians, therefore, to stop working for a living and much less time to stop living a life of faithfulness to the Lord. Acts 17:1–15 adds to this picture by pitting Paul against not only Jewish teaching on the Messiah, but also against the Roman imperial cult. And adding fuel to the fire of opposition to Paul were the non-Christian Jews in Thessalonica.

Paul fought Christian opponents on two fronts in the Corinthian letters (Chapter 4). First, the Corinthian church mistakenly believed that by virtue of the possession of the Spirit it had fully entered into the kingdom of God. This belief was no doubt encouraged by the Hellenistic religion that dominated the city of Corinth as well as the teaching of the merkabizers—Jewish Christian mystics. First Corinthians is therefore Paul's correction of such realized eschatology by reminding the believers in Corinth that this age had not yet been replaced by the age to come. Thus: The wisdom of the Spirit (of the age to come) is available only in the cross of Christ (the sufferings of the messianic woes that culminate this age); the resurrection of the body (of the age to come) has not yet happened for the Christian and therefore the believer must resist the temptation to commit immorality (associated with this age); neither has mystical union with Christ through baptism and the Lord's Supper (sacraments that bespeak the presence of the age to come) delivered the Christian from this age and the need to demonstrate personal faith and obedience to God; spiritual gifts (especially tongues, interpretation of tongues and miracles) are not an indication that Christians have become like angels; and, the general resurrection has not yet occurred. Moreover, Acts 17:16–34 contributes to the portrait of Paul's opposition in 1 Corinthians in terms of the teaching of the Athenian philosophers.

By the time of the writing of 2 Corinthians things had taken a turn for the worse in the Corinthian church, for Paul's opposition there had further stirred up trouble between Paul and the Corinthian believers. Paul's apostolic affliction became the target of attack by these intruders, who looked down upon him compared to their divine wonder-workings born out of mystic experience. Paul responded to such criticism by emphasizing, in 2 Corinthians, that Paul and the believer live in the tension between the two ages. Acts 18:1–28 contributes to that discussion by highlighting non-Christian Jewish opposition to Paul's ministry in Corinth, as does also the presence of the imperial cult. Chapter 5 summarizes 1 and 2 Corinthians in light of the background material uncovered in Chapter 4.

Like Galatians, Romans presents the Christian's justification as God's end-time acquittal in this present age (Chapter 6). The key verses of Romans—1:16–17—make this clear: faith in Jesus Christ brings with it the good news that sinners are now declared righteous before God. Such a theme is apocalyptic in orientation in that the righteousness associated in Second Temple Judaism with the age to come is already a reality in this present age for believers in Christ. But to make this point, Paul first has to show that the law of Moses was intended by God to reveal the fact that no human can merit God's favor because in fact no human can keep the Mosaic code. This truth drives the sinner—Jew and Gentile alike—to faith in Christ alone for justification. This message is one the non-*merkabah* Judaizers needed to hear. Moreover, Israel though not comprehending this spiritual axiom at the present time, will according to Paul embrace Jesus as its Messiah at the end of history. Finally, Romans makes the point that the righteousness of the age to come transforms the behavior of the Christian and the church in this evil age. Furthermore, Romans subtly undermines Roman imperial eschatology. Acts 28 also factors into this discussion, revealing how entrenched non-Christian Jews became toward Paul's apocalypse of Christ.

In Philippians 2:12–13 Paul exhorts the Christians at Philippi to work out their salvation (Chapter 7). For the apostle, such a challenge is rooted in the overlapping of the two ages, namely, believers are to demonstrate the lifestyle of Christ in this present age which will complete their entrance into the age to come. So, like Christ, Christians should particularly demonstrate a willingness to suffer the messianic woes like Christ did (but which the *merkabah* Judaizers discredited) and to treat others with the same selflessness that Christ showed while he was on earth, all the while rejoicing in the Lord. Moreover, both Philippians and Acts 16:11–40 provide a countercultural message to the Roman imperial eschatology.

In Second Temple Judaism, mysticism and apocalypticism were related, especially in the form of *merkabah* mysticism (Chapter 8). *Merkabah* mysticism taught that Jews could be caught up to heaven to gaze upon the throne of

God if they obeyed the law of Moses, fasted, and performed ascetic practices. There in heaven the mystic saw the reality of the age to come before it actually appeared on earth. In Colossians, Paul counters such *merkabah* mysticism of the Judaizing variety by asserting that Christians are caught up to the throne of God by worshipping Christ, the fullness of the Godhead; not by obeying the law of Moses. In fact, the law of Moses is a part of this age, not the age to come. There in heaven Christians presently reign with Christ and experience the unfolding of the age to come/kingdom of God. But such spiritual, mystical union with Christ on the throne of God must result in a righteous lifestyle lived on earth. This is the true wisdom of God. As we will also see, Hellenistic religion in the Lycus Valley also fed into the Colossian heresy that Paul refutes in his letter to the Colossian church. Beside all of that, Paul also had to contend with the imperial cult in the city of Colossae.

Although there is no explicit mention of apocalyptic ideas in Philemon, the letter is informed by an implicit eschatological principle—namely, in Christ there is a reversal of earthly status (Chapter 9). Thus it is that Paul can presume upon Philemon to set his slave Onesimus free because the dawning of the age to come has relativized race, gender, and status. That is to say, in Christ there is neither Jew nor Gentile, male nor female, slave nor free (Gal. 3:28).

While some scholars contend that Ephesians has capitulated to realized eschatology and a triumphalist view of the church, the truth is that Ephesians is a spiritual call to Christians to their battle stations—in heaven (Chapter 10). *of this book* In other words, Christians are in Christ and have therefore been raised to the heavenlies with him, and there they encounter both blessing and battle. The blessings in heaven include forgiveness, the indwelling of the Spirit, reigning with Christ, the new temple of God that is composed of Jew and Gentile, etc. These blessings in Christ bespeak the fact that the Christian and the church participate in the age to come that dawned in heaven with Christ's death and resurrection. But heaven is also the scene for the end-time holy war against Satan (cf. 1:3–14 with 6:10–20; etc.). It is there that the church is engaged in a death struggle against the enemies of God. This reality bespeaks the fact that the age to come is not yet complete, not even in heaven. But the battle is the Lord's and ultimately the church will win. This message is designed to strengthen the faith of the Ephesian believers in the face of Hellenistic religion and the Roman imperial cult (cf. Acts 19:1–41). Paul's message to the Ephesians also served to sever wisdom from the law of Moses—a notion sure to anger some Jews.

Those who reject Pauline authorship of the Pastoral Epistles do so largely because they believe those letters abandon Paul's eschatological hope of a <u>parousia</u> in favor of a realized eschatology associated with the first coming of Christ and that consequently the Pastorals acquiesce to the standard ethic of the Greco-Roman world (Chapter 11). But it is more accurate to say that the epiphany scheme in the Pastorals conveys the time period between the first and second coming of Christ. Thus the Pastorals are deeply imprinted by inaugurated eschatology and it is that which shapes the author's ethic—a clarion call to endure the messianic woes in the face of a world hostile to the gospel. This is hardly a "bourgeois Christianity" designed to accommodate the ancient Greco-Roman world. Acts 19—once again—throws light on the Ephesian setting, this time regarding the Pastorals, where Hellenistic religion and Roman imperial eschatology coexisted. It may be also that Paul's Jewish opponents, as reflected in the Pastoral Letters, drank deeply from the well of Philonic thought, as we will see.

This concluding chapter takes a step back by overviewing Paul's theology as a whole by using the seven typical systematic categories as a grid through which to interpret Paul's writings. We state in advance the main idea that emerges from our investigation, leaving the chapter as a whole to fill out the details:

I. Paul's Theology Proper
Paul viewed God through an apocalyptic lens: this age is evil and in these last days it is getting worse; the signs of the times are upon Christians and Christ will return at any moment; as a matter of fact, the only hope the church has is the parousia.

II. Paul's Christology
Concerning Paul's Christology, he believed that Jesus' death and resurrection inaugurated the age to come; Jesus' death and resurrection is being re-presented through him; and those who believe his message are united to Christ's death and resurrection. Consequently, the Christian lives in the intersection of the two ages—deliverance now but not yet.

31

III. Paul's Pneumatology

Paul's pneumatology is straightforward: the presence of the Holy Spirit in the believer and in the church is a key sign that the age to come has dawned; and the Spirit is received by faith in Christ alone, not by the works of the Torah. In point of fact, the Law stirs up the flesh. Only the Spirit can subdue the old nature with the obedience of the heart that comes from participating in the new covenant.

IV. Paul's Anthropology

The two Adams represent the two ages: The first Adam is the head of this age and the old humanity; while Christ, the last Adam, is the head of the age to come and the new humanity.

V. Paul's Soteriology (SAVIOR+WORD) STUDY OF DOCTRINE OF SALVATION

Paul's soteriology unfolds in three tenses, which is governed by the overlapping of the two ages. The Christian was justified before God at the moment of faith in Christ and now participates in the age to come. But the believer continues to live in this present age, which calls for daily sanctification. When Christ returns the believer will experience the full scope of salvation on resurrection day.

VI. Paul's Ecclesiology

Paul's ecclesiology is simple—the church is the eschatological people of God in Christ. Yet, no one metaphor is sufficient to capture the full-orbed picture of the church, for it ranges from the body of Christ to the bride of Christ to the restored Israel. Still, the multiple images of the church are rooted in eschatology.

VII. Paul's Eschatology

Paul's eschatology attests to the overlapping of the two ages in that the signs of the end times began with the first coming of Christ, but that they will not be completed until his return.

Conclusion to Paul's Theology

The conclusion of this work explores the spiritual and political reasons why

Paul's opponents rejected his apocalyptic gospel. Moreover, the already/not-yet aspects of the age to come hold the key for properly relating Paul's apocalyptic gospel to today.

I. Paul's Theology Proper

Paul viewed God through an apocalyptic lens: this age is evil and in these last days it is getting worse; the signs of the times are upon Christians and Christ will return at any moment; as a matter of fact, the only hope the church has is the parousia.

II. Paul's Christology

Concerning Paul's Christology, he believed that Jesus' death and resurrection inaugurated the age to come; Jesus' death and resurrection is being re-presented through him; and those who believe his message are united to Christ's death and resurrection. Consequently, the Christian lives in the intersection of the two ages—deliverance now but not yet.

III. Paul's Pneumatology

Paul's pneumatology is straightforward: the presence of the Holy Spirit in the believer and in the church is a key sign that the age to come has dawned; and the Spirit is received by faith in Christ alone, not by the works of the Torah. In point of fact, the Law stirs up the flesh. Only the Spirit can subdue the old nature with the obedience of the heart that comes from participating in the new covenant.

IV. Paul's Anthropology

The two Adams represent the two ages: The first Adam is the head of this age and the old humanity; while Christ, the last Adam, is the head of the age to come and the new humanity.

V. Paul's Soteriology

Paul's soteriology unfolds in three tenses, which is governed by the overlapping of the two ages. The Christian was justified before God at the moment of faith in Christ and now participates in the age to come. But the believer continues to live in this present age, which calls for daily sanctification. When Christ returns the believer will experience the full scope of salvation on resurrection day.

VI. Paul's Ecclesiology

Paul's ecclesiology is simple—the church is the eschatological people of God in Christ. Yet, no one metaphor is sufficient to capture the full-orbed picture of the church, for it ranges from the body of Christ to the bride of Christ to the restored Israel. Still, the multiple images of the church are rooted in eschatology.

VII. Paul's Eschatology

Paul's eschatology attests to the overlapping of the two ages in that the signs of the end times began with the first coming of Christ, but that they will not be completed until his return.

Conclusion to Paul's Theology

The conclusion of this work explores the spiritual and political reasons why Paul's opponents rejected his apocalyptic gospel. Moreover, the already/not-yet aspects of the age to come hold the key for properly relating Paul's apocalyptic gospel to today.

PART ONE

THE LIFE
and
LETTERS OF PAUL

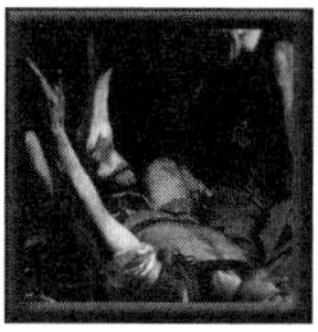

PAUL: AN APOCALYPTIC SEER

Based on Galatians 1, Romans 1, Paul's other letters (especially Ephesians 3), and Acts, this chapter presents the view that Paul's conversion and call were eschatologically driven. More particularly, the four components comprising Paul's message were apocalyptic in nature and were rooted in his conversion/call: Jesus is the Messiah; his death and resurrection inaugurated the age to come; this salvation is entered into by faith not by obedience to the law of Moses; and Paul's target audience was Gentiles. Moreover, these four eschatological components of Paul's message would become flash points with the other eschatological constructs highlighted above. *(pp 22-26)*

[margin handwriting: quoted from pages 27]

GALATIANS 1 AND PAUL'S APOCALYPTIC GOSPEL

In order to identify the heart of Paul's message, one must first visit Paul's autobiographical statements regarding his conversion to Jesus Christ, and simultaneously Paul's call to be an apostle. Such remarks are commonly recognized to occur in Galatians 1 and Romans 1. We begin with Galatians 1 since that is considered by many Pauline scholars to be the first of Paul's letters.[1] In particular,

---

1   This view usually presumes that Galatians was written in AD 48, *before* the Jerusalem Council in AD 49 (Acts 15). On this reading, Galatians 2:11–14 corresponds with Acts 11:27–30. The other major view of the date of Galatians is that it was written *after* the Jerusalem Council, around AD 54/55. This reading correlates Galatians 2:11–14 with Acts 15:1–30. We have opted for the last perspective (see my *The Reverse of the Curse: Paul, Wisdom, and the Law,* Wissenschaftliche Untersuchungen zum Neuen Testament 2/114 [Tübingen: Mohr Siebeck,

Chapter 1

Paul speaks of his conversion to Christ and his call to be an apostle in Galatians 1:1–5, 11–16a. From these verses, we see that Paul's conversion/call bequeathed to him a fourfold eschatological message.[2]

First, Paul's Damascus Road encounter revealed to Paul that Jesus is the Christ (vv. 12, 16; cf. v. 1).[3]

2000], pp. 335–36). Either way, Galatians 1 is Paul's earliest biographical statement concerning his conversion/call.

2   Two extensive matters related to Paul's Damascus Road encounter have occupied the attention of scholars, which we can only mention here. The first is whether the term "conversion" is an appropriate word for that experience. While some have called for the jettisoning of "conversion" as the correct nomenclature relative to Paul, opting instead for "call" (e.g., Krister Stendahl, "The Apostle Paul and the Introspective Conscience of the West," *Harvard Theological Review* 56 [1963], pp. 199–215; Paula Fredriksen, "Paul and Augustine: Conversion Narratives, Orthodox Traditions, and the Retrospective Self," *Journal for Theological Studies S* 37 [1986], pp. 3–34), three considerations suggest that the term is not out of order. (1) Alan E. Segal has demonstrated sociologically that Paul's belief in Jesus as Messiah provided his entrance into a new group, a reconstruction of reality on the apostle's part (*Paul the Convert. The Apostolate and Apostasy of Saul the Pharisee* [New Haven/London: Yale University Press, 1990, pp. 72–114, 285–300]). (2) Paul's own estimation of his Damascus Road encounter was that it entailed a radical transformation of his values (Gal. 1:10–24; Phil 3:2–11). (3) Mark A. Seifrid rightly notes that Paul gives himself and his churches an identity independent of Judaism, one that constituted the consummation of Jewish hope but which included Gentiles as well (Gal. 4:21–31; Rom. 9:23–36;1 Cor. 10:32; (*Justification by Faith. The Origin and Development of a Central Pauline Theme.* [Leiden: E. J. Brill: *Novum Testamentum*, 1992], p. 137). However, in labeling the Damascus Road encounter "conversion," we do not wish to minimize its prophetic call/commission character either (see Segal, *Paul*, pp. 6–9; cf. Karl Loav Sandnes, *Paul, One of the Prophets? A Contribution to the Apostle's Self-Understanding, Wissenschaftliche Untersuchungen zum Neuen Testament* 2/43 [Tübingen: J. C. B. Mohr/Paul Siebeck], 1991, pp. 58–76; cf. especially Gal. 1:11–17 with Jer. 1:5–11; Isa 6:1–9). A second issue surrounding Paul's conversion/call has to do with the question of whether or not it involved development in the apostle's thought. We believe that the impact of the Damascus Road experience on Paul's view of the Law and Gentiles was revolutionary and immediate. Nevertheless, such does not rule out development in Paul's thinking in terms of the scope of the Gentile mission nor in the sense that his conviction that the Law was now terminated became entrenched with his dealings with the Judaizers (see Martin Hengel, *Between Jesus and Paul: Studies in the Earliest History of Christianity*, trans. by John Bowden [Philadelphia: Fortress Press, 1983], pp. 49–54; Seyoon Kim, *The Origin of Paul's Gospel*, Wissenschaftliche Untersuchungen zum Neuen Testament 2/4 [Tübingen: J.C. B. Mohr/Paul Siebeck,1981], pp. 60–66).

3   Three comments regarding Galatians 1:16 are called for at this point: the occasion of the revelation; the content of it; and its form. First, that Paul in Galatians 1:16 is drawing on his Damascus Road experience is commonly recognized; cf. 1 Corinthians 9:1; 15:8; Acts 9:1–19; 22:3–16; 26:12–18; see, e.g., F.F. Bruce, *The Epistle to the Galatians*, New International Greek Testament Commentary (Grand Rapids, MI: Eerdmans, 1982), pp. 92–93; Kim, *The Origin of Paul's Gospel*, pp. 55–59; Richard N. Longnecker, *Galatians,* Word Biblical Commentary (Dallas: Word Books, 1990), pp. 31–32. Second, the content of the revelation Paul received

Obviously, "Christ" was an eschatologically laden term in Second Temple Judaism (from the time of Zerubbabel's Temple, 516/515 BC, to the destruction of Herod's Temple in AD 70). D.S. Russell provides a fine survey of the subject for both the Old Testament and early Judaism. The word "Messiah" (the Hebrew term) or "Christ" (the Greek term) means "anointed," with reference to one who is especially set apart for God's work. As such, this word is most often applied in the Old Testament to the kings of Israel (e.g., 2 Sam. 19:21; 23:1; Lam. 4:10) and, in the postexilic period, to the priests of God (Ps. 133:2; Zech. 4:14). Emerging out of the prophetic material toward the close of the Old Testament, however, is a more general messianic hope (though the word "Messiah" is not actually used for the concept) of a future Golden Age, the future kingdom of God, in which the fortunes of Israel will be restored and the surrounding nations judged (Isa. 40–66; Ezek. 40–48; Joel 3; Zech. 14). This era of justice and peace could be associated with a coming ideal ruler (Isa. 9:6; 11:1; Jer. 23:5; Mic. 5:2; Zech. 9:9).

---

was Jesus Christ, enthroned in heavenly glory. That Jesus Christ himself was the revelation Paul received at that time is confirmed by comparing Galatians 1:12 with 1:16. The grammatical debate over whether Ἰησου Χριστου (v. 12) is an objective genitive, i.e., the self-revelation of Christ (so E. D. Burton, *A Critical and Exegetical Commentary on the Epistle to the Galatians*. International Critical Commentary [Edinburgh: T & T Clark, 1921], pp. 41ff.), a subjective genitive, i.e., the gospel revealed by Christ (so, Longenecker, *Galatians*, p. 24) has been resolved by Kim as being both, who correctly observes that Paul usually defines the gospel Christologically (Rom. 1:3f; 1 Cor. 15:3–5; Gal. 1:16 [for the grammar of Gal. 1:16 see below]). Thus the gospel revealed was Jesus Christ himself (*The Origin of Paul's Gospel*, pp. 55–56, footnote 3). Third, the form, or the means, of the revelation of Christ to Paul recorded in Galatians 1:16 is debated, with two basic interpretations emerging. (1) ἐν ἐμοι is a simple dative with reference to an objective appearance, that is—"to me" (so, e.g. Christopher Rowland, *The Open Heaven: A Study of Apocalyptic in Judaism and Early Christianity* [London: Society for the Promotion of Christian Knowledge, 1982], p. 376). (2) The revelation was subjective—within me (so H.D. Betz, *Galatians: A Commentary on Paul's Letter to the Churches in Galatia*, Hermenia [Philadelphia: Fortress, 1979], p. 64; Bruce, *Galatians*, p. 93; Longenecker, *Galatians*, p. 32). The second view appeals to Galatians 2:20; 4:6 and the inward reality of Christian experience there portrayed as support of a similar reading of Galatians 1:16. Moreover, that opinion argues, whereas 1 Corinthians 9:1 and 15:8 use words derived from ὁραω (ἑορακα in the former)—which suggest an external vision—Galatians 1:16 does not, using instead ὀρθη; the latter verse is supposedly therefore not describing an objective vision (see, e.g. Longenecker *Galatians* pp. 31–32). Proponents of the first view, however, respond to the second interpretation thusly: (1) that ἐν ἐμοι is a simple dative is grammatically possible and, indeed, seems confirmed by the parallel phrase ἐν τοις ἐθνεσιν (v. 16); (2) for Paul to root his call in subjective experience would have been self-refuting to his purpose in Galatians 1. Besides seeing the risen Jesus seated on the divine chariot-throne, Kim makes a good case that Paul also heard the commissioning words of Christ, which subsequently drew the apostle's attention to Jeremiah 1:4–10; Isaiah 6:1–13; 49:1–6 (*The Origin of Paul's Gospel*, p. 57).

The conclusion D.S. Russell draws from the preceding data, then, is that the role of the Messiah in the Old Testament is somewhat restricted to a non-technical sense; that is, there is not some single individual expected as the Messiah, but rather a broad messianic expectation of the coming kingdom of God.

However, with the development of Judaism, particularly apocalyptic Judaism (200 BC–AD 100), the technical sense of Messiah as the long-awaited inaugurator of the kingdom of God developed, who is identified either as a Davidic-like king (*T. Jud.* 17:5–6; 22:2–3; 24:1–6; *Ps. Sol.* 17:23–51; 18:6–10), a Levitical priest (*T. Levi* 18:2–7; *T. Reub.* 6:5–12), or both (as in the Dead Sea Scrolls, *1QS* 9:11; *CD* 14:19; 19:10; *1QM* 12:10; 19:3). Also to be connected with the idea of the Messiah in Jewish apocalyptic literature is the figure of the heavenly Son of Man (Dan. 7:13; *1 Enoch* 37–73; *4 Ezra* 7:28–29; 12:32; 13:32, 37; *2 Bar.* 29:3; 30:1).[4] Apocra   259 v.11, 1st column.

Second, at his Damascus Road conversion/call Paul realized that Jesus the Christ inaugurated the age to come by his death and resurrection.

This claim is supported by four details in Galatians 1:1–5, 12–16a. (1) Verse 1 declares that God raised Jesus from the dead. Comparing this remark with 1 Corinthians 15, Paul's resurrection chapter, especially vv. 20–28, we see that Jesus' resurrection was the beginning of the general resurrection of humanity—the age to come—breaking into this present age (cf. Isa. 26:19; Dan. 12:2, 3; *2 Baruch* 21:23; *4 Ezra* 7:32; *1 Enoch* 83–90). (2) Galatians 1:4 states that the purpose of Jesus' death and resurrection was to rescue his followers from this "present evil age," the antithesis of the age to come. Compare this in Paul to: "this age" (Rom. 12:2; 1 Cor. 1:20; 2:6 (2x); 2:8; 3:18; 2 Cor. 4:14); "this present evil age" (Gal. 1:4); "this present age" (Eph. 1:21; 1 Tim. 6:17; 2 Tim. 4:10; Titus 2:12); "this present time" (Rom. 3:26; 8:18; 11:5; 2 Cor. 8:14); "this world" (1

---

4   D.S. Russell, *The Method and Message of Jewish Apocalyptic* (Philadelphia: Westminster, 1964), pp. 304–23. We should take a moment and note how Paul refers to Jesus. He calls him "Jesus" (his human name); "Christ" (the Greek counterpart to the Hebrew "Messiah," with reference to Jesus' deity); "Christ Jesus" (which may reflect Paul's mystical concept, "in Christ"); "in Christ" (some 164 times in Paul's letters), and "Lord Jesus Christ" (with "Lord" as the translation of the Old Testament "Yahweh"). In Galatians 1:15 Paul refers to Jesus as the Son (of God), another honorific title.

Cor. 3:19; 5:10; 7:31; Eph. 2:2); and by way of contrast, "the coming age" (Eph. 1:21).

(3) Paul's usage of the word "glory" in Galatians 1:5 taps into the Jewish apocalyptic notion of the glorious resurrection body of the righteous associated with the dawning of the age to come or the kingdom of God. That Paul saw Jesus enthroned in heavenly glory is indicated by the argumentation of 1 Corinthians 15:8ff., which describes the risen Christ in terms of a glorious body. This interpretation is corroborated by Acts 9:3; 22:6; 26:13, which record the risen Christ's appearance to Paul as accompanied by a brilliant light. If 2 Corinthians 4:6 is an allusion to the Damascus Road experience, it would also provide further evidence that Paul believed he witnessed the glorious Christ on the *merkabah* (throne) of God. Galatians 1:5 presumes that tradition.

(4) Paul labels Christ's revelation to him on the Damascus Road an "apocalypse" (Gal. 1:12, 16), a word patently eschatological. One thinks of the last book of the New Testament—the "Apocalypse"—given to John the seer. These four details, then, combine to indicate that, for Paul, Jesus' death and resurrection inaugurated the age to come.

The third eschatological component of Paul's message that was rooted in his conversion/call was his proclamation that entrance into the kingdom— salvation—is by grace, not by the law of Moses.
Galatians 1:3, 6–9, 11, 15 obviously connect the gospel Paul received from Christ on the Damascus Road with grace, as indeed the whole book of Galatians highlights. The gospel of peace is that humans are justified before God by faith in Christ alone, not by the works of the Torah.

But, contrary to Paul's gospel, Jews in the Second Temple period believed the real key to inaugurating the kingdom of God was their efforts to obey the Torah. If they kept the divine law God would send his kingdom, with or without a Messiah (e.g., see *CD* 4:17; *1QH* 1:32; *2 Bar.* 17:4–18:2; 51:3–7; *4 Ezra* 7:51, 89, 96; *Pirke Abot* 2:8; 6:7; *Sif. Deut.* 34; *b. San.* 97b; *p. Tan.* 64a). The last text expresses the idea succinctly albeit in negative fashion, "If Israel repented a single day, immediately would the Son of David come. If Israel observed a single Sabbath properly, immediately would the Son of David come."

Joseph Klausner's description of this conviction of Jews is pitted against Paul on this point:

> The Jewish Messiah is the redeemer of his people and redeemer of mankind. But he does not redeem them by his blood; instead he lends aid to their redemption by his great abilities and deeds. To be sure, Satan will be vanquished in the messianic age, not by the Messiah, but by God. Man must redeem himself from sin *not by faith alone*, but *by repentance and good works*; then God will redeem him from death and Satan. Each man is responsible for himself, and through his good deeds he must find atonement for his sins. He cannot lean upon the Messiah or upon the Messiah's suffering and death.[5]

Indeed, already in the Old Testament true obedience to the Law was expected to accompany the new covenant and the age to come (Jer. 31:31–34; Ezek. 36:24–32).

By way of contrast, Paul's message was that the age to come/salvation is entered into by faith in Christ alone.

Fourth, Paul was called to be the apostle to reach the Gentiles (Gal. 1:16).

Long ago Johannes Munck pointed out the eschatological nature of Paul's task. The Old Testament prophets predicted that in the end time Gentiles would stream into Jerusalem confessing Yahweh to be their God (Isa. 45:15; 60:15–17; Micah 4:13; cf. Tobit 3:11; Dead Sea Scrolls [*1QM* 12:13–15]). Munck argued that Paul was the point man in that endeavor and that when the nations were converted the end of history would come. Munck appealed to 2 Thessalonians 2:6; Mark 13:10/Matthew 24:14 in support of his theory.[6] We concur with Munck that Paul's apostleship to the Gentiles was eschatological in nature.[7]

---

5 Joseph Klausner, *The Idea of the Messiah in Israel. From Its Beginning to the Completion of the Mishnah*, trans. by W. F. Stipespring (New York: Macmillan, 1955), p.530.
6 Johannes Munck, *Paul and the Salvation of Mankind*, trans. by F.C. Clarke (Richmond, VA: John Knox, 1959).
7 There continues to be a debate among New Testament scholars as to whether or not "apostle" originally referred to the Jewish rabbinic institution of *shaliach,* whereby the decisions of the Sanhedrin (the ancient governing body of Israel, cf. the *Kinneset* today) were announced

ROMANS 1 AND PAUL'S APOCALYPTIC GOSPEL

The same fourfold eschatological message of Paul occurs in his other autobiographical statement about his conversion/call—Romans 1.

First, Paul calls Jesus the "Christ" (Rom. 1:1, 4, 6–8), as well as "Son" (1:3), "Son of God" (1:4), and "descendant of David" (1:3).

Concerning "Son"/"Son of God," such a title was applied in Judaism to the heavenly Messiah (see the Dead Sea Scrolls, *4Q* 246). And "descendant of David"—David's Son—was a near-equivalent for the Messiah to come at the end of history (see 2 Sam. 7). So Paul's equation of Jesus with the Christ, Son of God, and Son of David makes an eschatological statement: The long-awaited Messiah is here in Jesus.

Second, Romans 1 also acknowledges that Jesus' death/ resurrection was eschatological in import—it inaugurated the age to come, though Romans 1 draws on differing imagery than Galatians 1 to make that point.

Thus, when Paul speaks of the "gospel" in Romans 1:1, 3, 9, 16, he connects it with "salvation" (1:16) and "the righteousness of God" (1:17). These three terms take one back to Isaiah 40 and following. There Isaiah calls Israel's future restoration to her homeland from Babylonian exile "good news" (Isa. 46:13; 49:6; 52:7, 10) as a demonstration of the righteousness of God (Isa. 46:13; 51:5–6, 8). For ancient Israel, her future restoration and salvation was connected with the new covenant and the age to come/kingdom of God. For Paul, all of that is a present reality because of the death and resurrection of Jesus (Rom. 1:4).

Third, entrance into the age to come/the true restoration of Israel/salvation is based on faith in Christ alone, not on the works of the Torah (Rom. 1:16–17; cf. 1:18–3:31).

Indeed, Paul views such salvation in Christ as the fulfillment of the Abrahamic covenant as well as the prophesied new covenant (see Rom. 4).

---

throughout Israel by official representatives of the members of the Sanhedrin. These "sent ones" (apostles) should be treated as if they were the members of the Sanhedrin themselves. See the discussion by K. H. Rengstorf in *Theological Dictionary of the New Testament*, ed. by Gerhard Kittel, trans. by Geoffrey W. Bromiley (Grand Rapids, MI: Eerdmans, 1964; reprinted 1999), 1:407–47.

Fourth, Paul perceived his apostleship to the Gentiles as the end-time calling of converting the nations to Christ—the obedience of the Gentiles (Rom. 1:5, 16:26), again taking into consideration those Old Testament prophecies of the conversion of the nations at the end of history.[8]

PAUL'S APOCALYPTIC MESSAGE IN HIS OTHER LETTERS

Here we simply document the claim that Paul's fourfold eschatological message that was rooted in his conversion/call is pervasive in his letters.

First, Paul called Jesus the "Christ" throughout his letters, some 379 times.[9]

Second, Jesus' death and resurrection inaugurated the age to come.
For this, see Galatians 1:4–5; 2:15–21; 3:13–14; 4:4–6; 6:12–15; 1 Cor. 1:18–25; 15:3–4; 2 Cor. 5:14–17; Rom. 3:21–26; Phil. 2:5–11; Col. 1:13–23; Eph. 1:7–12; 2:11–12; Titus 2:11–14.[10]

Third, the age to come is entered into by faith in Christ apart from the Torah (Gal.; Rom.; Phil. 3:1–11).

Fourth, Paul was called to be the end-time apostle to the Gentiles (Gal. 1:1, 16a; Rom. 1:1–15; 16:24–27; Eph. 3:1–13; Col. 1:24–27).
We conclude this particular discussion of Paul's fourfold eschatological message by identifying their presence in Ephesians 3:1–13, another narrative of Paul's call to the gospel ministry. Although many interpreters do not include this text in Paul's conversion/call narratives because they do not support the Pauline authorship of Ephesians, we do include it here because we accept the letter as genuinely from Paul. Thus: (1) Paul calls Jesus "Christ" (Eph. 3:1, 4, 6, 8, 11). (2) Jesus' death and resurrection inaugurated the age to come, called "the mystery of Christ" (3:4; cf. v. 3; cf. 1:20–21). A mystery was an end-time

---

8 See my work, *Teach the Text: Romans* (Grand Rapids, MI: Baker, 2013), where I deal extensively with this aspect in Romans.
9 So Leon Morris, *The Epistle to the Romans* (Grand Rapids, MI: Eerdmans, 1992), p. 36.
10 The reader is referred to my discussion of these texts, which are clustered into three categories: Christ and sin; Christ and the flesh; Christ and the Law, in *The End of the Age Has Come*, pp. 76–97.

secret now revealed to God's spokesperson (see Dan. 2–7). (3) Specifically, the mystery Christ revealed to Paul was that Gentiles are now a part of the people of God (Eph. 3:1–13). (4) This gospel of the mystery of Christ is based on faith in Christ apart from the Torah (Eph. 3:2, 7; cf. 2:11–21).[11]

ACTS AND PAUL'S FOURFOLD APOCALYPTIC MESSAGE

The passages in Acts regarding Paul, especially his three conversion accounts (Acts 9:1–23; 22:3–16; 26:8–18), substantiate the above fourfold eschatological message.

First, upon his conversion/call on the Damascus Road Paul confessed that Jesus is "Christ" (Acts 9:22; 26:23), the "Son of God" (9:20), the "Lord" (22:17), the "righteous one" (22:14). Elsewhere in Acts, Paul calls Jesus "Savior" (13:23) and the "Lord Jesus Christ" (28:31).

Second, Paul in Acts understood that Jesus' death and resurrection inaugurated the age to come.

In his first sermon in Acts, Paul preached that Jesus had been raised from the dead (13:30). The resurrection of Jesus for Acts, like Paul, was the in-breaking of the end-time general resurrection into the present (see e.g. 1:3, 9–11; 2:24–36; 3:15–16; 7:55–56). Connected with this in Acts is a constellation of terms/ideas associated with the age to come now begun at the first coming of Christ that Paul mentions: light/the eschatological glory of the risen Christ (9:3; 22:6, 9, 11; 23:13); the coming of the Holy Spirit, the sign of the dawning of the eschaton (9:17; cf. 2:1–39—Peter's Pentecost sermon); the dawning of the kingdom of God (28:23, 32); the gospel (17:32) which, in Acts, is the true restoration of Israel (cf. 2:38–40; 3:19–26); forgiveness of sins to replace Israel's exile (see again 3:19–26; cf. 13:38); salvation (13:26; 28:24); eternal life (13:46–48); and the hope of the resurrection of the dead (23:6–8).

Indeed, Luke's portrayal of Paul's message that Jesus' death and

---

11 Philippians 3:1–11 is also autobiographical, but Paul only mentions his conversion, not his call to be an apostle, though he undoubtedly presumed the latter. We will examine this passage later in this work.

resurrection inaugurated the age to come fits in with Luke's overall presentation of the κηρυγμα, the preaching of the early church in Acts. Long ago C.H. Dodd demonstrated that the κηρυγμα in Acts (based on the sermons by Peter, Stephen, Paul, etc.) is thoroughly eschatological. He noted that therein there were at least five end-time aspects of Jesus' life, death and resurrection. First, in Jesus the messianic age has dawned (Acts 2:16; 3:18, 24) in his ministry, death and resurrection (Acts 2:23). Second, by his resurrection, Jesus has been exalted to the right hand of God as messianic head of the new people of God (Acts 2:33–36; 3:13). Third, the Holy Spirit is the sign of the presence of the eschaton as well as the proof that Jesus currently reigns in heaven in power and glory (Acts 2:33). Fourth, the messianic age will shortly reach its consummation in the return of Christ (Acts 3:21). Fifth, an invitation is always extended for the people to receive Christ and the life of the age to come (Acts 2:38–39).[12]

Third, Paul, along with the Jerusalem Apostles, recognized that the law of Moses was not the means to salvation but rather faith in Christ was the sole path to entering the age to come (Acts 13:39; 14:22; 15:9–10; 16:31; 20:24; 26:18).

Fourth, Paul was called to preach to the Gentiles to bring about the end-time conversion of the nations (9:15–16; 22:15, 21; 26:16–18, 23; 28:28).
Thus Acts, by including Paul's conversion/call testimonies confirms the apostle's fourfold eschatological message.

PAUL'S FOURFOLD ESCHATOLOGICAL MESSAGE AS FLASH POINTS WITH HIS OPPONENTS

Paul's fourfold eschatological message did not set well with his opponents. Indeed, they became flashpoints for his detractors. Here we anticipate some of our findings of the chapters to follow.

---

12 C. H. Dodd, *The Apostolic Preaching and Its Developments* (New York: Harper, 1944).

First, Paul's message that Jesus is the Christ, the only way to God, attracted opposition from non-Christian Jews, the Roman imperial cult, and Hellenistic religion.

Non-Christian Jews dogged Paul's footsteps on his missionary journeys because they abhorred the Christian's Christ, believing that such smacked of polytheism. Moreover, Judaism had no place in their theology for a suffering, crucified Messiah.[13] A suffering deliverer was hardly what Jews hoped for in a Messiah, especially since they longed for God to defeat their oppressors like Rome. And, according to Deuteronomy 21:23, a crucified Messiah was accursed by God. Already in the first century BC, the Dead Sea Scrolls

---

13 The notion of a suffering Messiah is not found in the Old Testament or in any texts of pre-Christian Judaism. Hermann L. Strack and Paul Billerbeck (*Kommentar zum Neuen Testament aus Talmud und Midrash*, 6 vols. in 7 [Munich: C. H. Beck, 1922–61], 2.273–299) say that the "Old Synagogue" knew of "a suffering Messiah, for whom no death was determined, i.e. the Messiah ben David" and a "dying Messiah, of whom no suffering was mentioned," i.e. the Messiah ben Joseph (ibid. pp. 273–274). Yet when they recite the passages from Rabbinic literature (ibid. pp. 282–291) that speak of the suffering of Messiah ben David, they are all drawn from late texts, which scarcely show that the expectations of such a figure existed among Palestinian Jews in or prior to the time of Jesus. The same has to be said of the texts about the dying Messiah ben Joseph (ibid. pp. 292–299). Str-B rightly reject the implication found at times in Christian commentators that Mark 8:31; Matt 16:21 refer to a "suffering Messiah," and the latter is not a "messianic" title without further ado. Where in pre-Christian Judaism does one find a "Son of Man" as an agent of Yahweh anointed for the salvation, deliverance of his people? True, in Tg. Jonathan the "servant" of Isa 52:13 is identified as "the Messiah": "See, my servant, the Messiah shall prosper; he will be exalted, great, very mighty," and 53:10c is made to read, "They will look upon the kingdom of their Messiah, many sons and daughters will be theirs." Yet no use of "Messiah" is made in the crucial verse, 53:12. It is not surprising that the "Servant" of Isaiah 52–53 was eventually identified with a messiah in the Jewish tradition; but it still remains to be shown that this identification existed in pre-Christian Judaism or in Judaism contemporary with the New Testament. Sometimes adherents of a pre-Christian origin of the suffering Messiah appeal to three texts thought to be important exceptions to the rule: *4 Ezra* 7:28–30; *Targum of Isaiah* 53; and the "Pierced Messiah" text in DSS (4Q285). The first mentions the death of the Messiah as the climax of the temporal messianic kingdom. However, it is important to note that there the Messiah does not suffer; rather, after having lived long and well for four hundred years, he simply dies with the rest of humanity. His death, therefore, had no apparent theological significance. Nor can the Aramaic translation (*Targum*) of Isaiah 53 be used as evidence for the concept of a suffering Messiah because it transposes (probably in reaction to Christianity) the afflictions of the suffering servant of Isaiah 53 *from* the Messiah *to* Israel or the surrounding Gentile nations (see again our comments above). Moreover, *4 Ezra* 7:28–30 and *Tg. Isaiah 53* are dated after the birth of Christ and cannot be used as testimony for pre-Christian Jewish messianic understanding. With regard to the Pierced Messiah Test, it cannot be invoked to support the idea of a suffering Messiah because it is the Messiah who inflicts suffering on his enemies rather than the reverse.

interpreted Deuteronomy 21:23 in terms of crucifixion and its attendant shame (see 11Q Temple 64:7–9; 4Q Nahum 1:7–8).

The Roman imperial cult opposed Paul and early Christianity because the latter supposedly offered a rival king to Caesar. That is why the Romans crucified Jesus. And Hellenistic religion with its syncretism cast aspersion toward Paul and Christianity because of the exclusivity of their message—Jesus alone, not a combination of Greco-Roman gods and eastern deities, is the way to salvation.

Second, Paul's inaugurated eschatology—with Jesus the Christ inaugurating the age to come—was in opposition to at least three groups in the apostle's day.
Besides their antipathy to a suffering, crucified Messiah, much of non-Christian Judaism held to consistent eschatology. That is, because non-Christian Jews did not believe the Messiah had arrived yet, the age to come was still forthcoming—though *merkabah* Judaism, as we will see later, did believe that the age to come is fully here through mystic experience. The authors of the Dead Sea Scrolls espoused this type of realized eschatology. Indeed, one group of Paul's opponents—*merkabah* Jewish Christianity—taught that through faith in Christ and obedience to the Torah the mystic was caught up to the heavenly throne where he or she fully experienced the age to come. Paul would have to combat such realized eschatology in 1 and 2 Corinthians, Philippians, and Colossians, as we will see. Hellenistic religion, in its own way, also championed realized eschatology, as we will observe in 1 and 2 Corinthians.

Paul's message that salvation is by faith in Christ apart from the Torah obviously did not go over well with non-Christian Judaism. Neither did it appeal to non-*merkabah* and *merkabah* Judaizers, who mixed faith in Christ with adherence to the law of Moses.

Paul's ministry to Gentiles also infuriated non-Christian Jews for two reasons: (1) The apostle's message that the Torah was finished obviously upset non-Christian Jews. (2) The mass conversion of Gentiles to the Christian faith threatened Jewish political clout in the cities where Paul preached the gospel. More on this later.

Moreover, Paul's claim of faith in Christ alone unsettled non-*merkabah* and *merkabah* Judaizers alike, for two related reasons: (1) Like their non-Christian kinsmen, Judaizers took umbrage at the thought that the Torah was finished. (2) It seems that the Judaizers were being pressed into the service of the Palestinian nomistic campaign in the late 40s and early 50s in Israel. Were the Judaizers on the side of their non-Christian brethren in their adherence to the Torah, or were they followers of Saul/Paul the apostate Pharisee who betrayed his Jewish heritage?[14] We will meet with this issue in our next chapter on Galatians.

CONCLUSION

This chapter identified the fourfold eschatological proclamation of Paul, stemming from his Damascus Road conversion/call: Jesus is the long-awaited Messiah of Israel, whose death and resurrection inaugurated the age to come, which is entered into by faith apart from the Law, and which includes Gentiles. We saw this to be the case for Galatians 1, Romans 1, and Ephesians 3. Moreover, Paul's fourfold message is pervasive in the rest of his writings. We also noted that the Acts material confirms that Paul did indeed preach the preceding fourfold message. Furthermore, those four components became flash points with Paul's opposition. We now turn to Paul's letters to highlight the conflict in eschatologies that Paul's apocalypse of Christ generated.

---

14 Acts 13:9 says that Saul was simultaneously called Paul, thus dispelling the common misconception that the apostle's name was changed from Saul to Paul at his conversion. It was normal in antiquity for Jews to have both Semitic and Roman names. A Roman name consisted of three parts; a first name (*praenomen*), a family name (*nomen*), and a surname (*cognomen*). Concerning the apostle, we only know the last of these—*Paulos*. See the discussions by Joseph A. Fitzmyer, *Paul and His Theology. A Brief Sketch*, 2nd ed. (Englewood Cliffs, NJ: Prentice-Hall, 1989), pp. 2–3 and D.A. Carson, Douglas J. Moo, and Leon Morris, *An Introduction to the New Testament* (Grand Rapids, MI: Zondervan, 1992), p. 216.

Chapter 2

GALATIANS

JUSTIFICATION BY FAITH—GOD'S

END-TIME VERDICT NOW

Galatians is perhaps Paul's earliest letter, and it sounds a theme dear to his heart: Sinners are justified by faith in Christ, apart from the law of Moses. According to the apostle to the Gentiles, being justified by faith in Christ is God's present end-time acquittal of the believer. Indeed, justification before God is a blessing that Judaism relegated to the age to come but which Paul contends is granted in this age to Jews and Gentiles alike. According to Paul, the law of Moses served its divinely intended purpose and has now run its course in this age. Paul develops this thesis vis-à-vis the non-*merkabah* Judaizers that harassed his churches in Galatia. This reading of Galatians is reinforced by Acts 13:13–15:35, which highlights the showdown between Paul's messianic eschatology and that of the Jewish synagogue. Also to be factored into this discussion is the role the imperial cult played in the crisis in Galatia.

This chapter unfolds in five points: a discussion of Paul's Judaizing opponents in the Galatian churches; an expose of the non-Christian Jewish opposition to Paul in Acts 13:13–15:35; a consideration of the role the imperial cult

(handwritten margin note: ITH + LAW)

played in Galatia; the resulting interplay of factors on the Galatian church; and a summary of the contents of Galatians.

PAUL'S NON-*MERKABAH* JUDAIZING OPPONENTS IN THE GALATIAN CHURCHES

This section naturally divides into two concerns: the identification of the Judaizing opponents, and the Judaizing message.

The Identification of the Judaizing Opponents

Attempting to reconstruct the events surrounding Paul's conflict with his opponents in the churches of Galatia is beset with problems: Who were the apostle's adversaries? What was the nature of the controversy? What is the relationship between Galatians 2 and Acts? Which hypothesis, if either, best accounts for the data in Galatians: the North or South Galatia theory? While space does not permit extended discussion of these issues, we will touch on these concerns along the way. Perhaps the best procedure to follow is to list and defend four interrelated propositions germane to the subject of the crisis in Galatia.

First, Paul's (and Barnabas') ministry to Gentiles was conducted in Antioch and their target group was the God-fearers.

Two claims inherent in this statement require explanation. (a) There was indeed a Gentile group in the first century AD identified as the God-fearers; (b) Paul and Barnabas ministered to such people in Antioch who fit that category.

(a) The traditional view concerning the God-fearers held that there was in late Second Temple Judaism a large number of Gentiles who were attracted to Judaism, but stopped short of conversion (i.e. becoming a proselyte) and, specifically, circumcision. Most of the evidence for the existence of such a group comes from Acts, where one finds these people called either οἱ φοβουμενοι τον θεον (fearers of God, 10:2, 22 [Cornelius]; 13:16, 26 [Paul in Pisidian Antioch]) or οἱ σεβομενοι τον θεον (worshippers of God, 13:43, 50 [Paul in Pisidian Antioch]; 16:14 [Lydia at Philippi]; 17:4 [Paul at Thessalonica], 17:17 [Paul at Athens]; 18:7 [and at Corinth]). But there is also evidence other than Acts upon which to base the theory that many God-worshipping Gentiles attached themselves to Jewish synagogues:

Josephus (*Ap.* 2.123, 209–10, 280, 282; cf. *J. W.* 2.462–63, 7.45); Philo (*Mos.* 2.17–20); Plutarch (*Cicero* 7.6); Juvenal 14.96–106; Cassius Dio 67.14.1–3; Suetonius (*Domitian* 12.2).[1]

(b) Based on the preceding data, the traditional view argued that the early Greek-speaking Jewish Christians—Paul and Barnabas included targeted such a group. More specifically, the God-fearers constituted an effective bridge between Jews and pagan Gentiles. Thomas M. Finn summarizes this view:

> Paul and his predecessors are evidence enough for the fact that Hellenistic Judaism was the principle bridge over which they traveled into the Gentile world. But can one be more specific? According to the *sensus receptus*, yes. The new religion was carried into the Greco-Roman world by those Gentiles who embraced monotheism, adopted a variety of Jewish observances short of circumcision, and frequented the synagogue—in short, by the God-fearers who became Christians in droves.[2]

Though some have denied that there was a God-fearing group in the first century, with the discovery of the Aphrodisias inscription[3] (which undeniably refers to Gentile God-fearers as a group attached to the synagogue thereby

---

1   On the definition and issues surrounding the term "God-fearer," the following should be consulted: Kirsopp Lake, "Proselytes and God-fearers" in *The Beginnings of Christianity: Part 1. The Acts of the Apostles*, ed. F. J. Foakes Jackson, K. Lake, 5 vols. (London: Macmillan, 1933), 5:74–96; A. T. Kraabel, "The God-fearers Meet the Beloved Disciple" in *The Future of Christianity: Essays in Honour of Helmut Koester*, ed. B. A. Pearson, A. T. Kraabel, G. W. E. Nickelsburg, and N. R. Peterson (Minneapolis: Fortress Press, 1991), pp. 276–84: Irina Levinskaya, *The Book of Acts in Its Diaspora Setting* (Grand Rapids, MI: Eerdmans, 1996) pp. 51–126.

2   Finn, "The God-fearers' Reconstruction," *Catholic Biblical Quarterly* 47 (1985), p. 76, though Finn accepts only with qualification that there was such a clear-cut category in the first century.

3   On the translation, date, purpose, and significance of this inscription for confirming the existence of the God-fearers see Paul R. Trebilco, *Jewish Communities in Asia Minor*, Society of New Testament Studies Monograph Series (Cambridge: University Press, 1991), pp. 152–55; Levinskaya, *Acts*, pp. 70–80. The Aphrodisias stele, dating to the third century AD, is inscribed on two faces (A and B) which consists of a group within the synagogue called the "decang," who were initiators and donors of a kind of soup-kitchen attached to the synagogue. Some fifty-two of the names are Gentiles and are listed on face B under the heading—και ὁσοι θεοσεβεισ. That they are called God-fearers is undeniable.

confirming similar usage of the term at Panticapaeum, Tralles, Sardis, Miletus, etc.), we now have archaeological and inscriptional evidence proving the existence of such a group back to the first century AD. It turns out, therefore, that Luke does not create the God-fearers out of thin air (as some have accused him of doing).

In light of Luke's vindication as a reliable historian, we are therefore permitted to factor his information into the discussion about Paul's ministry to the God-fearers in Antioch, our second point. That there was a significant number of God-fearers attached to the synagogues in Antioch is clear from Josephus' statement which observed that local Jews, "were constantly attracting to their religious ceremonies multitudes of Greeks, and these they had in some measure incorporated with themselves" (*J.W.* 7.32). Josephus' remark fits well with Luke's description of Antioch as the focal point of the preaching of the gospel to Gentiles (Acts 11:20–26); a mission begun by those Greek-speaking Jewish Christians fleeing from Saul's persecution in Jerusalem (Acts 8:4; 11:19–21) and developed by Barnabas and Paul (Acts 11:22–26; 15: 30–35). The success of Paul and Barnabas in evangelizing the Antiochene God-fearers set the stage for their subsequent ministry to the South Galatian churches of Antioch: Pisidia, Iconium, Lystra, and Derbe (cf. Gal. 2:7–8 with Acts 13:1–14:23). In those cities the God-fearers were again the main audience (Acts 13:16, 26, 43, 50) of Paul's (and Barnabas') law-free message (Acts 13:39). The above events best correlate with the following timeframe that Hengel and Schwemer have suggested:

- Conversion/call of Paul, ca. 33 (cf. Gal. 1:11–15).
- Paul in Damascus and Arabia, ca. 33–36 (cf. Gal. 1:16–17).
- Paul visits Peter in Jerusalem, ca. 36 (cf. Gal. 1:18–20).
- Mission of Paul in Tarsus and Cilicia, ca. 36/37 (cf. Gal. 1:21–23).
- Beginning of the mission of the Greek-speaking Jewish Christians to Antioch, ca. 36/37 (Acts 11:20–21).
- Paul/Barnabas in Antioch, ca. 39/40 (Acts 11:22–26).
- Paul/Barnabas' mission in Syria and Phoenicia, ca. 41 to 46/47 (Acts 11:27–12:25).

- First journey of Paul/Barnabas to Cyprus, Cilicia, and southern Galatia, ca. 46/47 (cf. Acts 13:1–14:25 with Gal. 2:1–2).[4]

Second, in reconstructing the historical overview of the crisis in Galatia we—in consonance with the majority opinion of scholarship—identify Paul's opponents as the Judaizers.

Richard Longenecker's summary assessment of the evidence reduces the choices to such a category. Thus, (a) The two-front theory of W. Lütgert and J. H. Ropes (a Judaizing group and pneumatic radical group) is ruled out by the fact that Paul addresses the Galatian converts as basically a homogenous congregation. (2) W. Schmital's Jewish-Christian Gnostic theory inappropriately passes over Galatians 3–4 and therefore wrongly reverses the situation to suggest that Paul's opponents accused him of being dependent on the Jerusalem apostles while they themselves were free from such authority. (3) J. Munck's hypothesis that the opponents were *Gentile* Christian Judaizers cannot explain Galatians 6:12 and Paul's reference there to his detractors desiring to avoid persecution associated with the cross, a statement best understood against the backdrop of Jews in some way connected with Jerusalem (on this point see below for more detail).[5]

On the other hand, the evidence for a Judaizing opponent is convincing (1) The adversaries were not indigenous to the situation for Paul repeatedly refers to them as distinguishable from the Galatian Christians (1:7–9; 3:1; 4:17; 5:7, 12; 6:12–13). (2) Paul's opponents presented his authority as inferior to the Jerusalem apostles (1:1–2:10). (3) The opponents' message centered on the need for Gentile Christians to observe the Law, symbolized in circumcision, in order to become the children of Abraham (3:6–4:31) and to overcome the deeds of the flesh (5:13–6:10). (4) Such Jewish Christians, as R. Jewett and others since him have demonstrated, most likely were part of a Palestinian nomistic campaign during the late 40s and early 50s which, fearing zealot reprisals, attempted to enforce circumcision on Gentile Christians (Gal. 1:6–10; 2:11–14; 4:17; 5:10–12;

---

4   Martin Hengel and Anna Marie Schwemer, *Paul Between Damascus and Antioch: The Unknown Years,* trans. John Bowden (Louisville KY: Westminster/John Knox Press, 1997), pp. xi-xiv.

5   Longenecker, *Galatians*, pp. xciv-vi.

6:12–13).[6] That Antioch would have attracted the attention of the Judaizers is not surprising because it was: (a) the center of the Gentile mission and hence a situation requiring monitoring by the Jerusalem congregation (see Acts 11:19–26; 15:1–2); (b) the capital of Syria, whose actions had far-reaching effects on Palestine (as witnessed in the rather recent crisis caused by Caligula, ca. 39).[7] It seems, then, that a contingent of Jewish Christians from Jerusalem, claiming the backing of James, came to Antioch (and later southern Galatia) with the purpose of convincing the God-fearing Gentile Christians there of the need to complete their spiritual progress by submitting to circumcision, and thereby the Torah. We may date this first intrusion of the Judaizers into Antioch at ca. 48/49.

Third, our adoption of the South Galatia theory does not militate against equating Galatians 2:1–10 with the Apostolic Council of Acts 15:1–30.
The debate over this issue is well-rehearsed and too extensive to be treated here. For our part, the following parallel points favor the identification of Galatians 2:1–10 with Acts 15:1–30. (1) Both describe a Jerusalem meeting which dealt with the question of Gentile Christians having to observe circumcision. (2) Both were prompted by Jewish Christian legalists. (3) Paul and Barnabas, on the one hand, and Peter and James, on the other hand, were the main participants in both. (4) Both accounts reached the same conclusion in favor of a law-free mission to Gentiles.

Differences between Galatians 2:1–10 and Acts 15:1–30 do not refute their identification. According to Galatians 2:2, Paul's role at the meeting was central. However, according to Acts 15:6–30, Paul was , according to Galatians 2:2, but overshadowed by Barnabas, Peter, and James, according to Acts 15:6–-30according to Galatians 2:2, the motivation for Paul's attendance was due to private revelation. However, according to Acts 15:2–3, Paul was a public representative of the Antioch church. The meeting is portrayed as having been private in Galatians 2:2, but billed as a public conference in Acts 15:6, 12.

6   Robert Jewett, "The Agitators and the Galatian Congregation," *New Testament Studies* (1971), pp. 198–212.
7   Emperor Caligula's instruction that a statue of himself be set up in the Jerusalem temple was sent to Petronius, the governor of Syria, whose responsibility it was to enforce the decree (see Philo, *Embassy to Gaius* 184–338; Josephus, *J.W.* 2.10.1–5/184–203; *Ant.* 18.8.2–9/261–309; Tacitus, *Histories* 5.9).

These differences are easily explained by Paul's concern to present himself as independent of the authority of the Jerusalem apostles. Furthermore, Paul's non-mention of the famine relief mission to Jerusalem is probably informed by the same motif; or, similarly, perhaps the trip did not assume polemical importance for Paul and his opponents. Finally, to the objection that it was self-refuting to Paul's argument with the Judaizers in Galatia not to mention the decision of the Apostolic Council (Acts 15:1–30), it should be observed that Paul, in actuality, does draw on that deliberation in Galatians 2:11–15—Peter's and Barnabas' actions were inconsistent precisely because they went against the council at Jerusalem. For Paul, however, the proof of his initial victory at the Jerusalem council was that the "pillar" apostles agreed with his law-free gospel to the Gentiles by not requiring Titus to be circumcised (Gal. 2:3). In conclusion, we may justifiably agree with the majority opinion: sometime during ca. 48/49, a Judaizing element infiltrated the Antioch church, much to the chagrin of Paul and Barnabas (Acts 14:26–15:2a), precipitating the Jerusalem Council (ca. 48/49; cf. Acts 15:2b–30 with Gal. 2:1–10). The decision reached there was a victory for Paul and the law-free gospel for the Gentiles.

Fourth, the issue was not thereby resolved.

The Judaizers struck again in Antioch (cf. Gal. 2:11–14 with Acts 15:35ff), this time persuading Peter and Barnabas with their arguments. That Paul failed to win the day in Antioch is indicated by the fact that he never mentions in the epistle to the Galatians that Peter and Barnabas recanted their new "nomist" stance. If they had, Paul certainly would have utilized such information to refute the Judaizing position. Consequently, the Antioch incident resulted in Paul's separation from Peter, Barnabas, and Antioch, prompting him to pursue the mission to the Gentiles independently. Along the way, the Judaizers extended their effort to South Galatia, most probably to the "daughter" churches of Antioch, appealing to James and their recent victory in Antioch as support for their nomistic message. Hence the writing of Galatians (ca. AD 54/55).

The Judaizing Message as Culled from Galatians

In the second point of this section we attempt to reconstruct the Judaizers' theology through a mirror-reading of Galatians—which, despite its inherent dangers, nevertheless provides evidence which we could not otherwise obtain. The following picture emerges in Galatians 1:1, 11–2:10 about the Judaizers: They portrayed Paul as deriving his message from the Jerusalem apostles, which consisted of faith in Christ plus the need to follow the Law, especially circumcision. But, according to 1:6–10, Paul abandoned the latter aspect because he did not want to offend the sensitivities of the Christian God-fearers. In other words, the apostle watered down the gospel in order to please the Gentiles. Based on this, then, perhaps we are to gather from Paul's comments there that the Judaizers indicated that the covenantal curses could be removed from Israel because Jesus the Messiah's death and resurrection inaugurated the long-awaited age to come—and with it, the beginnings of the eschatological restoration of Israel envisioned by the Old Testament prophets. Now because of his resurrection life, Christians—Jews and Gentiles alike—have a new-found power for obeying God's law, according to 2:19–20, thereby fully actualizing the age to come. However, Paul's antinomian message places Gentiles back under the slavery of sin and even makes Christ an instrument of unrighteousness, according to 2:17–18. In 3:1–5 one can detect the Judaizing message that the Spirit, the sign of the age to come, now resides within Christians and empowers them to perform genuine works of faith—in effect, the ethics of the new covenant. Furthermore, according to 3:6–9, even Gentiles can now become children of Abraham, if they will believe in Jesus Messiah and submit to circumcision. As such they, together with Jewish Christians, can experience the Deuteronomic blessings by obeying the Torah, because Christ has taken its curses unto himself, according to 3:10–14. In other words, the eschatological restoration of Israel has dawned and the nations can participate in Israel's salvation, provided they become like Jews. Gentiles no longer need to be enslaved to the curses of the covenant (pronounced on Israel's enemies) because they do not follow the Torah; now they can experience the new Exodus with its spiritual freedom born out of the dawning of the messianic age (4:1–7). To complete their salvation however, Gentiles believers must submit to circumcision, the dietary laws, and Sabbath-keeping (4:8–11). If they want to be the children of Abraham, then they must live like the children of Abraham, the descendants of Israel (4:21–31). With Christ and the Spirit, Gentiles can overcome the works of the flesh by permitting the Torah to inspire within them obedience to God, and hence participate in Israel's inheritance. Not to pursue this path, however, is to invite divine judgment (5:13–6:7). But the Christian message brings hope—Gentiles can become citizens of the new creation, the Israel God. For their part, they must exercise faith in Christ and accept the message of circumcision (6:11–18).

From this reading of the Judaizing theology in Galatians we discover a conflict in eschatologies between the Judaizers and Paul. The non-*merkabah* Judaizers: (1) believed Jesus the Messiah inaugurated the age to come, and with it the power to obey the Torah (1:1–5; 2:11–16; 4:1–7); (2) identified themselves with Christ and the new creation, the true Israel (6:15–16); (3) agreed that Jesus is the Messiah (3:6–14), as predicted in the Old Testament prophecies (3:19–25); (4) adhered to the Jewish calendar (4:10) and circumcision (5:2–12; 6:12–16).

For Paul's part, however, Jesus the Christ inaugurated the age to come by virtue of his death and resurrection (1:1–5) which is experienced by faith not the Torah (1:6 ff.), nor the Jewish calendar (4:10). Such a plan of salvation was predicted in the Old Testament (3–4), and comprises the new creation (6:15–16).

ACTS 13:13–15:35 AND PAUL'S NON-CHRISTIAN JEWISH OPPOSITION IN GALATIA

We make two points in this section: the theological reasons for the Jews' opposition to Paul's gospel in Galatia, and the political rationale for the Jewish persecution of Paul in Galatia.

First, the Jews in Galatia opposed Paul's gospel for theological reasons.

Paul and Barnabas first preached the gospel of Christ in the synagogues of Pisidian Antioch and Iconium. There in the synagogues in those towns the missionaries found an audience of both Jews and God-fearers (13:16, 26, 43, 50). Most Jews opposed Paul and Barnabas while many God-fearers embraced the gospel of Christ. When Paul and Barnabas went on to Lystra the Jews who opposed Paul earlier traveled to that town as well and stirred up the crowds to persecute Paul and Barnabas. Paul in 1 Corinthians 1:23 leaves no doubt as to why Jews rejected Paul's gospel—they were scandalized at the thought of a crucified Messiah. Using Acts 13:13–15:35, it would not be hard to extrapolate from this the eschatology of the non-Christian Jews in Galatia, which was antithetical to Paul's apocalypse of Christ. Recalling our comments in chapter 1 about Paul's fourfold eschatological message confirmed in Acts, as well as our introductory remarks about Paul's eschatology, the following chart reveals the contrasts between the eschatologies of Paul and the non-Christian Jews in Galatia opposed to him:

PAUL'S INAUGURATED ESCHATOLOGY	THE JEWS' CONSISTENT ESCHATOLOGY
1) The age to come has arrived in Jesus the Messiah (Acts 13:23, 26, 32, 34, 38, 39, 46–48)	1) The age to come has not arrived because the Messiah has not yet appeared, including Jesus (13:27–29, 41, 45–46, 50; 14:2, 5, 19)
2) The new creation has dawned and with it the long-awaited restoration of Israel as well as the end-time conversion of the Gentiles (13:24–25, 32–34, 46–48; 14:1, 27; 15:3–4; 15:7–18)	2) The new creation has not arrived; the restoration of Israel is not here and when it comes Gentiles will be ruled by Jews (13:46–48; 14:1–2, 27–15:1)
3) Jesus is the crucified Messiah, Davidic descendant but not political deliverer (13:29–37)	3) Jesus was crucified, so he was not the Messiah (13:27–29)
4) The OT predicts that the Messiah and the suffering servant are one and the same: the suffering Messiah (13:29 [Deut. 21:23]; 13:34 [Isa. 55:3]) is the Davidic Messiah (13:33 [Ps. 2:7]; 13:35 [Ps. 16:10])	4) The OT predicts that the Messiah will deliver Israel/Israel is the suffering servant not the Messiah. The Davidic Messiah is Israel's deliverer (13:33, 35)
5) Faith is the "ritual" by which one enters in to the age to come, not the Torah (13:38–41, 43; 14:3, 26–27; 15:6–11)	5) Circumcision, the sign of the Law, is the ritual for entering the age to come (13:38–39; cf. 15:1, 5, 10)

Second, the Jews in Galatia opposed Paul for a political reason.
Non-Christian Jews opposed Paul and Barnabas in Galatia, according to Acts 13:45, 50; 14:2, 4–5, 19. From Paul's speeches (Acts 13:16–41; 13:46–47; 15:6–11) and the speeches of Peter we have culled the theological reasons for the Jews' opposition to the gospel. But from the actions of those Jews against Paul and Barnabas recorded in Acts 13:45, 50; 14:2, 4–5, 19 we also find a political motivation—the Jews were jealous of Paul's sway over the Gentile God-fearers in the Galatian towns of Antioch Pisidian, Iconium, Lystra, and Derbe. Irina Levinskaya has made the case that the conversion of the God-fearers upset the balance of political power in the above towns:

> Luke records, with the insight of a good historian, a turning point in Jewish relations with their well-disposed Gentile neighbours: the beginning of a Christian mission to the Gentiles posed a serious problem for Jews. Before then, in the course of centuries of living among the Gentiles, they had achieved (at least in Asia Minor) a certain *status quo* which was now suddenly being challenged. Christian preachers were aiming at, and gaining, success among people whose social likes with the Jewish community secured Jewish life in the Gentile milieu. The Jewish community was forced to take measures to fight for influence over the God-fearers. As a response to the Christian mission, the Jews intensified relations with their sympathizers. M. Goodman found 'evidence of a Jewish mission to win gentile sympathizers in the first century'.[8]

These two reasons—theological and political—combined to unleash Jewish rejection in Galatia of Paul's apocalypse of Christ.

GALATIA AND THE IMPERIAL CULT

In this section, we continue to uncover the historical-cultural background of Paul's letter to the Galatians by examining the significant influence of the Roman imperial cult on Galatia, both Southern and Northern parts. We will do so by identifying the presence in Galatia of the five components of the realized eschatology of the imperial cult that we noted in our introduction: The new age has dawned, which is a new creation, through Caesar Augustus the

---

8   Irina Levinskaya, *The Book of Acts in Its First Century Setting*, pp. 124–25.

Savior; which was proclaimed in sacred writings, and which was popularized through temples, coins, games, oaths, etc.[9]

First, Caesar Augustus' birth was viewed by Romans as the dawning of the new age.

Two famous inscriptions bear this out. The Priene inscription, 9 BC, (discovered in Priene but also found in the cities of Apamea, Eumeneia, Dorylaeum, and Maeonia) suggests that the New Year should be realigned to coincide with Augustus' birthday, September 23:

> (It is difficult to tell) whether the birthday of the most divine Caesar … is something of greater pleasure or benefit, which we could rightly accept to be equivalent to the beginning of all things … and he restored, if not to its nature, at least to serviceability, every form, which was falling away and had carried over into misfortune; and he has given a different look to the whole world, which gladly would have accepted destruction had not Caesar been born for the common good of all things.[10]

Descriptions like, "the beginning of all things," "restored …" "different look to the whole world" indicate that Augustus' birth began the golden age.

The second famous inscription is by the Asian (Asia Minor) *koinon* (the college of imperial priests charged with propagating the worship of Caesar). It too dates to 9 BC:

> Since the Providence … that has [divinely] ordained our life, having harnessed her energy and liberality, has brought to life the most perfect good, Augustus, whom she filled with virtue … for the service of mankind, giving him, as it were, to us and our descendants a saviour … he who brings an end to war and will order [peace …], Caesar, who by his [epiphany …] surpassed the hopes … of all those who anticipated [good news …], not only [outstripping the benefactors]

---

9   I glean the following points from the massive evidence presented by Justin K. Hardin in his, *Galatians and the Imperial Cult*, Wissenschaftliche Untersuchungen zum Neuen Testament 2/227 (Tübingen: Mohr/Siebeck, 2008).

10   Quoted in Ibid, p. 32.

coming before him, but also leaving to no hope of greater benefactions in future; (And since) the [birthday] of the god initiated to the world the good news … resulting in him … (and since) Paullus Fabius Maximus … has invented an honour for Augustus that until now has been unknown to the Greeks—to begin time … from his birthday—for that reason with good fortune and safety … the Greeks of Asia have decided in all the cities, to begin the New Year with the 23rd September, which is the birthday of Augustus.[11]

Several words in this inscription remind one of the birth of Jesus ("Savior," "peace," "good news," "hope," cf. Luke 2:10–14) which inaugurated a new world order.

With regard to this new calendar heralding the new age with the birth of Augustus, the Galatian *koinon* decreed that the new Asian calendar should be the calendar of Galatia as well.[12]

Second, Augustus' birth and subsequent reign was thought to bring universal renewal.

The Roman poet Virgil wrote his fourth *Eclogue* in 40 BC anticipating such renewal. He spoke of a child who would usher in the golden age, a time when the earth would bring forth lavish fruit, the animals would also experience incessant fecundity, and the cattle would not fear huge lions (lines 18–30). When the child became an adult, the earth would experience its final renewal:

> The very trader will retire from the sea,
> nor will the ships bearing pine exchange goods;
> every land will bear all things …
> At this time, the hardy ploughman also will release the oxen's yoke.
> Nor will wool be taught to feign variegated colours,
> but the very ram in the meadows will change its fleece,
> at this time to a sweet-blushing purple, to a golden yellow;
> scarlet freely will clothe the grazing lambs.[13]

---

11 Ibid, pp. 23–33.
12 Ibid, p. 67.
13 Quoted in Ibid, p.35.

Virgil's later epic, the *Aeneid*, book six (19 BC) identified the prodigy as Augustus. Moreover, the golden age begun by Augustus was intimately connected with games. Thus in 17 BC Rome celebrated the return of the golden age when Augustus reinstated the secular games. Traditionally, the secular games were celebrated in response to the end of one age and the beginning of a new one, normally a span of one century. Under Augustus' leadership, however, it was determined that the new age began after 110 years, in 17 BC and for that celebration Augustus appointed the Roman poet Horace to compose an ode for the occasion. Horace did, calling it the *Carmen Saeculare* (*Song of the Age*). That piece praised Caesar Augustus as the bringer of the new age. Horace's *Song of the Age* was sung thereafter at the provincial games, including those celebrated in Northern Galatia—Pessinus and Tavium.[14]

Third, obviously the preceding inscriptions and songs hailed Caesar Augustus as the Savior who brought the golden age.

Such a conviction was echoed in South Galatia, where an inscription discovered read, "to Rome and the Imperator Caesar, Son of god, Augustus … their own Savior" (lines 1–4).[15] Moreover, the *Res Gestae* (*Divine Deeds*), a list of Augustus' divine deeds during his reign (published in AD 14 after his death, though composed by him before he died) were placed in the imperial sanctuaries across the province of Galatia, including Ancyra (North Galatia) and Pisidian Antioch (South Galatia).

Fourth, Roman sacred writings predicted the coming golden age under Augustus (Virgil's fourth* Eclogue*) and proclaimed it (Horace's* Song of the Age*), the latter of which was performed at the provincial games honoring Caesar, including in Galatia.

Fifth, the worship of Caesar was reinforced through games, coins, oaths, temples, etc., all of which occurred in Galatia.

We mentioned the provincial games in Galatia. To that can be added Galatian

---

14 Ibid, pp. 34–35, 67.
15 Ibid, p. 66.

coinage. The coinage from Pisidian Antioch displayed the emperor's image and also a Roman coin with the comet of Julius Caesar (the cosmological sign of the new age under Augustus) with the reverse side displaying a large eagle symbolizing Rome.[16] Moreover, the Galatian *koinon* (who presided in Ancyra, the capital of Galatia) dictated that the Galatians should pledge an oath to Caesar Augustus. Thus in Gangra in Galatian, an inscription was discovered dating to 3 BC containing an oath to Augustus to support him (lines 9–12, 18–21) and linking Augustus with other deities the Galatians swore allegiance to, "by Zeus, the sun, all the gods and goddesses, and Augustus himself" (lines 9–10).[17]

Simon R.F. Price has cataloged no less than seventy-seven temples built to the emperors in Asia Minor, often combined with temples to the Greco-Roman pantheon.[18] An impressive temple to Caesar Augustus was located in Pisidian Antioch, introduced by a triple-arched propylon, upon which stood statues of significant members of the imperial family. Augustus' *Res Gestae* was on the columns along with an inscription to "emperor Caesar Augustus, Son of god, Pontifex Maximus...."[19]

It seems clear from all of this that the realized eschatology of the imperial cult dominated the landscape and thinking of the province of Galatia.

THE RESULTING INTERPLAY CONCERNING THE GALATIAN CHURCHES

In this section we offer five statements that attempt to explain the crisis in the Galatian churches which takes into consideration our discussion in this chapter so far.

First, it is clear from Galatians 4:8–9 that the Galatian Christians once upon a time were pagans, no doubt worshipping the gods of the Greco-Roman pantheon and the Roman Caesar. (Recall above that the imperial cult was syncretistic.)* At that time, the Gentiles were under the sway of the *stoicheia* (4:9), the elements

the reconciliation or fusion of differing systems of belief. Usually results in a new belief system.

---

16 Ibid, p. 61.
17 Quoted in Ibid, p. 45.
18 Simon R.F. Price, *Rituals and Power: The Roman Imperial Cult in Asia Minor* (Cambridge: University Press, 1984), pp. 249, 274.
19 In Hardin, *Galatians and the Imperial Cult*, pp. 73–75.

of the world. Of the three main interpretations of this term—the natural elements of the world (i.e. earth, water, fire, and air), the elementary religious principles of the world, the demonic/elemental spirits attracting worship to the so-called gods—the third option most commends itself.[20] Thus the former pagan Galatians were probably under the influence of demons to worship the Greco-Roman pantheon and Caesar.

Second, but sometime in their past the Galatians became God-fearers and worshipped with Jews in the synagogues.

There is no hint in Galatians or in Acts 13–14 that the Galatian God-fearers suffered at the hands of the Roman authorities at that time. Neither is there any suggestion at this stage that the God-fearers were considered to be Jewish by Jews or Romans because the Galatian God-fearers had not been circumcised. (It is clear from Gal. 5:2–3 that the Galatians had not been circumcised as of the writing of Galatians). If the Galatians had been considered to be Jews (by being circumcised) then they would have been exempt from worshipping Caesar (see below). All of this leads one to believe that the Galatian God-fearers both worshipped God while still participating in the imperial cult. Three reasons suggest this to have been the case. (1) Becoming a God-fearer by nature involved compromise—on the one hand, Gentiles embraced Israel's God but, on the other hand, they did not embrace the whole of the Torah as represented in circumcision. (2) Some Christians in Revelation 2–3 pursued a similar strategy—worship Christ while paying lip service to Caesar. (3) Levinskaya documents cases in Asia Minor of God-fearers continuing to be polytheistic.21

Third, all of that changed when Paul and Barnabas arrived in Galatia preaching the gospel of Christ (Acts 13–14).

In accepting Paul's apocalypse of Christ, the Galatian God-fearers (and some Jews as well) will have necessarily made a break with both Judaism and the imperial cult. According to Paul's gospel one could follow Christ and no other; not the

---

20 See Peter T. O'Brien's *Colossians, Philemon.* Word Book Commentary 44 (Waco, TX: Word, 1982), pp. 129–32 for a summary of the perspectives and a defense of the third view.
21 See documentation in her *The Book of Acts in Its Diaspora Setting,* pp. 98–103.

law of Moses, nor the cult of Caesar. This, we believe, is what Paul is alluding to in Galatians 3:4 when he reminds the Galatian Christians how much they had suffered in the past. Their conversion to Christ and his exclusive claim would have put them at odds with the Jews, no doubt even causing them to be expelled from the synagogues (cf. John 9:22, 35), which often was accompanied by beatings (cf. 2 Cor. 11:24–25). The new Galatian Christians would have also been persecuted by Roman authorities for no longer participating in the imperial cult, a situation that later pertained to Christians in Asia Minor, hence the writing of Revelation. The Galatian believers would have renounced the worship of Caesar as Savior, inaugurator of the new age in embracing the worship of Christ. Paul understood this well, as Acts 14:22 attests, "we must go through many hardships to enter the kingdom of God;" that is, suffer the messianic woes (more on this in later chapters).

Fourth, the plot thickened when the Judaizers came to Galatia.

The Judaizers' arrival in Galatia offered the Galatian churches a way out of their persecution—continue to believe in Jesus but also submit to circumcision (like the Judaizers [Jewish Christians] had done back in Israel). If the Galatian churches did that, then Jews in Galatia would welcome them back as full Jewish brothers and they would be free of the imperial cult, because Jews were legally exempt from worshipping Caesar. As Bruce Winter argued, if the Galatians received circumcision they would appear to the civic authorities to be a Jewish group and thus a *religio licita* (a legal religion) in the eyes of Rome, a status that would protect the Galatians from the public worship of the emperor.[22]

Fifth, this was the occasion for the writing of the letter to the Galatian Christians.

Paul essentially exposes two errors in the Judaizers' message to the churches in Galatia. First, for the Galatians to embrace circumcision and the Torah it represented was ironically to go back to paganism because the law of Moses was also under the στοιχεια (Gal. 4:3). That is, just as the demonic spirits were behind pagan worship

---

22 Bruce W. Winter, "The Imperial Cult and Early Christians in Pisidian Antioch (Acts XIII 13–50 and Gal VI 11–18)," pp.67–75 in *Actes du 1er Congrès International sur Antioche de Pisidie*, Edited by T. Drew-Bear, p. 75, Mehmet Tashalan and Christine M. Thomas, Collection Archeologie et Historie de L'Antiquite Universite Lumiere-Lyon 2.5 Lyon: Kocaeli.

so were they behind the law of Moses. This is the connection between Paul's critique of the Torah in Galatians 4:1–7, 10a and the apostle's critique of paganism in 4:8–9. Indeed, according to v. 10, the Galatians were already returning to the Jewish calendar. The next step was submitting to circumcision.[23] It may also be that Paul's anger at the Galatian Christians for observing the Jewish calendar hinted at the imperial calendar the Galatians observed as pagans. The double *entendre* would have been biting—to follow the Jewish calendar was tantamount to resorting back to the pagan calendar of the imperial cult the Galatians once observed.[24] The second error in the Judaizing message that Paul exposes in Galatians is that the Judaizers harbored an ulterior motive—they wanted to convert the Gentile Galatians to circumcision and the Torah in order to spare themselves from persecution (Gal. 4:17–18; 6:12–13). Of whom were the Judaizers afraid? Most likely, they were afraid of the Jewish nomistic campaign back in Palestine. If the Judaizers could persuade the Galatians to be circumcised, then the pressure would be off the Judaizers when they returned to their homeland. It may be also, as Winter theorized, that the Judaizers wanted to be off the hook with the Romans in Galatia as well, and they would be if their fellow Christian Gentiles became Jewish Christians and thereby be made exempt from the worship of Caesar.

Having examined how the eschatology of Paul conflicted with the eschatologies of the Judaizers, non-Christian Jews, and the imperial cult, we are now in a better position to summarize the contents of Galatians.

SUMMARY OF GALATIANS

The theme of Galatians is justification by faith: God's end-time acquittal now. After Paul's introductory comments in 1:1–9, he provides three arguments in defense of the view that justification before God is based on faith in Christ alone and not the law of Moses. A more detailed outline is below with commentary following each point:

    A.   Introduction: 1:1–10

---

23 Though Exodus 12:43–51 declared that Gentiles had to be circumcised to observe the Jewish calendar, especially Passover, Hellenistic Judaism—Judaism outside Palestine—had learned that it needed to lighten requirements such as that on God-fearers (cf. Acts 15:19–21, 28–29).

24 See Hardin's treatment of this subject, *Galatians and the Imperial Cult*, pp. 122–27.

A. Introduction: 1:1–10

1. Salutation: 1:1–5

Like the rest of Paul's letters, Galatians begins with a salutation which identifies Paul as the author and the Galatian brothers (Christians) as the recipients. Paul introduces himself as an apostle of Christ, whose authority came directly from God, no doubt, at his conversion/call on the Damascus Road. The message Paul received at that time was that Jesus is the Messiah, whose death and resurrection inaugurated the age to come. The reader will recall here from our chapter 1 two of Paul's eschatological points—Jesus is the Messiah and he inaugurated the age to come. Paul then commends God's grace and peace through Christ to the Galatian churches.

2. Denunciation: 1:6–10

But, unlike Paul's other letters, the apostle offers no praise for the Galatian churches, because he fears they are apostatizing from Christ. "Deserting" (μετατίθημι, v. 6) is a word that taps into apocalyptic tradition—the end-time apostasy of God's people predicted in apocalyptic Judaism (Jubilees 23:14–23; *4 Ezra* 5:1–13; *1 Enoch* 91:3–10; etc.; cf. Matt. 24:10–13; Mark 13:20–23; Luke 21:34–36). The Galatians are doing this by embracing the Judaizing message— that justification before God is based on faith in Jesus Christ plus obedience to the law of Moses symbolized in circumcision. For Paul, this is a perversion of the gospel. Here we recall the third component of Paul's eschatological message: Faith in Christ alone is the means to justification and entrance into the age to come. In other words, faith in Christ projects for the believer God's end-time verdict of justification into the present. Conversely, the message of salvation via the Torah projects into the present for the non-believer and the apostate God's end-time verdict of condemnation. This is clear from the word Paul twice uses in vv. 8–9, "anathema." Two nuances inform this term. First, "anathema"/"curse" recalls the Deuteronomic curses pronounced on ancient Israel for disobeying the Torah. Deuteronomy 27–30 records the blessings pronounced upon Israel if she obeys the law of Moses but curses upon her if she does not. In a divine twist, Paul's gospel proclaims the reverse—if humans try to be justified by obeying the Law they place themselves under the Deuteronomic curses; only through faith in Christ could they experience the Deuteronomic blessings (see Gal. 3:10–14).[25] In Judaism, the Deuteronomic curses and blessings became associated with end-time divine condemnation and justification.[26]

Second, in 1 Corinthians 16:22 Paul offers a play on the word "anathema" signifying its eschatological implication—"If anyone does not love the Lord—a curse ("anathema") be on him. Come, O Lord" (*mar anathema*, Aramaic for "our Lord come"). In other words, the curse/anathema is associated with the judgment that will fall upon non-believers and apostates when Christ returns. For Galatians 1:8–9, that end-time condemnation is in danger of falling now on apostate Galatians.

B. 1:11–2:21: The Personal Argument for Justification by Faith

In Galatians 1:11–2:21, Paul relates his personal experience of how he came to see that justification is by faith in Christ alone apart from the works of Law. In Galatians 1:11–17, Paul relates to his audience that in the past as a Pharisee he was zealous for the Torah, surpassing even his peers to the point of perse-cuting Christians in Jerusalem (cf. Acts 8:1–3; 9:1–2; etc.). But on his way to Damascus to round up more Christians to harass, Paul/Saul met the risen Christ in a vision and was converted to him. There Paul exchanged his zeal for the Torah for faith in Christ alone, a message he was directly commissioned by God to share with Gentiles. Recall that these constituted the third and fourth eschatological components of the apostle's message. This was Paul's apocalypse of Christ.

Paul had fully formulated this message before going to Jerusalem to meet Peter and James. Paul conferred with no other apostle and no Judean church in

---

25 See my *Reverse of the Curse* for extensive documentation of this theme.
26 For this, see my co-authored work with Douglas Kennard, *Deliverance Now and Not Yet: The New Testament and the Great Tribulation* (New York: Peter Lang, 2004), pp. 125–27.

the matter (1:18–24; cf. Acts 9:26–30). The next time Paul went to Jerusalem was fourteen years later (cf. Gal. 2:1–10 with Acts 11:30). The reason for this visit seems to have been two-fold: First, Paul and Barnabas were sent by the church at Antioch to deliver financial relief to the Jerusalem church because of a recent famine in Jerusalem (cf. Gal. 2:10 with Acts 11:30). Second, the Judaizers had just appeared on the scene in Antioch with their message of justification by faith in Christ plus obedience to the Law (Gal. 2:4–5). So Paul and Barnabas traveled to Jerusalem to meet with the leaders of the Jerusalem church concerning the issue (including Peter and James, the half-brother of Jesus). That the Jerusalem apostles agreed with Paul's message of justification by faith in Christ alone is clear because they did not require Titus, a Gentile Christian, to be circumcised (Gal. 2:3–9). So this visit to Jerusalem further demonstrated that Paul received his message directly from God. And the other apostles concurred. Thus the Jerusalem council of Acts 15 solidified Paul's message of grace.

But Peter compromised the message of justification by faith alone later in Antioch (2:11–21). There he freely associated with Gentile Christians in the churches until the Judaizers came to town. At that point Peter stopped openly associating with Gentile Christians.

Paul called Peter on the carpet for his hypocrisy, and for dragging Barnabas and others down the same path. What Peter was actually doing was to compromise the gospel by aligning himself with the Judaizers' demand that Gentiles should be circumcised to be saved. But Peter himself had earlier confessed the impossibility of obeying the Torah (Acts 15:7–11). As Paul put it, by the works of the law of Moses no one can be justified; only through faith in Christ can one be accepted by God (vv. 15–16).[27] According to Paul in vv.

---

27 Paul's all-important phrase in Galatians 2:16; cf. 3:2, 5, 10; Rom. 3:20 "by the works of the law" (ἐξ ἐργων νομου) takes the reader into a landmine field of interpretation, with two leading views contending for acceptance among New Testament scholars. The old view of this phrase, championed by the likes of Augustine, Luther, and Calvin, was that by "works of the law" Paul means the law of Moses in its entirety and that no one is able to keep all the Torah in order to be justified before God on the last day. But with the groundbreaking article by Krister Stendahl, "The Apostle Paul and the Introspective Conscience of the West," a new interpretation toward Paul's view of the Law began to emerge: namely, before and after becoming a Christian Paul maintained a positive view of the Torah. It was only Lutheran exegesis that gave the false impression that Paul ever had a negative view of the Law. Three scholars in particular followed Stendahl's path of interpretation of Paul and thus the "New Perspective on Paul" was born. We list those three scholars here in chart form,

17–21, the Christian died to the law of Moses when Christ died on the cross and by his resurrection the Christian was freed from the Torah and sin to live by the grace of God. We might put it this way—for the Christian, God's end-time verdict of "not guilty" has been pronounced in this life because the believer is in Christ.

---

consisting of their respective slogans, their positions, as well as the traditional/old perspective's recent critique of those positions. Space constraints permit us to do little more:

NEW PERSPECTIVE LEADER	NEW PERSPECTIVE "SLOGAN"	NEW PERSPECTIVE POSITION	OLD/TRADITIONAL PERSPECTIVE CRITIQUE*
E. P. Sanders	"Covenantal Nomism"	Second Temple Judaism was not legalistic, but rather taught that Jews entered into the covenant by faith and remained in it by keeping the works of the Law	But this is still legalism because it synergistically combines grace (entering in the covenant by faith) with works (remaining in the covenant by the Law)
J.D.G. Dunn	"Works of the Law": the Jewish national markers of circumcision, dietary laws, and Sabbath-keeping	Paul is not criticizing the Law *per se* but the Law as being used by Jews as separating them from Gentiles by the national/covenant markers	But all occurrences of "works of the Law" in Paul equate that phrase with the entirety of the Torah; therefore Paul critiques not national markers, but individual attempts
N. T. Wright	"Righteousness of God"	For Paul, righteousness of God is God's faithfulness to his covenant people not the justification of the individual before God on the last day.	But it is impossible to avoid the justification of the individual in Paul's usage of the phrase, "righteousness of God" (see Rom. 1:16–17; 3:5, 21, 22, 25, 26; 10:3; 2 Cor. 5:21)

*For my part, I wholeheartedly support the traditional perspective toward Paul and the Law.

C. 3:1–4:31: The Doctrinal Argument for Justification by Faith

In Galatians 3:1–4:31, Paul roots the message of justification by faith alone in the Old Testament. In Galatians 3:1–5, Paul criticizes the Galatian churches for being hoodwinked by the Judaizer intruders. He reminds the Galatian believers that they received the end-time gift of the Holy Spirit (cf. Gal. 3:1–5 with Pentecost Acts 2) *before* the Judaizers came to town with their addition of the Torah to faith in Christ. If the Galatians had the Spirit already, why did they need the law of Moses? To accept the Torah as a condition of salvation was to forfeit possession of the Spirit. To accept the Torah was also to waste their suffering at the hands of the non-Christian Jews and the imperial cult when they became Christians (recall our discussion above).

Galatians 3:6–4:21 contains the doctrinal argument for justification by faith. Therein Paul contrasts Abraham's salvation by faith experience with the condemnation that comes from trying to be justified by the law of Moses.

In 3:6–9, Paul argues that Abraham was saved by faith (cf. v. 6 with Gen. 15:6) and that God's promise to Abraham's descendants, including Gentiles, was also that salvation is by faith (cf. vv. 7–9 with Gen. 12:3; 18:18; 22:18).

This is in contrast to the law of Moses, which only brings about condemnation before God—the covenant curses (Gal. 3:10–14). Here Paul reverses the Deuteronomic tradition:

DEUTERONOMY 27–30	GALATIANS 3:10–14
1) Obeying law of Moses brings blessings	1) Obeying law of Moses, which no one can do (Deut. 27:26; Lev. 18:5), brings curses
2) Disobeying law of Moses brings curses	2) Only faith in Christ brings blessings (which Paul roots in Hab. 2:4)

Those who trust in Christ, Gentiles included, share in the blessing promised to Abraham who himself was saved by faith in God's promise that he would make of Abraham a great nation.

Galatians 3:15–18 reiterates this point by arguing that the promise given to Abraham preceded the law of Moses by 430 years. Therefore salvation by faith trumps salvation by the Torah. Thus only those who are saved by faith in Christ constitute the true seed of Abraham (cf. 3:16 with Gen 12:7; 13:15; etc.).

Why then the Torah? Paul's answer in 3:19–25 is that the Torah was given to increase sin until the Messiah comes. That is, the Law was given to Moses by God through angels to show the human race its sin in order to drive individuals to the gospel of Christ.

As a result, the Galatian Christians are sons of God, no longer slaves to sin (3:25–4:7). But if they embrace the Judaizing message to be circumcised and follow the Jewish calendar, the Galatians may as well revert back to worshipping pagan gods, including Caesar (4:8–11). Recall again our discussion above.

Paul therefore appeals to the Galatian churches to resist the temptation to follow the Torah (3:12–20). They should rather follow Paul who suffered for the Galatians because he genuinely loved them. By way of contrast, the Judaizers harbor ulterior motives for enticing the Galatians to follow them (see once more our discussion above). Galatians 4:21–31 contains Paul's most famous allegory contrasting Isaac, the true son of Abraham, with Ishmael, the counterfeit child of Abraham. Most commentaries recognize that Paul here reverses the argument of the Judaizers. We first show their argument in chart form, then we show Paul's reversal of that argument on the following page.

Paul concludes his allegory by commanding the Galatians to cast out the Judaizers (just as Hagar and Ishmael were cast out by Abraham).

D. 5:1–6:10: The Ethical Argument for Justification by Faith

In Galatians 5:1–6, Paul makes the point that the gospel of faith in Christ sets sinners free from the enslavement of the Law. More specifically, God's grace in Christ by the power of the Spirit produces in the Christian's life righteousness and love. But the Galatians will throw this away if they submit to circumcision and thus the Torah.

In Galatians 5:7–12, Paul encourages the Galatians to embrace the sufferings of the cross even as Paul does. Such persecution results from Paul not preaching circumcision. In a similar manner, if the Galatians refuse to be circumcised they will be persecuted by Jews and Romans, as we saw above. But the gospel of grace should not lead to licentious living but rather love for others (Gal. 5:13–15), which is the fulfillment of the Law (cf. Lev. 19:18; Luke 10:25–28; Gal. 6:2).

JUDAIZERS

JEWS	GENTILES
Children of Isaac	Children of Ishmael
Free from slavery of sin	In bondage to sin
Because of the law of Moses	Because do not have the law of Moses

PAUL

JEWISH NON-CHRISTIANS	GENTILE CHRISTIANS
Children of Ishmael	Children of Isaac
From earthly Sinai	From heavenly Jerusalem
Bound to sin because the Law stirs up the flesh	Free from sin because of faith in Christ apart from the Law

Galatians 5:16–26 spells out the differences between living in the flesh (vv. 19–21) and walking in the Spirit (vv. 22–23). The former results from trying to obey the Torah, while the latter is the product of faith in Christ.

Galatians 6:1–10 contrasts the two destinies of those living in the flesh and those walking in the Spirit. The former caters to the sinful nature and will result in destruction. The latter loves others and will result in justification. For Paul, no doubt, the path to destruction is the course the Judaizers are treading; but Paul's gospel is the way to justification before God, beginning now.

E. 6:11–18: Conclusion

In the conclusion of Galatians, Paul takes a parting shot at the Judaizers, accusing them of inconsistency and ulterior motives in trying to get the Galatians to submit to circumcision (recall again our discussion above). For Paul's part, however, he will glory only in the cross of Christ. This is the basis of the true Israel, not the Torah and circumcision.

Conclusion

Our thesis for this chapter seems confirmed: Paul's eschatological message was in conflict with the eschatologies of his opponents: the Judaizers, non-Christian Jews, and the imperial cult. In one way or another, these groups opposed the scandal of the cross of Christ. The first two because it meant the end of the Torah and the last group because the one Rome crucified was the true Lord not Caesar.

Chapter 3

1 AND 2 THESSALONIANS

THE SIGNS OF THE TIMES, PAUL,

AND THE THESSALONIANS

First and 2 Thessalonians are often labeled as "eschatological letters of Paul," because eschatology dominates those correspondences. Thus every chapter of 1 Thessalonians ends with a reference to the second coming of Christ (1:9–10; 2:19–20; 3:13; 4:13–18; 5:23–24), while 2 Thessalonians is patently apocalyptic in its presentation of the signs of the times of Christ's return. But Paul's view of the end times was not the only eschatology in town; other end-time scenarios were popular in Thessalonica. This chapter will seek to demonstrate that Paul's eschatology was at odds in that city with the eschatologies of non-Christian Judaism, the Roman imperial cult, and Hellenistic religion. Before turning to that purpose, we first recount Paul's relationship with the Thessalonian church.

During Paul's second missionary journey, he and Silas traveled to the city of Thessalonica. There they preached in the synagogue to both Jews and God-fearers, meeting with the same results as they did in Galatia: some Jews and many God-fearers accepted the gospel while the majority of Jews rejected it. The latter group stirred up the town to oppose Paul and Silas. Things got so bad that the two missionaries had to leave Thessalonica for Berea under the cover of darkness (Acts 17:1–9). Even though the Bereans were more positive in response to Paul's gospel, the Jews from Thessalonica traveled to Berea and incited the townspeople there to turn against Paul and Silas. Silas and Timothy stayed in Berea but Paul was escorted to Athens for his safety (Acts 17:10–15). From there Paul traveled to nearby Corinth and wrote 1 Thessalonians sometime in AD 51.[1] The primary purpose of 1 Thessalonians was to steel the faith of the Thessalonian Christians in the face of persecution. Such persecution Paul seems to have understood to be the messianic woes/Great Tribulation (cf. 1 Thess. 5:3 with 2 Thess. 2:3–12).[2]

From 1 Thessalonians and Acts 17:1–9 we will see that Paul's opposition at Thessalonica was on two fronts: non-Christian Judaism and the Roman imperial cult. By the time Paul wrote 2 Thessalonians in AD 54 some six months later, the plot had thickened in Thessalonica.[3] Now someone within the church was stirring up trouble for Paul; someone, we will argue, that was influenced by Hellenistic religion. Paul was now having to confront three eschatological constructs. To put it another way Paul's apocalypse of Christ was in competition with the consistent eschatology of Judaism, the realized eschatology of the Roman imperial cult, and the realized eschatology of Hellenistic syncretistic religion. We now unpack this statement, taking each of Paul's eschatological rivals in the above order.

PAUL'S APOCALYPSE OF CHRIST VERSUS THE CONSISTENT ESCHATOLOGY OF JUDAISM IN THESSALONICA[4]

In our last chapter we were able to reconstruct the eschatology of the non-Christian Jews in Galatia. Based on 1 Thessalonians 2:14–16 and Acts

---

1   The point of departure for establishing the chronology of Paul's writings and linking it to Acts is the Gallio inscription discovered in Delphi, Greece. It dates Gallio's proconsulate in Corinth, Achaia to AD 52 (cf. Acts 18:12).

2   For documentation of this claim, I refer the reader to my, *The Glory of Adam and the Afflictions of the Righteous: Pauline Suffering in Context* (Lewiston, NY: Edwin Mellen Press,1993), pp. 291–312. See also our discussion below.

3   For documentation that Paul was indeed the author of 2 Thessalonians, see Ibid, pp. 291–92.

4   See Ben Witherington III's data regarding the strong presence of a Jewish population in Thessalonica, *1 and 2 Thessalonians: A Socio-Rhetorical Commentary* (Grand Rapids, MI: Eerdmans, 2006), pp. 7–9.

17:1–9, we can do the same for Thessalonica. We begin with 1 Thessalonians 2:14–16.

An Eschatological Reading of 1 Thessalonians 2:16

The two clauses in 2:16, "always heap up their sins to the limit" and "the wrath of God has come upon them at last" have occasioned much debate relative to the identity of the historical allusion behind the verse: Claudius's expulsion of the Jews from Rome (AD 49; Acts 18:2) shortly before the writing of 1 Thessalonians; the death of Agrippa (AD 44), Acts 12:20–23); the insurrection of Theudas (AD 49; Acts 5:36); the fall of Jerusalem (AD 70). None of these possibilities are fully convincing. The last one suffers from the problem of dating. The others do not seem to have been well enough known to fit Paul's casual reference here, which presupposes a widely held view. The best alternative, therefore, is that Paul is alluding to the commonly known apocalyptic tradition that the messianic woes were expected to overtake the people of God in the end times. After some introductory remarks on "wrath" in Romans 1:18, Ernest Best turns his attention to 1 Thessalonians 2:16, compiling the evidence for interpreting it eschatologically, particularly the words " the wrath of God has come upon them at last":

> The final clause of the verse has been taken in a number of different ways because its component parts are subject to varying interpretations. *The anger* can be taken either as an anger which will be disclosed at the End (cf. 1.10) or as an anger working itself out in the present to punish men (Rom. 1:18); it is doubtful if 1 Thess. 2:16 can be wholly cleared of eschatological qualification yet because (*a*) 1.10 does not precede it, (*b*) the definite article picks out a known phrase, (*c*) the whole tone of the letter is eschatological, and (*d*) v. 16b suggests the fulfillment of a measure, a limit; we are compelled to take it in the former sense.[5]

The resulting meaning of 2:16 for Best is as follows:

---

5   Ernest Best, *The First and Second Epistles to the Thessalonians.* Harper's New Testament Commentaries (N.Y.: Harper & Row, 1972), p. 119.

The clause … represents a complete reversal of values in Paul: the sufferings of Israel, the so-called Messianic Woes, were the herald of the End and God's anger would fall on their oppressors; now the Jews are not persecuted but the persecutors, not those expecting God's wrath to fall on others, but its recipients; the very people who were the object of God's grace (Rom. 9.4f.) are now the objects of his anger.[6]

To the above four reasons that Best supplies for interpreting 1 Thessalonians 2:16 as alluding to the messianic woes now come upon Israel, three more, we suggest, should be added. (*e*) First Thessalonians 2:15 highlights the death of Jesus which, as we contended elsewhere, signifies for Paul in general and 1 Thessalonians in specific Jesus's endurance of the messianic woes.[7] (*f*) First Thessalonians 2:15 draws on the eschatological notion emerging from the Old Testament that in the end times Gentiles would turn to God (Isa. 45:14–17, 20–25; 59:19–20; Micah 4:1–8). (*g*) First Thessalonians 2:15–16 and its condemnation of those Jews who rejected Jesus is to be understood as the actualization of the prophecy of end-time apostasy. Jewish apocalypticism expected that the end of history would witness a large-scale turning away from the faith by the people of God (*Jub.* 23:14–23; 1 *Enoch* 91:3–10; *4 Ezra* 5:1–13; etc.). This expectation was included in Christian apocalypticism as well (Mark 13:20–23; Matt. 24:10–13; Luke 21:19, 34–36). In fact, there are a number of New Testament texts which indicate the eschatological apostasy began with Israel's rejection of Jesus (Gal. 1:6–7; 2 Thess. 2:3–12; John 6:7; 13:2, 27; 14:30; 17:12 [with reference to Judas]; Rev. 13:15–18; etc.). It seems that it is this notion that Paul draws upon here in 1 Thessalonians 2:15–16.

A Deuteronomic Reading of 1 Thessalonians 2:16

Since the work of O. H. Steck, it has become more customary to view 1 Thessalonians 2:15–16 as impacted by the Deuteronomistic tradition. That motif can be reduced to four components: (1) Israel has been rebellious to God throughout its history; (2) God repeatedly sent his prophets to call the nation to repentance;

---

6   Ibid, p. 121.
7   See Pate, *The Glory of Adam and the Afflictions of the Righteous*, pp. 311–12.

(3) but Israel consistently rejected these divine spokesmen; (4) therefore God judged Israel by sending her into exile in 722 BC and, again, in 587 BC, a condition that persisted in Paul's day, despite Israel's apparent regathering to her land.

These four components of the Deuteronomistic tradition admirably explain 1 Thessalonians 2:15–16. Thus, (1) Paul accuses the Jews of his day of disobeying God in that they both reject Paul's gospel and attempt to prevent others from accepting the Christian faith. (2) and (3) In doing so they reject Jesus, the culmination of God's prophets, including Paul. (4) God's judgment, the Deuteronomic curses, continue to abide on Israel. As James M. Scott has carefully shown, Paul most probably has in mind here the stark reality that the exile continued to impinge on Israel's existence, the most recent expression of which was Roman occupation.[8] Best earlier approximated a Deuteronomistic reading of 1 Thessalonians 2:15–16, especially the phrase, "wrath has come upon them at last":

… the whole phrase 'while logically progressive, is regarded by the aorist collectively, a series of anaplērōsa being taken as one.' Paul is using words drawn from Gen. 15.16 (cf. Dan. 8.23; 2 Macc. 6.14) where they refer to the sins of the Amorites against Abraham the father of the Jews; he turns them against the Jews themselves. It suggests a definite measure of sins which when completed will be followed by God's judgment (v. 16a); cf. Col. 1.24 and the filling up of a measure of sufferings. It is the implication of vv. 15f that this measure is nearly filled up –Jesus and the prophets have been killed, Paul and his fellow Christian missionaries have been persecuted, and the preaching to the Gentiles is being hindered. There has been a terrifying consistency about the conduct of the Jews throughout their history; now it has reached its climax.[9]

8   James M. Scott, "Paul's Use of Deuteronomic Tradition(s)." *Journal of Biblical Literature* 112 (1993): pp. 645–65. Steck's work was programmatic for this interpretation of 1 Thessalonians 2:15–16, *Israel un das gewaltsame Geschick der Propheten: Untersuchungen zur Überlieferung des deuteronomistischen Geschichtsbildes im Alten Testament, Spätjudentum un Urchristentum,* (Israel and the Formation of the History of the Prophets: An Investigation in the Tradition of the Deuteronomistic Historical Image in the Old Testament, Late Judaism, and in Early Christianity), Wissenschaftliche Monographien zum Alten und Neuen Testament 23 (Neukirchen: Neukirchener Verlag, 1967).
9   Ernest Best, *The First and Second Epistles to the Thessalonians*, Harper's New Testament Commentaries (New York: Harper & Row, 1973), pp. 118–19.

THE MESSIANIC WOES AS THE CULMINATION
OF THE DEUTERONOMIC CURSES ON ISRAEL

The preceding two views of 1 Thessalonians 2:15–16 need not be contradictory; in actuality they cohere nicely in that Paul draws therein on the idea that the messianic woes were perceived to be the culmination of the Deuteronomic curses.[10] On this reading, the messianic woes that have fallen on Israel are completing the full measure of the Deuteronomic curses, because that nation has rejected its Messiah.

Two authors have recently put forth the preceding combination of views: David Wenham and N.T. Wright, whose arguments we now summarize. The former makes a good case for the hypothesis that Paul in 1 Thessalonians 2:16c—"wrath has come upon them at last"—draws on Luke 21:25—"There will be great distress on earth and *wrath against his people*" (emphasis is Wenham's). Wenham writes of this:

> The possibility that suggests itself is that here we have the tradition to which Paul alludes in 1 Thess. 2:16c. If it is, then what we effectively have in 1 Thes. 2:15, 16 is a combination of the sayings about the persecution of the prophets (seen in Matt. 23:32, 34–36/ Luke 11:48, 49–51) with the phrase about "wrath against his people" from the eschatological discourse as regarded in Luke. The combination is thoroughly intelligible, since the sayings about the prophets end with the warning of dire judgment coming on "this generation." Paul has thus interpreted that warning in terms of the eschatological discourse.[11]

In effect, without calling it such, Wenham is arguing here for the combination of Deuteronomistic and eschatological readings of 1 Thessalonians 2:16c. Of the evidence that he offers in support of his interpretation, the following is especially pertinent: (1) There is the similarity of the wording about "wrath" in 1 Thessalonians 2:16 and Luke 21:23. (2) It makes good sense of Paul's mysterious warning in 1 Thessalonians 2:16 if he is alluding to a known

---

10   See Pate and Kennard, *Deliverance Now and Not Yet,* pp. 29–115.
11   David Wenham, *Paul: Follower of Jesus or Founder of Christianity?* (Grand Rapids, MI: Eerdmans, 1995), p. 322.

tradition such as the eschatological discourse behind the Olivet Sermon. (3) The latter suggestion is all the more plausible in light of the commonalities between 1 Thessalonians 4–5 and the Olivet Discourse. (4) First Thessalonians 2:16, Romans 11:25 and Luke 21:23–24 share "the idea of judgment on the Jews and opportunity for the Gentiles coming together within an eschatological framework moving toward the "end."[12]

It could be objected, however, that the Lukan statement is a post-70 AD redaction of the Jesus tradition that post-dates Paul and therefore was unknown to the apostle. But N.T. Wright's research resolves such a potential dating problem by demonstrating that the merger of Deuteronomistic and eschatological traditions regarding the fall of Jerusalem go back to the historical Jesus, especially Mark 13:5–23. Concerning that passage, Wright uncovers three sets of Old Testament texts informing Mark 13:5–23, the first two of which deal with the Babylonian and Maccabean crises, respectively, while the third set keys in on Jerusalem as, not the victim of pagan aggression, but the enemy of the people of God.

First, Wright demonstrates that the messianic woes referred to in Mark 12:5–23 draw on those afflictions which attended the fall of Jerusalem to the Babylonians in 587 BC. So it is that the theme of the destruction of Jerusalem in Mark 13:2 echoes Micah 3:12; Jeremiah 7:14; 46:8; and Ezekiel 24:21. More specifically, the idea of internecine strife in Mark 13:12 recalls Micah 7:2–10. The reference in Mark 13:17 to those fleeing with children should be compared to Hosea 13:16 [MT 14:1]. The shortening of the days for the sake of the elect in Mark 13:20 reminds one of Isaiah 65:8; Mark 13:22 and the presence of the false prophets is rooted in, e.g., Deuteronomy 13 and Jeremiah 6:3f. The warning to run to the mountains before the invasion of Jerusalem in Mark 13:14 takes one to Ezekiel 7:12–16. In effect, then, what we have in Mark 13 is the apocalypticizing of the Deuteronomic curses.[13]

The second set of Old Testament passages informing Mark 13:5–23 are related, according to Wright, to the Maccabean crisis in 171–164 BC,

---

12 See Ibid, p. 322; cf. pp. 322–27.
13 For a discussion of some late Second Temple writings that apocalypticize the Deuteronomic curses and blessings (the former characterizing this age and the latter the age to come—see *1 Enoch*, the DSS, *4 Ezra, 2 Baruch*) consult Pate , *The Reverse of the Curse*, Part I.

namely, Daniel 9:24–27; 11:31–35: 12:10–11 (which speak of the coming anointed one's victory over Antiochus Epiphanes); compare also *1 Maccabees* 1:54–56; 62–64; *2 Maccabees* 8:17. Both of the previous crises—Babylonian and Maccabean—and the Old Testament texts they spawned, were obviously related to Israel's sin-exile-and restoration.[14]

Wright observes that a third set of Old Testament passages forms a part of the substructure of Mark 13:5–23, which reverses the story of Israel, namely, those texts accusing Jerusalem of itself being the enemy because of her idolatrous ways, thereby meriting her upcoming judgment: Isaiah 13; 6:9–11; 12:15; 14:4; 34:3–4; 48:20; 52:11–12; Ezekiel 32:5–8; Joel 2:10–11, 30–32; 3:14–15; Amos 8:9; Zephaniah 1:15; Zechariah 2:6–8; 14:2a, 3–5, 9.[15]

All of this is to say that the historical Jesus most probably combined Deuteronomistic and eschatological themes in his predictions regarding the fate of Jerusalem, a tradition drawn on by Paul in 1 Thessalonians 2:15–16. This co-joining of motifs is in keeping with those pre-Christian Jewish references that also interpreted the messianic woes as the culmination of the Deuteronomistic curses.[16]

We now note that there are two more points to the Deuteronomist tradition—number 5—Israel still has time to repent and if she does then, number 6—God will restore her to himself. Romans 11:25–27 attests to these last two points, as our later chapter will document. But here let us correlate the six points of the Deuteronomist tradition with the five points of the consistent eschatology of non-Christian Jews at the time of Paul:

14 See N. T. Wright, *Jesus and the Victory of God* (Minneapolis: Fortress Press, 1996), pp. 349–54.
15 Ibid, pp. 354–58.
16 For documentation of this point, see Pate and Kennard, *Deliverance and Not Yet*, pp. 29–115.

JEWISH ESCHATOLOGY	DEUTERONOMIC TRADITION
Hope for the age to come	#6 Restoration of Israel to replace #4 Israel's exile.
Hope for cosmic renewal	Again, #6, and #4.
Messiah will bring both	The Messiah will come to deliver Israel after she repents of her sin by obeying the Torah, #5
This is prophesied in the OT and Judaism	The Prophetic tradition and the Deuteronomic traditions are both affirmed in the OT and in Second Temple Judaism
But Israel must first obey the Torah and its ritual requirements	#1 Israel's repentance from sin and following the Torah means she will no longer reject the prophetic tradition, #2 and #3.

As we mentioned above, Paul's inaugurated eschatology was at odds with his kinsmen's consistent eschatology; indeed, Paul reversed the Deuteronomistic tradition. Thus:

JEWISH ESCHATOLOGY	PAUL'S APOCALYPSE OF CHRIST
1 and 2) Age to come not yet here nor cosmic renewal	1 and 2) Age to come/cosmic renewal has dawned
3) Messiah will deliver Israel and bring the age to come/restoration of Israel	3) Jesus is the suffering Messiah
4) Old Testament predicts the coming of the political Messiah (Isa. 2, etc.)	4) Old Testament predicts the coming of the suffering Messiah (cf. Acts 17:2–3 with Luke 24:26, 46–47; Isa. 53)
5) The restoration of Israel will happen when Jews obey the rituals of the Torah. Such obedience will replace the Deuteronomic curses with the Deuteronomic blessings/restoration	5) The true restoration of Israel and Gentiles (see 1 Thess. 2: 16; Acts 17:4, 12) happens only through faith in Christ, not the Torah. In actuality, obedience to the Law brings the Deuteronomic curses while faith in Christ brings the Deuteronomic blessings/restoration.

Paul's Apocalypse of Christ Versus
the Realized Eschatology of the Roman Imperial Cult

Recent studies on 1 and 2 Thessalonians have identified the presence of the Roman imperial cult at Thessalonica. We now correlate that evidence with the five components of the realized eschatology of Caesar worship.

The first and second eschatological components of the imperial cult—the primordial age has dawned and, with it, the beginning of cosmic renewal—are alluded to in Paul's usage of the word "gospel" in 1 Thessalonians 1:4; 2:4, 8–9; 3:1; 2 Thessalonians 1:8; 2:14. Εὐαγγελιον, it will be recalled, is the term used in the Priene inscription heralding the birth of Augustus. Moreover, "peace and safety" in 1 Thessalonians 5:3 no doubt allude to the peace and safety brought about by Augustus' *pax Romana*. Thus Witherington writes:

> There were inscriptions all over the empire attributing to Rome and its army bringing the "peace and security" to one region after another. For example, in Syria we have an inscription which reads "The Lord Marcus Flavius Bonus, the most illustrious Comes and Dux of the first legion, has ruled over us in peace and given constant peace and security to travelers and to the people" (OGIS 613). Velleius Paterculus says, "On that day there sprang up once more in parents the assurance of safety, order, peace and tranquility" (2.103.5). He adds that "The Pax Augusta which has spread to the regions of the east and the west, and to the bounds of the north and the south, preserves every corner of the world safe/secure from the fear of banditry" (2.126.3). Tacitus speaks of the time after the year of the three emperors as a time when security was restored and adds that the "security of peace" includes work without anxiety in the fields and in the homes (*Historia* 2.21.2; 2.12.1). Not to be plundered by robbers either at home or on journeys is "peace and security" (Josephus, *Antiquites* 14.158–60, 247). A variant of this slogan, "peace and concord," is found in inscriptions dating back to 139 BC and referring to a pact between Rome and the cities of Asia "preserving mutual goodwill with peace and all concord and friendship" (SIG 685.14–15). Paul must have thought "What foolish slogans and vain hopes when the day of the Lord is coming." He is critiquing the slogans and propaganda about the Pax Romana. It is on those who offer this rhetoric that destruction will come, which may suggest that Paul foresaw the same

future for Rome and those who cooperated with it as John of Patmos does in Revelation 6–19. Paul does not want his audience to be beguiled by such rhetoric, especially after he has been expelled and they have suffered persecution from those who are supposedly the bringers of "peace and security." It is the imperial propaganda and prophecies that Paul is offering a rebuttal to here.[17]

Added to the terms "gospel," "peace and safety," is the fact that all the Macedonians (of which Thessalonica was a part) chose to honor Augustus by declaring that they were inaugurating an "Augustan era," an era of unprecedented cooperation and commercial exchange between Macedonians and Romans.[18]

The third eschatological component of the imperial cult evidenced at Thessalonica was the identification of Augustus as the savior of the new age. Two titles of deity for Augustus were "Lord" (*kyrios*) and "Son of god." As Deissmann demonstrated long ago, *kyrios* was a title for Caesar that permeated the Roman Empire, especially east of Rome.[19] For the latter, see, for example, the inscription found at Cosa, ("[To Imperator Caesar], son of the deified, Augustus, pontifex maximus … son of a god Augustus").[20] Compare this to the inscription dedicating the temple to Augustus at Thessalonica, "In the time of priest and [Im]perator Caesar Augustus son [of god]…."[21] Paul's references to Jesus as "Lord" (1 Thessalonians 1:1, 8; 2:15, 19; 3:11–13; 4:2, 15 (2x); 16–17; 5:1, 9, 12, 23, 27–28; 2 Thess. 2:1; etc.) and "son" [of God] (1 Thess. 1:10) would have been an affront to Caesar.

Fourth, by Paul's time the Priene inscription (9 BC) was well known throughout the Roman Empire and was considered inspired prophecy, hailing the birth of Augustus. Interestingly enough Luke, the author of Luke

---

17 Witherington, *1 and 2 Thessalonians*, pp. 146–47.
18 See M. B. Sakellariou, *Macedonia: 4000 Years of Greek History and Civilization* (Athens: Ekdotike Athenon, 1983), pp. 195–96.
19 Adolf Deissmann, *Light From the Ancient East: The New Testament Illustrated by Recently Discovered Texts of the Graeco-Roman World*, trans. Lionel R. M. Strachan (New York: George H. Doran, 1927), pp. 349–67.
20 Quoted in Ben Witherington III's, *Conflict and Community in Corinth: A Socio-Rhetorical Commentary on 1 and 2 Corinthians* (Grand Rapids, MI: Eerdmans, 1995), p. 296, no.27.
21 Quoted in Gene L. Green, *1 and 2 Thessalonians*. The Pillar New Testament Commentary (Grand Rapids, MI: Eerdmans, 2002), p.39.

and Acts, alludes to the Priene inscription in his story of the birth of Jesus (see Luke 1–2), as has often been noted. This is the same Luke who records Paul's visit to Thessalonica and the resulting accusation made against Paul that he was disobeying the decrees of Caesar (Acts 17:7), on which see the next point.

Fifth, the imperial cult was cemented in the cultures of the Roman Empire via architecture, oaths, and celebrations. First and 2 Thessalonians, and Acts 17, attest to these aspects of the realized eschatology of the imperial cult. Thus, Witherington writes:

> The Thessalonians erected a statue of Augustus with the upraised right hand of a hero and a temple to Augustus as well (IG X.2.31–32), both of which Paul surely saw during his visit. The statue has been dated to the reign of Gaius (Caligula) or Claudius, and it is one of the few objects recovered at the city which can be dated with certainty to the time of Paul's visit. It is perhaps in the context of so effusive an outpouring of honors for Augustus that one should understand Paul's condemnation of those who promote "peace and security" (1 Thess. 5:3—a Julio-Claudian program of *pax et securitas?*). Even more interestingly, all the Macedonians chose to honor Augustus by declaring that they were inaugurating an "Augustan era".... Already, during the lifetime of Augustus there were priests of the imperial cult there, and the presence of the cult is shown by coins minted there which have identified Julius Caesar on one side and Augustus as "divi filius" on the other (IG X 2.1 31). We know of a Caesareum already built in the time of Augustus which had a sanctuary (*naos* – IG X.2.1.31).[22]

This may well be a part of the background of 2 Thessalonians 2 :2–3 where Paul refers to the lawless one exalting himself in the temple.

Furthermore, as has often been observed, 1 Thessalonians 4:15–17 contains three words that were associated with the arrival of the Roman Caesar to a town: *parousia* (coming, v. 15), *apantesis* (meet him, v. 17), and *kyrios* (Lord,

---

22 Witherington, *1 and 2 Thessalonians*, p. 5.

vv. 15, 16, 17). K. P. Donfried points this out, mounting the case that Paul's language in 1 Thessalonians was anti-imperialist, replacing Caesar with Jesus:

> If 1 Thessalonians is at all representative of [Paul's] original preaching then we certainly do find elements which could be understood or misunderstood in a distinctly political sense. In 2:12 God, according to the Apostle, calls the Thessalonian Christians "into his own kingdom"; in 5:3 there is a frontal attack on the *Pax et Securitas* program of the early Principate; and in the verses just preceding this attack one finds three heavily loaded political terms: *parousia*, *apantesis*, and *kyrios*. *Parousia* is related to "the 'visit' of the king, or some other official." When used as court language *parousia* refers to the arrival of Caesar, a king or an official. *Apentesis* refers to the citizens meeting a dignitary who is about to visit the city. These two terms are used in this way by Josephus (*Ant.* XI.327ff.) and also similarly referred to by such Greek writers as Chrysostom. The term *kyrios* especially when used in the same context as the two preceding terms, also has a definite political sense. People in the eastern Mediterranean applied the term *kyrios* to the Roman emperors from Augustus on…. All of this, coupled with the use of *euaggelion* and its possible association with the eastern ruler cult suggests that Paul and his associates could easily be understood as violating "the decrees of Caesar" in the most blatant manner.[23]

Moreover, Acts 17:6 relates that the Jews of Thessalonica accused Paul and Silas of disobeying the "decrees of Caesar." In all likelihood E. A. Judge is right that what is being referred to here is an oath of loyalty to Caesar and Rome administered by the politarchs. An example of such an oath that was administered in Paphlagonia reads:

> I swear … that I will support Caesar Augustus, his children and descendants throughout my life in word, deed and thought … that in whatsoever concerns them I will spare neither body nor soul nor life nor children … that whenever I see or hear of anything being said, planned or done against them I will report it

---

23 K. P. Donfried, "The Imperial Cult and Political Conflict in 1 Thessalonians," in *Paul and Empire,* ed. R. A. Horsley (Harrisburg, PA: Trinity Press, 1997), p. 217.

… and whomsoever they regard as enemies I will attack and pursue with arms
and the sword by land and by sea….[24]

These allusions in 1 and 2 Thessalonians, along with the material in Acts
17, indicate that Paul pitted Jesus Christ, the inaugurator of the age to come,
against any grandiose claims made by the imperial cult.

PAUL'S APOCALYPSE OF CHRIST VERSUS THE REALIZED ESCHATOLOGY OF HELLENISTIC RELIGION

In 1 Thessalonians 1:9 Paul rejoices that the Thessalonian believers left their
pagan worship of false gods (idols) to serve the true God in Christ. One part
of the pagan background of Paul's audience was the imperial cult. But as
Witherington points out, emperor worship in the first century was syncre-
tized with the Greco-Roman pantheon of gods as well as with the Hellenistic
mystery religions. At Thessalonica the mystery religions involved the worship of Cabirus (a local cult), the Greek cult of Dionysius and the foreign
cult of Isis and Serapis.[25] Syncretism is evident at Thessalonica. For example,
as the local coins show, the Roman emperor was deified as *kabeiros*.[26] Or the
phallus, the main symbol of the Cabirus cult, was also associated at Thessalonica with the Dionysius cult.[27] We also know that the Dionysius cult was
associated with wine, drunken orgies, and consequently ecstatic experience
in which the worshipper was thought to be united with Dionysius. Merged
with all of this at Thessalonica were astrological texts. Green records one
such text at Thessalonica:

> The experts in astrology tell of an early death for me; though it be so, I care
> nothing for that, Seleucus. All men have the same way down to Hades; if mine
> is quicker than others', I shall be face to face with Minos the sooner. Let us

---

24 E. A. Judge, "The Decrees of Caesar at Thessalonica," in *RTR* 30 (1971), p. 6.
25 Witherington, *1 and 2 Thessalonians*, pp. 5–6.
26 Ibid, p. 5, no. 27.
27 Green, *1 and 2 Thessalonians*, pp. 35–36.

drink, for surely it is a true saying that wine is like a horse for the highway, while your foot-traveller must go to Hades by a lane.[28]

Green supplies an ancient papyrus text that details how one can interpret astrological information:

> If in addition Mercury is in conjunction, and Saturn is irregularly situated … from an unfavorable position; if at the same time Mars is in opposition to Saturn, the aforesaid position being maintained (he will destroy?) profits of transactions. Saturn in triangular relation to Mars or in conjunction makes great kingdoms and empires. Venus in conjunction makes great kingdoms and empires. Venus in conjunction with Mars causes fornications and adulteries; if in addition Mercury is in conjunction with them, they in consequence makes scandals and lusts. If Mercury is in conjunction with Jupiter or appears in triangular relation, this causes favorable actions of commerce, or a man will gain his living by … or by reason, and … If Mars appears in triangular relation to Jupiter and Saturn, this causes great happiness, and will make acquisitions and … If while Jupiter and Saturn are in this position Mars comes into conjunction with either … after obtaining (wealth) and collecting a fortune he will spend it and lose it. If Jupiter, Mercury, and Venus are in conjunction, they cause glories and empires and great prosperity; and if the conjunction takes place at the morning rising (of Venus), they cause prosperity from youth upwards (*P. Tebtunis 276).*[29]

It is easy to see how such information could be viewed as prophetic in that they were thought to determine the future of individuals.

This religious pluralistic background seems to be behind Paul's warnings in several places in 1 and 2 Thessalonians. We noted above from 1 Thessalonians 1:9 that the Thessalonian believers were pagan before becoming God-fearers and then Christians (see Acts 17:1–9; cf. the Galatian churches). Paul's

---

28 Ibid, p. 36. In the ancient world, no distinction was made between astronomy and astrology.
29 Ibid, p. 37, no. 27.

exhortation in 1 Thessalonians 4:4 ("each man should control his σκεῦος")
is thought by some to allude to the phallus, the symbol of procreation and
new life in the Cabirus cult. This rendering would be in keeping with Paul's
exhortation in 1 Thessalonians 4:1–8 to holy living. In other words, the Thessalonians were not to resort back to the sexual immorality that characterized
their worship of Cabirus and Dionysius. First Thessalonians 5:5–8 may also
be Paul's invective against joining in with the nighttime drinking and orgies
that accompanied the Dionysius cult. Moreover, 1 Thessalonians 5:19 connects
prophecy and the Spirit, as does 2 Thessalonians 2:2–3. The latter text states
that someone in the Thessalonian church falsely appealed to Paul in support of
their prophecy that the Day of the Lord/parousia had already occurred. It is not
difficult to envision how this could have been so. The mystery religions at Thessalonica—especially Dionysius, and Isis/Serapis—taught that the worshipper
became united with the deity through ecstatic experience. This background,
plus Paul's teaching that the Thessalonians had received the Holy Spirit—the
sign of the age to come—(cf. 1 Thess. 1:5; 4:8; 5:19; 2 Thess. 2:2, 13 with Acts
2:1–21), could have easily caused a Thessalonian pagan turned Christian to
say that the parousia occurs when one has an ecstatic experience with the Holy
Spirit. We will see that this very notion was behind the realized eschatology of
the Corinthian church.

We conclude this section with a chart that shows how a Christian's past pagan
worship at Thessalonica could have produced a type of realized eschatology:

REALIZED ESCHATOLOGY OF HELLENISTIC RELIGION:	REALIZED ESCHATOLOGY OF THESSALONIAN PAGANISM EMBRACED BY CHRISTIANS:
(1) New age has dawned—symbolized by phallus in Cabirus/Dionysius cults	(1) New age dawned in Christ's first coming
(2) The cosmic joining of heaven and earth through mystic union between the worshipper and the deity (especially in Dionysius and Isis/Serapis cults)	(2) The second coming of Christ is realized now in ecstatic experience with the Spirit
(3) Savior is Dionysius, Cabirus, Isis, Serapis, Caesar	(3) Savior is Jesus Christ

(4) Sacred writing/astrological texts determine the future of individuals	(4) The Old Testament predicts the coming of the Spirit in the end times (Joel 2:28–32)
(5) Rituals—the drunken sex orgies of Dionysius	(5) Ritual ecstatic experience with the Spirit actualizes the parousia

Paul, however, begs to differ with his misinformed Christian brother. Paul wrote nothing about the parousia occurring in ecstatic experience with the Spirit (recall 2 Thess. 2:2–3). Indeed, the fact that Christians still die shows that the parousia has not yet occurred (1 Thess. 2:13–18). And there are certain signs that must happen before the second coming of Christ (see 2 Thess. 2:1–12). Thus the Thessalonian believers should get back to their jobs, for the return of paradise and the cessation of work have not yet happened (2 Thess. 3:6–15). Indeed, there is still much of the messianic woes to yet suffer (*ala* 1 and 2 Thessalonians). In others words, Paul's inaugurated eschatology is a healthy corrective—his eschatological reservation—to the false realized eschatology that caused an imbalance in the Thessalonian church.

A SUMMARY OF 1 AND 2 THESSALONIANS

First Thessalonians can be outlined as follows:

- A. 1:1–10: Paul's Thanksgiving for the Thessalonians
- B. 2:1–3:13: Paul's Explanation of His Actions
- C. 4:1–5:22: Paul's Exhortations to the Thessalonians

A. 1:1–10: Paul's Thanksgiving for the Thessalonians

Because Paul was not able to stay a long time with the Thessalonians after their conversion (see Acts 17:1–9), he was concerned about how their new-found faith was holding up under persecution. But Timothy's report to Paul related that the Thessalonian church was indeed faithful to Christ (1 Thess. 3:1–5). Hence the apostle's praise for the Thessalonians' faith that produced work, labor that resulted in love, and hope that inspired endurance (1 Thess. 1:2–3). This is because the Thessalonians experienced the end-time power of the Holy Spirit (v. 5). Such a dynamic enabled the Thessalonians to endure the messianic woes/Great Tribulation.

Chapter 3

Herein we see Paul's inaugurated eschatology—Christians participate in the age to come because of faith in Christ and the indwelling of the Spirit, yet they still are in this present age of the messianic woes (see 1 Thess. 1:12). This is what Jesus experienced and what Paul and the Thessalonians are encountering (vv. 6–10). The idea of suffering the messianic woes dominates Paul's discussion in 1 Thessalonians. For Paul and the Thessalonians it meant persecution at the hands of non-Christian Jews and the imperial cult (see 1 Thess. 2:14–16; Acts 17:1–9).

B. 2:1–3:13: Paul's Explanation of His Actions
In 1 Thessalonians 2:1–13 Paul recounts his ministry of suffering and hardship (2:1–2, 9). The hardships were the results of the persecution Paul encountered from Judaism and the imperial cult. No doubt his own labor at tentmaking also factored into Paul's experience.[30] All the while Paul served the Thessalonians out of pure motives (2:3–8, 10–13). Unlike some of the philosophical hucksters that charged their audience for their teachings, Paul did none of that.

Abraham J. Malherbe advanced the theory that 1 Thessalonians 1:6 and 2:14 are best understood from a philosophical perspective. He maintains the affliction suffered by the Thessalonians was the distress and anguish of heart experienced by persons who broke with their past as they received the gospel rather than some form of outward duress designed to prevent them from accepting the gospel.[31] Malherbe supports this interpretation by appealing to Greco-Roman philosophical texts like Epictetus' *Discourse* 1.6.38, 41–42; 2.17.18–19; Plutarch's *Progress in Virtue* 77EF; 78A-C; Philo's *On Virtues* 103; *Joseph and Asenath* 12.11; 13.1; etc.[32]

Those proposed parallels are intriguing, but not convincing. Charles W. Wanamaker provides three criticisms of Malherbe on this point:

(1) In 3:3 Paul uses *thlipis* of external oppression that his readers have undergone. It is questionable whether the same word would be used in two very

---

30 Ronald Hock points this out in *The Social Context of Paul's Ministry. Tentmaking and Apostleship* (Philadelphia: Fortress Press, 1980).
31 Abraham J. Malherbe, *Paul and the Thessalonians: The Philosophic Tradition of Pastoral Care* (Philadelphia; Fortress Press, 1987), pp. 46–47.
32 Ibid, pp. 37–46.

different senses in the same general context of the letter. (2) It is improbable that Paul meant that his converts had become imitators of the Lord by virtue of their inner sense of conflict at their time of conversion. Paul would hardly have wanted to suggest such internal ambivalence on the part of the Lord, whom they were imitating. (3) In v. 7 Paul proceeds to say that the Thessalonians' experience of "much distress" resulted in their becoming an example for all the believers in Macedonia and Achaia. This implies very strongly that in v. 6 Paul was speaking about more than mere "distress and anguish of heart."[33]

Wanamakers's own interpretation is a more plausible rendering of 1 Thessalonians 1:6 and 2:14. The former verse states that the Thessalonians became imitators of Paul and the Lord by enduring the opposition that they experienced at the time of their conversion. The latter verse adds the fact that the Thessalonian believers, through their faithful embracing of that persecution, imitated the Judean Christians. In particular, the Thessalonian believers (Gentiles by birth and lifestyle; see 1 Thess 1:9–10) suffered at the hands of their Gentile compatriots in a manner similar to the way Jewish Christians of Judea suffered at the hands of their Jewish countrymen. Wanamaker explains the analogy thusly: just as the Judaizers were responsible for the physical harassment of the Jewish Christians because of the latter's involvement in the Gentile mission, so the citizens of Thessalonica (who had strong ties to Rome and its imperial cult) persecuted the Gentile Christians there because of the latter's potential threat to Caesar's lordship which, in turn, jeopardized the city's relationship with Rome.[34] The point being made here, then, is that both groups, Jewish and Gentile Christians, encountered *physical* affliction at the hands of their own respective inhabitants. Wanamaker's conclusion about the eschatological nature of the Thessalonian Christians' suffering as reflected in 1 Thessalonian 1:6 and 4:2 seems correct, "Paul appears to have understood the continuing opposition of the Jews to

---

33 Charles W. Wanamaker, *The Epistles to the Thessalonians: A Commentary on the Greek Text,* The New International Greek Testament Commentary (Grand Rapids, MI: Eerdmans, 1990), p. 81.

34 Ibid, pp. 3–6, 113, 144.

the Christian mission and therefore to the will of God in terms of his apocalyptic framework."[35] This author concurs.

Moreover, like the Teacher of Righteousness who suffered for the Dead Sea Scrolls community, Paul endured the suffering of the messianic woes on behalf of the Thessalonians (cf. DSS [1QH 3:7–10; 7:20–22;CD 1;4QpPs 3:15–16 ; Col. 1:24). So also the Thessalonian church suffered at the hands of its townsmen—especially Gentiles—even as Paul and the Judean churches suffered at the hands of Jews. But the persecutors, both Jews and Gentiles, will do more than suffer the messianic woes, they will experience the wrath of God (1 Thess. 2:14–16); something which Christians will never know (1 Thess. 1:10; 5:9). In the meantime, Paul deeply wanted to revisit the Thessalonians but he was hindered by Satan and continued opposition from doing so. Nevertheless, the Thessalonians will be Paul's joy and glory at the parousia (2:17–20).

Paul had sent Timothy to encourage the Thessalonians to endure their trials. The fact that believers are destined to endure these afflictions taps into the Jewish-Christian apocalyptic expectation that true followers of God will first undergo the messianic woes/great tribulation before entering the kingdom of God (cf. 1 Thess. 3:1–5, with 1:12). Now that Timothy had returned to Paul with such a glowing report of the Thessalonians' endurance in the faith, Paul is encouraged to continue to persevere through his own apostolic hardships. Paul concludes this section of 1 Thessalonians by praying for his readers to be faithful to Christ until he returns with his holy angels (3:11–13).

C. 4:1–5:22: Paul's Exhortations to the Thessalonians
Paul exhorts the Thessalonian believers in three areas: their personal lives (4:1–12); the coming of Christ (4:13–5:11); and concerning church life (5:12–22).

In 4:1–12, Paul challenges the Thessalonian Christians to be done with their past pagan days of sexual debauchery. Lurking in the background ever ready to ensnare Paul's readers were the Hellenistic mystery religions of the cults of Cabirus, Dionysius, and Isis/Serapis. Rather, through the power of the Spirit the believers at Thessalonica should live holy lives, set apart to God. Moreover, they should quietly go about the business of genuinely loving one another and being

---

35 Ibid, p. 116.

faithful at their jobs. These actions of holiness, love, and faithfulness will earn the respect of onlookers towards the Christian faith.

Paul's exhortations regarding the parousia of Christ in 4:13–5:11 divide into two instructions: 4:13–18—the comfort that the hope of the parousia brings; and 5:1–11—the challenge that the imminence of the parousia instills.

Regarding 1 Thessalonians 4:13–18, the Christians at Thessalonica needed to be reminded that suffering and death was par for the course since they participated in the messianic woes. Thus they should not be surprised that death overtook some of their brethren. Neither were their deceased brothers and sisters in Christ eliminated from the kingdom of God because they died before the parousia. Actually, departed Christians will be the first to be resurrected at that event. Then those Christians still alive at the parousia will be raised to meet the Lord in the air. Together—departed and living Christians—will then escort Jesus to earth to establish his kingdom now made visible. This should comfort those believers regarding their departed Christian loved ones.

We conclude our summary of 1 Thessalonians 4:13–18 by making three comments. First, we earlier saw that Paul therein contrasts the parousia of Christ with the parousia of Caesar. Second, the Old Testament also factors into the background of vv. 13–18 for, as Witherington remarks:

It should be clear from the beginning of v. 16 that Christ is said to come *down* out of heaven and meet his followers somewhere else, in this case in the atmosphere, where there are clouds. There is likely an echo of Mic. 3 1.3 here: "For behold the Lord is coming forth out of his place, and will come down and tread upon the high places of the earth." Clouds are regularly said to accompany a theophany, when God comes down to the human level, not when humans are taken up into the presence of God in heaven (see Ex. 19.16; 40:34; 1 Kings 8.10–11; Ps. 97.2). Trumpet blasts also accompany theophanies (Ex. 19.16; Isa. 27.13; Joel 2.1; Zech. 9.14). The meeting does not take place in heaven, so there is no rapture into heaven here.[36]

---

36 Witherington, *1 and 2 Thessalonians*, p. 141.

Chapter 3

In other words, the parousia of Christ is the coming of God to earth.

Third, though the concept of a secret rapture of the church before the advent of the great tribulation followed by the visible second coming of Christ is enormously popular in American religion, there is no basis for such in 1 Thessalonians 4:13–18, the key passage in the debate. This is because Paul equates the "rapture" (1 Thess. 4:13–18) with the parousia/second coming of Christ. Douglas Moo shows this to be the case here because 1 Thessalonians 4:13–18 matches the descriptions of the parousia in 1 Thessalonians 5:1–11, 2 Thessalonians 2, and Jesus' Olivet Discourse. Thus:

> Paul clearly describes in these two passages what Jesus depicts as *one* event—showing that it is illegitimate to separate the Parousia of 1 Thessalonians 4 and the Parousia of 2 Thessalonians 2 in time *and* making it very overwhelmingly probable that Jesus addresses the *church* in the Olivet Discourse. For surely, if Paul addresses the church in the Thessalonian epistles, it is obvious that Jesus, who says virtually the same thing, is also addressing the church.[37]

OLIVET DISCOURSE	EVENT	PAUL
24:5 (Matthew)	Warning about deception	2 Thess. 2:2
24:5, 11, 24	Lawlessness, delusion of the non-elect, signs and wonders	2 Thess. 2:6–11
24:12	Apostasy	2 Thess. 2:3
24:15	Antichrist in the temple	2 Thess. 2:4
24:21–22	Tribulation preceding the end	2 Thess. 1:6–10
24:30–31	Parousia of Christ, on clouds, at the time of a trumpet blast, with angelic accompaniment	1 Thess. 4:14–16
24:30–31	In power	2 Thess. 2:8

37 Douglas J. Moo, in *The Rapture: Pre-, Mid-, or Post-Tribulational?*, by Gleason L. Archer, Paul D. Feinberg, Douglas J. Moo, and Richard R. Reiter (Grand Rapids, MI: Zondervan, 1984), p. 194.

OLIVET DISCOURSE	EVENT	PAUL
24:31	Gathering of believers	1 Thess. 4:16 2 Thess. 2:1
24:36, 42, 44, 50; 25:13	Unexpected and certain	1 Thess. 5:1–4
24:42–25:13	Exhortation to watch.	1 Thess. 5:6–8

In 1 Thessalonians 5:1–11, Paul exhorts his audience to alertness in preparation for the parousia of Christ. The Day of the Lord was an Old Testament concept going back to Amos 5:18. While ancient Israel expected that the Day of the Lord would be the coming of Yahweh to deliver Israel from her enemies, Amos declared just the opposite—Yahweh will come to judge Israel for her sin! Not covenant blessings upon Israel but covenant curses (cf. 1 Thess. 2:14–16). In the New Testament, the Day of the Lord is applied to Christ as well, whose parousia will spell judgment upon the church's enemies but deliverance for Christ's followers. It is clear from the close association of 1 Thessalonians 4:13–18/5:1–11 and 2 Thessalonians 2:1–2 that Paul equates the Day of the Lord with Jesus' parousia. From 1 Thessalonians 5:1–2 we learn that the messianic woes lead up to the parousia. Paul's metaphor of birth pangs was commonly associated in Jewish and Christian apocalyptic writings with the birth pangs of the Messiah, i.e., the messianic woes. While the unrighteous live driven by their passions, Paul challenges Christians to live as children of the light. The Dead Sea Scrolls also contrast the righteous and the unrighteous in terms of children of the light and children of darkness, respectively (1QM1:1; 13:1–18; 14:12–18; 1QS 1:9–10; 3:1–4:26). For Paul, the Thessalonians need to keep their pagan lifestyles encouraged by the mystery religions in the past. In doing so, Christians will not be caught off guard by the sudden appearance of Christ like the unrighteous will be (5:3–11).

Paul's third exhortation in this section of 1 Thessalonians relates to the Thessalonians' church life (5:12–22). In rapid succession the apostle exhorts the believers there to respect their leaders, be at peace with each other, get to work if they are idle, lift up the timid and weak, be patient and do not retaliate, be joyful and thankful, not to quench the Spirit's prophecies but rather assess the prophecies to make sure they are from the Lord. The last injunction became a major problem in the Thessalonian church because someone prophesied in Paul's name by word or letter that the parousia had already come with the reception of the Spirit. Paul would write 2 Thessalonians to clear up that misinformation.

Second Thessalonians can be outlined as follows:

A. 1:1–12: Paul's Thanksgiving and Intercession for the Thessalonian Believers
B. 2:1–17: Paul's Instruction to the Thessalonians Regarding the Signs of the Times before the Parousia
C. 3:1–5: Paul's Injunctions to and Criticisms of the Thessalonians in the Light of the Parousia

We now proceed to summarize these points.

A. 1:1–12: Paul's Thanksgiving and Intercession for the Thessalonian Believers

Regarding the former of these, Paul thanks God for his readers' faith, love, and perseverance in the gospel, much as he did in 1 Thessalonians 1:2–3. These qualities will serve the Thessalonian church well as it continues to endure the messianic woes/great tribulation. But such obedience on their part will be more than compensated when they receive the glorious kingdom of God at the parousia of Christ. Conversely, the Thessalonians' oppressors will be judged and sent into everlasting punishment at the return of Christ (1:4–10). Thus Paul prays that his audience will show itself worthy of that kingdom by being faithful to the gospel. All of this is rooted in God's grace (1:11–22).

B. 2:1–17: Paul's Instruction to the Thessalonians Regarding the Signs of the Times before the Parousia

As we mentioned earlier, it seems that someone or a group of members of the Thessalonian church had disseminated the misinformation that the parousia of Jesus occurred with the coming of the Spirit in ecstatic experience. In 2 Thessalonians 2, Paul corrects such realized eschatology with an explanation of his inaugurated eschatology—namely the parousia will not come until certain signs of the times occur, three in particular: apostasy (v. 3a) the removal of the restrainer, and the appearance of the man of lawlessness

(2:3–11). End-time apostasy, as we earlier documented, is a pervasive theme in Jewish apocalyptic literature (*Jubilees*; *4 Ezra* 5:1–12; *1 Enoch* 91:7; 93:9; DSS.; etc.) and in the New Testament (cf. Matt. 24:12; Acts 21:21 to 2 Tim. 3:1–9; Heb. 3:12). This activity is regularly associated with the rise of false prophets or teachers in the latter days (Mark 13:22; 1 Tim. 4:1–3; 2 Tim. 4:3–4), as it appears to be here.

The lawless one (2 Thess. 2:3b–5, 8–11) is a rival savior to Christ predicted to appear at the end of history (cf. 1 John 2:18; Rev. 6–19). Though Paul does not explicitly label this individual the "antichrist," that is probably who he has in mind here. This lawless one will exalt himself in the temple in an attempt to usurp the throne of God. Jewish readers would have immediately recalled Antiochus Epiphanes' sacrilege of the Jerusalem temple (Dan. 11:36), the Roman general Pompey's campaign in Judea in 63 BC which precipitated Jewish apostasy (Ps. 17:11–22) and, more recently, Emperor Caligula's decree in AD 39 that a statue of himself be placed in the Jerusalem temple (see Philo, *Embassy to Gaius*, 203–346). During the time when Paul wrote 1 and 2 Thessalonians, Claudius had a bronze coin issued in Philippi that equated himself with divinity. Later Caesar Nero abandoned all reserve and demanded to be worshiped as a god (see Rev. 13), and Emperor Domitian followed suit. The last two rulers targeted Christians because they would not bow before them. These infamous persons, along with the anti-imperial cult stance by Paul, combine to suggest that the apostle, like the book of Revelation, feared that the antichrist was about to dawn in the form of the Roman Emperor.[38]

The identification of the one who restrains the lawless man from appearing until God's appointed time is hotly debated: the Holy Spirit at the rapture of the church; the Roman government; Paul himself, or a holy angel like Michael. We have argued elsewhere that Michael, the angel of God, is the best option, especially when considering his role of deliverance on behalf of

---

38 Many dispensationalists argue that Paul in 2 Thessalonians 2:4 is predicting that the Jerusalem temple destroyed by the Romans in AD 70 will be rebuilt in the end times and there the antichrist will be enthroned as god. But this interpretation is highly debated. In my opinion, Paul more likely had in mind the ancient Jerusalem temple and the ancient Roman imperial cult, perhaps when Caligula decreed that a statue of him should be placed in that temple.

the people of God as spelled out in Daniel 12:1–2 and Revelation 12:7–9.[39] With Michael out of the way (at God's command) the lawless one will appear and through the power of Satan will dazzle many with his miracles and false teaching (2 Thess. 2:9–11).

In the meantime, the Thessalonians are to remain faithful to Paul's teaching and thus the true gospel of Christ (vv. 13–17). All of this to say, therefore, that the parousia has not yet occurred. Certain signs of the times still need to be fulfilled before that will happen.

C. 3:1–5: Paul's Injunctions to and Criticisms of the Thessalonians in the Light of the Parousia

At the same time, Paul encourages the Thessalonians to be faithful themselves to the gospel. And not to be idle. We have argued elsewhere that such inactivity stemmed from the realized eschatology that some in the church there had embraced. In other words, those who believed the parousia had already come through ecstatic experience with the Holy Spirit fancied themselves as enjoying paradise regained and, with it, the cessation of the curse of work (Gen. 3:17–19).[40] Paul closes 2 Thessalonians on a positive note (that the Lord will grant the church his peace during their trials) as well as to assure the church that he—Paul—is the author of 2 Thessalonians (3:16–18).

CONCLUSION

So Paul's inaugurated eschatology was in conflict with the eschatologies of at least three groups whose paths intersected with the Thessalonian Christians: the consistent eschatology of non-Christian Jews, and the realized eschatologies of the Roman imperial cult as well as Hellenistic religion. First and 2 Thessalonians, in one way or another as we have seen, challenged the church there to be faithful to Paul's apocalypse of Christ.

---

39 Pate, *The Glory of Adam,* pp. 297–99.
40 Ibid, p. 312.

1 AND 2 CORINTHIANS

PAUL'S ESCHATOLOGICAL RESERVATION

AND THE CORINTHIANS

According to Acts 18:1–8 Paul founded the church at Corinth on his second missionary journey. Later, in ca. AD 55 the apostle wrote our canonical 1 and 2 Corinthians to the church of Corinth. Corinth, at the time of Paul, was a metropolitan city with a three-quarters of a million population. Geographically, the city was strategically located just off of the Corinthian isthmus, a crossroads for travelers and traders. This isthmus joined the Peloponnesus to the central part of Greece. Corinth had two harbors: Cenchrea, six miles to the east of the Saronic Gulf; and Lechaeum, a mile and a half to the west on the Corinthian Gulf. Goods flowed across the isthmus on the *Diolkos*, a road by which smaller ships could be hauled fully loaded across the land bridge, and by which cargoes of larger ships could be transported by wagons from one side to the other.

Corinth's geography attracted various cultures (East and West), diverse religions (Aphrodite, the goddess of love; Asclepius, the god of healing; Dionysius, the god of wine; Judaism; the imperial cult merged with the worship of Apollo), and conflicting lifestyles (from the virtue of Greek wisdom to the scruples of Jewish diet to the prostitution of the priestess cult of Aphrodite). Little wonder, then, that the Corinthian church found itself in a cauldron of confusion, at times even fomenting against the apostle who founded it.

The occasion for the writing of 1 Corinthians was twofold. First, some members of Chloe's household at Corinth brought reports to Paul of the church's struggles (1 Cor. 1:11)—factions, immorality, litigation. Other members of the Corinthian church brought a letter from the congregation (1 Cor. 7:1) asking Paul's counsel on issues like marriage, eating meat, the Lord's Supper, spiritual gifts, the resurrection, and the collection for Jerusalem. By the time of the writing of 2 Corinthians the relationship between the Corinthian church and Paul had deteriorated to the point of a rupture. Fueling the fires of opposition to Paul was a group of individuals who called Paul's apostleship into question on the grounds he was not eloquent, had no mystic experience, and was weak because of his afflictions. Thus Paul wrote 2 Corinthians to shock the Corinthian church back into spiritual reality and back to a relationship with him. All total, Paul penned some four correspondences to the Corinthian church: the previous letter (1 Cor. 5:9–10), 1 Corinthians, a tearful letter (2 Cor. 2:2–4; 7:8) after a debacle visit to Corinth (2 Cor. 2:1), and 2 Corinthians.

What lay at the heart of the controversy between Paul and the Corinthian church he founded at Corinth? Simply put, Paul's inaugurated eschatology did not set well with the Corinthian church's realized eschatology, one fueled by the *merkabah* Judaizers. To make matters worse, the consistent eschatology of non-Christian Judaism, along with the realized eschatologies of the imperial cult and Hellenistic religion, also contributed to Paul's woes with the Corinthian Christians.

We now turn to these competing eschatologies after which, in the next chapter, we offer a summary of the contents of 1 and 2 Corinthians.

Paul Versus the Consistent Eschatology of Judaism at Corinth

In keeping with his policy of preaching in the synagogue when he first arrived in a new town, Acts 18:4 relates Paul's experience at the Corinthian synagogue.

There, as was his custom, Paul preached the gospel to Jews and God-fearers. Specifically, Paul tried to persuade Jew and God-fearer that Jesus is the Christ (Acts 18:5) but the Jews reacted abusively to Paul's message (v. 6). We find the reason for the Jewish antipathy to Paul stated by the apostle in 1 Corinthians 1:22–23—the message of a crucified Christ scandalized Jews. Despite the Jewish opposition to Paul in the synagogue in Corinth, Paul's message met with acceptance by the God-fearers there (Acts 18:6–11).

The consistent eschatology of Judaism we traced in Galatians and in 1 and 2 Thessalonians meets us here in 1 and 2 Corinthians as well, which was antithetical to Paul's inaugurated eschatology in Christ:

JEWS	PAUL
(1) The new age has not come	(1) The age to come has dawned in Jesus Christ (1 Cor. 10:11)
(2) Cosmic renewal has not occurred	(2) The new creation is in progress in Christ (2 Cor. 5:17)
(3) The Messiah has not come and certainly not a crucified Christ	(3) Jesus the crucified one is God's Messiah (1 Cor. 1:18–25)
(4) The OT predicts the coming of Messiah	(4) The OT promise of the new covenant of the Messiah is here in Jesus (2 Cor. 3:1–18)
(5) When Israel obeys the Torah, the Messiah will come	The age to come is entered into by faith in Christ, not by keeping the law of Moses (1 Cor. 7:19; 15:56–57; 2 Cor. 3:1–4:6)

PAUL VERSUS THE REALIZED ESCHATOLOGY OF THE IMPERIAL CULT

The ancient city of Corinth experienced two stages of growth. The first was from its founding in the tenth century BC until its destruction in 146 BC by the Roman consul L. Mummius. During that long period Corinth was a Greek-styled city. But, after its destruction in 146 BC and century-old ruin, Julius Caesar shortly before his death in March 44 BC ordered Corinth to be rebuilt as a Roman colony. This meant that the architecture of the city took on a Roman look, that it would be ruled by a Roman form of government with Roman officials, and the city would be colonized by Romans—chiefly some of Caesar's veteran soldiers, along with urban plebians, freedmen and freedwomen from Rome itself, and some Romaized Greeks (Strabo 8.6.23; 17.3.15). Driving this new Roman Corinth was the imperial cult.

The Imperial Cult at Corinth
Ben Witherington lists the evidence of such in Corinth:

- Cult personnel such as the *flamen* [which stoked the flames of sacrificial altars to Caesar], *pontifex* [priest], and *augstali* [a lower class of freed slaves devoted to Caesar] are mentioned in Corinthian inscriptions.
- By AD 50 two additional sets of imperial games had been instituted in Corinth and apparently elsewhere as well: the Caesarea to honor the deified Augustus, and the imperial contests to honor the current emperor.
- A statue of Augustus about to offer a sacrifice was found in the Julian basilica in Corinth.
- Coins portraying emperors and images of Roman peace and plenty were minted in Corinth and replaced earlier coins with images of local deities, as Corinth's Romanness was increasingly stressed in the first century AD.
- A statue has been found with an inscription on its base honoring a priestess of the providence of Augustus (that is, Tiberius).
- The remains of a Roman-style temple, Temple F—apparently dedicated to Venus, the patroness of Julius Caesar's family—have been found.
- The archaeological evidence suggests that in the first century of the common era, the whole of downtown Corinth was gradually realigned architecturally to form a huge, composite, splendid monument to the imperial family, with an altar to Julius Caesar in the center, numerous imperial statues, and a huge temple dedicated to the *genus*, or family, of the Julians. Anyone who visited Corinth in the mid to late first century AD would have confronted a breathtaking panorama in the center of town testifying to the victory of the Roman imperial rulers and the glorious arrival of salvation for the Roman people (among whom Corinthian citizens counted themselves, since Corinth was a Roman colony). This salvation amounted to the present blessings of safety, health, and wealth

for Corinth, and it was the more well-to-do families who got the lion's share of the benefit and who would have supplied from their numbers the priests and priestesses for the imperial cult. Virgil's famous Fourth *Eclogue* celebrated the edenic conditions supposedly created by Augustus and the *pax Romana*. In view of the economic prosperity of Roman Corinth, there was special reason to believe in the Roman imperial eschatology there, especially on the part of those who had benefited most from Roman rule.[1]

Realized Eschatology and the Imperial Cult at Corinth

It is not difficult to see the realized eschatology of the imperial cult in the preceding evidence at Corinth:

A. The new age has dawned, and with it...
B. Cosmic renewal (the wealth of Corinth was thanks to the emperor's favor) and *pax Romana*
C. The savior is Augustus and the imperial line that followed him (statue to Augustus, coins proclaiming his deity, a temple to Augustus, monument to the imperial family).
D. Sacred writings confirm that Caesar is the Savior (Virgil's Fourth *Eclogue*).
E. There were celebrations of Augustus's redemption (two sets of imperial games to honor the deified Caesar—Caesarea and imperial contests to honor the current emperor).

Paul's Critique of the Imperial Cult in the Corinthian Church

But Paul begs to differ with the realized eschatology of the imperial cult. Thus Jesus the crucified one (by Rome) is the true savior (1 Cor. 1:18). Indeed Caesar's *pax Romana* will be short-lived due to Christ's parousia (1 Cor. 15:23) and his handing over of the kingdom of this world to the Father (1 Cor. 15:24–28; cf. 2 Cor. 2:14–17). This was prophesied in the Old Testament (cf. Ps. 110:1; Dan. 2:44 with 1 Cor. 15:24–28). Jesus' lordship is celebrated in baptism (1 Cor. 10:1–11) and in the Lord's Supper (1 Cor. 11:23–26).

---

1   Ben Witherington III, *Conflict & Community in Corinth: A Socio-Rhetorical Commentary on 1 and 2 Corinthians* (Grand Rapids, MI: Eerdmans, 1995), pp. 296–97.

Witherington encapsulates the clash of eschatologies here: "Paul seeks to replace the present imperial eschatology of some Corinthians with his own 'already ... not yet' Christ-centered eschatology."[2] The previous two eschatologies—Jewish and Roman—merged in the events recorded in Acts 18:12–17. Luke reports that the Jews in Corinth appealed to Gallio, proconsul of Achaea (of which Corinth was the capital city), to support their persecution of Paul and Christianity. What the Jews were pushing for was to have Gallio rule that Christianity was not Jewish and therefore was not a legal religion. In other words, the Jews were trying to disassociate Judaism from Christianity so that Christians would not be exempt from worshipping Caesar. But Gallio foiled the Corinthian Jews' plan by ruling that Christianity was an in-house Jewish matter, something not to be ruled upon by the Roman procurator. That is to say, Gallio judged that Christianity was still a branch of Judaism and therefore was exempt from the imperial cult.

Acts 18:1–2 also factors into this discussion. There we read that Caesar Claudius (the current emperor at the time of Paul's visit to Corinth) decreed that all Jews leave Rome. We learn from the Roman historian Suetonius (Claudius, 25) that Roman Jews were fighting over one named "*Chrestus*" (Latin) probably a misspelling of "*Christos*" (Greek). Most likely, what happened was that Roman Jewish Christians and non-Christian Jews were debating whether Jesus was the Christ. Because Rome did not yet distinguish between Jewish Christians and non-Christian Jews, Caesar Claudius thought the argument was an in-house matter for Jews to decide. He therefore expelled the whole lot of the Jews from Rome in AD 49. In other words, Claudius like Gallio, considered Christianity a branch of Judaism and therefore a legal religion.

Such a favorable ruling was only temporary, however. With Rome's hatred for the crucified Christ fresh in its memory, Paul's critique of the imperial message,[3] and the fall of Jerusalem in AD 70 that revealed that Christianity and

---

2   Ibid, p. 298.

3   Seyoon Kim offers an important caveat regarding the argument that Paul's and Luke's main message in their writings was to castigate the Roman Empire, offering instead the more balanced thesis that Paul and Luke, on the one hand, appreciated the Roman world while, on the other hand, disagreeing with the worship of Caesar, *Christ and Caesar: The Gospel and the Roman Empire in the Writings of Paul and Luke* (Grand Rapids, MI: Eerdmans, 2008).

Judaism were very much different, Rome's ire was raised against Christianity. Indeed, already in the early 60s, Emperor Nero found the Christians to be a perfect scapegoat for his burning of Rome. Rome's growing opposition to the Christian faith would come to a head in Domitian's pogrom against John's churches in Asia Minor in the 90s.

Paul Versus the Realized Eschatology of the Merkabah Judaizers

Since Christopher Forbes' devastating critique of the supposed Hellenistic background to the erroneous teaching that plagued the Corinthian church, more and more scholars are turning to the revived theory that Palestinian Judaism of the mystic kind was the real source of Paul's headache with the Corinthian Christians.[4] We align ourselves with that position in this section as we argue that Paul's apocalypse of Christ was a corrective to the realized eschatology of the *merkabah* Judaizers that intruded upon the Corinthian congregation (though we still think that Hellenistic religion influenced the Corinthian church; see our discussion below).[5] To develop this thesis we will need to focus on the ancient Jewish equation of wisdom and law. Simply put, numerous Jewish writings after the close of the Old Testament argued that the Torah was God's wisdom. That is, that God's pre-existent wisdom is now manifested in the law of Moses (Sirach, *Baruch*, *Psalms of Solomon*, Wisdom of Solomon, *4 Maccabees*, the *Third Sibylline Oracle*, the *Letter of Aristeas*, *The Testaments of the Twelve Patriarchs*, the Dead Sea Scrolls, *4 Ezra, 2 Baruch*).[6] Moreover, I have argued elsewhere that the pre-Christian Paul bought into the idea that God's wisdom is equated with the Torah. That can be seen from Paul's autobiographical remarks in Galatians 1:13–14; 4:4–6; Philippians 3:6; 1 Corinthians 1:20; and Romans 2:17–20.[7] We offer here our assessment of 1 Corinthians 1:20 in that light because such a verse in the past was often viewed

---

4   Christopher Forbes, *Prophecy and Inspired Speech in Early Christianity and its Hellenistic Environment* (Peabody, MA: Hendrickson, 1997).
5   The following point on the Jewish nature of Paul's opposition in the Corinthian church is an adaptation of my *The Reverse of the Curse*, pp. 277–304.
6   For documentation of this, the reader is referred to the first part of my *Reverse of the Curse*, pp. 21–128.
7   Ibid, pp. 129–70.

through a Hellenistic lens—the debater is the Greek rhetorician. But Martin Hengel effectively argued rather that 1 Corinthians 1:20 is rooted in Judaism:

> In my view 1 Cor. 1.20 sheds brief light on this spiritual milieu of the Pharisaic school which Paul himself experienced, with the following 'triad' … wise man, scribe, debater. These are designations from the Pharisaic *bet midrash* [house of study]. The Corinthians understand these terms, which are hardly comprehensible to a pagan Greek in their real—Jewish—significance, because of course during his eighteen-month stay there Paul will have told them of his former study of the law and thus at the same time of his mistaken way (cf. 1 Cor. 15.9). In other words, 1 Cor. 1.20 has an autobiographical background. What was formerly the aim of his own profession here becomes the embodiment of the wisdom of this world, because Paul once himself took offence at the cross, as his contemporary representatives did (and, apart from him, still do).[8]

The preceding background of Paul seems confirmed by the fact that the term σοφός (wise) is pervasive in *Sirach* (e.g., 1:1, 3–4, 6; 24:1, 25; 51:13), and that the word γραμματεύς (scribe) occurs also therein (10:5; 38:24; 44:4), both of which are connected with the house of discipline (51:23). Given this backdrop of 1 Corinthians 1:20, the σοφός is the Jewish sage who decides *halakhah* (legal matters regarding the Torah), which is related to the scribe, the interpreter of the Torah. In other words, we have here the wisdom teacher in the Torah School whose task it is to propound and defend the Pharisaic interpretation of the Law.[9] If this is the case, as it seems likely to be, then in this biographical allusion we meet with the pre-Christian Paul's association of wisdom and Law.

But Paul's conversion to Christ brought him to see that Jesus Christ is the wisdom of God and that the Torah is finished in the plan of God. We explore this thesis below relative to 1 and 2 Corinthians. We turn now to 1 Corinthians 1:24, 30; 2:6–10; 8:6; 10:4. We will put forth three arguments regarding those

---

8   Martin Hengel, *The Pre-Christian Paul*. Trs. By John Bowden (Philadelphia/London: Trinity Press International/SCM, 1991), p. 42.
9   Contrast this view with M. M. Mitchell's argument that the wise and the debater refer only to the Greek orator, *Paul and the Rhetoric of Reconciliation: An Exegetical Investigation of the Language and Composition of 1 Corinthians* (Louisville, KY: Westminster/John Knox, 1991), pp. 87–88.

passages: (a) Christ is therein portrayed as the preexistent wisdom of God, (b) who has brought the Torah to its end; (c) indeed, Paul uses the wisdom theme in those passages and their context to argue that the Deuteronomic curses and blessings were reversed at the cross.

Christ, God's Preexistent Wisdom

In this section we put forth the evidence for viewing 1:24, 30; 2:6–10; 8:6; 10:4 as expressions of Paul's wisdom Christology.

1 Corinthians 1:24, 30; 2:6–10

The statements that Christ is "wisdom" (1:24) and "wisdom of God" (1:30) clearly and explicitly link Christ and wisdom. It is a commonplace among scholars to see in this linkage a crediting to Christ key functions of wisdom from the Jewish sapiential tradition, including five interrelated ideas: (1) Just as wisdom is perceived as bringing salvation to her followers (e.g., *1 Enoch* 51:1–5; 58:1–6; *4 Macc.* 18:4), so Jesus Christ proffers redemption to his followers (1 Cor. 1:24, 30). (2) Paul's talk about Christ being God's mystery, hidden before time began (v. 7) which is now revealed to those who love him (vv. 9–10), is of the same thought world as wisdom being the mystery of God (*Sir.* 4:18; 14:10; *Wis.* 6:22; 7:21). *First Enoch* is especially illuminating in this regard for it associates wisdom with the secrets to be revealed in the last days but which are now present in heaven and to which the righteous alone are made privy (*1 Enoch* 2:6–9; 37:2–5; 38:3; 39:4–5, 9; 48:6–7; 62:7; etc.). (3) Paul's stress on the revelatory character of wisdom as dependent on the Spirit (1 Cor. 2:10–16) is in the line of Jewish sapiential tradition which asserted that wisdom could only be known through God's Spirit (*Wis.* 7:27; 9:17; *Sir.* 24:33; 1QH 12:11–15; 13:19–20; etc.). (4) Paul's mention of the rejection of wisdom by the rulers of this world (1 Cor. 2:8) reminds one of the idea in Jewish sapiential literature of wisdom being rejected by the nations (*Sir.* 24:6–7; *1 Enoch* 42:1–3; 63:2). (5) The possibility that there are levels of Christian maturity, with the "perfect ones" heading the list, is reminiscent of the idea that those who possess God's wisdom are mature (*Sir.* 4:8; 31:10; 44:17; *Wis.* 6:15; 9:6; DSS [1QSa 1:27; CD 12:18–19]).

1 Corinthians 8:6

There are three parallels between 1 Corinthians 8:6 and Jewish sapiential tradition indicating that this text too expresses Paul's wisdom Christology. (1) The language of God the creator ("from whom are all things") and redeemer ("for whom we exist") is also predicated of Christ ("through whom are all things," creator; "through whom we exist,' redeemer). The application of the ideas of creator and redeemer to wisdom is replete in Jewish sapiential literature (e.g., *Wis.* 7:26/9:9; 8:1, 4, 7; *Sir.* 1:4; cf. Philo [*QodDet* 54, 84]). (2) The connection between knowledge (1 Cor. 8:1) and wisdom (1 Cor. 8:6) is also plentiful in Jewish sapiential material, as R. Horsley has shown (e.g., *Wis.* 7:15–17; 10:10; 15:3).[10] Paul's association of knowledge and wisdom (which is probably based on the Corinthians' prior connection of the two) reminds one of this background. (3) Paul's remarks about idolatry point, as Ben F. Witherington III has observed, to Jewish polemics against idols which pit the false knowledge of pagans against the true wisdom of God (e.g., Jer. 10:1–16; *Wis.* 13:10–14).[11] The net result of these parallels between Christ and the wisdom of God is striking, as Witherington notes:

> Paul [is] drawing on the Jewish Shema and putting Jesus right in the midst of the most fundamental assertion in the early Judaism of its monotheistic faith. I would suggest that … here he is reading the Shema through the later sapiential reflections on monotheism, wisdom, and idolatry…. Paul is taking what was formerly said of God the *Father*, and *Sophia*, and now saying the same of the Father and Jesus Christ.[12]

1 Corinthians 10:4
It is a commonplace for commentators to interpret the phrase, "the rock was Christ" (v. 4), in the light of Jewish sapiential traditions.[13] Paul's midrash (interpretation) displays interesting parallels with other Jewish writings that equate the rock in the wilderness with wisdom (*Wis.* 10:17–18; 11:4; Philo [*Leg. Alleg.* 2:86]), and is not far removed from other texts that associate that rock with the

---

10 See R. A. Horsley, "Pneumatikos Versus Psychikos: Distinctions of Spiritual Status among the Corinthians," in *Harvard Theological Review* 69 (1976), pp. 269–88.
11 Ben F. Witherington III, *Jesus the Sage* (Philadelphia: Fortress Press, 1994), pp. 315–16.
12 Ibid, p. 316.
13 See Pate, *The Reverse of the Curse*, p. 280.

shekinah (cloud of glory, *b. Suk.* 3:11; *Tg. on Num.* 21:19–20). Paul's meaning in 1 Corinthians 10:4, then, is that Christ, God's wisdom, provided sustenance (physical and spiritual) for the Israelites in the wilderness. In other words, Paul believed that Christ was God's preexistent wisdom. His intervention at various points in history reminds one of the help wisdom gave to God's people along the way as recorded in *Wisdom of Solomon* 10–11. Otherwise the force of Paul's argument against the Corinthians is lost. For, just as Christ sustained the Isra- elites in the desert but which did not prevent them from falling into unbelief, so a similar scenario was impending for the Corinthians. Perhaps the major difference for Paul between the divine wisdom in Old Testament history and in the apostle's days of eschatological fulfillment (1 Cor. 10:11) was that Christ now indwells the hearts of God's people (see 1 Cor. 3:16–17; 6:19–20; 2 Cor. 6:14–7:1; 8:9; and perhaps 1 Cor. 10:16–17). We may conclude this section by joining together 1 Corinthians 8:6 and 10:4, taking note of Witherington's comments on these two verses:

> What is especially striking about both 1 Cor. 8:6 and 10:4 is that Paul is willing to take not just marginal ideas or events, but the very heart of the Jewish faith, its Shema and the Exodus—Sinai events that made them into the unique people of God they became, and redefine these additions in the light of what Paul now believed to be true about Christ. Paul does not fully draw our the im- plications of the pre-existence of Christ here, but this text shows he is already thinking along such lines.[14]

PAUL'S NEGATIVE PORTRAYAL OF THE LAW IN 1 CORINTHIANS

Having demonstrated from 1 Corinthians 1:24, 30; 2:6–10; 8:6; 10:4 that Paul believed Christ to be the pre-existent wisdom of God, we now turn to the apos- tle's understanding of the Law. We will argue that Pauline opposition in the church at Corinth stemmed from the Peter party, particularly in its positive association of wisdom and Law. If this is accurate, then Paul's separation of the two can be seen as a rejection of that approach which viewed the Torah as the embodiment of wisdom and as mediated by the Spirit. We will develop that

---

14 Witherington, *Jesus the Sage*, p. 318.

thesis in three steps: (1) the identification of the Peter party as the source of Paul's opposition in the church at Corinth; (2) Paul's disassociation of wisdom and Law in 1 Corinthians; (3) Torah-centered wisdom mediated by the Spirit as the connecting link among four major influences on the Corinthian church (eschatological, sapiential, rhetorical, mystical).

The Peter Party and Paul's Opposition in 1 Corinthians

It is typical for modern scholarship to divide the schisms of 1 Corinthians 1:12 into two basic groups.[15] The identification of those two opposing sides, however, has been much debated. The Tübingen school, led by F. C. Baur, divided the groups between Paul and Apollos on the one side and Peter and Christ on the other side.[16] This hypothesis dominated discussions of 1 Corinthians in the nineteenth and early twentieth centuries, but has been roundly criticized in modern times because of the apparent absence of a Judaizing influence in that letter. Currently the pendulum has swung toward the Apollos theory, holding that neither Christ nor even Peter factor into the equation; rather, the two groups at odds are the followers of Paul and admirers of Apollos.[17] We summarize the evidence for each viewpoint below.

The identification of a Peter party as the source of the Pauline opposition in 1 Corinthians was popularized by F. C. Baur. More recently, C. K. Barrett has expanded upon this view, offering the following supplemental arguments:[18]

A. The unnamed person in 1 Corinthians 3:10–17 who is attempting to build on Paul's foundation is Peter.

B. First Corinthians 5:9–13 may echo the controversy at Antioch (Gal. 2:11f.), portraying Paul's idea of what was a "kosher" table for Christians.

---

15 For a helpful survey of the literature on this subject, see Michael D. Goulder's "*Sophia* in 1 Corinthians," *New Testament Studies* 37 (1991), pp. 516–20.

16 F. C. Baur, "Die Christuspartei in der Korinthischen Gemeinde, der Gegensatz des paulinischen und petrinischen Christentums in der Ältesten Kirchen,der Apostel Petrus in Rom.," ("The Christparty in the Corinthian Congregation, the Opposition of Pauline and Petrine Christianity in the Old Church, the Apostle Peter in Rome") *TZ* 4 (1831), pp. 61–206.

17 See Horsley, "Wisdom" as an example of this approach.

18 C. K. Barrett, "Cephas and Corinth", in *Essays on Paul* (Philadelphia: Westminster Press, 1982), pp. 40–59.

C. 1 Corinthians 6:1–8 (especially vv. 1–6) might be explained by litigation against Paul by the Peter party.

D. 1 Corinthians 7 represents the differing perspectives of Paul (a celibate) and Peter (who was married).

E. 1 Corinthians 8–10 is informed by Jewish dietary concerns, most probably raised by the Peter party.

F. 1 Corinthians 11:17–34 may also be informed by the issue of what constitutes a "kosher" table.

The identification of an Apollos party as the source of Pauline opposition in 1 Corinthians has enjoyed a rather large following among scholars over the last decade or so.[19] The catalyst for the rise of this theory has been the recent tendency of interpreters to root 1 Corinthians 1–4 and its talk of knowledge/wisdom in Hellenistic Jewish wisdom material.[20] This being the case, Apollos, or an Apollos faction, became a likely candidate as the source of Pauline opposition. Two broad pieces of evidence are appealed to in support of this view. (a) Comparing Acts 18:24–28 and 1 Corinthians 1–4 suggests a number of parallels between those two texts regarding Apollos:[21] (1) Acts 18:24 describes Apollos as ἀνηρ λογιος ("man of words"), suggesting he was eloquent and possibly proficient in Greco-Roman rhetoric. This background may inform Paul's redefinition of the term σοφια λογου ("wisdom of word") in 1 Corinthians 1–4. (2) The Acts material depicts Apollos as a person possessed by the Spirit, which might account for the Corinthians' emphasis on the Spirit as hinted at in 1 Corinthians 1–4. (3) According to Acts 18:24–28, Apollos was deficient in his understanding of baptism—he knew only John's baptism—but concerning which Aquila and Priscilla helped to complete his education. This might explain the rise of the issue of baptism in 1 Corinthians 1:10–17 ("I belong to Apollos," "I belong to Paul," v. 12). (b) Three texts in 1 Corinthians itself are appealed to in order to support the theory of an Apollos faction in Corinth.[22] (1) It is argued that because Paul goes to

---

19   See again Horsley, "Wisdom"; see also Ben F. Witherington III, *Jesus the Sage,* pp. 299–318.

20   See Horsley, "Wisdom," and B. A. Pearson, *Pneumatikos-Psychikos Terminology in 1 Corinthians* (Missoula, MT: Scholars Press, 1973).

21   Witherington, *Jesus the Sage*, pp. 300–1.

22   Ibid, pp. 300–3, 306.

some lengths in 1 Corinthians 3 to stress that he and Apollos are working together in harmony that this implies a rivalry existed between the two in the church at Corinth (see especially 1 Cor. 3:4, 21). (2) 1 Corinthians 4:6b states that the nub of the problem was that the Corinthians were pitting one apostle against the other which, in the context of 3:1–4:6, seems to point to Apollos and Paul. (3) First Corinthians 16:12 is invoked as further indication that tension existed in Corinth between the followers of Apollos and those of Paul; hence Apollos' reticence to return to that church.

Those advocating the Petrine party theory, however, offer the following four rebuttals to the Apollos faction hypothesis which seem to tip the scales in their favor, with which we concur. The first response concerns the three texts appealed to in 1 Corinthians. We may take chapter 3 and 4:6 together, since the latter verse is critical to the interpretation of the former passage. The key word for these two texts is in 4:6, μετασχηματίζω "transferred?"). Those who hold to an Apollos faction versus a Paul party argue that the term means "figure of speech." P. Lampe expresses the resulting implication for chapter 3 and 4:6:

> For your sake I have clothed the thoughts of 3:5–4:2 in … disguised speech about planting and watering, about preparing a foundation, building on it, and about examining a steward's housekeeping. And I have applied these disguised metaphors to me and Apollos … that you may learn not to be puffed up in favor of one (apostle) against another."[23]

David Hall, however, decisively refutes this rendering of μετασχηματίζω, marshaling the following evidence:[24] First, the term in ancient Greek texts consistently meant "to change the form of something" (e.g., Philo [*Aet. Mund.* 79]; Plutarch [*Moralia* 680A]; Josephus [*Ant.* 7.257]). The common element in the Greek texts is that of one thing being changed into something new. This, indeed, is how Paul uses the word elsewhere (see 2 Cor. 1:13–14; Phil. 3:21). Second, this meaning, however, is

---

23 P. Lampe, "Theological Wisdom and the 'Word about the Cross': The Rhetorical Scheme in 1 Corinthians 1–4," *Interpretation* 44.2 (1990), p. 129.

24 David R. Hall, "A Disguise for the Wise: *METACHĒMATIZMOZ* in 1 Corinthians 4.6," *New Testament Studies* 40 (1994), pp. 143–49.

rejected by modern interpreters on the basis that its original nuance does not fit the context of 1 Corinthians 3:1–4:6.[25] But Hall refutes this objection by demonstrating that whenever the verb μετασχηματίζω is followed by εἰς, the preposition introduces the end product of the transformation (e.g., *4 Macc.* 9:22; 2 Cor. 11:13–14); compare other Greek verbs compounded with μετα and followed by εἰς (John 5:24; Rom. 1:26; 2 Cor. 3:18; James 4:9; 1 John 3:14; Jude 4). In all these cases the μετα-compound with εἰς indicates an actual change from one state into another, not just a figure of speech. A. Robertson and A. Plummer catch the significance of all of this when they write of 1 Corinthians 3:1–4:6, "I have transferred these warnings to myself and Apollos for the purpose of covert allusion."[26] The meaning of μετασχηματίζω consists, therefore, in putting forth the names of those who were not really responsible for the division in Corinth (Paul and Apollos) instead of the names of others who were more to blame.[27] Hall applies these observations to 1 Corinthians 3:1–4:6, arguing that they make good sense of that text:

[Chapter 3] verses 4 to 9... describe Paul and Apollos as fellow-servants, who are caring for God's garden and God's building. The rest of the chapter contains a warning to those who are damaging that building by poor workmanship. The link between the two sections is verse 10, in which Paul makes two statements. First he declares that he laid the foundation on which another … is building. This echoes the argument of verses 4–9: just as I planted and Apollos watered, so I have laid the foundation and another builds on it. But then Paul continues: 'let each person … observe how he is building.' This implies a number of builders—some using good materials, some bad. On Chrysostom's theory this is a natural extension of the argument, since the description of Paul

---

25 See W. Bauer, W. F. Arndt, F. W. Gingrich, F. Danker, eds., *Greek-English Lexicon of the New Testament* (Chicago: University of Chicago Press, 1979), p. 513 regarding 1 Corinthians 4:6.
26 A. Robertson and A. Plummer, *First Epistle of St. Paul to the Corinthians*, ICC (New York: Charles Scribner's Sons, 1911), p. 81.
27 As Hall demonstrates, this was the earliest recorded understanding of this verse; see Chrysostom, MPG 61.24; see Hall for more early references to this understanding, "A Disguise for the Wise," pp. 143–44.

and Apollos in verses 4–9 was a covert allusion to the wisdom-teachers criticized in verses 10–20.[28]

Third, drawing on the grammatical fact that μετασχηματιζω followed by ἐις emphasizes the end product, Hall rightly rejects the idea that the change referred to in 1 Corinthians 4:6 is the changing metaphors in 1 Corinthians 3. Rather, the transformation is not from one metaphor to another but from one set of people (the real cause of division) into Paul and Apollos (the ones not responsible for the division). Fourth, in answer to the contention that "these" in 1 Corinthians 4:6 refers to the change of metaphors in 1 Corinthians 3, Hall correctly argues that "these" refers to the whole unit of 1:10–4:5.[29] That is to say, "these things" refer not to the metaphors of 1 Corinthians 3, but to the divisions attested to in 1:12 and following.

If these arguments of Hall are sound, then the theory of an Apollos party versus Paul is effectively dismissed. Who, then, is the real source of the Pauline opposition covertly alluded to in 1 Corinthians 3:1–4:6? M. Goulder provides a plausible answer—Peter: "So Paul says he is transforming 'these things' on to himself and Apollos—that is, the real issue was between the two of them and Cephas, but he has changed it to be as between himself and Apollos, for pastoral reasons." Goulder supports his viewpoint with several arguments emerging from 1 Corinthians 3:1–4:6. First, the seriousness of the criticism of Paul is better explained by a Peter-versus-Paul controversy. Comparing 1 Corinthians 4:6 with 9:3 reveals that Paul's apostleship is indeed being judged and the latter passage leads to a discussion of Paul's rights as compared to the apostle Peter's (9:4–5, 12). Goulder writes of this connection of 4:6 and 9:3ff:

> It is not easy to see how anyone could have drawn a distinction in apostolic authority between Paul and Apollos to the latter's advantage, while it is only too easy to see that such a distinction could have been drawn between Paul and Cephas. Indeed, this could well account for the critics being puffed up in ch. 4: they said to the Paulines, 'Our leader is an apostle, yours is not.' It is also easy to

---

28 Ibid, p. 145.
29 Ibid. p. 147.

read 9:4–5, 12 as a sour comment on Peter: 'Have we not the right to eat and drink? Have we not the right to take round a Christian wife, like the other apostles, and Cephas?... If others share in this right over you, do not we more?' The unnecessary 'and Cephas' sounds like the bitter reflection of many 'judgments' on Paul. The argument implies that only apostles had the right to free hospitality, and suggests that it has been exercised by an apostle other than Paul, and perhaps his wife. Perhaps people said, 'Cephas was a true apostle, and the church paid for him, and his wife too.' Such a reading is strengthened by the presence of a passage of similarly sour, anti-Petrine tone in Gal. 2.[30]

Second, drawing on the last statement, such a reading of 1 Corinthians 3:1–4:6 is strengthened by the anti-Petrine tone of Galatians 2.[31] Third, utilizing the insight of C. K. Barrett, Goulder notes that in 1 Corinthians 3:10 Paul, by contrasting his laying the foundation for the Corinthian church (which is Christ alone) with the work of the "other" who builds on it, is covertly taking exception to the assumption that Cephas, the rock, was the foundation of the church (Matt. 16:18).[32]

With regard to the remaining text in 1 Corinthians appealed to in order to defend an Apollos versus Paul division, 16:12 calls for comment. However, a straightforward reading of that verse does not suggest that there was any real tension between Paul and Apollos, as Goulder observes. He offers three points in this regard. First, Paul mentions Apollos in 16:12 in the same paragraph as Timothy, both of whom the apostle seems positive about. Furthermore, if Paul did not trust Apollos or truly believed there was an Apollos faction in the church at Corinth, surely he would not have urged him to go there. Second, the clause, "he was not willing to go," refers not to Apollos' will but God's will, for θϵλμα ("will") is never used of the human will in the New Testament (e.g., Matt. 18:14; Rom. 2:18). That being the case, it is not Apollos' reticence to return to Corinth that Paul speaks of in 16:12 but God's decision to prevent him from doing so.

---

30 Goulder, "*SOPHIA* in 1 Corinthians", p. 517.
31 Ibid., p. 517.
32 Barrett, *Commentary on the First Epistle to the Corinthians*, Harper's New Testament Commentaries (New York: Harper & Row, 1968), pp. 87–88; cf. Goulder, 519–20.

Third, Acts 18, written later than 1 Corinthians by Luke, a Pauline Christian, portrays Apollos as an asset, not a liability, to the Pauline movement.[33]

With regard to the comparison of Acts 18:24–28 and 1 Corinthians 1–4, we suspect that both texts present a *complimentary*, not competitive, relationship between Paul and Apollos. But what about the appeal to the Greco-Roman rhetorical tradition reflected in 1 Corinthians 1–4 and Acts 18:24–28? At the end of the day, this evidence seems to constitute the heart of the reason for appealing to an Apollos faction versus Paul. In our estimation, the rhetorical tradition is definitely present in 1 Corinthians 1–4, and throughout the Corinthian correspondences.[34] But it is a *non sequitur* to deduce from this that Apollos, a Hellenistic Jew from Alexandria, was the sole catalyst for such an influence. Palestinian Jews also employed Greco-Roman rhetoric to articulate and propagate the Torah among Gentiles. Three pieces of evidence can be adduced to support this contention. First, it is very interesting that the description Luke applies to Apollos in Acts 18:24, ἀνηρ λογοις ("man of words"), is the same nomenclature Josephus applies to Palestinian Jews in the Maccabean period, ἀνηρ λογοις (*Ant.* 17.149). The former (Apollos) used rhetorical eloquence to expound his messianic belief while the latter (the brightest of the Palestinian Jewish young men) used rhetorical eloquence to defend the Torah in their battle against the advances of Hellenism (cf. *Sir.* 39:6 and its reference to the scribe as possessing in the Torah ῥηματα σοφιας ("words of wisdom"). This observation (that Palestinian Jews could use the Greco-Roman rhetorical tradition for their own purposes) is in keeping with the current scholarly consensus that Hellenism deeply impacted Palestinian Judaism.[35]

Second, it is a least clear that Paul's opponents in 2 Corinthians claimed to be Palestinian Jews (see 2 Cor. 11:22) and that, despite this, they were enamored with the Greco-Roman rhetorical tradition, including the art of persuasion (e.g., 2 Cor. 5:11; 10:1–6, 11; 11:5–6); contrasting their own philosophical school with others in order to devalue them (2 Cor. 10:12–18); surrounding themselves with, and

33 Goulder, p. 518.
34 Witherington, *Jesus the Sage*, pp. 299–307. To this must also be added the work by Duane A. Litfin, *St. Paul's Theology of Proclamation: 1 Corinthians 1–4 and Greco-Roman Rhetoric*, Society for New Testament Studies Monograph Studies 79 (Cambridge: University Press, 1994).
35 Martin Hengel, *Judaism and Hellenism*.

accepting the support of, well-to-do patrons (2 Cor. 2:17; 8–9); and possibly portraying themselves as "divine men" workers (2 Cor. 3:1–4:6; 11:13–14; 12:1–10).

Third, if indeed the apostle Paul—Hellenist and Roman citizen that he was—received significant training in Jerusalem (see Acts 22:3), then he himself becomes an example of a "Palestinian" Jew employing Greco-Roman rhetorical tradition. This is attested to, for example, (a) in the way he refuses the patronage of the Corinthian church, in good Socratic anti-Sophist fashion (1 Cor. 9:15–18; 2 Cor. 8–9); (b) in his employment of the *peristasis* ("affliction") lists, Socrates, the suffering sage, being the celebrated illustration of such (1 Cor. 4:9–13; 15:30–31; 2 Cor. 4:7–15; 6:4–10; 11:23–12:10; etc.); and (c) in his masterful usage of the fool's speech, like Socrates of old (2 Corinthians 10–13). Thus Paul's method of proclaiming his message (which of course was different from the Torah-keeping message of Palestinian Jews since his conversion) was not unimpacted by ancient rhetoric.

The evidence mounts in favor of a Petrine party versus Paul in Corinth, as Gerd Lüdemann has judiciously shown, when one compares 1 Corinthians 9 and 15. A comparison of the anti-Paulinism reflected in these two passages points toward a Peter faction as its source:

A. In both instances Paul sees himself as dealing with people who dispute his apostolic authority. The basis of the objection in 1 Corinthians 9 was his refusing to accept support from the church, while in 1 Corinthians 15 it was argued that the apostolic circle had already been closed before Paul was converted.

B. The disputing of Paul's apostleship occurs each time with some reference to the Jerusalem authorities (1 Corinthians 9: the rest of the apostles, the brothers of Jesus, Cephas; 1 Corinthians 15: Cephas, the five hundred brethren, James, all the apostles).

C. In both cases Paul uses the same arguments to defend himself: (a) he appeals to his vision of Christ (9:1; 15:8) and (b) he introduces his missionary word as confirmation (9:1f.; 15:10).[36]

To quote Lüdemann, "In my opinion, these three points make the conclusion

---

36 Gerd Lüdemann, *Opposition to Paul in Jewish Christianity*, trans. by. M. Eugene Boring (Minneapolis: Fortress Press, 1989), p. 74.

necessary that the anti-Paulinism of 1 Corinthians 9 and the anti-Paulinism of 1 Corinthians 15 belong together and thus that its advocates belong to one and the same group."[37] For Lüdemann, that group is the Petrine faction.[38]

The remaining key criticism of a Petrine base to the anti-Paulinism in Corinth is the old argument raised by W. Lügert in 1908 that there is no apparent Judaizing presence in the Corinthian letters, especially relative to the issues of the Law, circumcision, and dietary regulations.[39] In light of recent research, however, this criticism will not stand. We consider briefly each of these three topics. With regard to the Law, although 1 Corinthians contains only five passages referring to either the "commandments" or to the "Law" (7:19; 9:8–9; 9:19–23; 14:21; 15:56), there is evidence that the Torah nevertheless played a significant role in Paul's dealings with the Corinthians. This is especially the case for 1 Corinthians 1–4. M. Goulder has offered a very plausible interpretation of the key words occurring in 1 Corinthians 1–4, "words of wisdom" (1:17; 2:1, 4–5, 13). He reasons that they refer to a way of life in accordance with the Torah (*Sir.* 24:11, 23l; *Bar.* 3:9–4:3; *4 Macc.* 1:16; etc.). Goulder argues that the phrase "words of wisdom" was a common designation for Jewish *halakhic* ("legal") interpretations of the law (*b. Kid.* 49b; *Sir.* 39:6; *1 Enoch* 99:10; *m. Ned.* 9:3; 11:7; etc.).[40] For Goulder, the most logical source of this perspective in the church at Corinth was the Petrine party.[41] Paul, of course, disapproved of such a viewpoint.[42] It would seem, then, that the Torah occupied the forefront of 1 Corinthians (chapters 1–4) even as it would later do in 2 Corinthians (see especially 2:17–4:6). We will return to Goulder's theory later.

With regard to circumcision, it is true that such an issue did not loom large at Corinth, but there is still Paul's bombshell statement in 1 Corinthians 7:19, "For neither circumcision accounts for anything nor uncircumcision, but keeping the commandments of God." On any reading of this text, verse

---

37 Ibid.
38 Ibid, pp. 75–80.
39 W. Lütgert, *Freiheitspredigt und Schwarmgeister in Korinth: Ein Beitrag zur Charakteristik der Christuspartei* (*Freedompreaching and Enthusiasts in Corinth: An Investigation into the Character of the Christparty*) (Gütersloh: C. Bertelsmann, 1908), pp. 47ff.
40 Goulder, "SOPHIA in 1 Corinthians." pp.516-34.
41 Ibid, pp. 523–24.
42 Ibid, pp. 524–27.

19 would have hardly been innocuous to a Jew in Paul's day, for the statement at the very least relativizes circumcision, if not actually pits it against the law of God. We are not left to our imagination about how ancient Jews might respond to this kind of statement. What Trypho the Jew told Justin Martyr the Christian could equally apply to Paul:

> You who claim to be pious and believe yourselves to be different from the others do not segregate yourselves from them, nor do you observe a manner of life different from that of the Gentiles, for you do not keep the feasts or sabbaths, nor do you practise the rite of circumcision. You place your hope in a crucified man, and still expect to receive favours from God when you disregard his commandments. Have you not read that the male who is not circumcised on the eighth day shall be cut off from his people? [43]

For Trypho, no male Christian could claim to keep God's commandments unless he had obeyed the injunction to become circumcised. Seen in this light, Paul's statement in 1 Corinthians 7:19 can be understood as a calculated criticism designed to preempt any Judaizing tendency on the part of certain Corinthian Christians.

Concerning the Jewish dietary regulations, while 1 Corinthians 8, 10 is normally perceived as addressing the Gentile setting of meats offered to idols; this should not be misconstrued to rule out Jewish concerns as well, especially the *kashrut* system. The question of whether or not meats were kosher inevitably affected the Jewish Christian element in the Corinthian church. This would have been so at both the common fellowship meals (cf. Gal. 2) and at the *agape* feast/Eucharist. Goulder writes of this unavoidable concern in the Corinthian church:

> What could not be evaded was the food laws, because there was a weekly common meal at the eucharist, and with wealthy Christians like Erastus and Gaius at Corinth, this would include meat (cf. Rom. 14). With meat would inevitably arise the questions, where was this bought? Is it kosher? Gentile Christians could read Lev. 17:14 and maintain with perfect truth that they

43 Justin Martyr, *Dialogue 10*; quoted in Frank Thielman, "The Coherence of Paul's View of the Law," in *New Testament Studies* 38 (1992), p. 238.

had seen the animal killed with a knife, and the blood run away; but this could never satisfy Jewish Christians who knew how many complications were involved before one could safely eat meat.[44]

We now summarize the preceding section. In essence, four pieces of evidence have been adduced in favor of tracing the anti-Pauline opposition in Corinth to a Peter faction: (1) 1 Corinthians 3–4:6 covertly points to a Peter-versus-Paul debate, while 1 Corinthians 16:12 depicts a harmonious relationship between Paul and Apollos. Acts 18:24–28 and 1 Corinthians 3–4:6 attest to the last point. (2) Concerning again the last two texts, Hellenistic Judaism was not alone in its utilization of Greco-Roman rhetorical tradition; Palestinian Judaism did the same with regard to defending the Torah. (3) First Corinthians 9 and 15 jointly point in the direction of a Petrine anti-Pauline faction in Corinth. (4) There is a Judaizing presence in 1 Corinthians after all, specifically involving the Law, circumcision, and the dietary regulations. We turn our attention now to Paul's disassociation of wisdom and law in 1 Corinthians.

Paul's Disassociation of Wisdom and Law in 1 Corinthians

We are arguing that the source of the anti-Pauline opposition at Corinth was rooted in the Peter party, whose theological platform involved adherence to the Torah. It will be recalled that Goulder makes the interesting point that the phrase, "words of wisdom," specifies the nature of the Petrines' message—*Sophia* (wisdom) was their way of interpreting and applying the Torah. Some of the extrabiblical passages Goulder produces merit mentioning at this juncture. According to *m. 'Aboth* 1.1, Moses was believed to have received both written law and its interpretation on Sinai and the latter came to be the core of the oral law in time. *B. Kiddushin* 49b makes the same point, "What is meant by Torah? The interpretation of the Torah." There follows this statement a question to the effect of who is competent to make this interpretation, and the answer is provided, "One who can be asked a matter of wisdom in any place, and he can answer it." These "words of wisdom" in the Greek are ῥηματα /λογοις/σοφιας. *Sirach* 39.6 echoes this sentiment; speaking of the scribe of the Torah, it says that "he

---

44 Goulder, "SOPHIA in 1 Corinthians," pp. 528–29.

1 and 2 Corinthians

shall pour forth his "ῥηματα σοφια," the context of which reveals that they proceed from the scribe's learning in the Law and tradition. *First Enoch* 99:10 continues this theme, "Blessed are all those who accept the words of wisdom and understand them, and follow the paths of the Most High"—that is to say, the words of wisdom show the way of God. *M. Ned.* 9.3; 11.7 also use the same phrase, "words of the wise," for *halakhic* interpretations of the Torah.[45]

Goulder convincingly sets 1 Corinthians 1–4 against this background, demonstrating that the association of σοφια and λογος occurs in Paul's polemical barbs at his detractors in Corinth. Paul preached the gospel, not λογου σοφιας (1:17); Paul did not come to the Corinthians proclaiming σοφιας λογοις (2:1); nor was Paul's preaching or the persuading of people by σοφιας λογοις (2:4); otherwise the Corinthians' faith might rest in human σοφιας λογου (2:5); but Paul does not want their faith to reside in σοφια λογου (2:13). Comparing these polemical passages with the Corinthians' emphasis on the spiritual gift of the λογος σοφιας (12:8; cf. 1:5) leads Goulder to say that the Petrine Christians in Corinth were delivering *halakhah* (legal pronouncements) as under the inspiration of the Spirit, words of wisdom interpreting and applying the Torah.[46]

Though Goulder does not call it such, his presentation of Paul's refutation of the Petrine party's espousal of *halakhah* interpretation (wisdom) of the Torah amounts to a critique of the association of wisdom and Law. We suggest this is evident in 1 Corinthians 1:19ff. In 1 Corinthians 1:19 Paul rejects the wisdom of the wise, invoking Isaiah 29:14 against it, "I will destroy the wisdom of the wise." First Corinthians 1:20 specifies the nature of such wisdom, "Where is the wise man? Where is the scribe? Where is the debater of this age?" Here Goulder approvingly draws on the work of Adolf Schlatter, which roots all three of the aforementioned terms in Judaism: the *hakam*, the Jewish sage who decided *halakah*; the *sofer*, the interpreter of the Torah; and the *daršan* or *doreš* who sought out the seventy faces of Scripture.[47] If this is correct (or even partially correct), then vv. 19–20 can be perceived to be Paul's attempt to distance divine wisdom from the Torah (cf. v. 18). Moreover, the context of vv. 19–20 includes vv. 24 and 30 (cf. 8:6; 10:4), statements we earlier rooted in Paul's wisdom Christology. These combined observations lead

---

45 Ibid, p. 522.
46 Ibid, pp. 522–23.
47 Ibid, p. 524.

to the reasonable conclusion that Paul believed divine wisdom resided solely in Jesus Christ and was not to be equated with the Law, or its *halakhah*. More on this below when we treat Paul's reversal of the Deuteronomic curses and blessings. In this, Paul will have recanted his earlier preconversion belief that wisdom and law are equated (recall our earlier comments).

Torah-Centered Wisdom Mediated by the Spirit and 1 Corinthians

Intimately related to the nature of Pauline opposition at Corinth is the identification of the major strands of influence upon that church's thinking. Four recur in the scholarly discussion of the subject: eschatological, sapiential, rhetorical, and mystical. We will now put forth the theory that Torah-centered wisdom mediated by the Spirit adequately accounts for each of these influences, the source of which can well be traced to the Petrine party.

Since A. C. Thiselton's seminal article, it has become characteristic of interpreters to link the Corinthian problem with "over-realized" eschatology. That author summarizes the data thusly:

> The Corinthians apparently believed that the kingdom of God had fully come and that they, as saints, were already reigning and judging in it (4:5, 8). Viewing their possession of the Spirit and his attendant charismatic gifts to them as proof of the arrival of the eschaton (chaps. 12–14), nothing remained for them to do but to enjoy the blessings of freedom (cf. their eating of meat offered to idols [chaps. 8, 10]) and liberation from the body (manifested in such diverse aberrant behavior as libertinism [chaps. 5–6] and asceticism [chap. 7]). They probably believed that baptism magically associated them with Christ and the Spirit, and that the Lord's Supper protected them from all physical harm (chaps. 10, 11). In essence, the Corinthians thought they had attained the status of the angels (hence their claim to speak in angelic language [chap. 13]; their sexual abstinence in marriage [chap. 7; cf. Luke 20:34f.]; their egalitarian attitudes toward males and females [cf. chaps. 11, 14 and the equal role of women in the worship services]; etc.).[48]

---

48 A. C. Thiselton, "Realized Eschatology at Corinth," *New Testament Studies* 24 (1978), pp. 519–26.

This enthusiast tendency is not unrelated to the Torah, wisdom, and the Spirit, for one of the common Jewish expectations concerning the arrival of the age to come was that it would be accompanied by true obedience to the Torah (based on the power of God's Spirit; see Jer. 31:31–34; Ezek. 36:2–32). Furthermore, as Witherington demonstrates, Jewish wisdom traditions connected *sophia* and apocalypticism. His discussion of this matter deserves quoting:

> Corinthians were steeped in Hellenistic Jewish Wisdom and were taking the promises made in that material quite seriously. They had a kingdom mentality believing that through the Spirit and the Wisdom it conveyed they had already arrived and even obtained the state of perfection, for they themselves were *sophoi* and as *M. Berak.* 2:2 say, "It is the task of the wise person to take on the [yoke of the] kingdom of heaven." Again the close connection made between Wisdom and the Spirit in Wis. 1:6; 7:7, 23–24 as in 1 Corinthians must be stressed. Through the Spirit at least some of the Corinthians believed they were already *teleioi*, already having esoteric knowledge and wisdom about God and the power that comes with it.[49]

Moreover, Palestinian Jewish writers could interpret wisdom and law apocalyptically (e.g., Daniel, *1 Enoch*, *4 Ezra*, *2 Bar.*, Dead Sea Scrolls—obeying the Torah in this age guarantees one life in the age to come). It is reasonable to think that a similar linkage informed the Corinthian church, especially as advocated by the Petrine (Palestinian) party. In other words, they believed that because they possessed the Spirit (wisdom) of the end-times, they were now capable of obeying God's law and were thereby reigning with Christ. As is the case for the other influences to be identified, Paul's refutation of such realized eschatology is to be found in his emphasis on the cross of Christ (1 Cor. 1:18–4:21). For Paul, the cross, particularly as the suffering identified with it is re-presented through the apostle and all true believers, testifies to the fact that this age is a continuing reality and has not yet been fully replaced by the age to come. This is Paul's eschatological reservation.[50]

It will be clear from the previous point that there was a sapiential underpinning

---

49 Witherington, *Jesus the Sage*, pp. 303–4.
50 Pate, *The Glory of Adam*, pp. 94–105.

to the Corinthians' theology as well. They prided themselves in their "heavenly" wisdom which, if Goulder is accurate in his interpretation of the phrase "words of wisdom," will have involved the equation of wisdom and Torah and its *halakhah* as mediated to them by the Spirit (see Paul's critique of this in 1 Corinthians 2:6–16).[51]

We have already called attention to the influence of the Greco-Roman rhetorical tradition on the Corinthians' theology, especially their usage of the art of persuasion for the apparent purpose of articulating the Torah. It is not difficult to imagine that the Petrine party, in particular, fancied itself as being empowered by the Spirit to win people over to the obedience of the Torah, and thus true wisdom, the inevitable result of genuine faith in Christ (cf. Acts 15:1–12; Gal. 2:11–21; James 2:14–26). For Paul, however, attempting to keep the Law is ultimately self-defeating because it stirs up sin in the individual which, in turn, brings about death (1 Cor. 15:56). The only solution is faith in Christ and his gospel alone (1 Cor. 15:1–4). Moreover, in proclaiming this message, Paul refused to employ the ornamentation of the rhetorician lest the people's trust be in humans and not in God (1 Cor. 1:18–2:5). Paul's confidence was only in the cross, foolish though it is to the natural person (1 Cor. 2:6–16).

The fourth significant influence on the Corinthians' theology was mysticism. Although Lütgert tried to distinguish between "nomistic" and "charismatic" Jews,[52] that separation will no longer stand in light of recent research on Jewish *merkabah* mysticism. Such teaching probably goes back to Paul's day, which we summarize here. This teaching emphasized ascetic-mystic visionary experiences of the throne of God, patterned somewhat after Ezekiel 1:15–26. In order to achieve this "beatific vision," the worshipper was required to observe scrupulously the Old Testament law, especially rituals of purification. Furthermore, the seeker engaged in a period of asceticism (estimated to be twelve or forty days). Then the heavenly mystic ascent was attempted, all the while showing deference to the angels who led the mystic along the journey. The path to the abode of God led through some seven heavens, each controlled by an *archon* or angel. Within the seventh heaven,

---

51   See my discussion of this passage from that perspective in *The Reverse of the Curse*, pp. 295–96.
52   Lütgert, *Freiheitspredit … in Korinth*, pp. 47ff.

the mystic had to pass through seven halls or palaces (*hekalot*), each one of which was guarded by an angelic gatekeeper. Only after negotiating this heavenly maze could the worshipper view the glorious divine throne and participate with the angels in the worship of God. This emphasis on angels in *merkabah* (throne) mysticism, however, too easily moved from worshipping *with* angels to actually worshipping the angels. Also, it was inevitable that the seven heavens or the seven palaces would be correlated with the seven planetary spheres ruled by their respective lords, so popular in ancient astrology.

It is not hard to see a connection between Jewish *merkabah* mysticism and the Corinthian problem. Some of the Corinthians apparently believed that it was their mystic ascent to the throne of God in the Spirit that mediated to them tongues, healings, and miracles. It can be surmised that they, too—especially if there was a Petrine faction in the church of Corinth—viewed strict observance of the Torah as the means for generating their mystic ascent to the third heaven. Such an experience, they may have claimed, granted them wisdom and knowledge (1 Corinthians 12–14). Paul, of course, counteracts this brand of spirituality with his message of the cross. It is the cross that fills out the true meaning of God's mystery (1 Cor. 2:6–16) and is the epitome of spirituality, not some supposed heavenly trip (2 Cor. 12:1–10). Stated another way: Paul, too, like the Corinthians, had his share of mystic experiences, but the revelation of the glorious, risen Christ to him was paradoxically manifested through the apostle's afflictions. It was that which legitimated Paul as a servant of God.

1 CORINTHIANS 1:18–3:20 AND PAUL'S REVERSAL OF THE DEUTERONOMIC CURSES AND BLESSINGS

In this section we build on the previous points by arguing that Paul utilizes the wisdom motif especially in 1 Corinthians 1:18–3:20 (the key passage in the discussion) in order to reverse the Deuteronomic curses and blessings. We also factor 2 Corinthians into this discussion.

The Background of 1 Corinthians 1:18–3:20

Older attempts to interpret 1 Corinthians 1:18–3:20 against the backdrop of

Gnosticism[53] rightly gave way to a more Jewish understanding of that text, which rooted wisdom in the Old Testament, and especially (Essene [Dead Sea Scrolls]) apocalypticism.[54] James A. Davis pursued the matter further by contending that the nature of the problem in the Corinthian church as expressed by Paul in 1:18–3:20 stemmed from the Corinthians' equation of divine wisdom with the Torah.[55] In our opinion Davis is quite correct in this regard, and his thesis makes more sense of 1 Corinthians 1:18–3:20 than recent attempts which exclusively relate the situation to Greco-Roman rhetoric.[56] Davis uncovers the flow of thought reflected in 1:18–3:20, which is informed by the Corinthians' positive association of wisdom and the Torah, and against which Paul begs to differ: (a) True wisdom is the Torah (1 Cor. 1:18–20),[57] (b) the obedience of which brings perfection (1:26–31; 2:6–16),[58] (c) the power for which is produced by the Spirit (3:1–5).[59] Against this, Paul counters that Christ, not the Torah, is the hidden wisdom of God, whose death has annulled the Law. To continue to maintain that the Torah is the means for growth toward perfection, as the Corinthians do, is to be misled by the wisdom of the world; a similar error the political rulers who crucified Jesus made. Furthermore, the one who enables people to comprehend God's paradoxical wisdom displayed at the cross is the Spirit. Martin Hengel had earlier arrived at a similar interpretation of 1 Corinthians 1:18–30 in observing that Paul claimed therein that, "the true will of God was no longer embodied in the Torah of Sinai, but in the teaching of the Messiah Jesus, and his accursed death on a cross (Deut. 21.23), could, and indeed must put in

53 The classic work in this regards was by Ulrich Wilckens, *Weisheit und Torheit: Eine exegetisch-religionsgeschichtliche Untersuchung zu 1. Kor. 1 und 2 (Wisdom and Torah: An Exegetical-religion History Investigation of 1 Corinthians 1 and 2)*, Beiträge zur historischen Theologie 26 (Tübingen: J. C. B. Mohr, 1959).
54 First argued by E. Earle Ellis, "Wisdom' and 'Knowledge' in 1 Corinthians." *Tyndale Bulletin* 25 (1974), pp. 82–98.
55 James A. Davis, *Wisdom and Spirit: An Investigation of 1 Corinthians 1:18–3:20 against the Background of Jewish Sapiential Traditions in the Greco-Roman Period.* (Lanham, MD: University Press of America, 1984).
56 See, for example, Witherington (*Jesus the Sage*) and Horsley ("Wisdom").
57 Davis, *Wisdom and Spirit*, pp. 72–73.
58 Ibid, pp, 74–78.
59 Ibid, pp. 78–80.

question the law of Moses as the *ultimate* authority."[60] In the ensuing discussion, we should like to move this perspective to another level by arguing that in 1 Corinthians 1:18–3:20 Paul reverses the Deuteronomic curses and blessings.

The Deuteronomic Tradition as the Textual Underpinning of 1 Corinthians 1:18–3:20

Our suggestion here is that the Deuteronomic tradition forms the exegetical substructure of 1 Corinthians 1:18–3:20, an assumption that the Corinthians accepted. At least the following Old Testament verses are utilized in that passage: Isaiah 29:14 (1 Cor. 1:19); Job 12:17; Isaiah 44:25; Jeremiah 8:9 (1 Cor. 1:20); Deuteronomy 21:22–23 (1 Cor. 1:23; 2:2); Jeremiah 9:23–24 (1 Cor. 1:31); Isaiah 64:4 (1 Cor. 2:9a); Deuteronomy 5:10; 7:9; cf. Isaiah 65:17 (1 Cor. 2:9b); Isaiah 40:13 (1 Cor. 2:16); Job 5:13 (1 Cor. 3:19); Psalm 94:11 (1 Cor. 20). Certain observations emerge from these texts in their Old Testament setting, moving from the general (numbers 1, 2) to the specific (numbers 3, 4, 5): (1) Mere human wisdom is ineffective (Ps. 94:11). (2) God's wisdom subverts conventional wisdom (Job 5:13; 12:17). (3) The wisdom of Israel's leaders, which perverted God's word to the nation, will incur divine judgment on the people—the Deuteronomic curses (Isa. 29:14; 44:25; Jer. 8:9; 9:23–24). (4) One day, however, Israel will repent, obey the Law, and love God from the heart and thus be restored to her land—the Deuteronomic blessings (Deut. 7:9; cf. 5:10; Isa. 64:4; 65:17). (5) Those who were killed and hung on a tree because of a capital offense were to be removed so as not to bring impurity and thus the divine curse on the land (Deut. 21:23). From these remarks one can see that the textual underpinning of 1 Corinthians 1:18–3:20 is very much in keeping with the Deuteronomic tradition, particularly the sin-exile-restoration pattern of the story of Israel. Indeed such a backdrop is consonant with those attempts to argue that 1:18–3:20 is a *haggadic* (story/sermon) homily associated with the ancient synagogue's commemoration of the fall of Jerusalem

---

60 Martin Hengel, *The Son of God: The Origin of Christology and the History of Jewish-Hellenistic Religion,* trans. by J. Bowden (London: SCM, 1976), p. 58.

in 587 BC.[61] Moreover, the view we are here offering of 1 Corinthians 1:18–3:20 is also able to accommodate those authors who interpret 1 Corinthians 2:6–9 against the backdrop of Jewish apocalyptic materials such as *1 Enoch*[62] and the Dead Sea Scrolls,[63] in the following way—1 Corinthians 1:18–3:20, like those Jewish apocalyptic works mentioned above, plays off of the positive association of wisdom and the Law, such that to obey the Torah is to replace the Deuteronomic curses of this age with the covenantal blessings of the age to come. This perspective makes particularly good sense of 1 Corinthians 2:9: the promise of the nation's restoration—the reinheritance of the land (what cannot be imagined because of its wonder; Isa. 64:4 [cf. 65:17]) is contingent on Israel's love for and obedience to God's law (for those who love him; Deut. 7:9; cf. 5:10). We, therefore, agree with those who claim that the Corinthians equated Christ with divine wisdom who embodied the Torah,[64] and we suggest that the Deuteronomistic tradition informs 1 Corinthians 1:18–3:20 such that the Corinthians, influenced by the Peter party, believed that Christ, the wisdom of God, provided the power by his Spirit to obey the Torah. In doing so the Corinthians fancied themselves to have inherited the Deuteronomic blessings of the age to come. As such they formed the spiritual elite of the church at Corinth.

Paul's Reverse of the Deuteronomic Tradition in 1 Corinthians 1:18–3:20

Paul's allusion to Deuteronomy 21:23 in 1 Corinthians 1:23; 2:2 is not haphazard. We suggest that its net result on the other Old Testament passages he utilizes in 1 Corinthians 1:18–3:20 is to reverse the Deuteronomic curses and blessings (cf. what his usage of Deut. 21:23 does to the Old Testament texts quoted in Gal. 3:10–13). That is to say, Christ took the Deuteronomic curses upon himself on the cross in order to dispense the Deuteronomic blessings on

---

61 W. Wuellner, "Haggadic Homily Genre in 1 Corinthians 1–3," in *Journal of Biblical Literature* 89 (1970), pp. 199–204.

62 R. G. Hamerton-Kelly, *Pre-Existence, Wisdom and the Son of Man: A Study of the Idea of Pre-Existence in the New Testament*, Society for New Testament Studies Monograph Series 21 (Cambridge: University Press, 1973), pp. 112ff.

63 Markus Bockmuehl, *Revelation and Mystery in Ancient Judaism and Pauline Christianity*, Wissenschaftliche Untersuchungen zum Neuen Testament 2/36 (Tübingen: J. C. B. Mohr/ Paul Siebeck, 1990), pp. 158–65.

64 Hengel, *The Son of God*, p. 74; Davis, *Wisdom and Spirit*, pp. 74ff.; Kim, *The Origin of Paul's Gospel*, pp. 127ff., 258–60.

those who believe the gospel. According to Paul, therefore, for the Corinthians to revert to the Torah was to depreciate the full significance of Christ's death and resurrection; it was, in actuality, to forego the covenantal blessings. What one discovers in 1 Corinthians 1:18–3:20, then, is Paul's announcement that the Deuteronomic curses abide on those who attempt to be justified by the works of the Law, which are manifested through their rejection of the cross (1:18, 20–21; 2:7–8, 14–16). Ironically, the message of a crucified Messiah—scandal though it was to the Jews (1:23)—is precisely the divine means for receiving the covenantal blessings, according to the apostle Paul (1:24–31; 2:5–10). This line of thinking is reminiscent of Romans 1:18–3:31 with its declaration that both Jew and Gentile are under divine judgment because they do not obey the Torah (cf. 1 Cor. 1:23), but that both can be saved through faith in Christ alone (cf. 1 Cor. 1:24). In effect, then, Paul's message of the cross in 1 Corinthians 1:18–3:20 both replaces Torah with faith and Jewish particularism with a gospel for all.

2 Corinthians 3:1–4:6

Second Corinthians 3:1–4:6 needs to be factored into this discussion. Second Corinthians 3:1–4:6 presents an antithetical Moses typology. Seyoon Kim's chart of contrasts between the Mosaic covenant and the new covenant in Christ is a helpful summary of 2 Corinthians 3:1–4:6:[65]

THE MINISTRY OF THE OLD COVENANT	THE MINISTRY OF THE NEW COVENANT
1. It is a written code (3:6f.): of death (3:6) of condemnation (3:9) in the process of abolition (3:11) of less glory	It is of the Spirit (3:6, 8): of life (3:6) of righteousness (3:9) permanent (3:11) of greater glory (3:7–11)
2. Moses, its minister, veiled himself in order to prevent the Israelites from seeing the end of the covenant which was being abolished (3:13)	Paul, its minister, acts with confidence, hope, freedom, and frankness (3:4, 12; 4:1ff.)

---

65 Kim, *The Origin of Paul's Gospel*, p. 214.

- In consequence the old covenant remains veiled (3:14)	- The new covenant reveals the glory of God (3:16–18; 4:4, 6)
- Its adherents, the Israelites, are also veiled in their hearts, so that they cannot understand the revelation of God (3:14f.; 4:3f.)	- Its adherents, the Christians, have their veil removed in Christ, and see the glory of the Lord,
-Implied: the glory and image of God were restored to Israel on Sinai; but they lost them through sin. The observance of the Law restores them.[65]	- and are transformed into the image of Christ who operates as the Spirit (3:16–18; 4:4–6).

Although an increasing number of recent interpreters argue that Paul does not say in 2 Corinthians 3:1–4:6 that the Law and the old covenant is annulled,[66] the following four points made by Ben F. Witherington III seem to suggest otherwise,[67] as indeed a straightforward reading of the previous contrasts might have indicated. (a) Paul is not merely talking here about a legalistic approach or attitude to the Mosaic law. The contrast is between the actual effect of the Mosaic law on humans (death, 3:6; condemnation, 3:9) as opposed to the opposite result of the Spirit and Christ on people (life, 3:6; righteousness, 3:9; enlightenment and spiritual obtuseness removed, 3:15). This contrast in effect is similar to what Paul says in Romans 2–3; 7–8. To read a passage like *Exodus Rabbah* 4:1 (on Ex. 31:18) is to appreciate the uniqueness of Paul's stance regarding the result of the Torah, "While Israel stood below engraving idols to provoke their Creator to anger … God sat on high engraving tablets which would give them life." (b) Paul's usage of the verb, καταργεω ("abolish"), in various forms in 2 Corinthians 3:1–4:6 (3:7, 11, 13–14) is critical to the discussion. Twenty-two of its twenty-seven occurrences in the New Testament are found in the undisputed Pauline letters and always refer to something replaced, invalidated or abolished, not merely to something faded.[68] Consistency would dictate that Paul uses the word here with the same intended meaning. (c) The third point has to do with the removal of the veil over the hearts

---

66 Most notably Scott J. Hafemann, *Paul, Moses, and the History of Israel: The Letter/Spirit Contrast and the Argument from Scripture in 2 Corinthians 3*, Wissenchaftlichen Untersuchungen zum Neuen Testament 81 (Tübingen: J. C. B. Mohr/Paul Siebeck, 1995).

67 Ben F. Witherington III, *Jesus, Paul, and the End of the World: A Comparative Study in New Testament Eschatology* (Downers Grove, IL: InterVarsity Press), pp. 110–11.

68 Ibid, pp. 110–11.

of unbelievers, thanks to the working of Christ and the Spirit. This, too, indicates that the Mosaic law and covenant have reached their end. Witherington writes of this:

> … only Christ the Lord or the Spirit can take away the veil over the hearts of the Israelites. But when the veil is taken away, what does Paul think the Israelites will see? His arguments suggest that they will see that the Mosaic law has a temporary, not a permanent glory, unlike the new covenant (v. 11) … and thus a temporal and temporary part to play in the divine economy of salvation. His argument suggests that they will see the Mosaic covenant, far from giving life, had just the opposite effect on fallen human beings. When the veil, or hardheartedness, is removed, though the law will be seen as a good and glorious thing in and of itself, it will also be seen to have had bad effects, and thus in the end needed to be superseded by a more effective covenant that gives life and righteousness.[69]

(d) In view of the fact that the neuter participle in v. 11, to $\kappa\alpha\tau\alpha\rho\gamma\text{ου}\mu\epsilon\text{νον}$ ("what faded), in accordance with the neuter substantive in v. 10, to $\delta\epsilon\delta\text{οχασμενον}$ ("what had glory), should be interpreted as applying to the entire old covenant, then it is likely that Paul in v. 14 says that the old covenant, not just the veil, is passing away.

(3) In light of the previous discussion, we may now add a further contrast to those already delineated in 2 Corinthians 3:1–4:6—the law of Moses and Christ, the wisdom of God. Kim captures this point well:

> That at the Damascus revelation Paul realized that Christ had superseded the Torah and is therefore the true wisdom, can be clearly seen in 2 Cor. 3.4–4.6…. Paul realized this truth and received the ministry of the new covenant of Christ's gospel when he saw the surpassing light of the glory of God in the face of Christ who appeared to him while he was treading the road to Damascus in blind obedience to the Torah. If the Torah as God's revelation had formerly been supposed by him to be light and to give man light (cf. Pss. 19.8; 119.130; Prov. 6.23; 2 Bar. 17f.; Wis. 18.4; Sifre Num. 6.25; etc.), Paul now saw the

---

69 Ibid.

perfect revelation of God in the person of Christ which is the true divine light, the creation light (esp. 2 Cor. 4.6). This Corinthians passage indicates not only that at the Damascus revelation Paul realized that Christ had superseded the Torah but also that at the same time he perceived Christ as the true wisdom.[70]

5. Jewish Merkabah and 2 Corinthians 12:1–10

That we are on the right track of rooting 1 and 2 Corinthians in a Jewish, rather than Hellenistic, setting is confirmed by 2 Corinthians 12:1–10. Second Corinthians 12:1–10 records Paul's mystic experience of being caught up to the throne of God, which finds key parallels to Jewish *merkabah* texts contemporaneous with Paul. Thus:

a. The mystic is caught up to the throne of God (*1 Enoch* 71:3):
   - Archangel Michael seizes Enoch by the hand and lifts him up.
   - According to Paul's account, he is "caught up" (v. 2–3).
b. The traveler journeys through a plurality of heavens (*2 Enoch* 3–20):
   - Gates between the heavens are guarded by archangels and are passed only by saying the names of the guardian and showing the proper symbol.
   - Paul travels to the third heaven and paradise (v. 2–3).
c. The traveler sees various hidden things (i.e. cosmic phenomena (*1 Enoch* 72–80), and supernatural beings (*2 Enoch* 20–22):
   - Paul sees "visions and revelations."
d. The journey discloses secrets, i.e., mysteries are revealed (*3 Apoc. Bar.* 1:6–7), and books (*2 Esdr.* 14:44–46) and tablets (*T. Levi* 5:5) that contain secrets are inscribed:
   - Paul says he heard "unutterable utterances which a human being is not permitted to speak" (v. 4).
e. The meaning of this revelation is interpreted by an angel:
   - In apocalyptic literature this is accomplished by a dialogue between the traveler and his heavenly guide (*1 Enoch* 72:1).

---

70 Kim, *The Origin of Paul's Gospel*, p. 128.

- Some sort of communication to Paul is implied in the fact that Paul heard utterances (v. 4).
f. In *merkabah* mysticism there is an element of danger associated with making these heavenly journeys (*Chagigah* 2:3–4; 14–15b):
  - Some think that Paul continues a theme of the "greatness" of his revelations and that this is what led to his "thorn in the flesh" (v. 7–10).

But Paul's purpose in relating this mystic experience was ironic—he divulged this story precisely to refute his opponent's boasting in *merkabah* mysticism. Rather than bask in his heavenly encounter with the throne of God, Paul boasted in his sufferings. Only through his apostolic afflictions could the strength of Christ be perfected. Moreover Paul pit his inaugurated eschatology against the realized eschatology of the *merkabah* Judaizers:

MERKABAH JUDAIZERS	PAUL
1) The age to come is completely here by virtue of the coming of Christ and the indwelling Spirit	1) The age to come has dawned (1 Cor. 10:11; 2 Cor. 3:1–4:6) but it is not yet complete, as sufferings indicate (2 Cor. 4:7–5:21)
2) By the Spirit the mystic is caught up to the throne of God to see divine glory (the merger of heaven and earth)	2) Christians have divine glory but in vessels of clay— their bodies (2 Cor. 4:7–18)
3) Jesus is the Savior who makes this possible	3) Jesus is the Christ whose Spirit and glory indwell the Christian (the age to come has dawned) but so are the sufferings of Jesus manifested in the Christian in this age (2 Cor. 1–2, 4–5, 10–13).
4) The new covenant texts of the Old Testament (Jer. 31; Ezek. 36; Joel 2) predict this will come, which is now fully realized in Christ	4) The new covenant texts are being fulfilled in the Christian (2. Cor. 3:1–4:6) but not yet fully realized (2 Cor. 4:7–5:21)
5) Being caught up to the *merkabah* is conditioned upon obeying the Torah and fasting.	5) Experiencing the age to come is based on faith in Christ, not the law of Moses (2 Cor. 3:1–4:6)

In essence, then, Palestinian Jewish Christians following Peter as their hero and claiming mystic experience and ecstatic Pentecostal speech undermined Paul's apostolic authority upon their intrusion in the Corinthian church. 1 and 2 Corinthians are Paul's response to the realized eschatology of those "merkabizers," all the while doing battle with the realized eschatology of the Roman imperial cult and the consistent eschatology of the non-Christian Jews, and, as we will now see, the realized eschatology of Hellenistic religion.

PAUL VERSUS THE REALIZED ESCHATOLOGY OF HELLENISTIC RELIGION

But the Corinthians' realized eschatology was also due to Hellenistic syncretistic religion. Thus one can see the influence of Greek philosophy on the Corinthian church, especially its obsession with oratory like the local Sophists who awed the crowds and charged them heftily for doing so (see 1 Cor. 1–4; 2 Cor. 10–13). And then Platonic philosophy factored into the Corinthian Christians' chagrin at the thought of a bodily resurrection (see 1 Cor. 15). Some of the Greco-Roman pantheon also made their presence felt in the Corinthian church, which was tempted to return to its immoral flings with the Aphrodite (Venus) prostitute priestesses (see 1 Cor. 6), or eat meats offered to Apollos and Asclepion in their temples (see 1 Cor. 8, 10), or fancied itself to be prophets like the Sibyls at the Delphi oracle (see 1 Cor. 14), or participate in the Pan-Hellenic games at the Poseidon (Neptune) complex.

These components of Hellenistic syncretistic religion set the table for the powerful influence of the mystery religions at Corinth like the cults of Dionysius (Bacchus) and Isis. The former was noted for its drunken orgies and ecstatic speech (see 1 Cor. 13–14). The latter, the Isis cult, deserves special attention here because one of the most celebrated descriptions of this mystery is provided by Apuleius's *Metamorphoses* (the *Golden Ass*) which situates its story in Corinth and nearby Cenchreae. Apuleius's story of the young man Lucius turned into a donkey by a formula gone awry is an entertaining, albeit at times lewd, tale. But for our purposes, we may focus on Book XI, the last book of this novel for there one meets with the five components of the realized eschatology of the mystery religion of Isis.[71] We supply a self-explanatory chart

---

71 Though Apuleius wrote his *Metamorphosis* in the second century AD, there is no reason to doubt the prevalence of the Isis myth in Corinth during Paul's time there, especially since the Isis myth was one of the most pervasive mystery religions of all. We should also mention that it is not Paul who is being influenced by this mystery religion (recall our rejection of the mystery religions' influence on Paul's theology in our introduction) but rather Isis' influence on the Corinthians.

below with four columns that compare the Isis mystery in *Metamorphosis* with the Corinthian church's realized eschatology (Columns 1–3). Then we supply Paul's rebuttal based on his inaugurated eschatology (Column 4):

REALIZED ESCHATOLOGY OF MYSTERY RELIGIONS	REALIZED ESCHATOLOGY OF *METAMORPHOSIS* BOOK XI	CORINTHIAN CHURCH'S REALIZED ESCHATOLOGY	PAUL'S REBUTTAL TO THE CORINTHIANS: INAUGURATED ESCHATOLOGY
1) New age dawned	Isis-mother of universe is the first offspring of the ages (XI. 5) who brings salvation (XI. 12) /rebirth in Isis (XI. 25)	Age to come fully here: Corinthians reign in the kingdom of God (1 Cor. 4:5, 8), are like angels (1 Cor. 7, 13), and are free from the body (1 Cor. 5–6)	Age to come dawned but not complete, therefore: Christians don't reign yet (1 Cor. 4), need to be holy (1 Cor. 6) and need to be married to resist immorality (1 Cor. 7)
2) Cosmic/ universal renewal	Through the mystery rites—the initiate joins the gods (XI. W1), is glorious (XI. 10) like the stars (XI. 10), and receives unutterable secrets (XI. 23)	Through the Spirit and the Torah (2 Cor. 3:1–4:6) believers are mystically caught up to heaven (2 Cor. 12:1–10) where they speak like angels (1 Cor. 13:1)	Prophecy and tongues will not be needed after the parousia (1 Cor. 23); this age of suffering continues (2 Cor. 1–2; 4:7–5:21; 10–13).
3) Savior	Isis, the savior (XI. 25) who embodies all gods (XI. 5–6) and rules with Osiris (XI. 30)	Jesus and the Spirit	Jesus Christ by faith apart from the Torah (2 Cor. 3:1–4:6)
4) Predicted through the sacred texts	Isis priests give divine promises/ dreams/oracles to her followers (XI. 13)	This is the fulfillment of new covenant prophecies like Jer. 31, Ezek. 36, Joel 2.	New covenant prophecies of Jer. 31, Ezek. 36, Joel 2 dawned but not complete (2 Cor. 4:7–5:21)
5) New age celebrated through rituals	Initiates join a processional that makes an offering to Isis (XI. 16), abstains from eating meat for 10 days (XI. 22, 28), participates in a ritual bath (XI. 23), etc.	Baptism and the Lord's Supper magically protect them (1 Cor. 10, 11)	Baptism and the Lord's Supper will not magically protect Corinthians (1 Cor. 10–11)

CONCLUSION

This lengthy chapter identified several eschatologies Paul combated in 1 and 2 Corinthians (cf. Acts 18): the consistent eschatology of Judaism, the realized eschatology of the Roman imperial cult, the realized eschatology of the *merkabah* Judaizers, and the realized eschatology of the Hellenistic syncretistic religion, especially the Isis cult as portrayed in Apuleius' *Metamorphosis*. At the end of the day, the one thing these syncretistic religions—Jewish, Roman, Greek—could not tolerate about Paul was the exclusivity of his message: the crucified Christ. The next chapter offers a summary of the contents of 1 and 2 Corinthians.

Chapter 5

A SUMMARY OF
1 AND 2 CORINTHIANS

We will summarize 1 and 2 Corinthians on the assumption put forth in the last chapter: that the Corinthian church fancied itself as fully realized spiritually. Such realized eschatology was the product of two major influences—*merkabah* Judaizers from Palestine, and Hellenistic syncretistic religion from Corinth, especially mystery religions like the Isis cult. To deal with the latter necessarily meant also critiquing Greek philosophy, the Greco-Roman pantheon, and the imperial cult. Paul opposed the preceding spiritual ideologies with his apocalypse of the crucified Christ.

1 CORINTHIANS

First Corinthians can be outlined along the theme of problems in the church:

A. 1:1–4:21: Factions in the Church
B. 5:1–6:20: Immorality and Litigation in the Church
C. 7:1–40: Six Issues in the Church Related to Marriage
D. 8:1–11:16: Eating Meats Dedicated to Idols, a Magical View of Baptism, Inappropriate Worship
E. 11:17–34: Abuse of the Lord's Supper
F. 12:1–14:40: Abuse of Spiritual Gifts in the Church

We now address these concerns.

A. 1:1–4:21: Factions in the Church

Paul's introduction both acknowledges that the Corinthian Christians are in Christ but still need to be holy (1:1–3) and that they are gifted spiritually but still await the parousia (1:4–9). So from the get-go, the apostle introduces his eschatological reservation as a corrective to the Corinthians' realized eschatology—that is, he supplies the "not yet" (the need to be holy/the parousia is still forthcoming) to their "already" (they are in Christ/spiritually gifted in eloquence and knowledge).

Then Paul turns his attention to the problem of factions in the Corinthians church (1:10–4:20). Although Paul mentions four factions—Paul, Apollos, Cephas/Peter, and Christ—we argued in the last chapter that the main division was between followers of Paul and followers of Peter (not that there wasn't a group that lauded Apollos and another that applauded Christ). The background we uncovered in the last chapter helps to explain the origin of the divisions in the Corinthian church, especially between the Pauline and Petrine groups. First, the well-known tendency of Greek philosophical schools to compete with one another no doubt predisposed the self-engrossed Corinthians to do the same—not so much the schools of Plato, Zeno, Aristotle, etc., but the schools of Peter, Paul, Apollos, and Christ. Second, this was reinforced by the mystery religions, like Isis which practiced its own form of baptism (ritual baths as part of the preparation for mystic experience; recall *Metamorphosis* XI). As far as the Corinthian church was concerned, the hero you championed—Peter, Paul, etc.—was the name into whom you were baptized. But Paul calls such thinking ludicrous, because all Christians are baptized into only one name—Christ. Third, Paul counters the Corinthian believers' love for words—*logos* (born out of infatuation with the philosophical oratory of the Greek Sophist philosophical school), combined with the Corinthians' adherence to wisdom—*sophia* (Torah as the wisdom of God) with his message of the crucified Christ.

In 1:18–2:5 Paul opposes divine wisdom to human wisdom by supplying three examples of that contrast. First, the cross of Christ is antithetical to the wisdom of this age (1:18–2:5). The crucifixion of Christ scandalized the Jews for two reasons: The cross was an affront to their hope for a military deliverer, and it spelled the end of the Torah. Christ, not the law of Moses, is the wisdom of God. The foolishness of the cross also offended the Greek's love for eloquence and knowledge, as the Sophists supposedly displayed. But in reality, Jesus's crucifixion was the power and wisdom of God, the only means to salvation.

Second, the status of the Corinthians believers also illustrated the contrast between divine wisdom and human wisdom (1:26–31). The majority of the Corinthian Christians were from the lower classes, not the patrons of society. But the fact that God saves undesirables—like most in the church of Corinth—and not the wealthy and powerful bespeaks the superiority of divine wisdom.

The third contrast between divine wisdom and human wisdom was the preaching of Paul (2:1–5). Paul's message resulted in the conversion of the Corinthians precisely because his "style," unlike the Sophists, matched the cross—weak and faltering. Yet God's Spirit was unleashed through the apostle because he emulated the cross.

In chapter 2:6–16 Paul discusses how God discloses his wisdom—it is by the Spirit based on the cross of Christ. Those who embrace the crucifixion of Christ belong to the age to come and truly know God by his Spirit. But those who reject the cross, beginning with the Jewish and Roman leaders who had Jesus executed, belong to this age and do not really know God. Neither the Sophists nor the Judaizers receive divine revelation.

After chiding the Corinthians Christians for acting like non-Christians enamored with the world's wisdom (3:1–4) Paul then offers five images that present Christ-centered leadership (3:5–4:21). The agricultural image demonstrates that Paul, Apollos, and any minister of the gospel are servants fulfilling their respective roles but it is God that gives spiritual growth (3:5–8). The architectural metaphor points out that Christ is the foundation of the church and leaders must build on that with the gospel of the cross (costly stones) not human wisdom (wood, hay, stubble), (3:9–23). The financial picture reminds the Corinthians that ministers are to be faithful stewards of the truth of God (4:1–7). The gladiatorial image sarcastically contrasts the Corinthians' "perfection" with the apostles who are in the fight of their lives defending the cross of Christ. Thus Paul introduces the "not yet" aspect of eschatology into the discussion—embracing persecution for the gospel's sake—into the "already" aspect of the Corinthians' triumphalist "gospel" (4:8–13). The familial metaphor portrays Paul as the spiritual father of the Corinthian believers, which gives him the divine authority to challenge the church to imitate his commitment to the cross (4:14–21). The preceding five images were offered by Paul to jolt the Corinthian church into the reality that their divisive spirit was born out of exalting human leaders over the cross of Christ, God's wisdom.

B. 5:1–6:20: Immorality and Litigation in the Church

In 5:1–6:20 Paul addresses two areas of inappropriate behavior by the Corinthian believers. In 5:1–13 we see that the church encouraged immoral behavior by one of the members that would not be sanctioned by even pagans—a man was having an affair with his stepmother. Such incest was condemned by Jews (Lev. 18:8; Deut. 22:30; 27:20) and Romans (for example, Cicero). The church could applaud the man's actions because they believed, like Plato, that the body doesn't matter and that only the soul/spirit counts before God. And since the Corinthians fancied themselves as already raised from the dead by virtue of their possession of the Spirit (see 1 Cor. 15), no action could jeopardize their standing with God. Paul, however, had other ideas, condemning the man by delivering him over to Satan.

In 6:1–11 Paul chastises the Corinthian church because some of its members were suing each other in the court system. The apostle delivers two reprimands to the Corinthians for doing so. First, since they will one day rule with Christ in the kingdom judging the world and angels, why do they now go to court to let the world judge them? Second, their litigation against each other hurts the testimony of Christ. Most likely, the Corinthian believers took each other to court to display their rhetorical abilities—something Sophists taught the rank and file to do in defending themselves in court. But, from Paul's perspective, the Corinthian immorality and legal suits brought into question whether or not they had even entered the kingdom of God yet, must less reigned in it.

Paul condemns the church's immorality again in 1 Corinthians 6:12–20. Probably the Corinthians were being influenced by two factors here—their past adultery with the Aphrodite prostitute priestesses had beckoned them once again, and their false confidence that the actions committed in their bodies could not hurt their souls because they possessed the Spirit. Paul counters such error by commanding the Corinthian church to treat their bodies as the temple of the Holy Spirit. One also hears in this challenge the practice of sacral manumission. Slaves in the Roman Empire could buy their freedom by dedicating themselves to a temple deity. Paul alludes to this custom by reminding the Corinthian believers that they were bought with the blood of Christ and now they belonged to him, the true deity.

C. 7:1–40: Six Issues in the Church Related to Marriage

In 1 Corinthians 7 Paul answers questions raised of him by the church at Corinth related to marriage. Six matters are addressed by Paul. We agree with Gordon Fee that the problems were due to realized eschatology. The Corinthians believed that because the Spirit had come, and with it the full realization of the age to come, they were reigning in the kingdom like the angels. Therefore, the physical aspect of marriage was no longer necessary. We touch upon each of the six matters by outlining the respective problems and Paul's principles of solution:

1. The problem—overrealized eschatology and Hellenistic thinking— because the Spirit has come, and with it the age to come, the Christian is now fully in the kingdom of God, and therefore spiritual; the physical no longer is needed or desirable.
2. The principle—eschatological reservation—Christians live in tension between the ages:
   a. Already the age to come has dawned (v. 29), "time is shortened" (v. 31), "this age is passing away."
   b. Not yet complete—still in this age—proof is present suffering—v. 26
   c. Therefore remain in present status—vv. 8, 17–24, 29–31, 40
3. Particulars—six instances—apply problem/principle
   d. Vv. 1–7—married
      1) Problem—v. 1—"not touch woman"=angelic existence, there-fore not married nor sexual relations ("spiritual marriage")
      2) Principle—in between times—remain married, fulfilling each other sexually
   e. b. Vv. 8–9—unmarried (single or widows)
      1) Problem—v. 9—fine to marry—physical aspect of marriage okay, though Paul prefers single status, if a person's gift (v. 7)
      2) Principle—v. 8—remain unmarried—(if gifted to do so, v.7)

    f. Vv. 10–11—married (both believers—don't divorce)
       1) Problem—dissolving marriages and sexual relationships—because angelic existence
       2) Principle—remain married
    g. Vv. 12–16—to those with unbelieving spouses
       1) Problem—thought divorce would remove unbelieving spouse's bad influence on their spirituality and have heavenly existence
       2) Principle—remain; Paul stresses positive influence of believer on unbeliever (open to sanctifying influence of the gospel) not negative influence of the unbeliever
    h. Vv. 25–38—single woman (virgins and fathers or man betrothed to?)
       1) Problem—not get married and have sexual relations—hinders spirituality
       2) Principle—remain single but:
          a) Not for moral reasons (marriage fine)—vv. 28a, 35–36, 38a
          b) But eschatological reasons—end is near—vv. 26, 29, 31, for in heaven present status (marriage, single, circumcision, free, slavery) will be dissolved
    i. Vv. 39–40—married and widow
       1) Married, v. 39a
          a) Problem—angelic-like existence renders marriage now irrelevant
          b) Principle—remain married—marriage fine
       2) Widows, vv. 39–40
          a) Principle—angelic existence renders marriage irrelevant
          b) Principle—fine to remarry in Lord—v. 36b, but preferable to remain single, v. 40

D. 8:1–11:16: Eating Meats Dedicated to Idols, a Magical View of Baptism, Inappropriate Worship

In 1 Corinthians 8:1–11:16, the apostle addresses three interrelated issues, each stemming from the Corinthians' realized eschatology rooted in Hellenistic syncretistic religion: meat offered to idols, a magical view of baptism, and inappropriate conduct in the worship services.

Paul addresses the issue of eating meats offered to idols in 1 Corinthians 8:1–13 and in 10:14–11:1. There are two situations rooted in ancient Corinth's culture that inform Paul's comments on the matter. The first is the fact that any meat bought in Corinth would have been purchased in the marketplace, and would have been earlier dedicated to one of the pagan gods. This was so because the priests of those pagan temples would have sacrificed meat to their respective deities—Apollo, Dionysius, Isis, Poseidon, Caesar, etc.—eaten a portion of the meat, and sold it to the marketplace. That meat would have then been mixed with any other meat to be sold in the *macellum* (marketplace). Therefore, Christians who bought meat would not have been able to discriminate between meat offered to a pagan deity and meat that was not. Paul's answer to this issue in 1 Corinthians 8:1–6 and 10:23–30 is that since there is no god but the true God, the meat offered to pagan deities was in reality offered to no deity. Therefore, believers can eat that meat in good conscience either in private or in the home of another believer. But the Christian must avoid that meat if it offends the conscience of another believer.

The second situation that informed the issue of eating meats dedicated to idols was the regular occasion when individuals attended the feasts at the pagan temples. In 1 Corinthians 8:7–13 and 10:14–22, Paul forbids Christians from attending those feasts held at the pagan temples. This was to invite demonic control over the believer's life.

In 1 Corinthians 9:1–27 Paul elaborates upon the importance of not offending the conscience of another Christian, especially in the matter of eating meats offered to idols. Paul used his own right to accept payment for his apostolic service (9:1–12a, 13, 14) but forewent that right for the sake of the gospel as an illustration (9:12b, 15–27). Lurking in the background of this discussion was the Sophists' custom of charging for their services rendered. But for Paul not to do so to illustrate the free nature of the gospel, caused the Corinthians to doubt his right to be an apostle. Consequently, 1 Corinthians 9:1–27 is devoted also to Paul's defense of his apostleship.

First Corinthians 10:1–13 is also rooted in the Corinthians' realized eschatology stemming from Hellenistic syncretistic religion, especially the Dionysius cult. The issue there was the Corinthians' magical view of baptism for, like the mystery religions, especially the Dionysius cult, baptism, or ritual bathing, was a part of the initiation rites into the cult, and therefore signified union with the deity (recall Apuleius' *Metamorphosis*, XI. 23). The Corinthians transferred such an understanding to Christian baptism, apparently believing that their baptism into Christ and the Spirit signified that they were fully in the kingdom of God. Indeed, baptism magically protected them from all ills of this age. Paul agrees that faith in Christ and baptism does place the believer into the age to come (1 Cor. 10:1–13), but Paul disagrees that the age to come is fully realized now. Paul reminds the Corinthians that the ancient Israelites were baptized into Moses at the Exodus but that most of them still died in the wilderness before reaching the promised land (1 Cor. 10:1–11a). Therefore, let the Corinthians learn that baptism did not magically protect them; they still needed to resist the temptations of this present age, from which God can deliver them (1 Cor. 10:12–13).

The third interrelated issue Paul addresses in this section of 1 Corinthians, besides eating meats dedicated to idols and a magical view of baptism, was the inappropriate actions of some folk in the church worship services (1 Cor. 11:2–16). Specifically, women seemed to be prophesying in worship services with unveiled heads. Probably they were imitating Isis priestesses whose heads were uncovered and hair unloosed when they performed rituals in that cult. It may even be that the Isis priestess's unveiled head intended to reverse gender distinctions. This background makes sense of Paul's two arguments in this passage. First, the differentiation of the sexes is divinely ordained (vv. 3–6). Second, so also is the subordination of the sexes (female to males in worship, vv. 7–16). These two instructions by Paul provide his eschatological reservation to the Corinthian church's realized eschatology: The age to come has dawned, hence the reason women can prophesy like men; but the age to come is not complete, therefore Christian women must not prophesy with unveiled heads which could be interpreted as usurping God's priority in creation.

E. 11:17–34: Abuse of the Lord's Supper
In 1 Corinthians 11:17–34, Paul corrects the abuse of the Lord's Supper in the worship setting of the Corinthian church. It seems that the Corinthians celebrated a "potluck meal" (an agape meal, cf. 1 Cor. 11:17–22, 33–34 with

Jude 12) before observing the Lord's Supper. But the more well-to-do believers (patrons) got to the agape feast earlier and ate most of the food and
drank most of the wine, leaving little for the less fortunate believers to partake
in when they arrived after work. Such discrimination in the body of Christ
was apparently causing the more well-to-do to get sick and even die due to
the judgment of God upon them. Such drastic divine measures shocked the
Corinthian church into realizing that the Lord's Supper, like baptism, did
not magically protect them. Furthermore God's judgment was also a way of
saying the age to come had not fully arrived.

F. 12:1–14:40: Abuse of Spiritual Gifts in the Church

In 1 Corinthians 12:1–14:40, Paul corrects the Corinthian church's misun-
derstanding about spiritual gifts, tongues in particular. All indication is that
the church emphasized tongues, along with knowledge and wisdom, over the
other gifts due to at least two influences. First, the Sophists' stress on knowledge and wisdom enamored the church with those abilities. Second, ecstatic
speech as the sign of the Pentecostal gift of tongues also greatly impressed
the Corinthian believers. We argued in the last chapter that the *merkabah*
Judaizers combined both tongues and knowledge/wisdom in their appeal to
the church. All of this caused the Corinthians to think they were spiritually
perfect, like the angels (1 Cor. 13:1). Paul therefore corrects such misinformation in 12:1–14:40, in three ways.

First, in 12:1–29 Paul teaches that there is a diversity of spiritual gifts,
not just one—tongues. He makes three points in this regard: (1) Diversity belongs to the Godhead (12:1–11). (2) Diversity characterizes the human body
(12:12–26). (3) Diversity characterizes the body of Christ (12:27–31).

Second, in 13:1–13 Paul exalts love over the gifts, even over prophecy,
tongues, and knowledge. Indeed when the perfect comes (the parousia), love
is the only quality that will last.

Third, in 14:1–40 Paul makes two general points: (1) Prophecy is pref-
erable to tongues in public worship because the former can be understood
whereas the latter cannot be without interpretation/translation (14:1–25). (2)
All of the gifts—prophecy and tongues included—should be exercised properly in the worship service (14:26–40). Thus, those who speak in tongues must

have someone interpret that message; and those exercising prophecy (which needed no interpretation) should do so in order, not simultaneously.

Paul concludes his instruction to the church concerning worship by challenging women to be silent in the worship service (vv. 34–35). These controversial words probably mean no more than that Christian wives, enjoying their freedom in Christ to prophesy and speak tongues, should be careful not to let things get out of control by becoming overly enthusiastic to the point of being boisterous in the worship services. Rather than all speak at once, the ladies should discuss spiritual matters at home with their husbands.

G. 15:1–58: Problems over the Resurrection of the Body

The issue that Paul deals with in 1 Corinthians 15 is the Corinthian denial of the resurrection body of the believer. There were probably two aspects to that denial. First, influenced by the Platonic disparagement of the body, the Corinthian believers seemed to have taught only the immortality of the soul. Second, the Corinthians thought that their possession of the Spirit meant that they were already raised to immortality; hence their present earthly bodies did not matter. Consequently they could indulge the passions of the body or deny its legitimate needs. Paul refutes such thinking in three steps. First, the apostle argues that Christ's body was resurrected from the dead (15:1–11). Second, Paul argues that if Christians are not raised from the dead then neither was Christ raised from the dead (15:12–19). Moreover, Christians have not yet received their resurrection bodies, so the kingdom of God is not fully here (15:20–28). Third, Paul describes the nature of the future resurrection body—it will be both corporal and spiritual (vv. 35–44), like Christ's glorious body, the second Adam (vv. 45–49). This will occur at the parousia and not before (vv. 50–58). At that time Christ will be shown to be Lord, not Caesar.

H. 16:1–4: The Matter of the Collection for the Jerusalem Saints

The one topic in 1 Corinthians that was not a matter of controversy was the Gentile collection for the poor Jewish Christians in Jerusalem (16:1–4). The Corinthians had asked Paul for some guidelines in putting together that offering. The offering was for the poor saints in Jerusalem, perhaps because of the famine mentioned in Acts 11:27–30. The apostle Paul collected relief money from his Gentile churches to help the Jerusalem church. In doing so, the Gentile churches showed their unity with the mother church in Jerusalem (see 2 Cor. 8:4; 9:13; Rom. 15:26). It was probably the case that Paul viewed this gift as the fulfillment of Old Testament prophecy that in the end times the Gentiles would stream into Jerusalem to worship the one true God (recall the earlier references we mentioned). The apostle to the Gentiles hoped this offering would be the catalyst for the conversion of the Gentiles which, in turn, he hoped would precipitate the conversion of Israel to Jesus Messiah (cf. Rom. 11:11–27 with Rom. 15:14–33). Herein we find the already/not yet aspect of Paul's eschatology: the age to come has dawned in that Gentiles in Christ are streaming to the one true God but not yet has Israel been restored to God in Christ.

Having said that, we note the three guidelines Paul gives in 16:1–4 to the Corinthian church for the collection for Jerusalem. First, it should be based on proportionate giving. Second, the offering should be saved at home: the first day of the week (Sunday). Third, when Paul comes to Corinth, he and others will collect the offering to take it to Jerusalem.

I. 16:5–24: Conclusion

Paul concludes the letter in 16:5–24 by giving the Corinthian church his travel plans, (vv. 5–12), by challenging the Corinthian church to stand firm in the gospel (vv. 13–18), and by offering a concluding greeting (vv. 19–24).

2 CORINTHIANS

Many scholars posit that the following events led to the writing of 2 Corinthians: First Corinthians did not bring the positive results that Paul had intended, so he paid Corinth a second visit (2 Cor. 2:1–2; cf. 12:14; 13:1). That visit was a debacle in terms of Paul and the Corinthian church being reconciled. After the apostle left Corinth, he wrote a tearful letter to the church (2 Cor. 2:3–4). Some scholars think the tearful letter is 2 Corinthians 10–13, since those chapters are very harsh on the Corinthians. Other scholars think the tearful letter is lost. Either way, the tearful letter seems to have been effective, bringing the Corinthian church to repentance and even reconciliation with Paul. The apostle then penned 2 Corinthians. Still, in 2 Corinthians Paul feels the need to defend his apostleship, no doubt in the face of his opponents there—the *merkabah* Judaizers.[1] These critics had ratcheted up their attacks on Paul, necessitating from him a forceful response in 2 Corinthians. The letter conveys three points, all in defense of Paul's apostleship:

A. 1:1–7:16: Paul Defends His Apostolic Conduct and Afflictions
B. 8:1–9:15: Paul Defends His Integrity Regarding the Gentile Collection for the Jerusalem Church
C. 10:1–13:14: Paul Defends His Apostolic Authority

We turn now to these three points.

A. 1:1–7:16: Paul Defends His Apostolic Conduct and Afflictions

Paul broaches the theme for 2 Corinthians in 1:1–11: His afflictions legitimate him as an apostle. This perspective was against Paul's opponents' teaching which called into question Paul's apostolic authority because he suffered much (cf. 2 Cor. 10–13). Rather, they claimed, if Paul were a true apostle then he would be a wonder-worker who was above illness and trouble and an eloquent speaker like them. Paul begins to counter that thinking so rooted in realized eschatology by continuing his theme of the eschatological reservation. On the one hand, the age of salvation has dawned, but Christians must still endure the messianic woes because the age to come is not complete (vv. 3–7). Indeed, Paul nearly lost his life for his faith in Ephesus, but God preserved him (vv. 8–11).

In 2 Corinthians 1:12–2:13, Paul defends his decision not to return to the Corinthian church after the painful visit. He determined that another personal encounter might be too harsh for the church. So instead, the apostle sent his tearful letter to the congregation there. That letter accomplished the

---

1   Many scholars argue that the nature of Paul's opposition in 1 Corinthians was an in-house group but that by the time of the writing of 2 Corinthians, outsiders from Palestine entered into the Corinthian congregation for the purpose of undermining Paul's apostleship. Our last chapter, however, argued that the Palestinian *merkabah* Judaizers associated with 2 Corinthians were also behind the campaign against Paul in 1 Corinthians. We should also mention here that the Peter party was probably to be identified with the "merkabizers", but that need not mean that Peter would have supported their opposition to Paul. Often the followers of a famous leader go beyond the dictates of the leader; compare Calvinists and Calvin or Lutherans and Luther.

intended goal of bringing the believers to repentance and a restored relationship with Paul. Scholars debate the specifics here. Did the Corinthian church repent of its loose morals that had allowed incest in the church (recall 1 Cor. 5) and expel the man from the fellowship? Or was it that the church, led by an instigator, offended Paul during his recent trip (hence the name "painful visit") but now the culprit and the church repented? It is difficult to decide between those options. But, either way, the church came to realize that it had disrespected Paul and repented of it.

In 2:14–7:16, Paul defends his paradoxical ministry: one of life/death (2:14–17), glory/suffering (3:1–7:3), and joy/sorrow (7:2–16). The paradoxes resulted from the overlapping of the two ages: the dawning of the age to come— life, glory, joy; the incomplete nature of the age to come—death, suffering, and sorrow. Paul describes his apostleship as paradoxical in order to counter the realized eschatology of the *merkabah* Judaizers.

Second Corinthians 2:14–17 portrays Paul's ministry as that of a captive to Christ. The background is the Roman triumph processional. The Roman general would be honored after a major military victory by Rome throwing a parade for the hero. In the parade would be his soldiers, who would smell the sweet savor of sacrificed animals which to them signified victory. But the captives in the parade would smell the same sacrifice, realizing with horror that the smell was the scent of death that would meet them at the parade's end. Paul likens his gospel to those two opposite reactions—life for the victors in Christ but death for the enemies of Christ. But Paul goes even further by internalizing those two opposite reactions: He has *both* become a captive of Christ, which spells his death, and a victor in Christ, which signifies his life.[2] Thus Paul's ministry was a paradoxical display of life and death. Is there also a hint here that one day the Roman Caesar will see the tables turned and become himself a captive of Christ?

Paul's defense of his paradoxical ministry continues in 3:1–7:3: the glory of the new covenant and age to come that Paul preaches (3:1–4:6) occurs in the

---

2   Scott J. Hafemann has persuasively made the case for this double nuance in, *Suffering and the Spirit: An Exegetical Study of II Corinthians 2:14–3:3 within the Context of the Corinthian Correspondence*, Wissenschaftliche Untersuchungen zum Neuen Testament 2/19 (Tübingen: J. C. B. Mohr/Paul Siebeck, 1986).

context of the sufferings of this age (4:7–7:3). In 3:1–4:6 Paul contrasts his ministry of the new covenant in Christ with Moses and the old covenant of the Law:

MOSES	PAUL
Old Covenant (v. 14)	New Covenant (v. 6; cf. Jer. 31:31–34; Ezek. 36:25–28
Tablets of Stone (letter) (vv. 1–3)	Written on heart by Spirit (v. 36)
Condemnation (vv. 4–7, 9)	Righteousness/life (vv. 8, 9)
Temporary glory (vv. 7–11)	Eternal glory (vv. 11b, 17, 18; 4:1–6)
Spiritual blindness (vv. 12–15)	Spiritual understanding (v. 16)

But such a message of the arrival of the new covenant in Christ occurs in the midst of Paul's apostolic affliction (4:7–7:3). Note therefore the running antitheses in 4:7–5:19:

Glory of the Age to Come in the Inner Person	Sufferings of This Age Regarding the Outer Person
1. not crushed (4:8a)	1. afflicted (4:8a)
2. not driven to despair (4:8b)	2. perplexed (4:8b)
3. not forsaken (4:9a)	3. persecuted (4:9b)
4. not destroyed (4:9b)	4. struck down (4:9b)
5. life manifested in our bodies (4:10)	5. carrying Jesus' death (4:10)
6. Jesus' life manifested in our flesh (4:11)	6. being given up to death (4:11)
7. inner nature is renewed every day (4:16)	7. outer nature is wasting away (4:16)
8. eternal weight of glory (4:17)	8. slight momentary affliction (4:17)
9. eternal things that are unseen (4:18)	9. transient things that are seen (4:18)
10. building from God (5:1)	10. earthly tent (5:1)
11. putting on the heavenly dwelling (5:2–3)	11. groaning at nakedness (5:2–3)
12. being further clothed (5:4b)	12. sigh with anxiety in this tent (5:4a)
13. swallowed up by life (5:4b)	13. what is mortal (5:4b)
14. Spirit as a guarantee (5:5)	14. what is mortal (5:4)
15. of good courage (5:6)	15. home in the body/ away from the Lord (5:6)
16. walk by faith (5:7)	16. walk by sight (5:7)
17. at home with the Lord (5:8)	17. in the body (5:8)
18. no longer regarded from a human point of view (5:16)	18. regarding from a human point of view (5:16)
19. new creation in Christ (5:17)	19. old creation in Adam (5:17)
20. message of reconciliation (5:19)	20. trespass (5:19)

Paul concludes his description of his paradoxical ministry of the glory of the age to come in the midst of the suffering of this age by challenging the Corinthian church to accept him as a legitimate apostle (5:20–7:3), for to be reconciled to Paul (6:3–13) is to be reconciled to Christ the suffering servant (5:20–6:2). And the way the Corinthians can be reconciled to Paul is by expelling from the Corinthian church the false apostles who criticize Paul (6:14–7:3).

In 7:4–14, Paul describes his paradoxical ministry in terms of joy in the midst of sorrow. More particularly, Paul's tearful letter to the Corinthian church (which brought sorrow to both the church and Paul) resulted in repentance and subsequent joy for the church and Paul.

B. 8:1–9:15: Paul Defends His Integrity Regarding the Gentile Collection for the Jerusalem Church

We met with the topic of the Gentile collection for the Jerusalem church back in 1 Corinthians 16. Paul devotes fuller discussion to that matter here in 2 Corinthians 8–9.

In 8:1–5 Paul extols the example of the Macedonian churches because they sacrificially gave to the collection for the poor saints in Jerusalem. In 8:6–15, Paul challenges the church at Corinth to finish what they started regarding that offering. Why did the Corinthian church suspend collecting the relief fund? Perhaps they forgot, or possibly they ran out of money, or did they now think they were fully in the kingdom and earthly items like money no longer mattered? And, then again, maybe the false apostles cast suspicion on Paul's motives for asking for the collection. Our guess is the last two mentioned possibilities are as good an explanation as any.

To ensure Paul's integrity in this matter, Paul reports that Titus and two anonymous but trusted brothers in Christ will facilitate taking the collection, along with Paul, to the Jerusalem congregation (8:16–24). Paul exerts social pressure on the church at Corinth in the province of Achaia by relating to them that it would be embarrassing if the Macedonian churches (Philippi, Thessalonica, etc.) learned that the Corinthian congregation did not keep their promise to give to the Jerusalem saints (9:1–5).

In 9:6–15 Paul reminds the Corinthian believers of the guidelines for the collection (give liberally and cheerfully, vv. 6–7); he encourages them concerning God's power to provide for them because they provided for others (vv. 8–10; cf. Phil. 4:11–13); and he mentions that the collection will contribute to the needs of others (v. 12a) and bring glory to God (vv. 11–15). All of this is motivated by the self-giving of the Lord Jesus Christ (2 Cor. 8:9).

C. 10:1–13:14: Paul Defends His Apostolic Authority

The gloves come off in 2 Corinthians 10–13, as Paul vigorously defends his apostolic authority. The key to grasping these chapters is to recognize therein Paul's anti-Sophistic approach to self-praise. Bruce Winter has demonstrated from 10:10; 11:6; and 12:14–18 that the essential criticism of Paul by his opponents runs as follows:

> that Paul is no expert of *Sophia* (wisdom), as is shown by his personal appearance and his weak and uncouth delivery (his *hypokrisis*), that he is inconsistent, one way in his letters and the opposite when present in Corinth, and that he is underhanded in his financial dealings: his refusal of support as proof that he is no rhetor and no *apostolos*.[3]

Second Corinthians 10–13 is Paul's response to those criticisms. Thus in 10:1–6, Paul announces that though he is weak in person and rhetoric, he is nevertheless strong in the Lord. In 10:7–11, Paul says that he is a true apostle of the Lord, and that when he revisits the Corinthian church he will demonstrate that spiritual authority if they push him to do so. So Paul does boast, but it is in the Lord, not according to human standard (10:12–18). In 11:1–6, the apostle chides the Corinthians who supposedly have wisdom but, in reality, are gullible to the wiles of the super, or false, apostles.

Thus in 10:1–11:6 Paul responds to the first two criticisms above regarding his weak and inconsistent presence. His answer is very much like his opening comments in 1 Corinthians 1–4: Paul will only glory in the "foolishness" and "weakness" of the cross. In 2 Corinthians 11:7–15, Paul answers the

---

3   B. W. Winter, *Are Philo and Paul among the Sophists? A Hellenistic Jewish and a Christian Response to a First Century Movement* (dissertation, MacQuarrie University, 1988).

third accusation of his Sophist-like opponents—he did not accept payment from the Corinthians, not because he didn't deserve to do so, but because Paul wanted to illustrate that the gospel is free of charge. This, coupled with his defense of his responsible handling of the Gentile offering in 2 Corinthians 8–9, fully answered his critics on the issue of finances.

Second Corinthians 11:16–12:13 is round two of Paul's fight with his critics. It is Paul's "Fool's Speech," a speech in which Paul boasts in his weakness. Boasting in oneself to impress an audience was a favorite technique of the Sophists; hence Socrates' invective against them. Such boasting was also a common stock feature among non-Sophist philosophers (Plutarch's, *On Inoffensive Self-Praise*; Dio Chrysostom, 32.39; Cicero, *De. Inv.* 1.16.22; Quintilian's handbook on rhetoric, *Inst. Or.* 11.3.12f). Caesar Augustus does the same in his *res gestae* (divine acts). Thus:

> The accomplishments of the deified Augustus by which he subjected the whole world to the empire of the Roman People, and the expenses which he incurred for the state and the Roman People....
>
> When I was nineteen years old, by my own deliberation and at my own expense, I raised an army by which I brought the Republic, oppressed by the denomination of a faction, into a condition of freedom. For that reason the senate by honorary decrees enrolled me into its order in the consulship of Gaius..., assigning me consular position ... and giving me imperium....
>
> Wars on land and sea both domestic and foreign throughout the whole world I often waged and as a victor I spared all citizens.... I captured six hundred ships, apart from those which were smaller than triremes.
>
> Twice I celebrated ovations and three curule triumphs, and I was acclaimed twenty-one times imperator. When the senate decreed more triumphs for me, all of them I declined ... Because of the things which I or legates of mine, acting under my auspices, accomplished successfully on land and sea, fifty-five times the senate decreed thanksgiving should be offered to the immortal gods....

I did not refuse in the great scarcity of grain, the superintendency of the grain-supply, which I administered in such a way that within a few days I freed the whole state from fear and immediate danger at my own expense and care....

To the Roman plebs man for man I paid out three hundred sesterces in accordance with the testament of my father and in my own name I gave each four hundred sesterces from the spoils of war when I was a consul for the fifth time (29 BC)....

I pacified the seas, freed it of pirates. In that war the slaves, who had fled from their master and had taken up arms against the republic, I captured about thirty thousand of them and turned them over to their masters for punishment....

In my sixth and seventh colonies of soldiers in Africa, Sicily, Macedonia, the two Spains, Achaia, Asia, Syria....

In my sixth and seventh consulships (28–27 BC) after I had extinguished the civil wars and by the consent of all had acquired control of everything, I transferred the Republic from my power to the discretion of the senate and the Roman People. In return for this service of mine by senatorial decree I was called Augustus ... and a golden shield in the Curia Iulia was put in place, which the senate and the Roman People gave to me because of my courage, clemency, justice and piety....

When I was in my thirteenth consulship, the senate and the equestrian order and the Roman People as a whole called me the father of my country....[4]

Paul too parades such boasting (11:16–22), not in his strengths, but in his weaknesses. Thus in 11:23–33, Paul supplies his catalogue of afflictions. In 12:1–13, the apostle recounts his mystical trip to heaven but only as a parody of *merkabah* mysticism to illustrate his weakness. And it is precisely in Paul's weakness that Christ's strength is perfected.

In 12:14–21, Paul expresses his genuine care for the Corinthians as a spiritual father along with his concern that the false apostles have caused a relapse

---

4   Quoted in Witherington, *1 and 2 Corinthians*, pp. 451–52.

in the church's spiritual walk. These super apostles (11:5, 13–14) have deceived the Corinthian believers into exchanging a glorious, non-crucified Jesus for Jesus the suffering servant (11:4–5). The former Jesus the false apostles preach; the latter Jesus—the true gospel—the apostle Paul emulates.

In 13:1–10, Paul warns the Corinthian church that, if it does not repent, his next visit with the congregation will show the power of God, but it will be by way of judgment upon them. In 13:11–13, 2 Corinthians is concluded with a final exhortation and a benediction.

CONCLUSION

First and 2 Corinthians, through and through, are Paul's criticism of the realized eschatology of the church at Corinth. Because of *merkabah* Judaizers, the Corinthians mistakenly thought they were fully in the kingdom of God; raised to heaven via possession of the Spirit. Paul's eschatological corrective to this is: The age to come has indeed dawned, but it is not yet complete. Before the kingdom of God fully arrives, the Corinthians will first have to follow Jesus the suffering servant, and his chosen apostle, Paul. This is Paul's apocalypse of Christ, the crucified Messiah who offended non-Christians Jews, power-crazed Caesar, merkabizers, and Hellenistic syncretistic religion.

Chapter 6

ROMANS

THE RIGHTEOUSNESS OF GOD

AND PAUL'S APOCALYPTIC GOSPEL

TO THE CHURCHES AT ROME

The book of Romans has dramatically shaped church history like no other biblical work, transforming the lives of Augustine, Luther, Wesley, Barth, and countless others. We owe that influence to Romans' message of justification by faith.

Scholars agree that Paul wrote Romans on his third missionary trip, between AD 55 and 58, from Corinth (cf. Rom. 16:1, 23 with Acts 20:1–3). The recipients of the letter were both Jewish and Gentile, for both groups of Christians are addressed throughout the letter (1:1–16; 2:1–3:20; 9–11; 14:1–15:13). Probably the church in Rome was founded by those Roman Jews visiting Jerusalem on the day of Pentecost who became Christians (Acts 2) and then returned home to their synagogues with their newly acquired faith in Jesus Christ. No doubt the Christian Jews tried to convert-fellow Jews and Gentile God-fearers in the Roman synagogues.

These early Christians established some five house churches in Rome

(Rom. 16:5, 10, 11, 14, 15) between AD 30 and 55. The Gentile Christians became the dominant group in the Roman house churches after Emperor Claudius's edict to eject all Jews from Rome in AD 49 (see Acts 18:1–2; Suetonius, *Claudius* 25.4; see also our discussion below).

Most interpreters of Romans look to Romans 1:16–17 as the theme of the letter. In our view, Paul is drawing therein on the theme of the story of Israel. Simply put, the story of Israel is the Old Testament plot of Israel's repeated sins against God, and his sending Israel away into exile because of that—to Assyria in 721 BC and then to Babylonia in 587 BC; but there was always the divine promise that Israel will be restored to her land if she repents. It is interesting that every key word in Romans 1:16–17 is rooted in the third point of the story of Israel just mentioned—Israel's promised restoration. Thus, the words "gospel," "power," and "salvation" would have immediately called to mind Isaiah chapters 40–66 and the promise of the good news of God that he will restore Israel to her land; this is nothing less than the power of God to save his people and it will be a demonstration of God's righteousness (see, for example, Isaiah 46:13; 51:5–8). And when Israel is restored to God and her land, then the nations of the world will come to believe in Israel's God and stream into Jerusalem to worship him (see Isa. 45:15; 60:15–17; Micah 4:13; etc.). In other words, "first the Jew" would be restored/saved and "then the Gentile." However, in the meantime according to Habakkuk 2:4, the faithful Jew is to wait on the Lord for the day of Israel's restoration by obeying the Torah.

Paul, however, tweaks—actually, changes—the Old Testament story of Israel as reflected in Romans 1:16–17. Thus, for the apostle to the Gentiles, the good news of the power of God's salvation and righteousness is not the physical and geographical restoration of Jews to their homeland but rather the spiritual conversion of sinners precisely because they stop trusting in the works of the law of Moses and place their faith in Jesus Christ alone. Moreover, the order of the restoration of Israel and the conversion of the Gentiles is reversed by Paul: First comes the conversion of the nations, and then the restoration of Israel (see our comments on Romans 1:1–15; 11:52–27; etc.).

With this background in mind for Romans 1:16–17, we propose that the outline of Romans matches the covenant components of Deuteronomy. Note the covenant structure of Deuteronomy:

(1) *Preamble* (Deut. 1:1–5): accentuates the most intimate name of God—Yahweh.

(2) *Historical Prologue* (Deut. 1:6–3:29): provides a wonderful description of Yahweh's saving acts on behalf of Israel.

(3) *Stipulations* (Deut. 4–26): are divided into two classifications—the ten commandments (chaps. 4–11) and those general commandments specified in terms of Israel's relationship with God and others (chaps. 12–26).

(4) *Curses and Blessings* (Deut. 27–30): The curses were pronounced by the Levites on Mount Ebal if Israel should prove to be disobedient to the Torah; while the blessings for following the Law were pronounced by priests on Mount Gerizim upon Israel if she should be obedient to Yahweh stipulations. The blessings and curses alternate like an antiphonal chorus culminating in Deuteronomy 30:15–20, which presents the "two ways" tradition: the way of obedience and covenantal blessings and the way of disobedience and covenantal curses.

(5) *Document Clause* (Deut. 31:9, 24–26): which specifies that the Law on the tablets of stone be placed inside the ark of the covenant for safekeeping. Indeed Joshua 24 reminds Israelites in the days of Joshua that the law of Moses is on stone as a public witness for all to see.

(6) *Appeal to Witnesses* (Deut. 31:26–32:47): In establishing the covenant, Yahweh appeals not to pagan deities because he alone is God, but rather to history which is a witness of God's faithfulness to his covenant with Israel. Thus:

COVENANT FORMAT	DEUTERONOMY
1) Preamble	1) 1:1–5
2) Historical Prologue	2) 1:6–3:29
3) Stipulations	3) Chaps. 4–26
4) Curses/Blessings	4) Chaps. 27–30
5) Document Clause	5) 31:9, 24–26
6) Appeal to Witnesses	6) 31:26–32:47

We contend that the book of Romans amazingly follows the form of Deuteronomy, except that Paul subverts the old covenant of Moses by replacing it with the new covenant of Christ. Thus:

Old Covenant Replaced by the New Covenant of the Gospel of Christ, according to Romans

OLD COVENANT OF ISRAEL	NEW COVENANT IN ROMANS
1) Preamble	1) Rom. 1:1–15 (conversion of Gentiles before the restoration of Israel)
2) Historical Prologue	2) Rom. 1:16–17 (spiritual, not physical or geographical, restoration in Christ)
3) Stipulations	3) Rom. 1:18–4:25 (faith in Christ not the law of Moses)
4) Blessings	4) Rom. 5–8 (covenantal blessings on believing Gentiles)
5) Curses	5) Rom. 9–11 (covenantal curses on unbelieving Israel)
6) Appeal to Witnesses	6) Rom. 12:1–15:33 (renewal of the covenant ceremony)
7) Document Clause	7) Rom. 16 (on a letter not on stone)

But, before summarizing Romans along the lines of the covenant format, we highlight four eschatological constructs Paul counters in his epistle to the Romans: the imperial cult, Hellenistic syncretistic religion, non-Christian Judaism, and non-*merkabah* Judaizers.

ESCHATOLOGIES IN CONFLICT IN ROME

In this section we highlight the various eschatological systems in Rome that posed opposition to Paul's apocalypse of Christ: the realized eschatology of the Roman imperial cult, the realized eschatology of Hellenistic religion, the consistent eschatology of non-Christian Judaism, and the inaugurated eschatology of non-*merkabah* Judaizers. The last-mentioned system was the immediate reason for the writing of Romans.

The Realized Eschatology of the Imperial Cult

It should not occasion surprise that the imperial cult thrived in Rome, the capital of the Roman Empire. We might organize the data of the presence of the imperial cult in Rome around our customary five points of realized eschatology.

First, Augustus' *pax Romana* that spread across the world was on display at Rome. Robert Jewett writes of Augustus:

> An extensive building program paid by the emperor and his wealthy supports transformed Rome into a gleaming city of marble that grew to house a million people. Under his loyal son-in-law Agrippa, a new aqueduct was built along with numerous public fountains; temples were restored; public gardens, baths, and theaters were erected; and the city administration was reorganized with fire brigades and police protection; enhanced grain deliveries to Roman citizens were also provided. All of the improvements served to demonstrate that the golden age of peace and plenty had finally arrived. In place of the chaotic warren of streets and alleys that was difficult to administer, Augustus organized 265 neighborhoods with elected leaders and local shrines containing altars to the local Lares and to the emperor's genius, thus linking leading craftsmen into his system of honorable governance. The beneficiaries of the vast program of renewal were the citizens of Rome but not the slaves and immigrants who made up the bulk of the early Christian congregations.[1]

Second, Augustus's prowess lent cosmic significance to Rome in two ways. (1) Augustus had coins minted in Rome of his Zodiac sign, Capricorn, and horn

---

1 Robert Jewett, *Romans* (Minneapolis: Fortress Press, 2007), p.47. The following data regarding the imperial cult at Rome is culled from Davina C. Lopez, *Apostle to the Conquered: Reimagining Paul's Mission* (Minneapolis: Fortress Press, 2008), pp. 26–118; Marcus J. Borg and John Dominic Crossan, *The First Paul: Reclaiming the Radical Visionary Behind the Church's Conservative Icon* (San Francisco: HarperCollins Publishers, 2009), pp. 93–121; and Ramsay MacMullen's entire work, *Romanization in the Time of Augustus* (New Haven, CT/London: Yale University Press, 2000), documents the profound effect the reign of Augustus had on the then-known world.

of plenty. This showed that Augustus' peace was foretold in the stars of astrology. (2) Augustus adopted the sun god Apollo as his "alter ego," which meant that in Octavian Augustus heaven and earth were joined. The combination of Augustus and Apollo is illustrated in at least three ways: an icon of Apollo was placed beside Augustus' statue, the *Prima Porta* statue; a lyre-playing Apollo can be seen from a wall painting from Augustus's own Palentine palace; Augustus built a new temple to Apollo in a prominent place on Palentine Hill.

Nearer to Paul's day, emperors Claudius and Nero tried to continue Augustus's building programs hailing the arrival of the golden age, though under the madman Nero it became clear that the golden era was not fully here.

Third, Augustus was the savior who brought *pax Romana*. Even Rome, which in the past hated the divinization of humans, fell under the sway of Augustus. Thus Augustus had his statue placed by the speaker's rostrum in the forum. He was called, "Son of the Divine Savior." He melted down sixty silver statues of himself. His *pietas* (commitment to traditional values and religion) manifested itself in renovating some eighty-two temples along with the building of new temples to Apollo, Jupiter, Asclepius, Isis, and others. He was the *pontifex maximus* (the chief priest). Indeed, in the aforementioned temples Augustus' statue appeared, with veil and toga. And at his death Augustus was voted the eternal honor of a god by the Roman senate. Such an *apotheosis* (the transference of the emperor to the abode of the gods) devolved onto succeeding Roman emperors.

Fourth, after Julius Caesar's assassination in March 44 BC, a comet appeared in the sky, which the Romans interpreted as a sign of Julius' *apotheosis*. Eighteen-year-old Octavian accepted the comet as a sign that he would now inaugurate the tenth and final age. This was confirmed by the *Sibylline* oracles, which hailed Octavian as "Son of a divine one" or "Son of god." Thereafter Augustus displayed the comet on coins. These coins were minted in Rome and they portrayed Augustus placing the star upon Julius Caesar. The obvious implication for all to read was that if Julius was now divine, so was his adopted son Octavian. Thus Augustus and Rome believed that it was predicted in the stars that he should be the bearer of the golden age.

Fifth, Rome was replete with accolades that hailed Augustus as inaugurator of the golden age: the sacred games began to be celebrated in Rome in 18 BC;

Augustus built temples to himself—Jupiter, Isis, Asclepius, and others—to parade his *pietas*; he embraced the title *pontifex maximus* (chief priest). All of these and more reinforced for the citizens of Rome that Augustus was the savior.

Although Paul was no political revolutionary (see Rom. 13:1–7) still his message in Romans undercut the imperial cult. In Romans 1:16–17, Paul declares that he is not ashamed to preach the gospel in Rome for the gospel is the power of God unto salvation. In these verses Paul takes issue with the first two points of the eschatology of the imperial cult. The good news/the gospel is being made right before God not embracing Caesar's golden age. Furthermore, true salvation results from the gospel of Christ not the imperial cult (cf. Rom. 10:9). In Romans 10:9–15, the apostle counters the other three eschatological points of the imperial cult: Jesus, not Caesar is Lord; the Old Testament predicted the coming of Jesus the Lord; and followers of Jesus proclaim his lordship in baptism.

The Realized Eschatology of Hellenistic Religion at Rome

Hellenistic religion was alive and well at Rome, thanks to Caesar Augustus. He built temples to Jupiter, Asclepius, and Isis. Augustus first adopted Apollos as his second identity and later added Dionysius to his repertoire of deities. The emperor's commitment to *pietas* as *pontifex maximus* legitimated Hellenistic religion in a forceful way. Thus the mystery religions of Isis and Dionysius found a home in Rome. The mystic was joined with those deities thereby transcending the gap between heaven and earth. Astrology and Sibyl oracles alike hailed the arrival of the mysteries. And the worshipper celebrated their union with the deity by baptism and sacred meals (cf. Apuleius's *Metamorphosis*).

As has been known for years, the mystery religions stand behind Romans 6[2] and perhaps Romans 14–15. The former speaks of the Christian's union with Christ via baptism and of the salvation that results. In that passage, Paul seems to reject the mystery religions: it is baptism into Christ's death that brings salvation not union with Isis or Dionysius; the resurrection

---

2   Recall our comments in the introduction of this work that distanced Paul from the mystery religions in terms of his own theology. But this does not rule out the strong possibility that Paul's audiences like the churches at Corinth and Rome were influenced by the mystery religions, and by Hellenistic religion in general.

of the believer has not yet occurred (see. Rom. 6:5) thus opposing the realized eschatology of the mysteries; and union with Christ brings holiness not drunkenness and debauchery. It may be that Romans 14–15 touches upon the problem of eating meats dedicated to Hellenistic deities as 1 Corinthians 8 and 10 did, though there are significant differences between the two Pauline texts. Possibly, the Romans passage alludes to Jewish Christians' scruples against eating meats because they were dedicated to the Hellenistic deities and then sold in the marketplace.

The Consistent Eschatology of Non-Christian Judaism at Rome

We know that there was a substantial population of Jews in Rome, and Acts 28:17–27 confirms that. Moreover, we know that God-fearers were associated with the synagogues in the capital city, as Acts 28:28 also indicates. Romans presumes the Jewish presence in Rome, and we may cull from Paul's letter and Acts 28 the eschatology of his Jewish compatriots in that city.

First, Jews in Rome contrasted this age begun by Adam with the coming of the age to come or the kingdom of God. Paul speaks of the first of these realities in Romans 5:12–14 and the second in Romans 5:15–21 which Christ has initiated. Moreover, Paul speaks of the presence of the kingdom of God in Christ in Romans 14:17 and also in Acts 28:23, 31. Thus in Romans 5:12–21 Paul contrasts the cosmic effects of Adam and Christ: One brought condemnation, while the other brought justification before God.

In Romans 9:5 Paul draws on Israel's hope of the coming Messiah whom the apostle equates with Jesus. So for Paul, Jesus Christ has inaugurated the age to come for those whose faith is in him. But we know from the Roman historian Suetonius that Roman Jews rejected Jesus as the Christ. Suetonius reports that emperor Claudius expelled all Jews from Rome in AD 49 over one "*Chrestus*." It is likely that *Chrestus* (Latin) is a misspelling of *Christos* (Greek). That is, non-Jewish Christians in Rome disagreed with Jewish Christians regarding the latter's claim that Jesus is the Christ. Claudius decided to kick all Jews out of Rome to solve the problem. Thus Paul's inaugurated eschatology based on Jesus Christ conflicted with the consistent eschatology of the Jews who rejected Jesus as their Messiah.

Throughout Romans, especially Romans 4 and 8–11, Paul argues that Jesus is the Messiah predicted in the Old Testament (cf. Acts 28:23). But the Jews did not agree. Moreover, Paul announced that the law of Moses found its fulfillment in Christ and is finished in the plan of God (see Rom. 2:1–3:31; 4:1–23; 7:1–3; 8:3–4; 10:4). Only faith in Christ is the means to justification, God's end-time decision now for the believer (Rom. 1:16–17; 5:1; 8:1). This too the Jews rejected.

The Inaugurated Eschatology of the Non-Merkabah Judaizers at Rome
Of all the detractors to his gospel that Paul deals with in Rome, the non-merkabah Judaizers take center stage. We don't know if these Jewish Christian legalists had arrived at Rome yet but, judging from the way they dogged Paul's footsteps, if they had not visited Rome yet they soon would to oppose Paul's brand of eschatology. We can surmise from Romans their five point message.

First, these Judaizers believed that the age to come had arrived (Rom. 13:8–14), which included the restoration of Israel (Rom. 1:16–17). Second, such a new age was cosmic in scope—Christ replaced Adam in God's scheme of things (Rom. 5:12–21).

Third, Jesus is the long-awaited Messiah of Israel (Rom. 9:1–5). Fourth, Jesus Christ has inaugurated the new covenant of the Spirit predicted in the Old Testament (cf. Rom. 8:1–16 with Joel 2:28–32; Jer. 31:31–37; Ezek. 36:24–26). Fifth, with the power of the Spirit, Christians (Jew and Gentile alike) can finally obey the Torah (see again Rom. 8:1–10; cf. Rom. 9:1–5), and live under the sign of the covenant, circumcision (2:25–28).

But Paul's letter to the Romans disagrees. Yes, the age to come is here in Christ the second Adam, but it is spiritual in nature, not geographical (Rom. 1:16–17; 9:6–29), and it is entered into by faith alone (Rom. 1:16–17; 2:1–3:21; 4:1–23; 7:1–3; 8:3–4; 10:4). Indeed, it is this message of justification by faith alone that Abraham, Moses, and the prophets witnessed to (see 4:1–23; 10:5–13; 3:21, respectively). Circumcision is not the sign of the new covenant, faith in Christ is (2:25–28). As we will see in the next section, Paul's letter to the Roman Christians is a sustained attempt to refute the Judaizers, like Galatians.

SUMMARY OF THE CONTENTS OF ROMANS
In summarizing the contents of Romans we will follow the outline presented earlier that contrasts the new covenant of the gospel with the old covenant of the

Law. Doing so will accentuate Paul's critique of the Judaizers and non-Christian Judaism.

A. 1:1–15: The Preamble of the New Covenant in Christ

Romans 1:1–15 introduces Paul's letter to the Roman Christians. We believe these verses correspond to the preamble component of the Deuteronomic covenant and Paul equates Jesus with God, the author of the new covenant. Jesus is the Messiah, the Son of God that the Old Testament predicted would come to bring about the restoration of Israel (1:1–4). Yet, Paul introduces a twist to that story: He, Paul, is called to be the catalyst for the end-time conversion of the Gentiles (1:5–15) which reverses the order of salvation history. In other words, the Old Testament envisions that in the end times first Israel will be restored to her land and God, and then the Gentiles will stream into Jerusalem to worship Israel's God (Isa. 45:15; 60:15–17; Micah 4:13; etc). But Paul reverses that order: The conversion of the Gentiles (to which Paul is called to accomplish) is now preceding the restoration of Israel.

B. 1:16–17: The Historical Prologue of the New Covenant in Christ

The historical prologue of the covenant highlighted God's saving actions on behalf of ancient Israel. Paul draws on that theme in Romans 1:16–17, the key verses of Romans. Three major interpretive insights emerge from these theologically dense and much-debated verses. First, we join the chorus of those who root the major key terms in Romans 1:16–17 in the Old Testament promise of the restoration of Israel, especially Isaiah. Note the following connections:

ROMANS 1:16–17	THE RESTORATION OF ISRAEL, ESPECIALLY AS RECORDED IN ISAIAH
"not ashamed" (cf. 1:16 with 9:33; 10:16)	Isaiah 28:16 (in the sense that he who trusts in the Lord will not be disappointed, that is, will participate in Israel's restoration)
"gospel"	Isaiah 40:9; 52:7; 60:6; 61:1; Joel 2:32; Nah. 1:15 (the good news of Israel's return to her land)

ROMANS 1:16–17	THE RESTORATION OF ISRAEL, ESPECIALLY AS RECORDED IN ISAIAH
"power"	Exodus 9:16; Psalms 77:14–15; 140:7 (God's saving action at the exodus, a motif applied to the return of Israel from exile in Isa. 43:2, 16–19; 52:10–12; etc.)
"salvation"	Isaiah 12:2; 25:9; 46:13; 49:6; 52:7, 10 (God's deliverance of Israel from the exile)
"righteousness"	Isaiah 46:13; 51:5, 6, 8; Micah 6:5; 7:9 (God's faithfulness to his covenant with Israel by restoring her to himself)
"revealed"	Isaiah 22:14; 40:5; 43:12; 53:1; 56:1; 65:1 (in the sense that the restoration of Israel will reveal God's righteousness and his faithfulness to his covenant with Israel)
"faith"	Habakkuk 2:4 (in the sense that the righteous one is the one who trusts in the Lord to bring Israel out of exile back to her homeland

Second, that the threefold story of Israel is the key to interpreting Romans 1:16–17 is confirmed by observing that the rest of Romans draws heavily upon that theme. Note the following quotations that cluster into the three stages of the story of Israel:

Romans and the sin of Israel

ROMANS	SIN OF ISRAEL
1:21	Jeremiah 2:5; 17:9—Israel's idolatry against God
2:24	Isaiah 52:5; Ezekiel 36:22—Israel's sin is dishonoring God's name among the Gentiles

3:17	Isaiah 59:7–8—Israel's sin
8:22	Jeremiah 12:4—the land of Israel is cursed because of the nation's sin
10:21	Isaiah 65:2—Israel's sin

Romans and the exile/judgment of Israel

ROMANS	THE EXILE/JUDGMENT UPON ISRAEL BECAUSE OF HER SIN
2:1–5	Wisdom of Solomon 3:9–10; 11:9–10; 12:22; 15:2—Israel was overconfident that God will not punish her for her sin; but he did.
9:20	Isaiah 10:15; 29:16; 45:9; 64:8; Jeremiah 18:6—God is the potter and Israel is the clay; therefore God will judge Israel as he wishes because of her sin against him
11:8	Isaiah 29:10—Israel's eyes are blinded and her heart hardened because God has judged her because of her sin

God will restore Israel to her land if she repents

ROMANS	THE PROMISE OF ISRAEL'S RESTORATION
4:25	Isaiah 53:5—the suffering servant is the reason for Israel's restoration, whom Paul equates with Jesus Christ
8:33	Isaiah 50:8–9—the sufferings of the righteous servant are the basis for God's forgiveness of Israel's sin
8:36	Isaiah 53:7–8—the suffering servant is like a sheep led to the slaughter, whose affliction is the basis of Israel's restoration to God; Paul applies this to Jesus Christ
9:25–27	Hosea 1:10; 2:23—God will restore Israel to himself as his children

ROMANS	THE PROMISE OF ISRAEL'S RESTORATION
9:27	Isaiah 10:22–23—a righteous remnant of Jews will return to their homeland
9:33	Isaiah 8:14; 28:16—Paul says that Jesus Christ is the stumbling stone that is nevertheless the basis of Israel's restoration
9:33/10:11	Isaiah 28:16—the righteous Jew will not be ashamed for trusting the Lord because they will return to their homeland
10:13	Joel 2:32—all who call upon the name of the Lord in repentance will experience the restoration of Israel
10:14–15	Isaiah 52:7—the good news of the restoration of Israel/return to her land
10:16	Isaiah 53:1—the need to believe the good news of God's restoration
10:20	Isaiah 65:1—Gentiles will believe in the Lord when Israel is restored
11:26	Isaiah 47:17—God will deliver Israel by restoring her to her land
11:27	Isaiah 59:20–21;cf. 27:9—when God delivers Israel by restoring her, he will establish a (new) covenant with Israel
14:11	Isaiah 54:23—at her restoration, Israel will bow before God
15:12	Isaiah 61:10—Gentiles will hope in the Davidic Messiah at the restoration of Israel
15:21	Isaiah 52:15—the Gentiles will be converted to God at the time of the restoration of Israel

Chapter 6

Two other significant observations surface from the theme of the restoration of Israel in the preceding chart: (1) The restoration of Israel will witness the establishment of a new covenant (compare: Romans 11:27 with Isaiah 27:9; 59:20–21; Romans 2:14–15; 2:29; 8:1; 9:4 with Jeremiah 31:31–33; Ezekiel 36:24–3). (2) The restoration of Israel will include the conversion of the Gentiles (see the chart references already cited).

Third, uncovering the story of Israel, especially the restoration of Israel, as the immediate background to Romans 1:16–17 helps to resolve three critical issues therein: the meaning of the phrase "righteousness of God"; the meaning of the words, "faith to faith"; and how Romans 1:17 relates to Habakkuk 2:4. We now briefly address these concerns with the story of Israel's restoration in mind.

Much ink has been spilled over the phrase "righteousness of God," with essentially two interpretations ruling the day: the forensic view and the transformative view.[3] The first view understands the righteousness of God to be God's legal declaration that the believer in Jesus is righteous before God; that is, God's righteousness is imputed to the sinner's standing before God. The primary support for such a perspective is to be found in Paul's emphasis in Romans on faith as the sole means to acquiring God's righteousness (cf. 1:17 with 3:21–22; 4:3, 5, 6, 9, 11, 13, 22; 9:30–31; 10:3, 4, 6, 10; see also Gal. 2:20–21; 3:6, 21–22; 5:5; Phil. 3:9). To be sure, Paul refers to faith as the basis of receiving God's righteousness three times in Romans 1:16–17 alone. The other view of the phrase "righteousness of God" is that it refers to the action of God in transforming the sinner. In support of this view one could point to the apostle's words in v. 16—the gospel is the saving power of God. Moreover, as we mentioned before, all of the key terms in Romans 1:16–17, including "righteousness," are essentially rooted in Isaiah's good news that God is faithful to his covenant people Israel and that he will restore them to himself. Commentaries these days are reticent to choose between these two options because both are grounded in Romans 1:16–17 and its Old Testament

3   See the discussions and bibliographies in Douglas J. Moo, *The Epistle to the Romans*. The New International Commentary on the New Testament (Grand Rapids, MI: Eerdmans, 1996), pp. 70–75, 79–91; Thomas R. Schreiner, *Romans*, The Exegetical Commentary on the New Testament (Grand Rapids, MI: Baker, 1998), pp. 63–70; James D. G. Dunn, *Romans 1–8*, Word Biblical Commentary vol. 38a (Nashville, TN: Thomas Nelson, 1988), pp. 40–43; Jewett, *Romans*, pp.141–44.

moorings. Thus the righteousness of God is God's saving act of fulfilling his promise to restore Israel and convert Gentiles based exclusively on faith in Jesus Christ. With this conclusion we agree.

What does the phrase, "from faith unto faith" mean? Various explanations have been offered concerning these words: from the faith of the Old Testament to the faith of the New Testament; from the faith of the Law to the faith of the gospel; from the faithfulness of God to the faith of human beings; from beginning to end, salvation is by faith. The last-mentioned possibility is the one most defended today, because of the emphasis on faith and believing in Romans 1:16–17. We agree with this conclusion and would add one important detail: for the Old Testament covenant, keeping the law of Moses was the way to ensure that the Israelite remained in a right relationship with God[4] but, for Paul, one receives the righteousness of God by believing in Jesus Christ, not by obeying the Torah. Moreover, the restoration of Israel is no longer geographical in orientation nor exclusive in membership. Rather it is spiritual in nature and encompasses all the nations.

Three questions await the reader of Habakkuk 2:4 as quoted by Paul in Romans 1:17: First, why does Paul omit the personal pronoun—"my"—from the Septuagint (LXX) of Habakkuk 2:4 "But the righteous shall live by *my* [God's] faithfulness" (contrast the Hebrew [Masoretic Text/MT], "But the righteous by *his* [the Israelite] faith/faithfulness shall live")? The answer seems to be that Paul wants to make it clear that it is the faith of the individual that he has in mind [so the MT not LXX]. Second, what does "by faith" modify: "the just/righteous by faith shall live" or "the righteous shall live by faith"? The former seems to be the most correct, since Romans 1:18–4:25 highlights faith as the means to justification while Romans 5–8 seems to emphasize eternal life as the gift of justification. Third, are Habakkuk and Paul at odds with each other? That is, does Habakkuk 2:4 buy into the idea that obeying the Law is the

---

4   E. P. Sanders famously called this "covenantal nomism" in his work, *Paul and Palestinian Judaism: A Comparison of Religions* (Philadelphia: Fortress, 1977). In doing so Sanders initiated the movement now labeled "the new perspective on Paul." We interacted with this school of thought earlier in our chapter on Galatians, and found it wanting.

way to stay in covenant with God? There does seem to be tension between Habakkuk and Paul here: for the former, obedience to the Law is the means to being faithful to God; for the latter faith in Christ is the means to be justified. But this is no real contradiction because both inspired authors emphasize that faith resulting in faithfulness is the means to receiving God's approval (cf. Romans 3:21–22).

We see in all of this that Romans 1:16–17 nicely corresponds to the historical prologue section of the covenant format: God in Christ has been faithful to his Old Testament promises to Israel and Gentiles, but based on faith not on the Law.

We conclude our discussion of Romans thus far by recalling from our earlier chapter that the fourfold eschatological message of Paul occurs in Romans 1: Jesus is the Christ, whose death and resurrection inaugurated the age to come, the stipulation of which is faith apart from the Torah, including Paul's target audience, the Gentiles.

C. 1:18–4:25: Stipulation: Salvation Is by Faith in Christ, Not by the Law of Moses

Before Paul discusses in depth the good news of justification before God, he first exposes the bad news of justification before God. The bad news unfolds in Romans 1:18–3:20. The good news occurs in 3:21–4:25.

The bad news about justification is that no human is deserving of salvation before God—and certainly not pagan Gentiles who suppress the truth that God is the creator and expects righteousness from his creation. Rather, pagan Gentiles worship the creation rather than the creator, and their lives demonstrate the disastrous consequences (1:18–32).

But neither are God's Old Testament people, the Jews, justified before God. This unfortunate state of affairs pertains because they try to earn salvation from God by obeying the Torah. Indeed, the very sins Jews accuse Gentiles of committing the Jews commit as well (2:1–4). But God is not partial; he will condemn both Gentile and Jew for not following the divine law. Gentiles are condemned because they do not adhere to natural law and Jews are culpable because they do not obey the Mosaic law (2:5–16). In fact, Israel's disobedience actually leads

Gentiles to blaspheme God (2:17–24). Therefore, the Jews may as well discard the practice of circumcision, the sign of their covenant with God (2:25–19).

From what Paul has said thus far in Romans, Jews might expect to hear Paul say that Israel was no longer the people of God. But Paul's answer is surprising and nuanced: God has not abandoned his covenant with Israel—*spiritual* Israel, that is (3:1–8). In Romans 9:6–29 Paul will define spiritual Israel as the remnant—those Jews who walked with God by faith.

Paul saves the worst of the bad news about justification for last: No one will be justified before God by observing the works of the law of Moses, because the Torah actually stirs up disobedience to God (3:9–20).

In Romans 3:21–4:25, Paul explains the good news regarding justification before God—it is received by faith alone. In 3:21–31 Paul provides an explanation of the good news of justification by faith, while in 4:1–25 he provides the prime example in the Old Testament of justification by faith.

In 3:21–31, Paul explains that even the Old Testament—the origin of the Torah—witnesses to the reality that salvation is by faith and not the works of the Torah, in two ways. First, that no one in the Old Testament was saved by keeping the Mosaic law is clear from the fact that ancient Israel constantly sacrificed animals for its disobedience to the Torah and even the sacrificial system did not fully and permanently offer forgiveness. Such perfect atonement would come only with the death and resurrection of Jesus (3:21–26). Second, since God is one, his plan of salvation for Jew and Gentile must be unified—and only justification by faith, not the works of the Law, applies to both Gentile and Jew (3:27–31).

In Romans 4:1–25, Paul provides exhibit A as the Old Testament example that justification is by faith—Abraham, the father of Israel. According to 4:1–8, Abraham was a sinner and could only be justified before God by faith (see Gen. 15:6). According to 4:9–12, Abraham was justified by faith before he was circumcised. Therefore faith precedes circumcision, the symbol of the Torah. According to 4:13–17, God's promise to bless the world (Jew and Gentile) is fulfilled by faith, not the Law. Finally, in Romans 4:18–25 Paul implies that God's word created faith in Abraham and continues to do so in the Christian, which eliminates any human boasting before God.

Thus, Romans 1:18–4:25 makes the point that faith in Christ as the stipulation of the new covenant has replaced the Law and the old covenant of Moses.

D. 5:1–8:39: The New Covenant Blessings on Believing Gentiles

Romans 5:1–8:39 highlights a number of end-time, new-covenant blessings that rest on the Christian. The majority of Jews rejected the gospel of Christ in Paul's day, but Gentiles seem to have converted to Christianity *en masse.* How ironic: The end-time blessings promised to Israel devolved onto Gentiles.

In Romans 5:1–11, Paul assures his audience that justification before God by faith alone has brought to them peace with God, hope for tomorrow, and love as the new motivation for their lives. Such love is based on the reconciling work of Christ's death. Peace, hope, and love: these are blessings that accompany the new covenant.

According to Romans 5:12–21, Christians have become a part of the new humanity in that they have been transferred from the realm of Adam to the realm of Christ, the new Adam. The background to vv. 12–21 is interesting: Israel, the supposed replacement of Adam, is itself still in Adam. Only in Christ can the Adamic old humanity be replaced with the eschatological humanity.

Chapter 6:1–23 indicates that the new humanity in Christ has a new-found power to obey God through Christ, because the power of Adam's sin is broken.

Romans 7:1–25 documents that the believer is free from the Torah through union with Christ. Whereas in the past Paul's audience was enslaved to Adam and disobedience because of the Law, now in Christ believers are free to obey God. Even the struggle between the old and new natures within the Christian is proof they are in Christ. That is, believers live in the overlapping of the two ages—Adam and this age of sin, Christ and the obedience of the age to come.

But the eschatological battle that wages within the Christian does not result in a stalemate, because the believer possesses the Holy Spirit, the gift of the end times *par excellence,* according to Romans 8:1–16. The Spirit enables Christians to obey God and thus live a life of righteousness by faith. This is something the Law and the old covenant could never do. But the Spirit of the new covenant has changed all that.

In Romans 8:17–39, Paul discloses that the glory of the age to come resides in the hearts of believers even though they presently suffer the messianic woes that conclude this present age of evil. And one day, when Christ returns such glory will transform the believer's earthly body, for nothing can separate them from the love of God in Christ.

E. 9:1–11:36: Curses of the Covenant for Unbelieving Israel

If the new covenant blessings rest on believing Gentiles, then—according to Romans 9–11 at the present time—the curses of the old covenant are being poured out on non-believing Jews. In chapter 9:1–29, Paul contrasts the blessings that once resided on Israel (9:1–5) with the curses that now have become her lot (9:6–29). More specifically, God's blessings rest on the remnant of Israel, (9:6) those who believed God. Note the following chart:

VERSES	BLESSINGS ON THOSE WHO BELIEVED	CURSES ON THOSE WHO DID NOT BELIEVE
vv. 7–9	Isaac	Ishmael
vv. 10–13	Jacob	Esau
vv. 14–18	Moses	Pharaoh
vv. 19–29	Spiritual Israel	National Israel

According to Romans 9:30–10:4, the irony is that Gentiles are enjoying the blessings of the new covenant because they trust in Christ not the Torah, whereas unbelieving Jews are encountering the covenant curses because they are trusting in the law of Moses.

But the fault is not Moses or his law, because already in the Pentateuch Moses realized that salvation comes not from the Torah but by faith, according to Romans 10:15–13. Indeed, Moses and the Old Testament prophets predicted that unbelieving Israel will be sent into exile, while believing Gentiles will participate in the restoration once restricted to Jews (10:14–21).

But in 11:1–36, Paul makes the point that God has not finished with unbelieving Israel. That is to say, Paul believes that the Old Testament prophecies proclaiming the future conversion of the Gentiles are coming true, but not after Israel's restoration to God but before it. Paul calls this a "mystery" and is convinced that such a turning to God on the part of the Gentiles will make Jews jealous of the Gentiles' reception of Israel's messiah. He offers three comments in that regard. First, the fact that a remnant of Jews, Paul included, believe in Christ is a foretaste of the future conversion of Israel to Christ (11:1–10). Second, in the mystery of God, believing Gentiles will stir up Israel to jealousy to "reclaim" their Messiah (11:11–24; 28–36). Third, in the future the nation of Israel will indeed accept Jesus as their Messiah. In point of fact, it is the present end-time conversion of the Gentiles that will be the catalyst to restore Israel to God in Christ. At that time the new covenant blessings will finally rest on Israel (11:25–27).

F. 12:1–15:33: Appeal to Witnesses

In the Old Testament covenant ceremony, Moses sacrificed an animal and scattered its blood on the gathered Jews to indicate that they were separating themselves unto God as his witnesses (Exodus 24:1–8). Using figurative language, Paul does something similar when he challenges the Roman Christians to become living sacrifices for God by being witnesses of the eschatological covenant (12:1–2; 15:14–16). How are the Roman Christians to do this? By: using their spiritual gifts for God and the church (12:3–8), living Christlike lives before the watching world (12:9–21), obeying the government (13:1–7), loving others, the fulfillment of the Law (13:8–10), expecting the return of Christ (13:11–14), being unified through giving to the Jerusalem church in its time of need (14:1–15:33; cf. 1 Cor. 16:1–4; 2 Cor. 8–9). In effect, Romans 12:1–15:33 is the new covenant renewal ceremony in which Paul challenges the Roman believers to accept the terms of the covenant by being witnesses to Christ in a watching world, just as ancient Israel was to be a witness to the nations.

G. 16:1–26: The Document Clause

In the Old Testament, the terms of the covenant were publicly displayed for

Israel to be reminded of her relationship with God—in the temple or on a stone/ stela. In Romans 16, we learn that Paul's patron, Phoebe, will deliver the epistle of Romans to the Roman Christians and have it read to the congregations. Paul's letter, then, is the document clause of the new covenant, available for all to hear, read, and respond to.

Conclusion

In this chapter we have seen that Paul's apocalypse of Christ met with opposition in the capital city of the Roman Empire, from the imperial cult, Hellenistic religion, non-Christian Judaism, and non-*merkabah* Judaizers. Though Paul would meet his death in Rome at the hands of Nero in the 60s, before it was over Paul would have the last word because the mighty Roman Empire would bow in defeat before the cross of Christ in 313, when Constantine converted to Christianity.

PHILIPPIANS

REJOICING IN SUFFERING

AND THE ALREADY/NOT YET

The topic of suffering is integral to Paul's letter to the Philippian church. Suffering, for Paul, is to be equated with the messianic woes that are concluding this present evil age. But the power of Christ's resurrection has inaugurated the age to come within this present age. To better appreciate Paul's inaugurated eschatology, we first must excavate the background informing Paul's letter to the Philippians. Two key influences are at work which notably contribute to the suffering of Paul and the Philippian believers: the realized eschatologies of the Roman imperial cult, and *merkabah* Judaizers.

THE TWOFOLD INFLUENCE ON PHILIPPIANS

In this section, as we have done for previous chapters, we uncover the key religious beliefs that sparked Paul's letter, in this case Philippians: the imperial cult and *merkabah* Judaizers. The former was the dominant influence in the city of Philippi dating back to 42 BC, while the latter posed a recent intrusion into the church at Philippi.

The Realized Eschatology of the Imperial Cult as Background to Paul's Letter to the Philippian Church

The five components of the realized eschatology of the imperial cult can be culled from both the Philippian letter and the city of Philippi itself.

First, Philippians 4:7 asserts that what people need is the peace of God (implied), not *pax Romana*. God's peace guarding the Christian alludes to the Roman garrison housed in Philippi to keep the peace of Rome, the *pax romana*, for the benefit of the Roman Empire. The city of Philippi enjoyed a special relationship with Rome since 42 BC when, on the plains near Philippi, Octavian and Mark Antony defeated Brutus and Cassius, Julius Caesar's assassins. Consequently Philippi became a Roman colony (cf. Acts 16:12). Later, when Octavian/Augustus defeated Antony and Cleopatra at the battle of Actium in 31 BC, Augustus became the unquestioned ruler of the Roman Empire. He renamed Philippi, *Colonia Iulia Augusta Philippensis*. G. Walter Hansen writes of the privileges accorded to Philippi as a Roman colony:

> In the colony of Philippi renamed by Augustus after the Julian family (*Colonia Iulia Augusta Philippensis*), Roman aristocracy flourished and Roman architecture became the standard. More Roman soldiers were given allotments in Philippi. Since it was a Roman colony, the citizens of Philippi enjoyed all the privileges and rights of Roman citizens: they were exempt from taxes and governed under Roman law, the *ius Italicum*. Philippi was modeled after the mother city, Rome. Roman arches, bath-houses, forums, and temples dominated Philippi at the time of Paul. In a Greek-speaking province, Latin became the official language of Philippi. Although Greek, Phyrgian, and Egyptian gods had their temples in Philippi, the imperial cult was the most prominent in the city. With impressive altars and temples dedicated to the emperor and members of his family, the city's religious life centered on the worship of the emperor. Withdrawal from participation in the imperial cult was viewed as subversive activity.[1]

Paul himself alludes to Philippi as a Roman colony in Philippians 3:20

---

1   G. Walter Hansen, *The Letter to the Philippians* (Grand Rapids, MI/Cambridge: Eerdmans, 2009), pp. 2–3.

(cf. 1:27), for the word "citizenship"/"commonwealth" (πολιτευμα) tapped into the Philippians' pride that their city was "Rome" away from Rome, a little Italy, since its members were Roman citizens with all due rights. *Pax Romana* was alive and well in Philippi.

Second, the cosmic dimension of Augustus' era of peace is drawn upon by Paul in Philippians 2:9–11, if by way of contrast. One of the themes that forms the backdrop to Philippians 2:9–11 is the imperial cult. Paul's talk about Jesus being given universal authority, such that all who bow before him experience salvation, alludes to Caesar Augustus bringing peace and salvation to the world through submission to him. Thus imperial coins contained the inscription, "The Emperor, Caesar, Son of a god, the god Augustus, of every land and sea the overseer." Or, "Nero, the Lord of all the world." Even Philo, the Jewish philosopher, agreed:

> So that the whole human race exhausted by mutual slaughter was on the verge of utter destruction, had it not been for one man and leader Augustus whom men fitly call the averter of evil.... This is he who not only loosed but broke the chains which had shackled and pressed so hard on the habitable world ... who reclaimed every state to liberty, who had led disorder into order.... He was also the first and the greatest and the common benefactor in that he displaced the rule of many and committed the ship of the commonwealth to be steered by a single pilot.... It is not well that many lords should rule.[2]

In other words, Augustus was seen as bringing heaven on earth through his *pax Romana*; and the nations who bowed before Caesar were the recipients of cosmic renewal, Philippi included.

Third, Philippians 2:11 and 3:20 ascribe to Jesus two names already reserved for the Roman emperor—Lord (*kurios*); "Nero, the Lord [*kurios*] of all the world" and Savior (Augustus was proclaimed "Savior of the world"). Indeed, Deissmann's *Light from the Ancient East* supplies many divine titles for Caesar—Lord, Savior, God, Son of God.[3]

---

2   Philo, *De Legatione ad Gaium*, 144–9, trans. by F. H. Colson; quoted in Peter Oakes, *Philippians: From People to Letter*, Society for the New Testament Studies Monograph Series 110 (Cambridge: Cambridge University Press, 2001), p. 161.

3   Deissmann, *Light from the Ancient East*, pp. 338–78.

Fourth, we have already called attention to texts that predicted Augustus would bring about the golden age (the Priene Inscription, the *Sibylline Oracles*, Livy, Horace). Here we mention one more—Virgil's *Aeneid*, books 6 and 8. Book 6:788–807 casts Augustus as a new Romulus, founder of the golden age of Rome:

> Turn here now your two-eyed gazed, and behold this nation (*gentem*), the Romans that are yours. Here is Caesar and all the descendants (*progenies*) destined to pass under heaven's great sphere. This man, he is the one you often hear promised to you, Augustus Caesar, divine offspring (*divi genus*), who will again make a golden age in Latium amid fields once ruled by Saturn; he will extend empire beyond the Garamats and the Indians to a land which lies beyond our stars, beyond the paths of year and sun where sky-bearing Atlas wheels on his shoulders the blazing star-studded sphere. Against his coming both Caspian realms and the Maeotic land even now shudder at the oracles of their gods, and the mouths of sevenfold Nile quiver in alarm. Not even Hercules traversed so much of the earth's extent, though he pierced the stag of brazen foot, quieted the woods of Erymanthus, and made Lerna tremble at his bow; nor either, who guides his chariot with vine-leaf reigns, triumphant Bacchus, driving his tigers down from Nysa's lofty peak. And do we still hesitate to spread out virtue by our works, or hold back in fear from occupying Ausonian land.[4]

In Book 8:713–29, Virgil portrays Augustus as the last man standing with the gods as the emperor enters Rome in triumph as the unrivaled ruler of the world:

> But Caesar, entering the walls of Rome in triple triumph, was dedicating to Italy's gods his immortal votive gift—three hundred mighty shrines throughout the city. The streets were ringing with gladness and games and shouting; in all the temples was a band of matrons, in all were altars, and before the altars slain steers covered the ground. He himself, seated at the snowy threshold of shining Phoebus, reviews the gifts of people in long line, as different custom of dress and arms as in languages. Here Mulciber had portrayed the Nomad race

---

4   Quoted by Davina Lopez, *Apostle to the Conquered: Reimagining Paul's Mission* (Minneapolis: Fortress Press, 2008), p.78.

and the ungirt Africans, here the Leleges and Carians and quivered Gelonians, Euphrates moved now with humbler waves and the Morini were there, furthest on mankind, and the Rhine of double-horn, and undominated Dahae, and Arazes chafing at his bridge.[5]

The occasion for these divine predictions about Augustus' coming *pax Romana* was his victory over Antony and Cleopatra at the battle of Actium in 31 BC, not far south of Philippi on the coast of Greece.

Fifth, as Hansen notes, Philippi contained impressive altars and temples dedicated to the emperor and members of his family. The city's religious life centered on the worship of the emperor.[6]

Judging from his letter to the Philippians and Acts 16 Paul, though a Roman citizen (see Acts 16:37–38), would have none of the imperial cult. First, the new age is here in Christ, not Caesar (Phil. 4:7). Second, at Jesus' parousia he will establish his commonwealth by conquering the nations, Rome included (Phil. 2:9–11; 3:20). Third, this is so because Jesus Christ is the true Lord (Phil. 2:11) and Savior (Phil. 3:20). Fourth, his universal rule and peace was predicted by the Old Testament prophets (cf. Phil. 2:10–11 with Isa. 45:23). Fifth, rather than submit to the imperial cult and all of its celebrative trappings, the Philippian Christians should submit to Christ as Lord (Phil. 2:6–11). This, no doubt, lay behind the Philippians' accusation that Paul and Silas were advocating customs at odds with Roman lifestyle (Acts 16:20–21). In other words, Paul's apocalypse of Christ was a direct affront to the worship and celebration of Caesar.

The Realized Eschatology of the Merkabah Judaizers as Background to Paul's Letter to the Philippians

There does not seem to have been a sizeable Jewish population in Philippi during Paul's ministry there. Acts 16:13–15 records the conversion of Lydia, a God-fearer, to Christ. However, the fact that Paul met her worshipping by a river implies there was no synagogue in town, for Jews and God-fearers worshipped at

5   Quoted in Ibid, pp. 84–5.
6   Hansen, *The Letter to the Philippians*, p. 3.

a river (it symbolized purity) when there were not ten Jewish males to constitute a synagogue. Moreover, the derogatory remark by the Philippian townspeople about Paul and Silas being Jewish might also suggest that Jews would have been considered outsiders to Philippi (Acts 16:20–21).

But, judging from Paul's letter to the Philippians, a Jewish presence had begun to make itself known in the church, notably *merkabah* Judaizers. It is not difficult to cull from Paul's letter their message of eschatology.

First, they taught that Jesus is the Christ, whose Spirit now empowers Jews and Gentiles to truly obey the Torah, symbolized in circumcision (Phil. 3:1–6). Obeying the law of Moses by the power of Christ and the Spirit brings spiritual perfection (Phil. 3:12–16). Although the *merkabah* influence on these Judaizers is not spelled out as it is in 1 and 2 Corinthians—or, as we will see, in Colossians—there are indications in Philippians 3:12–16 that Paul's Jewish opponents did claim they reached perfection in mystic experience: (1) They used the term "perfect" (τελιος, vv. 12, 15), a word used in the mystery religions for the spiritual state the worshipper reached when in union with the deity. (2) The "upward call," as A. Lincoln has argued, is probably an allusion to heaven, Paradise in particular (vv. 13, 14; cf. *3 Baruch* 4:15; 2 Cor. 12:1–10, explicitly *merkabah* texts).[7] (3) Philippians 3:15–16 makes a veiled reference to the Judaizers having received divine revelation, reinforcing their perfectionist assumptions.

Second, these *merkabah* Judaizers argued that Jerusalem was heaven on earth; that the kingdom had come to the Jerusalem church (Phil. 3:20; cf. Gal. 4:21–31). Thus Jerusalem was the place where heaven and earth met—where cosmic harmony in Christ abode.

Third, these Judaizers confessed Jesus to be the Christ, the Savior (Phil. 2:6–11; 3:20–21) and the indwelling of Spirit to be the end-time gift *par excellence* (Phil. 3:3).

Fourth, consequently the Judaizers will have viewed the mother church in Jerusalem, the indwelling of the Spirit, circumcision, and the Torah as

---

7   Andrew T. Lincoln, *Paradise Now and Not Yet: Studies in the Role of the Heavenly Dimension in Paul's Thought with Special Reference to his Eschatology*, Society for the New Testament Studies Monograph Series 43 (Cambridge: Cambridge University Press, 1981), pp. 94–95.

indicating that the long-awaited restoration of Israel had occurred (see again 3:1–6; 20–21).

Fifth, the Judaizers who infiltrated the Philippian church exalted circumcision as the key celebration of the message of Christ and the Spirit (3:3; cf. v. 19).

But Paul begged to disagree with the *merkabizers*. First, Jesus Christ did inaugurate the age of the Spirit, but not to obey the Law. Rather, faith in Christ actually liberates the believer from the Torah (3:1–11). And, since the parousia has not yet occurred, there is no perfection in this life (3:12–16).

Second, Jerusalem is not a sacred place uniting heaven and earth. Rather Jerusalem is merely earthly, not spiritual or heavenly (3:20). Rather the Christian should focus on heaven and Christ's imminent return (3:21).

Third, although the Judaizers claim Jesus is Christ they are actually enemies of the cross, because they fail to perceive that Jesus' death brought an end to the Torah and circumcision as a means of salvation (3:18–19).

Fourth, rather than the restoration of Israel having occurred in Jerusalem, Paul claims that the current generation of Jews and Judaizers remain under the covenant curses because they are a crooked generation (cf. 2:14–15 with Deut. 31:30–32:47). Restoration to God comes only through Christ—not Jerusalem, the Torah, nor circumcision.

Fifth, in fact Paul makes some nasty remarks about circumcision and the Torah. Rather than these be celebrations of Israel's and the church's faith, those who practice them are unclean "dogs" (the same label Jews applied to Gentiles), because they try to practice the works of the Torah, and do nothing more than mutilate their flesh when they are circumcised (3:21). Contrary to the Jews and Judaizers, Christians are the ones who worship God in the Spirit by faith, not by confidence in the flesh (3:3–11).

Paul continues to heap invectives on the Judaizing celebration of circumcision in 3:19—to glory in their shame (circumcision was seen as a shameful act by Gentiles) and to exalt the dietary laws was to invite divine judgment, not celebration (3:19).

SURVEY OF PHILIPPIANS

We propose to summarize the content of Philippians by proceeding along three lines. First, we will discuss Paul's inaugurated eschatology by noting the already/

not-yet aspects of his message in the letter. Second, we will observe how the topic of suffering interacts with the imperial cult and the Judaizers. Then we will summarize in a more systematic way the contents of Philippians.

Paul's Inaugurated Eschatology

Philippians 2:6–11 indicates that the cross of Christ (vv. 6–8) and his resurrection initiated the age to come (vv. 9–11). Currently, the believer lives in between those two ages. Consequently, several end-time blessings belong now to the Christian. (1) Joy is an eschatological blessing associated with the dawning of the age to come (e.g. 1:4, 18, 26; 2:2; 3:1; 4:4, 10). (2) The resurrection of Jesus brought about the dawning of the age to come in heaven (1:21; 3:20a). (3) Salvation is a present eschatological reality for believers in Christ (2:12). (4) The power of Christ's resurrection is operative in the lives of Christians (3:10–11). (5) The peace of God, an end-time blessing, is now the possession of the believer (4:6).

However, these blessings of the age to come are not yet fully realized for the Christian; they occur in the midst of this present age, especially the messianic woes that mark the transition between the two ages. Thus: (1) Joy occurs in the midst of suffering and persecution (1:4–6; 1:18–21; 1:27–30; 3:1–2/10–11; 4:4–5). (2) While the resurrection of Jesus inaugurated the age to come in heaven (the blissful place awaiting the soul of the departed Christian), the resurrection body of the righteous that will finalize the age to come still awaits the parousia (cf. 1:21; 3:20a with 3:20b–21). (3) The salvation of the age to come still must be worked out in this present age (2:12–13). (4) The power of the resurrected Jesus is available to the Christian, but until the parousia such power ironically enables Christians to share in the suffering of Christ's cross and the messianic woes (3:10–11). (5) The peace of God associated with the age to come does indwell the believer, but it is not complete yet because the parousia is no more than near, not here (4:4–7).

Paul's Comments on Suffering, the Imperial Cult, and the Judaizers

Paul's comments on suffering dominate his letter to the Philippians. There are two angles to this topic. First, Paul encourages the Philippian church to expect to suffer for Christ in the face of persecution because it does not submit to the worship of Caesar. This is what is happening to Paul as well (1:13–28; 2:17). Paul's reminder that the Philippians can expect to suffer for Christ (1:28–29) stems from the Jewish-Christian expectation that the godly will suffer persecution for their faith in the end times as a part of the messianic woes. One can especially see this in the book of Revelation, which equates Christian suffering at the hands of the imperial cult with the messianic woes/ great tribulation.

Second, Paul's talk about suffering in the Christian life feeds into his eschatological reservation regarding the realized eschatology of the *merkabah* Judaizers who infiltrated the Philippian church (1:15–17; 3:10–11, 12–17). The fact that Christians still suffer demonstrates that, even though the age to come has dawned, Christians still live in this present evil age.

For Paul, the Christian who accepts suffering as God's will for them thereby embraces the cross of Christ (3:10–11). Conversely, the suffering inflicted by the imperial cult on the believer along with the aversion to suffering communicated in the realized eschatology of the Judaizers proceed from the same reality—both disdain the cross (3:18).

SUMMARY OF PHILIPPIANS

Paul's inaugurated eschatology and the topic of suffering form the backdrop for the Philippian letter, which we now summarize. We may outline the book thusly:

A. 1:1–2: Greetings
B. 1:3–11: Thanksgiving and Prayer for the Philippians
C. 1:12–26: Paul's Personal Circumstances
D. 1:27–2:18: Exhortations
E. 2:19–30: Paul's Associates in the Gospel
F. 3:1–4:1: Warnings against Judaizers and Antinomians
G. 4:2–23: Final Exhortations, Thanks, and Conclusion

A. 1:1–2: Greetings

Paul and Timothy (Timothy may have co-authored the letter with Paul) greet the Philippian church, with whom the two had such intimate dealings. Acts 16:11–40 records Paul's founding of the church at Philippi. By the time of the writing of the letter, two offices helped to govern the local church there: overseer/elder/bishop (all the same office; see Acts 20:27–28; 1 Peter 5:1–2),[8] and deacon.

B. 1:3–11: Thanksgiving and Prayer for the Philippians

In vv. 3–11, Paul conveys his affection for the Philippian church by thanking God for them and praying for them. Paul thanks God for the believers at Philippi for their fellowship in the gospel with him (vv. 3–8). Paul prays that the Philippian church will grow in discernment, no doubt relative to the dangers of the imperial cult and the Judaizers (vv. 9–11). God's wisdom will help the Philippians to see through the blasphemy of the worship of Caesar and the heresy of the Judaizing message. We detect in v. 6 Paul's inaugurated eschatology: God has begun the good work of salvation in the Philippian Christians (the age to come has dawned) and he will complete it at the return of Christ (the age to come will only be complete then).

C. 1:12–26: Paul's Personal Circumstances

Paul is joyful despite being under house arrest in Rome, for two reasons. First, he is evangelizing the Praetorian Guard (the palace guard, vv. 12–13) and second, his incarceration is emboldening fellow believers to preach the gospel (v. 14). The latter category contains two groups of people—those who preach Christ out of pure motives and those who preach Christ to get back at Paul (vv. 15–18). It may be that the ones who preach with the impure motive of getting back at Paul are the Judaizers who, now that Paul is under arrest and not able to visit Philippi, can propagate their works salvation message among the believers there.

For Paul's part, he wants to live for Christ in life or in death (vv. 19–26). Here we see Paul's inaugurated eschatology at work again: if Paul dies for Christ the apostle will go to heaven to be with him, whose death and resurrection inaugurated the age to come in heaven. But, still Paul would have to wait for the parousia to receive his resurrection body. This is the "not yet" of eschatology. Paul then encourages the Philippian church to be faithful to the gospel despite persecution from the imperial cult. Such persecution is a part of

---

8   It was not until the second century that the office of bishop (monarchial episcopate) ruled over several churches in an area.

the messianic woes/great tribulation. But at the end of the day the Christian through Christ will triumph over Caesar (vv. 27–30).

D. 1:27–2:18: Exhortations

In 2:1–5, Paul exhorts the Philippian believers to be at one (cf. 4:1–3). The servant attitude that such action requires is illustrated in 2:6–11, the marvelous *kenosis* ("empty") hymn. Debate has raged over the background of the *kenosis* hymn, with several possibilities competing for attention: the Redeemed Redeemer of the History of Religions of School; Wisdom; the Jesus tradition (especially the Upper Room episode of the washing of the disciples' feet); the Suffering Servant of Isaiah 52–53; Jewish angelology; Adam (as described in Gen. 1–3 or as portrayed in non-canonical Jewish speculation, or both); and the imperial cult. If there is a growing consensus among scholars today concerning the background of the hymn, it would seem to be with regard to the Adamic background, though not necessarily mutually exclusive of some of the other alternatives. Seen in this light, one can argue that the hymn contrasts the choices of Adam and Christ in that it presents the latter as the restorer of the former's lost glory. There are four aspects to these archetypal choices. The following chart highlights those elements.

SCRIPTURE	ADAM	CHRIST
1) vv. 6–7a	Although Adam shared in the glory of God, he was not content but grasped after equality with God by exalting himself	Although Christ exuded the glory of God, he did not count equality with God something to be used for his own advantage, but emptied himself
2) v. 7b	Was in the likeness of God	Became a servant by taking on the likeness of man
3) v. 8	Disobedient	Obedient
4) vv. 9–11	God humbled him: -Loss of dominion -Loss of glory	God exalted him: -Restoration of dominion -Restoration of glory

Thus Christ, the suffering servant, died on the cross for the sins of humanity and was raised to glory. Now as the new Adam he is destined to rule the cosmos, including Caesar and his realm. Christ's death and resurrection brought about nothing less than the shift of the two ages.

According to 2:12–13, Christians belong to the age to come, but they must live out their salvation in the context of this present age. Not Israel, which is still under the covenant curses, but Christians are experiencing the blessings of the covenant, according to vv. 14–15. Along the way they, like Paul, should be prepared to suffer for the cause of Christ (v. 17).

E. 2:19–30: Paul's Associates in the Gospel

Two illustrations of suffering for the cause of Christ proceeding from a deep love for the Philippian church are presented in vv. 19–30: Timothy and Epaphroditus. The former is Paul's spiritual son, who like his mentor and Jesus has a genuine concern for others, including the Philippian church (vv. 19–24). The latter, probably a member of the church at Philippi, became ill in his service to Paul and the Philippians (vv. 25–30).

F. 3:1–4:1: Warnings against Judaizers and Antinomians

In 3:1–11 Paul contrasts his message of faith-righteousness with the Judaizers' message of works-righteousness. Before his conversion Paul followed the path of works-righteousness, but that only led to a dead-end street before God. Now Paul can only proclaim the gospel of Christ—faith in him alone is the means for receiving divine righteousness (vv. 1–11).

We can detect in these verses Paul's fourfold eschatological message. First, Jesus is the Christ (vv. 7–10). Second, his death and resurrection inaugurated the age to come (vv. 10–11). Third, one enters into the age to come, or receives justification of the age to come now, by faith in Christ not the works of the Torah. Fourth, Paul now ministers especially to Gentiles. Indeed, the irony is that Gentiles ("dogs" the Jews called them, v. 2) have become the true circumcision, or the people of God, while unbelieving Jews have lost that status.

In vv. 3:12–21 Paul further warns the Philippian church regarding the Judaizers by raising his eschatological reservation as a barrier to the *merkabizers'* realized eschatology. Their message that circumcision and the Law plus faith in

Christ brings them destruction, not perfection. These enemies of the cross are earthbound, not heavenly oriented. In 4:1 Paul exhorts the Philippian church to resist these Judaizers and remain true to the gospel.

G. 4:2–23: Final Exhortations, Thanks, and Conclusion

Paul concludes his letter by making three points. First, the Philippians should rejoice in the fact that the parousia is imminent (4:4–7). That should also motivate them to devote themselves to unity (4:2–3) and purity (4:8–9). Second, Paul thanks the Philippian church for its sacrificial and gracious financial gift to him (vv. 10–18). Because of this God will supply all their needs (v. 19). Third, Paul offers a doxology to God (v. 20).

CONCLUSION

We conclude our discussion of Philippians by noting that Paul's inaugurated eschatology was in opposition to the realized eschatologies of the imperial cult and the *merkabah* Judaizers. The new age lies neither in Augustus' exploits nor Moses' regulations. Rather the new age lies in Christ the crucified Lord, a scandal to both Romans and Jews, but the power and wisdom of God.

COLOSSIANS

HELLENISTIC RELIGION, *MERKABAH*

MYSTICISM, IMPERIAL CULT,

AND THE COLOSSIAN HERESY

Besides the authorship of Colossians, the greatest debate associated with that letter is the nature of the Colossian heresy. What exactly posed such a theological threat to the church at Colossae, thus precipitating Paul's letter?[1] Did the Colossian heresy (spelled out in Colossians 2:6–23) consist of

---

1   The reasons for advocating Pauline composition of the letter to Colossae need to be highlighted. They are based on more recent discussions of the issue and thus proceed beyond the virtual impasse with regard to style and vocabulary. See the discussions by W. Kummel, *Introduction to the New Testament*, tr. Howard Clark Kee (Nashville, TN: Abingdon, 1973) pp. 240–241; Peter T. O'Brien, *Colossians, Philemon,* Word Biblical Commentary 44 (Waco, TX: Word Books, 1982), pp. xli–xlix; Donald Guthrie, *New Testament Introduction* (Downers Grove, IL: Intervarsity Press, 1970), pp. 551–554; and Eduard Lohse, *Colossians and Philemon,* Hermeneia (Philadelphia: Fortress Press, 1972), pp. 84–91. The evidence can be presented here in broad strokes. First, there is the historical evidence. Wedderburn's judicious conclusion concerning the relationship between the date of the earthquake in the city of Colossae in AD 60–61 and an early dating of the Colossian letter is hard to deny:

> The idea of a later pseudonymous letter written to a city that was in ruins and to a church there that perhaps no longer existed and which Paul never visited (Col 2:1) seems too

Hellenistic religion? Or was it *merkabah* mysticism? Or was it the Roman imperial cult? We will see that all three teachings informed the theological dangers Paul exposes in his letter to the Colossians. But Paul opposes his apocalypse of Christ to the realized eschatology of those three ideologies. After discussing the Colossian heresy, we will then summarize the contents of the letter.

THE COLOSSIAN HERESY

In discussing the nature of the Colossian heresy, we will survey each of the major contenders according to their order of appearance in the scholarly literature. The only candidate we will decline to survey is Gnosticism which, due to its second century origins and mosaic description, is no longer viewed by scholars as a viable candidate to be the Colossian heresy.

Hellenistic Religion

The Gnostic interpretation of the Colossian heresy, proposed by J. B. Lightfoot and Martin Dibelius at the end of the nineteenth century and the turn of the twentieth century, gave way to the mystery-religions interpretation. Clinton E. Arnold has documented the influence of local Hellenistic syncretistic religion upon the Colossian heresy, including the Isis and Mithras mysteries. First we list the parallels between the Isis mystery and the Colossian heresy, then we note the parallels between the Mithras cult and Colossians 2:6–23. After that, we rearrange the parallels noted by Arnold to correspond with the five components of

---

macabre to be likely, especially since the letter makes no mention of this disaster that had overtaken the city. This silence is even stranger if the letter is written soon after the earthquake, and, even if Colossae was relatively untouched by the earthquake, the church there was in touch with that in Laodicea (Col 4:16); it is unlikely that it remained oblivious to the latter's fortunes or that the writer of Colossians would wish it to be so (A. J. M. Wedderburn, *Baptism and Redemption: Studies in Pauline Theology against its Graeco-Roman Background*, Wissenschaftlichen Untersuchungen zum Neuen Testament 44 [Tübingen: J. C. B. Mohr, 1987], pp. 70–71).

Wedderburn's own tentative solution is that Colossians was written by a close follower of Paul during the apostle's lifetime, perhaps in a situation where Paul's imprisonment (Col. 4:3, 10, 18) meant that he had to leave the composition of the letters to Colossae and Philemon to his associates (Weddernburn, *Baptism and Resurrection*, p. 71). Yet, in the opinion of this writer, Wedderburn's hypothesis is, in actuality, a revival of the amanuensis theory (note the reference to Timothy in Col. 1:14 or to Epaphras in 4:23) and, for all practical purposes, places the letter under Paul's auspices and approval.

realized eschatology and the mystery religions that we have become accustomed to expect.

Isis and the Colossian Heresy

Arnold finds the following comparisons between the Isis mystery in the eleventh book of Apuleius's *Metamorphosis* and the Colossian heresy:[2]

A. "Entering" (ἐμβατευω) in Colossians 2:18 corresponds to the Isis initiate entering into the underground sanctuary to be united with Isis in worship (*Met.* 11.22).

B. The initiate experienced visions of Isis when they entered the threshold of the sanctuary (cf. Col. 2:18 with *Met.* 11.22).

C. The initiate had a vision of passing through the four elements—spirit, fire, water, and earth—which were gods to be feared in the journey (cf. Col. 2:18, 20 with *Met.* book 11).

Second, there is the theological evidence. Two categories, in particular, fall under this rubric: eschatology and ecclesiology. Concerning the former of these, O'Brien and Andrew T. Lincoln have provided healthy correctives to the older, much hackneyed assertion that in Colossians, Paul's "already/not yet" tension has given a way to a realized eschatology (O'Brien, *Colossians*, pp. xlvi–xlvii; Lincoln, *Paradise Now and Not Yet*, pp. 122–134). Rather, these two authors have carefully established the fact that Paul's eschatological tension remains intact in Colossians. Both the "not yet" (futurist) aspect is present (Col. 1:22, 29; 3:1–11) as well as the "already" (realized) aspect (Col. 1:9–14; 2:8–15). If the latter pole is emphasized in the letter, it is due more to the refutation of false teaching at Colossae that undermined the Colossian Christians' exalted position in Christ, than to different authorship. Concerning the ecclesiology of the letter and the oft-made claim that Colossians 1:15–20's portrayal of Christ as head of the cosmic body (redacted and interpreted as the church, v. 18) is indebted to a late-first-century incipient Gnosticism, two replies can be underscored. a) It does not seem to be the case that 1:18 is a redaction (an assumption usually dependent upon the hypothesis that the hymn is Gnostic in origin). Moreover, the cosmic proportion of Christ's body described in Colossians 1:18 could just have easily originated in Jewish discussions about the cosmic size and/or corporate personality of Adam, now applied to Christ. b) The very theory that the Colossian heresy stemmed from Gnosticism has, itself, given way to a more accurate identification of the error; it is at least Jewish mystical, *merkabah* experience that has drawn fire from Paul, as will be seen below. Such a tradition can be traced to the first century AD (*1 Enoch* 14:8–23 is probably the earliest example of *merkabah* mysticism and dates to at least the first century AD) and provides a closer contact point than does Gnosticism. All of that to say that Paul is as good a candidate as any to be the author of Colossians.

2   Clinton E. Arnold, *The Interface between Christianity and Folk Belief in Colossae* (Grand Rapids, MI: Baker, 1996), pp. 133–36.

D. Fasting and prohibitions attended the mystery rites to attain the purity needed to unite with Isis (cf. Col. 2:16, 18, 21, 23 with *Met.* 11.23).

E. The sacred tradition of the initiation rite of the Isis mystery was passed along from one initiate to the next. Compare Colossians 2:23 with *Met.* 11.22, "The day is at hand for which you have longed with constant prayers, the day when you shall enter … into the most sacred mysteries of the holy rites." These sacred texts can also be found in Plutarch, *De. Is. Et Os.* 4.352c-d; 7.353b.

F. Upon being united with the deity, the initiate overcame the gods over the four elements (cf. Col. 1:16; 2:8, 10, 15, 20). Dibelius summarizes this aspect of the initiation:

Insofar as Lucius traverses this was [to the underworld and through the heavens] unharmed, he proves himself charmed against chthonic, earthly, and heavenly powers. The deification at the end of the ceremony imparts confirmation and duration to this superiority…. Thus the initiate becomes a participant in the cosmic rule of his goddess…. This freedom from the rule of the cosmic powers means freedom also from the coercion of fate…. One sees what significance is here attributed to the Isis mystery: the rule of the cosmic powers and the blind Fortuna represented by them is replaced by the rule of the gracious *Fortuna videns* [Fortune who sees], whom all those powers obey, Isis.[3]

Mithras and the Colossian Heresy
The Great Paris Magical Papyrus (PGM IV. 475–829) is thought to contain an actual liturgy of the mysteries of the Mithras cult. Arnold describes the text:

The text prescribes the proper rites and invocations for a prospective initiate to become immortal … (11. 477–78). The process involves a visionary ascent to heaven and a mystery rite in which an ointment is created and applied. The result is the initiate's immortality (… 11. 647–48, 741, 771). This is imparted through union with the deity: when Mithras appears to the initiate, he or she responds by

---

3   Quoted in Ibid, p. 135.

saying, "dwell with me in my soul" (... [1. 710]). The experience is described throughout as a rebirth (... 1. 501; 11. 508–509, 647; ... 11. 517–19).[4]

Arnold notes the following parallels between the Mithras liturgy and the Colossian heresy:

1. The liturgy was received as sacred tradition (cf. Col. 2:8 with I. 476).
2. The initiation provides deliverance from dreaded fate and the threat of hostile supernatural powers (cf. Col. 1:16; 2:8, 10, 15, 20 cf. with I. 475; II 605–606; etc.).
3. The four elements are assumed to prevent immortalization (cf. Col. 2:8, 20 with I. 501).
4. The initiate in the Mithras liturgy experienced visions of gods, angels, and astral powers (cf. Col. 2:18 with II. 713–15).
5. An angel is said to have revealed the Mithra mystery traditions (cf. Col. 2:8, 18 with I. 483).
6. Dietary and purity regulations are imposed on the fellow initiate (cf. Col. 2:16, 21 with II. 734–36, 783–84).

We may now correlate the above parallels with the five components of the realized eschatology of Hellenistic syncretistic religion, especially the Isis and Mithra mysteries:

REALIZED ESCHATOLOGY	ISIS CULT	MITHRAS LITURGY
1) New age has dawned	#6—life	#7—immortality
2) Cosmic	#1, #2, #6—mystic union with Isis	#5, #6—mystic union with Mithras
3) Savior	Isis	Mithras
4) Sacred Prediction	#5—sacred tradition about the initiation passed on	#1—sacred tradition about the initiation passed on
5) Celebrations	#4—fasting and prohibitions	#6—dietary and purity regulations

---

4   Ibid, p. 138.

Paul's Rebuttal to the Isis and Mithras Cults

We may find in Colossians Paul's opposition to the above expressions of Hellenistic religions at the following points:

- The new age has dawned in Christ, the fullness of God (Col. 1:12, 15–20; 2:9).
- It is through union with Christ by faith alone that the believer is exalted to heaven (Col. 3:1–4).
- Jesus is the Savior, not Isis or Mithras, nor any other supposed Hellenistic god (Col. 1:15–20). Jesus has triumphed over the demonic powers (Col. 2:8, 15, 20).
- The mystery of Christ in the believer is the fulfillment of Old Testament prophecy (cf. 1:23–27 with Rom. 16:25–27).
- Faith in Christ, not pagan ritual (or the Law; see below), is the key to salvation (Col. 2:8–23).

Merkabah Mysticism

It is popular these days in scholarly circles to interpret the Dead Sea Scrolls (hereafter DSS) and some of Paul's opponents as being heavily influenced by *merkabah* mysticism. This is especially the case for the Songs of Sabbath Sacrifice (4Q400–405, 11Q17), which describe the angelic liturgy as followed by the Qumran sectaries. John Stugnell, the publisher of these fragments, identifies the form of these songs:

> The first line of a typical section runs, "By a sage. The song of the Sabbath sacrifice for the seventh Sabbath on the 16th of the 2nd month. Praise God all ye angels …" and then the *Maskil* (sage) exhorts the angels, under numerous names, to various forms of praise. These then are elements in the liturgy of the Sabbath offering, composed by a *Maskil* for every Sabbath of the year according to the Essene calendar; according to one's judgment on another disputed issue one will see in them songs which accompanied the sacrifice schematically performed at Qumran or songs by which these sacrifices were spiritually replaced.[5]

---

5   John Strugnell, "The Angelic Liturgy at Qumran –4 Q Serek Sirot 'Olat Hassabat", *Congress Volume*, Oxford, 1959, VT Supplements 7 (Leiden: Brill, 1960), pp. 318-45; p. 320.

Neil S. Fujita provides a useful summary of the *merkabah* components occurring in these liturgical songs: Essenes join the angels in worshipping God via the Sabbath liturgy, with the angels serving as priests in the heavenly temple (which itself enshrines seven sanctuaries) and the Torah as the means for encountering the heavenly throne.

More and more scholars also perceive *merkabah* mysticism to be an important backdrop to the Colossian heresy, particularly as it is portrayed in Colossians 2:8–23. That passage affords striking similarities between *merkabah* mysticism and the Colossian error: mysticism (Col. 2:2–3, 18), legalism (Col. 2:13–14, 18, 20) and the glorious throne of God (Col. 3:1–4).

It should be noted that a common theme occurring in Jewish *merkabah*, especially the Angelic Liturgy (4QShirShabb) of Qumran and the Colossian heresy, is angelology. Such a topic provides intriguing points of comparison between the DSS and Paul's refutation of the aberrant teaching in the Colossian church. I will therefore devote this section to an investigation of three aspects of angelology found in the DSS, especially the Angelic Liturgy, which also surface in Colossians 2:8–23 and its context: mysticism—angelic worship; legalism—angelic revelation; and asceticism—angelic purity.

Mysticism: Angelic Worship

The mystical nature informing the Colossian heresy is highlighted by two phrases, θρησκεια των ἀγγελιων—"worship of angels"—and ἁ ἑορακεν ἐμβατευων—"the things which he had seen upon entering" (Col. 2:18). The meanings of both phrases have been debated but something of a scholarly consensus is now being reached in rooting them in Jewish *merkabah* mysticism.

"*The worship of angels.*" This phrase in the past was interpreted to mean the worship or veneration of angels. Three pieces of data were often appealed to in support of this viewpoint:

- Grammatically, the phrase in the Greek is an objective genitive—the angels are the objects of the worship.
- Colossians 2:15, with its declaration that Christ triumphed over the rulers and authorities (presumably fallen angels), is enlisted as evidence

that the Colossian Christians were tempted to worship hostile angels, despite the fact that they were defeated at the cross.

- Extrabiblical literature approximately contemporary with Paul's day is drawn on in support of the theory that the angelic veneration existed in Judaism, *Kerygma Petrou*; *Apology of Aristides* 14:4; Celsus (in Origen *Contra Celsum* 1:26, 5:6); *Pseudo Philo* 13:6; *1 Enoch* 48:5; 62:6, 9 (which envisions the worship of the heavenly Son of Man, assuming that such a personage was an angel) and *Tosefta Hullin* 2:18.

- The other interpretation of Colossians 2:18 is that it refers to humans joining—not worshipping—the angels in their adoration of God, particularly in mystic ascent. Four pieces of evidence convince most recent scholars that this is the correct rendering.

  - Grammatically, it is more likely that the phrase "worship of angels" is a subjective genitive, thus denoting worship offered by angels to God (cf. *4 Macc* 5:7).

  - While Colossians 2:18 almost certainly alludes to evil angels triumphed over at the cross, good angels which worship God need not be ruled out in Colossians 2:18.

  - While the aforementioned texts may point to the worship of angels in some Jewish circles, more characteristic of ancient Judaism was the warning precisely against such type of activity (Deut. 4:19; 17:3; Jer. 8:2; 19:13; Zeph. 6:15; *Apoc. Zeph.* 6:15; *Apoc. Abr.* 17:2; Philo *Fug.* 212; *De Somnis* 1.232, 238; *Asc. Is.* 7:21; *Psuedo Philo* 34:2; cf. Rev. 19:10; 22:9).

  - Early Jewish-Christian literature is replete with references to angels worshipping God (e.g., Isa. 6:2–3; Dan. 7:10; *1 Enoch* 14:17–23; 36:49, 39–40; 61:10–12; *2 Enoch* 20–21; *Apoc. Abr.* 17–18; *T. Levi* 3:3–8; Luke 2:14; Phil. 2:10–11; Rev. 4–5; *Asc. Is* 1–9). More germane to Colossians 2:18 is the evidence from apocalyptic and mystical Jewish circles, which attests to a desire on the part of humans to join angels in worshipping God (Ps. 29:1–2; 148:1–2; *T. Job* 48–50; *Apoc. Abr.* 17; *Asc. Is.* 7:13–9:33; *Apoc. Zeph.* 8:3–4).

- Most interesting of all is the evidence that such worship was coveted in the Qumran community. James D. G. Dunn writes of this:

According to 1QSa 2:8–9 the rules for the congregation of the last days would have to be strict, "for the Angels of Holiness are [with] their [congregation]." But the implication of other references is that these rules were already in operation, indicating that the Qumran community saw itself as a priestly community whose holiness was defined by the presence of the angels (cf. particularly 4QCD and 1 QM 7:4–6 with Lev. 21:17–21). So explicitly in 1QH 3:32–22: "thou hast cleansed a perverse spirit of great sin … that it may enter in community with the congregation of the Sons of Heaven" (similarly 1QH 11:10–13). More to the immediate point, in 1QSb 4:25–26 one of the blessings of the priest is: "May you be as an Angel of the Presence in the Abode of Holiness to the glory of the God of [hosts].… May you attend upon the service in the Temple of the Kingdom and decree destiny in company with the Angels of the Presence." Most interesting of all are the recently published complete (but often fragmentary) texts of the Songs of the Sabbath Sacrifice (4Q 400–405), which contain songs of praise to be offered to God by angels in the heavenly temple during the first thirteen Sabbaths of the year and in which it is clear enough (since the Songs presumably belonged to the liturgy) that the community itself (or at least its priests) joined with the angels in reciting these songs of heavenly worship.[6]

Thus, another plausible background for the phrase in Colossians 2:18, "the worship of angels" is Jewish *merkabah* mysticism, in particular the variety expressed in the DSS.

"The things which he had seen upon entering." The best background of the phrase "the things which he had seen upon entering," as Dunn and Thomas J. Sappington demonstrate, is the mystic ascent of the righteous leading into the heavenly temple portrayed in Jewish apocalyptic materials. There the worshipper joined with the angels in praise to God (*1 Enoch* 14:8–13; *2 Enoch* 3; *3*

---

6   James D. G. Dunn, *The Epistles to the Colossians and to Philemon*. New International Greek Testament Commentary (Grand Rapids, MI: Eerdmans, 1996) p. 181.

Enoch 2:2; 3:1–2; *T. Levi* 5:5–7; cf. Rev. 4:1–2).[7] The words "the things seen," a prominent way to refer to the heavenly vision of angels during the course of mystic ascent in apocalyptic texts (*1 Enoch* 14; *T. Abr.* 10; Rev. 4–5; cf. 2 Cor. 12:2–4), confirm this suggestion. And as was the case for the phrase "the worship of angels," so here a viable background is the *merkabah* mysticism evident in the DSS. Dunn calls attention to this aspect of the Songs of the Sabbath Sacrifice, noting that heaven therein is depicted as a temple into which the angels entered for the purpose of worshipping God. Thus, 4Q405 14:1—15:3–4 exclaims, "Their wonderful praise is for the God of gods … and they sing … the vestibules by which they enter, the spirits of the most holy inner Temple." Similarly, 4Q405 23.1:8–10 says, "When the gods of knowledge enter by the doors of glory, and when the holy angels depart towards their realm, the entrance doors and the gates of exit proclaim the glory of the King. Blessing and praising all the spirits of God when they depart and enter by the gates."[8]

In light of the discussion above, a viable background for the phrases "worship of angels" and "the things which he had seen upon entering" seems to be *merkabah* mysticism, in particular the kind espoused in the Songs of Sabbath Sacrifice. It is quite reasonable, therefore, to imagine a Jewish synagogue in Colossae claiming that its Sabbath worship participated in the worship of angels and thereby making inroads into the church. Paul, however, criticizes such mysticism with four comments in Colossians 2:18–19:

- Such worship is, in actuality, idle self-deceit ("puffed up without reason").
- Rather than taking them on a mystic heavenly journey, such teaching is to be characterized as the "sensuous mind." According to Hellenism, the mind was the higher part of the human being—the medium for entering heavenly realms—whereas the body was inferior and earthbound. In essence, Paul equates such "higher reason" with the flesh. Dunn notes, "To speak of the 'mind of flesh' was therefore in

---

7 Ibid., p. 184; and Thomas J. Sappington, *Revelation and Redemption at Colossae*, Journal for the Study of the New Testament 53 (Sheffield: JSOT Press, 1991), pp. 155–58.
8 Ibid, p. 183.

effect to deny that this Colossian worship with angels could ever have 'lifted off' from earth: even his mind was 'flesh' fast bound to earth.[9]

- Such an aberrant belief diminished the supremacy of Christ, the head of the church and the world (cf. Col. 1:15–20), and destroyed the unity of the church with its division of Christians into the categories of those who had mystic experiences and those who did not.

- It should also be noted in this connection that the Angelic Liturgy describes the angels as guarding "the temples of the King […] in their territory and in their inheritance" (4Q400 1:1:13.). It may well be, therefore, that the Songs of the Sabbath Sacrifice identify mystic experience under the supervision of angels as the means for entering into heaven, the spiritualized rendition or possibly a foretaste of the end-time possession of the land of Israel, the Deuteronomic rest. Indeed, according to Joshua 5:13–15, the angelic warrior—the "commander of the army of the Lord"—guided the Israelites in their conquest of Canaan. The War Scroll applies that motif to Michael, the Essenes' apocalyptic advocate (1QM 1:1–4, 11:11: 13:10–12; 17:7). It is most interesting in this regard to read of the inheritance of the saints in Colossians 1:9–14. In light of Paul's polemic against angels in Colossians 1:16; 2:8, 14–15 and 20, perhaps we are to understand the apostle as detracting attention from the role of angels in acquiring the heavenly rest. Rather, the Colossian church should focus on Christ. This interpretation is in keeping with the fact that "entrance" (ἐμβατευον, Col. 2:18) occurs in Judaism with reference to possessing Canaan.

Legalism: Angelic Revelation

A mirror-image reading of Colossians has suggested to a number of commentators that the Colossian heresy emphasized the capacity of humans to receive angelic, heavenly revelation via mystical experiences. Two components of that supposed divine disclosure surface in Paul's letter to the church at Colossae: wisdom (Col. 1:9, 15–20, 26–27:2:3, 23) and Law (Col. 2:8–23). More particularly, Paul seems to refute the prevalent Jewish notion that heavenly wisdom comes

---

9   Ibid, p. 183.

through obeying the Mosaic law (cf. *Sir* 24:23–26; *Bar* 3:36–4:1; *1 Enoch* 42; *4 Ezra* 4:5–5:13; *2 Apoc. Bar.* 38:1–4; 44:14; 48:24; 51:3–4; 77:15–16; 1QH 4:9–12; 6:10–12; 11:7–10; 12:11–13; 16:11–12; 1QS 5:8–10; 9:13; 11:15–18; Demons of Death 2:1–4; 4QMMT 113–12).My own analysis of these texts in another study demonstrates that there is a strong Deuteronomistic connection between wisdom and Law therein: if Israel wants to be restored to the land, it must follow God's wisdom, which is manifested through the Torah.[10]

The DSS are especially relevant to this discussion, for writings such as the *Hodayot* and the Rule of the Community, which equate divine wisdom with the Mosiac law, do so in the context of worshiping with the angels. Also of special interest in this matter are the Songs of Sabbath Sacrifice or the Angelic Liturgy (4Q400–405; 11Q17), which envision the Qumran covenanters as joining in the angelic worship of God, who is seated on the glorious chariot throne (cf. 4Q405 20–22; 1–4; 11Q17).

Interestingly enough, the themes wisdom and Law repeatedly occur in the Angelic Liturgy. To encounter the heavenly presence of God is to be made privy to his wisdom (variously called "knowledge and council" [e.g. 4Q400 1.1:5]; "wondrous mysteries" [4Q401 12.2:2]; "plan" [4Q 402 4.6]; "hidden things" [4Q402 4.11]; "wonderful revelations" [4Q402 4.14]; "wonderful words" [4Q403 1:1–46]), which involves obeying God's law based on Qumran sectarian interpretation and labeled "precepts which are engraved ordinances" (e.g., 4Q400 1.1.4–6); "stipulations" (e.g., 4Q202 1.3); and "commandments" (4Q402 4.2). To do this is to participate in the inheritance, the heavenly rest (4Q400 1:1–13).

Those DSS texts associating wisdom and Law, especially the *Hodayot*, the Rule of Community and the Angelic Liturgy, provide a very plausible backdrop against which to interpret Paul's letter to the church at Colossae. Two rejoinders to the Colossian heresy can therefore be culled from the apostle's comments:

- Divine wisdom is revealed in Christ, not mystic experience.
- Christ, God's wisdom, is received by faith, not by works of the Law.

---

10 Pate, *The Reverse of the Curse*, Part I, pp. 21-128.

Divine wisdom is revealed in Christ, not mystic experience. In several key texts in the epistle to the Colossians, Paul presents his belief that Christ is the wisdom of God, probably to counter the notion that the Torah is the locus of divine wisdom (Col. 1:9, 15–20, 26–27; 2:3). It is valuable to summarize those passages here in light of the preceding discussion.

Most probably, as a number of scholars have suggested, Colossians 1:9 is a statement made in contrast to the Jewish belief that divine wisdom is revealed through the Torah (see Deut. 4; *Wis* 15:2–3; *4 Ezra* 8:12; as well as the references already mentioned above). The DSS strengthen this hypothesis, especially since these documents, in associating wisdom and Law, root obedience to the new covenant in the eschatological reality of the Spirit, who is the medium for mystic experience (e.g., 1QH 4:9–12; 6:10–12; 1QS 5:8–10; 9:13). Paul's prayer for the Colossian Christians as specified in 1:9 can be understood, therefore, as contradicting claims like those made in the DSS. Only through Christ can one access divine wisdom and true understanding of the Spirit, "that you may be filled with the knowledge of God's will in all spiritual wisdom and understanding." According to Colossians 1:9–14, this is the only legitimate way to gain the heavenly inheritance.

Colossians 1:15–20 has long been thought by scholars to be a hymn; however, one may delineate its structure. Furthermore, it is safe to say that the majority of interpreters of this passage identify personified/hypostatized wisdom as the best conceptual background for understanding the hymn. They rightly point to the following descriptions: εἰκων του θεου του αορατου (v. 15; cf. *Wis 7:26*) πρωτοτοκος πασης κτισεως (v. 15; cf. Prov. 8:22; *Sir.* 1:4; *Wis.* 9:9; Philo [*Conf. Ling.* 146; *Agric.* 51; *Som.* 1:215]); ἐν αὐτω ἐκτισθη τα παντα (Col. 1:16; cf. Prov. 8:27–30; Irenaeus *Haer.* 189, 199) and perhaps ἀρχη (Col. 1:18; cf. Gen. 1:1 as mediated through Prov. 8:22).

It seems that in presenting Christ—God's wisdom—as cocreator and redeemer, Paul is severing the Jewish connection between wisdom and Law. First, according to Colossians 1:15–17, Christ was preexistent with God and cocreator of the universe. This statement is a frontal assault on those Jewish texts which predicated preexistence and cocreatorship of the Torah (e.g., *Jub.* 16:29; 31:32; 39:7; *Sir.* 16:29). Second, according to Colossians 1:18–20, Christ is the means for humans to be reconciled to God, not the Law. Such denigration of the Law would have been antithetical to much Jewish thinking (e.g., *Bar.* 51:7; *Sir.* 15:15; 45:5; 1QS 3:17–4:26). According to Colossians 2:13–14, the Law alienated people from each other and from God; yet Christ's death on the cross has removed the enmity of the Law.

As N. T. Wright perceptively argued, the wisdom background of Colossians 1:15–20 is itself deeply influenced by the story of Israel's sin-exile-restoration.[11] On this reading, the first part of the hymn (Col. 1:15–17) is steeped in the Jewish concept that God's wisdom is manifested through the Torah, the cocreator of the world and the special possession of Israel. This is intimately related to the prevalent idea among Jews that the world was made for Israel (see, e.g., *4 Ezra* 6:54–59; 7:11; *2 Apoc. Bar.* 14:18–19; 15:7; 21:24; *Pirke Aboth* 6:11–12; *Pss. Sol.* 18:4). The second part of the hymn (Col. 1:18–20) draws on the notion that Israel's reconciliation with God and deliverance from sin and exile is conditioned on her obedience to the Torah. Indeed, the same idea is latent in Colossians 1:9–14: adherence to the Torah, God's wisdom, is the means for implementing the restoration and deliverance from exile. Paul's take on the matter, however, is rather that Christ is divine wisdom, not the Torah, and he, not Israel, is the co-creator and goal of creation (Col. 1:15–17). His death alone, not following the Law, is the means for forgiveness of sin and the end of spiritual exile from God. Furthermore, such reconciliation applies to the cosmos, not just the nation of Israel (Col. 1:18–20).

Colossians 1:26–28 contains significant vocabulary which also occurs in the DSS: *mystery, hidden, revealed, wisdom, mature.* For Paul, however, these terms center on Christ, whereas for the DSS they focus on the Law. Those contrasts can be summarized as follows:

Both Paul and the Qumran community share the same conceptual world informing the term *mystery* (μυστηριον, Col. 1:26; cf. Rom. 11:25–26; 16:25–26; Eph. 1:9–10; 3:3–6; *r'z*, 1QS 3:23; 4:18; 1QpHab 7:5; 1Q27), which is the apocalyptic notion that the divine plan for the end times is now being revealed to the righteous. But the context of that mystery differs for Paul and Qumran. For the Essenes, the eschatological mystery is that the DSS sectaries

---

11   N. T. Wright, *The Climax of the Covenant: Christ and the Law in Pauline Theology* (Edinburgh: T & T Clark, 1991), pp. 109–110, 118.

are true Israel, while all outside that community are lost. For the apostle, however the divine mystery is that God is forming his new people from both Jew and Gentile (Col. 1:26–27). And for the Qumran community, the Law is the fence that protects it from the contamination of the world, while for Paul it is a barrier between people groups that God removed through the cross of Christ (Col. 2:13–14).

- Related to the last point, both Paul and Qumran employ the words *hidden-revealed* but with reverse intent. The DSS understand the terms *hidden-revealed* (*nistar/nigleh*) to refer to the Law. While the Mosaic Law had been revealed to (but spurned by) all Jews, the hidden meaning of the Law (the sectarian interpretation of the Torah by the teacher of Righteousness and the Qumranic leadership) is the exclusive property of the DSS covenanters (1QS 5:7–11; CD 3:12–16). This, of course, is a message of particularism. In utter contrast to the preceding understanding of the terms, for Paul the mystery of the inclusive nature of the people of God (composed of both Jew and Gentile) was hidden (ἀποκεκρυμμενον) in past ages but now has been revealed (ἐφαωερωθη) in Christ, not the Law (Col. 1:26; 2:3). This is a message of universal appeal.
- Both writings utilize the term *wisdom* (σοφια [Col. 1:28] *hokmâh* [e.g., 1QS 4:3, 18, 24; CD 2:3]) but from differing vantage points. As we noted above, according to the DSS divine wisdom resides in the Law but according to Paul it indwells in Christ (Col 1:15–20; 2:3) who inhabits his people (Col. 1:27–28).
- Both Paul and the DSS describe the status of the righteous as "mature" (*teleion* [Col. 1:28], *tāmîn* [1QS 2:2; 3:9–11, 9:9–10, 19, 12QpHab 7:1–5]), but the means for arriving at that position is at odds. For the DSS, perfection is achieved by obeying the sectaries' interpretation of the Law; for Paul, however, it is received by faith in Christ alone.

Colossians 2:3 speaks of treasures of wisdom and hidden knowledge, a concept that appears in Jewish apocalyptic texts which describe wisdom as hidden away in heaven (*1 Enoch* 42; *4 Ezra* 4:5–5:13; *2 Apoc. Bar.* 48:33–36;

cf. Job 28; Prov. 1:20–33; *Sit* 1:1–10). Because such wisdom is in heaven, it requires mystic experience to be grasped. In the preceding apocalyptic works, mystic ascent for the purpose of gaining divine wisdom goes hand in hand with God's revelation of that wisdom through the Law. The one—mystic ascent—is the means for better understanding the other—God's law, the embodiment of wisdom (e.g., *2 Apoc. Bar.* 44:14–15; 54:13–14). As noted earlier, a similar combination informs the DSS, especially the Rule of Community, *Hoydayot,* and the Angelic Liturgy. It may be, therefore, that Paul's statement in Colossians 2:3 that the treasure of wisdom resides in Christ alone was designed to counter the above thinking associated with writings like the DSS (cf. Col. 2:23).

Christ, God's wisdom, is received by faith, not the works of the Law. Paul's disassociation of wisdom and the Law continues to occupy our attention as this section highlights the legalistic aspects of the Colossian heresy. At least four considerations in this epistle point to the law of Moses as factoring into the problem.

Three nationalistic marks of Judaism are criticized by Paul in Colossians 2:8–23: circumcision (cc. 11–12), dietary laws (vv. 16, 21), and Sabbath-keeping (v. 16). Thus Dunn writes:

> None of the features of the teaching alluded to in 2:8–23 resist being understood in Jewish terms, and several can only or most plausibly be understood in Jewish terms. To be more precise, the division of the world into "circumcision and uncircumcision" (2:11–13; 3:11) and the observance of the Sabbath (2:16) would generally be recognized in the ancient world as distinctively Jewish, as indeed food and purity rules (2:16, 21) when set alongside circumcision and Sabbath (see on 2:11, 16, 21); so distinctively Jewish are they, indeed that any non-Jew adopting them would be said to be "judaizing" (adopting a Jewish way of life).[12]

The phrase "festivals, new moons, or sabbaths" was the typical Jewish language for the main festivals of Judaism (1 Chron. 23:31; 2 Chron. 2:3; 31:4; Neh. 10:33; Isa. 1:13–14; Ezek. 45:17; Hos. 2:11; *1 Macc* 10:34). Interestingly

---

12 Dunn, *Epistles to the Colossians and to Philemon,* p. 34.

enough, the Qumran community claimed to have received special revelation regarding "the holy Sabbaths and glorious feasts" and also the new moon (CD 3:14–15; 1QS 9:26–10:8; 1QM 2:4–6).

The two terms in Colossians 2:14—the "bond" or record (χειρογραφον) and the "decrees" or legal demands (δογμασιν)—contribute to the theory that it is the law of Moses that Paul criticizes in his exposé of the Colossian heresy. The word "bond" is most probably to be identified with the Jewish idea of a heavenly book or record of good and evil deeds performed by humans while on earth, to be assessed at the final judgment (Ex. 32:32–33; Ps. 69:28; Dan. 12:1; Rev. 3:5; 20:12; *1 Enoch* 89:61–64, 70–71; 108:7; *Apoc. Zeph.* 7:1–8; *T. Abr.* (rescension A) 12:7–18; 13:9–14; (rescension B) 10:7–11:7; *2 Enoch* 53:2–3; *Apoc. Paul*). According to Colossians 2:14, such a heavenly record serves to condemn humans.

The word "decrees" is the criterion against which to evaluate a person's deeds, which most likely is the law of Moses (3 *Macc* 1:3; Philo [*Le.g. All.* 1:55; *Gig.* 52]; Josephus *Ag. Ap. 1:42)*. That this interpretation is on target is demonstrated by the verbal form δογματιζω in Colossians 2:20, which alludes to the Jewish regulations of the Law (cf. Eph. 2:15). Thus the decrees intended by Paul are the *halakhic* rulings denounced in Colossians 2:11–12, 16, 21–22: circumcision, dietary laws, and Sabbath observance.

The enigmatic phrase "the elements of the world" or " the elemental spirits of the universe" (Col. 2:8, 20; cf. Gal. 4:3, 9) has generated three competing interpretations:

- The "principle" interpretation
- The "cosmological" view
- The "personalized-cosmological" interpretation

The second view, that the *stocheia* are the four basic components of the universe (earth, water, air and fire), has been essentially abandoned in the twentieth century. This is so because, among other reasons, the elements of the world almost certainly are to be equated with the rulers and authorities over whom Christ triumphed at the cross (Col. 2:15). The first view, that the *stoicheia* are the rudimentary principles of learning, the alphabet (cf. Heb. 5:12), is a viable interpretation, but again because of the personal nature of the rulers and authorities referred to in Colossians 2:15 it is a minority position.

The majority view today is the third perspective, the "personalized-cosmological" reading. There are primarily two variations within this approach, both of which associate the "elements" with angels.

One interpretation is that the elements are the angels that served as mediators of the Mosaic Law. Dunn observes that this view is precisely the same phrase used in Galatians 4:3, 9, where it is clearly linked into the Jewish law, understood as itself a kind of power set in charge of Israel like a slave-custodian or guardian (Gal. 3:23–25; 4:1–3) and given "through angels" (Gal. 3:19). The close association of the thought here with talk of Jewish festivals (Col. 2:16; cf. Gal. 4:10) and the "worship of angels" (Col. 2:18) strongly suggests the same connotation of the phrase for Colossians 2:8, 20.[13]

This understanding accords well with a comparative analysis of Hebrews and the DSS, relative to the giving of the Law through angels (contrast Heb. 1:5–2:18 with 4Q400–405).

The other variation within the personalized-cosmological view is that the elements of the world refer to angelic beings associated with the planetary bodies that exert control over humans (e.g. *Jub.* 2:2; *1 Enoch* 4:1; *T. Abr.* 13:11). It is again noteworthy that the Qumran community espoused such thinking connecting, as it did, angels with the courses of the stars and their calendar. Thus horoscope texts have been discovered among the DSS (4Q186; 4QMess Ar). Moreover, Josephus described the Essenes as believers in fate (*Ant.* 13.6.9 [172]) and could even claim that they prayed to the sun (*J. W.* 2.8.5 [128]). The preceding views need not, therefore, be mutually exclusive, for in the DSS one finds a combination of the two: the Law was mediated through angels, and following that Law (that is, the sectarian interpretation of it) harmonizes one with the heavenly bodies which are joining the heavenly hosts in worship of God, which anticipates the restoration of true Israel. Paul, however, refutes such thinking. Christ, as divine wisdom, alone should be the object of the Colossians' worship, not some heavenly trip based on scrupulous observance of the Torah.

---

13   Ibid, p. 50.

Asceticism: Angelic Purity

The last key component of the Colossian heresy is asceticism—"Do not handle, Do not taste, Do not touch" (Col. 2:21). These regulations have to do with Jewish laws of purity. Handle and touch refer to physical contact with impure objects or people (e.g., Lev. 5:2–3; 7:19, 21; 11:8; Num. 19:11–13) while taste applies to food taboos (cf. Matt. 27:34; Luke 14:24; John 2:9; Acts 10:10–14; 20:11; 23:14). The word ταπεινοφροσυνη in Colossians 2:23 suggests that such prohibitions were taken to great lengths. F. O. Francis's research on the term shows that while the word includes fasting, it encompasses a still broader range of bodily disciplines such as abstinence and stations.[14]

Such asceticism characterized the Colossians' understanding of worship, which Paul pejoratively labels having "an appearance of wisdom in promoting rigor of devotion." Most probably, therefore, the Colossian heresy taught that mystic ascent leading to worship with the angels was accomplished through severe treatment of the body. Thomas J. Sappington's study demonstrates that a prominent feature of mystic ascent as portrayed in Jewish *merkabah* texts was asceticism, including fasting (e.g., for three weeks) and sexual abstinence.[15]

With the DSS, however, we reach the epitome of asceticism in order to achieve heavenly worship with the angels. Dunn expresses the point well, calling attention to passages like Rule of the Community 6–7, which emphasizes the purity of the Essenes, and the Temple Scroll 47:3–5: "The city which I will sanctify, causing my name and sanctuary to abide [in it], shall be holy and pure of all impiety with which they can become impure. Whatever is in it shall be pure. Whatever enters is shall be pure." Likewise, the Songs of Sabbath Sacrifice asserts, "there is no unclean thing in their holy places" (4Q400 1:1:14)[16].

It is significant that a number of terms Paul employs in Colossians to describe Christians are also used in the DSS with reference to certain qualities Qumran members shared with angels: "saints" (cf. Col. 1:2 with 1QM 3:5); "inheritance" (cf. Col. 1:12 with 1QS 11:7–8); "light" as opposed to "darkness"

---

14 F. O. Francis, "Humility and Angelic Worship in Colossians 2:18," in *Conflict at Colossae*, F. O. Francis and Wayne Meeks, eds., Society of Biblical Literature Monograph Series 4 (Missoula, MT: Scholars Press, 1975), p. 168.
15 Sappington, *Revelation*, pp. 65–70.
16 Dunn, *The Epistles to Colossians and to Philemon*, pp. 191–192.

(cf. Col. 1:12–13 with 1QS 3:20–24; cf. 1QM 1:1; 8:14; 13:5–16). It should be noted in this context that the Angelic Liturgy presents the Essenes as priests (Zadokites?) probably under the influence of Ezekiel 44:10–16, whose outstanding characteristic of ritual purity (see again, e.g., 4Q400 1:1:14) qualified them to participate in the heavenly inheritance (4Q400 1:1:13).

Taken together, the preceding data suggests that the Colossian error was similar to the DSS teaching that ascetic observance of the Law admitted one into the presence of angels and the heavenly inheritance. More than that, the initiate apparently achieved the level of purity the angels enjoyed. Paul, of course, begs to differ with such a view on two counts. First, for the apostle, the true people of God include Gentiles (see Col. 1:2, 12–13, 24–29), whereas the Qumran community excluded all Gentiles and even nonobservant Jews. Second, for Paul, Christ is received by faith, not the works of the Law, as promoted by Essenes.

We may now categorize the previous data concerning *merkabah* mysticism as detected in the Colossian heresy according to the five components of realized eschatology. The *merkabah* Judaizers taught that:

A) The new age has dawned in Christ (Col. 1:12).
B) It is cosmic in that the believer in Jesus is caught up to the throne to see God and to experience the worship of angels (Col. 2:8, 15, 18, 20). In other words, mystic vision joins heaven and earth for the worshipper.
C) Jesus is the Christ (Col. 1:15–20).
D) Jesus is the wisdom of God prophesied in the Old Testament and in Second Temple Judaism (Col. 1:9, 15–20; 2:9, 16 with Prov. 8; *Baruch*; *Wisdom of Solomon*; *Sirach*; etc.)
E) Jesus as the wisdom of God empowers his followers to obey the law of Moses (Col. 2:16–23).

But Paul begs to differ with the Colossian heresy. Thus:

A) Jesus has inaugurated the age to come, but it is not yet fully realized (Col. 1:12–14; 3:1–11).

B) The believer does not need mystic experience with the angels nor with the heavenly throne, because all they need they have in Christ who resides in them (Col. 2:9).

C) Jesus is the Christ, the wisdom of God, not the Torah (Col.1:9, 15–20; 2:9–12).

D) Jesus is the embodiment of the long-awaited wisdom of Israel (1:15–20).

E) Faith in Christ has replaced the law of Moses (2:6–8, 13–23). Indeed, the Torah is associated God's enemy, the elements of the world (Col. 2:8, 20). Rather, the believer's baptism into Christ and the new covenant signifies a break with circumcision, the sign of the old covenant (Col. 2:11–12).

The Imperial Cult

Harry O. Maier has uncovered allusions to the imperial cult in Paul's letter to the Colossian church, which we categorize according to the realized eschatology that the Roman imperial cult espoused[17]:

A) Colossians 1:20b and 3:15 allude to the *pax Romana* established by Augustus.

B) Augustus' *pax Romana* was viewed as cosmic in scope. Caesar Augustus conquered Rome's enemies (Col. 2:15) and pacified them, bringing them into harmony with Rome and the world (Col. 1:19). Caesar even harmonized the races (Col. 3:11) and families (Col. 3:18–4:1). Indeed, Caesar was pictured as seated on the heavenly throne with the Greco-Roman gods (recall the *Gemma Augustea*).

C) Not only was Augustus considered the savior god who brought a new, cosmic age, so was Nero perceived in a similar light (Capurnius Siculus, *Ecl.* 4.142–46, where Nero is called "Jupiter"). Elsewhere Nero is called a "god" (Lucan, *Bell. Civ.* 1.60–66).

---

17 The following is a digest of Harry O. Maier's article, "A Sly Civility: Colossians and Empire," in *Journal for the Study of the New Testament* 27.3 (2005), pp. 323–49.

D) Recall as well the texts predicting the coming salvation of Caesar (Virgil; Horrace) and astrology (the comet).

E) The Roman triumphant processional reinforced Caesar's lordship over the earth (Col. 2:15).

Maier goes on to argue that Paul in Colossians begs to disagree with the imperial cult. Thus:

A) Jesus Christ alone has brought peace with God and humans (Col. 1:20b; 3:15).

B) Christ, not Caesar, defeated his supernatural enemies on the cross (Col. 2:15; cf. 2:8, 20) and will one day reconcile the world to God (Col. 1:15–20), including bringing harmony to the races (Col. 3:11) and the household (Col. 3:18–4:1).

C) Christ has been raised to the throne of God (Col. 1:18–20; 2:12) and has exalted Christians with him (Col. 2:12; Col. 3:1–4), although the age to come will not be complete under the parousia.

D) Christ is the predicted Messiah (Col. 1:13), the wisdom of God longed-for by Israel (Col. 1:15–20; 2:9).

E) Christians celebrate their union and triumph with Christ in baptism (Col. 2:11–12).

Thus, like the other letters of Paul we have examined in this work, Colossians too witnesses to the confluence of various religious traditions that wrecked havoc on the people of God. In Colossians, the realized eschatologies of Hellenistic religion, *merkabah* Judaizers, and the imperial cult combined to deliver a knockout punch to the Christian faith there at Colossae. No wonder Paul comes out swinging in Colossians in defense of his apocalypse of Christ.

SURVEY OF COLOSSIANS

Assuming Paul wrote the letter of Colossians, it would have been written along with the other prison epistles (Philippians, Ephesians, Philemon) probably from Rome in about AD 60–62. Colossae was located along with

Laodicea and Hieropolis (4:13) in the Lycus Valley in the central highlands of Asia Minor. Colossae lay on the great East-West trade route leading from Ephesus on the Aegean Sea to the Euphrates River. During Paul's three-year ministry in Ephesus (Acts 19:1–41), Epaphras was converted and apparently went on to found the church at Colossae (1:7–8; 4:12–13). Perhaps as a result of Epaphras' efforts or the work of other converts of Paul, churches were also established in Laodicea and Hierapolis (4:13). The Colossian church had become the target of heretical teaching which ultimately led to the writing of the Colossian letter. The main purpose of this letter is to counter the Colossian heresy. We may outline the letter thusly:

A. 1:1–14: Introduction
B. 1:15–23: The Supremacy of Christ
C. 1:24–2:7: Paul's Labor for the Church
D. 2:8–23: Paul's Critique of the Colossian Heresy
E. 3:1–4:6: Ethics of the Christian Life
F. 4:7–18: Final Greetings

A. 1:1–14: Introduction

Paul's introduction to the Colossian church consists of his: greetings (1:1–2), thanksgiving (1:3–8), and prayer for the Colossians (1:9–14).

Paul sends greetings to the church at Colossae from Timothy and himself. Paul reminds the Colossian believers that he is an apostle by the will of God, so (implied) they need to side with his teaching rather than those who were promoting the Colossian heresy. Paul calls the Colossian Christians "holy and faithful brothers in Christ," which is what he hopes the recipients will show themselves to be concerning the true gospel.

The overlapping of the two ages informs Paul's thanksgiving for the Colossians in 1:3–8. Thus the hope that is stored up for them in heaven (the age to come is not yet complete) stirs up faith in Christ and love for the saints in the present (the age to come has dawned).

Paul's prayer for the Colossian church in 1:9–14 highlights a number of blessings that are theirs because they are citizens of the kingdom of the Messiah: spiritual power, redemption, and forgiveness of sin. But the growth of the

Colossians is not complete. They need wisdom in Christ to ward off heresy, patience to endure their challenges, and they need to live like Christ.

B. 1:15–23: The Supremacy of Christ

Colossians 1:15–23 divides into two parts: Paul's hymn to Christ (1:15–20), and Paul's challenge to the Colossians in the light of the hymn (1:21–23).

Paul's magnificent hymn to Christ in vv. 15–20 highlights the supremacy of Christ. Since we have already examined the wisdom background of this piece, here we simply outline and summarize the passage. The hymn divides into two stanzas: Christ is exalted above creation (vv. 15–17); Christ is exalted in the church (vv. 18–20). Verses 17–20 equate Christ with God the creator. Christ is the outward expression of the invisible God. As such, Christ is preeminent ("firstborn") over creation. Indeed, God created the world through Christ, and in him all creation holds together. By this statement Paul wants the Colossian church to realize that Christ is superior to everything and everybody, including angels, demons, and Caesar. In verses 18–20, Paul asserts that Jesus is the Lord of the church by virtue of his resurrection from the dead. So exalted is Christ that the fullness of God dwells in him. And by Jesus' death on the cross God will put the world to rights and reconcile all of existence to himself. Not *pax Romana,* not mystic experience with angels, nor the Torah will accomplish this reconciliation, but only Jesus Christ. He is superior to all.

In light of Christ's preeminence over all creation, Paul challenges the Colossian believers to remain faithful to Christ (vv. 21–23).

C. 1:24–2:7: Paul's Labor for the Church

Paul's labor for the church is for the Gentiles in general (vv. 24–29) and for the Christians in the Lycus Valley in particular (2:1–7). In vv. 1:24–29 Paul talks about his call to be an apostle to the Gentile world. Paul's apostolic suffering and God's deliverance of him time and time again is a picture to the Gentile world of the death and resurrection of Christ. Paul's suffering, which is the cost for getting the gospel to the Gentiles, does not complete the atonement of Christ because that is already finished. Rather Paul suffers the messianic woes so that the church will suffer less of them. Apocalyptic Judaism taught that there was a quota of messianic woes to be endured and Paul hopes that his afflictions will make a dent in that quota so the church will not have to suffer as much.

The mystery that Paul speaks of here is the Old Testament promise that Gentiles will convert to Yahweh at the end of history, except that Paul reverses the order of that mystery: not restoration of Israel first, then the conversion of the Gentiles but the opposite. To this end of evangelizing the Gentiles Paul devotes all his energy. One can detect in Colossians 1 the fourfold apocalyptic message of Paul (cf. Gal. 1; Rom. 1; Eph. 3): Jesus is the Christ (1:1, 3, 7, 22, 24, 27–28), whose death and resurrection inaugurated the age to come, the kingdom of God (1:13–14, 18–20, 22). Moreover, salvation is based on faith, not the Torah (1:5, 23). Paul's calling is to spread that message to the Gentile world (1:24–29).

In Colossians 2:1–7, Paul focuses on the Gentile Christians in the Lycus Valley. In these verses Paul challenges the churches there to be faithful to the truth that Christ is the fullness of God. Christ is preexistent wisdom, not the Torah. Christ as the mystery of God should be the object of believers' worship not mystic union with angels. And Christ is Lord, not Caesar. These opening comments set the stage for Paul's critique of the Colossian heresy.

D. 2:8–23: Paul's Critique of the Colossian Heresy

Here we summarize our preceding findings above.

The deceptive philosophy that was wooing the Colossians was not divine in origin. Rather it was mere human tradition connected with pagan gods involving even the Torah used wrongly as a works salvation (v. 8). Paul reminds the Colossian Christians that all they needed was Christ, the fullness of God. Their union with his death and resurrection was superior to any union with the so-called deities of the mystery religions, whether Isis, Mithras, or Caesar (vv. 9–12).

Indeed, Christ's death on the cross absorbed the sins committed against the law of Moses and his resurrection triumphed over the demonic world that had misused the Torah as an instrument of works-salvation. Moreover, not Caesar's triumph over his enemies, but Christ's victory over all would-be contenders for his throne, is Paul's message (vv. 13–15).

Neither were the rituals associated with the Torah nor the ascetic rites that accompanied the mystery religions the means for heavenly worship. That only comes through union with Christ, the head of the cosmos and the church (vv. 16–19). Indeed, since the Colossians believers died with Christ, they also died to the Law, the worship with/of angels, regulations of the mystery religions, and even celebrations proclaiming Caesar to be Lord.

E. 3:1–4:6: Ethics of the Christian Life

In Colossians 3:1–4:6, Paul offers ethical challenges to the Colossian church: to individuals (3:1–17); for households (3:18–4:1) and to all (4:2–7).

Regarding individual ethics (3:1–17), Paul grounds the Christian lifestyle in inaugurated eschatology, which is put here in chart form:

THE AGE TO COME HAS DAWNED	THE AGE TO COME IS NOT COMPLETE
The already aspect of the age to come: Christians have been raised with Christ (3:1–3) and therefore should put on Christian graces (3:12–17)	The not yet aspect of the age to come: because the parousia has yet to happen (3:4), Christians must put off the sins of this age (3:5–11).

Regarding Christian ethics for the household (3:18–4:1), Paul alters the Roman household code of conduct by introducing reciprocity into the respective duties of the family. This too is influenced by Paul's inaugurated eschatology:

THE AGE TO COME HAS DAWNED	THE AGE TO COME IS NOT COMPLETE
The kingdom of God has dawned and thus introduces reciprocity as a sign of equality regarding the roles of husbands, fathers, masters: • Husbands, love your wives • Fathers, do not provoke your children • Masters, be fair to slaves because you too have a master	The kingdom of God is not complete, so hierarchy still remains for wives, children, and slaves: • Wives, submit to your husbands • Children, honor your parents • Slaves, obey your masters

Colossians 4:2–7 issues ethics for all Christians: They should be prayerful, wise, and filled with grace.

F. 4:7–18: Final Greetings

Paul sends greetings from his co-workers to the Colossian church from Jewish Christians: Tychicus, Onesimus (see Philemon), Aristarchus, Mark (now reclaimed for the ministry, see Acts 15:37–41), Justus, and from Gentile Christians: Epaphras, Luke, Demas.

Paul concludes his letter by asking that the letter to the Colossians be read to their sister church at Laodicea (vv. 15–16). Paul challenges Archippus (the pastor of the church at Laodicea?) to fulfill his ministry there. And then Paul, imprisoned for the gospel, sends his final greeting to the Colossian believers.

CONCLUSION TO COLOSSIANS

In summary, this chapter has identified three eschatological challenges to the Christian faith that contributed to the Colossian heresy: Hellenistic religion, Merkabah mysticism, and the imperial cult. For Paul, however, Jesus Christ trumps any of these would-be claimants for the worship of the Colossian Christians. And rightly so, for Paul rather presents Jesus Christ as the Messiah of Israel, the Savior of the world, and the Lord of the universe.

PHILEMON
AND THE OVERLAPPING
OF THE TWO AGES

This brief chapter surveys Paul's letter to Philemon. Paul wrote this short letter at the same time as Colossians ca. AD 60–62. Paul wrote this letter to Philemon, a believer in Colosse who was a slave owner (cf. Col. 4:1). One of Philemon's slaves, Onesimus, had apparently stolen from him (cf. v. 18) and then run away, which under Roman law was punishable by death. But Onesimus met Paul and through his ministry became a Christian (see v. 10). Now he was willing to return to his master, and Paul writes this personal appeal to ask that Onesimus be accepted back as a Christian brother (v. 16). We treat first the background issue of slavery according to Paul's perspective in 1 Corinthians 7:22–23 and Philemon, along with the related topic of the *Haustafeln*. Then we survey Philemon.

SLAVERY AND THE *HAUSTAFELN*

Slavery was tragically a basic element in Greco-Roman society, reaching its highest proportion in the first centuries BC and AD. Estimates vary that from one-fifth to one-third of the population was enslaved. The slave revolts in Italy and Sicily in the late republic confirm widespread social discontent at the time. Cato's account of slave labor in agriculture reveals a taskmaster mentality reminiscent of pre-Civil War American slavery. Seneca relates that a proposal in the Roman senate that slaves be required to follow a distinctive dress code was defeated, lest the slaves discover how numerous they were.

Slavery was a despicable institution, devaluing the dignity of the human being. The legal status of a slave was that of a "thing." Aristotle defined a slave as "living property" (*Politics* I.ii.4–51253b) and as a "living tool and the tool a lifeless slave" (*Nicomanean Ethics* VIII.ii). In short, the slave was subject to the absolute power of his or her master.

Although early Christianity did not officially challenge slavery, the gospel thankfully did sow the seeds that later produced its overthrow (or apparent overthrow). Paul's writings in particular, especially Galatians 3:28, have contributed much to the cause of freedom. However, the fact that Paul was a child of his day unavoidably influenced his presentation of the issue. We find, therefore, a nuanced call in his letters for social equality that was shaped by the idea of the overlapping of the two ages. Three passages necessitate comment regarding this matter.

1 Corinthians 7:22–23

This passage applies the already/not yet eschatological tension to the ancient institution of slavery. It is uncomfortably straightforward concerning the latter emphasis: "each one should remain in the situation which he was in when God called him" (v. 20; cf. vv. 17, 24). That is, Paul suggests that slaves should not aspire to obtaining freedom. He does not call the church to challenge or overthrow slavery; to have done so would have provoked the wrath of Rome on the newly established Christian religion. Paul realized that societal institutions, slavery included, would continue to remain intact in his day, and thus Christians would have to cope with the political realities of this age.

But as Scott Bartchy has carefully detailed, Paul's main point in 1 Corinthians 7:17–24 was not to absolutize social standings. In Paul's day, slaves could be freed by the process of manumission, and he in no way opposed that procedure. Bartchy shows that a slave could reject the offer of manumission. Thus, Paul did not intend to suggest that slaves should weigh the choice between freedom and slavery; rather, when they were able to become free, they should make the most of the opportunity.[1] In effect, what Paul does here is to *relativize* social standings. Slaves needed to realize that they were freedmen in Christ, and the free needed to see that they were slaves to Christ (vv. 21–22). In other words, the apostle's point is not that change is disallowed, but that it is immaterial spiritually. Seeing that one's earthly situation presents no disadvantage in fellowship with God, each person is challenged to live the Christian life at the level with which he or she is identified. This is the already aspect of Paul's eschatology—in Christ there is no slave or free.

Philemon

Philemon, like Galatians 3:28 and 1 Corinthians 7:21–22, has received bad press in its history of interpretation, particularly regarding the institution of slavery. It was used by the anti-abolitionists in America prior to the Civil War. But this is surely a wrong reading of the letter. In fact, the correct understanding of Philemon is to view it through Paul's lens of the overlapping of the two ages. The not-yet aspect is admittedly there, for Paul does indeed send Onesimus back to Philemon, changed man that he was (vv. 12–16). While Paul sincerely hopes that the slave's owner, Philemon, will not require it, and while Paul expects that the new relationship between the converted slave and master will take priority over social status, Onesimus may have to resume his servitude to Philemon in Colossae.

But Paul is not content to leave the matter there, he relativizes class status. He reverses the roles, calling himself a slave or prisoner of Christ (vv. 9–10, 13) and Onesimus a brother (v. 16). Furthermore, as a master communicator, Paul subtly tries to influence Philemon toward releasing Onesimus in a number of ways: (1) Paul hopes that Philemon will permit Onesimus to remain with him in the ministry (v. 13), which implies Onesimus' freedom. (2) Paul reminds Philemon that he owes him (Paul) a favor—since Philemon can thank Paul for his salvation (implied), he should set Onesimus free (v. 19). (3) Paul expresses his confidence in Philemon's judgment, "You will do even more than I ask" (v. 21; cf. v. 8). That is, Philemon will do more than just take Onesimus back

---

1   S. Scott Bartchy, *First-Century Slavery and I Corinthians 7:21,* Society of Biblical Literature Dissertation S 2 (Missoula, MT: Scholars Press, 1971), pp. 62–120.

with open arms—he will let him go free. (4) Probably Paul sagely relied on social pressure to help motivate Philemon to free Onesimus, inasmuch as the apostle expected that his letters would be read publicly in the house church settings and to be received as the word of God (cf. v. 2 with 1 Thess. 2:13; 5:27). Philemon would thus have felt social pressure to let Onesimus go. All these factors bear witness to the already aspect of Paul's eschatology: the age to come in which there is no class distinction has arrived in Christ.

The Haustafeln

Martin Luther first coined the word *Haustafeln,* a word meaning "house-table" or "household codes." Today the term is used for those New Testament passages that delineate the structure of Greco-Roman society, bringing to bear on it Christian conduct: Ephesians 5:22–6:9; Colossians 3:18–4:1; Titus 2:1–10; 1 Peter 2:18–3:7. One of the most insightful works done on this subject is David L. Balch's *Let Wives Be Submissive to Their Husbands.*[2] Although Balch works primarily with the husband-wife role as delineated in 1 Peter 3:1–7, his research is equally applicable to the topic of slavery as put forth in Ephesians 6:5–9; Colossians 3:22–4:1; Titus 2:9–10. Though he does not call it such, it is the eschatological tension of the intersection of the two ages that informs these *Haustafeln.*

Balch convincingly proves that the origin of the threefold division inherent to the *Haustafeln* (husbands and wives; parents and children; masters and slaves) is Greek, not Jewish or Christian. This categorization, with its attendant class status and accompanying prejudicial attitudes, can be traced back to Plato (*Laws* 627A; *Timaeus* 90c) and his student Aristotle (*Politics* I 1253a; *Nicomanean Ethics* VIII 1160b–1161a10). The emphasis in those philosophers' statements on the subject is less than positive.[3] The upshot of their comments is to stress the role of the subservient side of the ledger: Wives are to submit to their husbands;

---

2   David L. Balch, *Let Wives Be Submissive to Their Husbands,* Society of Biblical Literature Monograph Series 26 (Chico, CA: Scholars Press, 1981).

3   For example, Plato writes of children that it is "the claim of parents to rule over offspring" (*Laws* 627a); of slaves, "slaves ought to be ruled, and masters ought to rule" (*Laws* 627a); and of women, "On the subject of animals, then, the following remarks are offered: Of the men who come into the world, those who were cowards or led unrighteous lives may with reason be supposed to have changed into the nature of women in the second generation" (*Timaeus* 90c).

children are to obey their parents; slaves are to serve their masters. This mentality was bequeathed to later Roman society, especially in the absolute power conveyed to the father of the household (*paterfamilias*). Even Philo and Josephus, famous Jewish writers contemporaneous with Paul, were not able to extricate themselves from such a patriarchal attitude.[4]

This, argues Balch, is the setting in which early Christianity found itself. How was it to respond to the prevailing social norms of the day? Balch's answer is insightful—the New Testament writers utilize the *Haustafeln* in an apologetic manner. Recognizing Rome's suspicion of Christianity's message of egalitarianism (e.g., the widespread formula of Gal. 3:28; cf. also 2 Cor. 5:17) and recalling the imperial government's recent strictures on some mystery religions' espousal of equal status for all its members, the New Testament authors continued to employ the *Haustafeln* in their writings in order to alleviate any suspicion on Rome's part that Christianity desired to disrupt the fabric of society. We believe that Paul's attitude of slaves submitting to authority is sufficiently explained by Balch's thesis. It expresses the not-yet aspect of Paul's eschatology; submission and authority are facts of the age.

However, early Christianity was not content to leave the issue there. Balch goes on to demonstrate that the New Testament writers significantly qualify the *Haustafeln* by introducing into it for the first time the principle of reciprocity. The "superior" side of the ledger has its obligations, too. As Christians, husbands should love their wives; fathers are not to provoke their children; masters must treat their servants fairly. Interestingly enough, Ephesians 6:9 and Colossians 4:1 relativize the last category by reminding masters that they themselves will give an account to their heavenly Lord concerning how they treated their servants.

This principle of reciprocity surely stemmed from Paul's eschatological perspective: because the kingdom of God has dawned, there are no second-class citizens in its realm. All are equal in position before God. Nevertheless, the tension in Paul's thought remains: equality and authority attest to the reality

---

4   For Philo, see *Special Laws* II 225–27; III 169–71; *The Decalogue* 165–67. For Josephus, see *Against Apion* II. 199. For further discussion, see Balch, *Let Wives Be Submissive to Their Husbands*, pp. 52–56,

that the age to come exists in the midst of this present age. Such a tension continues into modern times.

SURVEY OF PHILEMON

Philemon can be outlined as follows:

A. Vv. 1–3: Greetings
B. Vv. 4–7: Thanksgiving and Prayer
C. Vv. 8–21: Paul's Plea for Onesimus
D. Vv. 22–25: Final Request, Greetings, and Benediction

A. Vv. 1–3: Greetings

Paul writes his letter to Philemon from a Roman (?) prison, along with Timothy's support. Philemon and Apphia (Philemon's wife) hosted a church in their home. They may have been the patrons of the congregation or the pastors, or both. Archippus was challenged in Colossians to fulfill his ministry to Laodicea (cf. Col. 4:17 with Philem. 2). Paul greets these people with God's grace and peace in Christ.

B. Vv. 4–7: Thanksgiving and Prayer

When Paul prayed for Philemon, Apphia, and Archippus he thanked God for their faith in Christ and for their love for all the saints. The more these Christian leaders share their faith the more they will experience God's goodness. Paul prays that they will continue to refresh Christians.

C. Vv. 8–21: Paul's Plea for Onesimus

In vv. 8–11, Paul reminds Philemon of the former's apostolic authority which gave Paul the right to command Philemon to welcome back Onesimus without qualification. But Paul rather appealed to Philemon on the basis of love and his suffering in prison for the gospel. Moreover, Onesimus (whose name meant "profitable") in the past proved useless to Philemon because he stole from him (v.18). But now Paul has led Onesimus to the Lord and he is ready to live up to his name.

In vv. 12–16, Paul expresses his affection for Philemon as his spiritual son. Since becoming a believer, Onesimus has served Paul in prison. Paul would have liked to have Onesimus' help in the future, but he wanted first to seek Philemon's input on the matter. Indeed, Philemon can receive Onesimus back, not as a slave, but as a brother in Christ and find him useful for years to come.

In vv. 17–21, Paul offers to pay any damages incurred by Onesimus' past behavior. If this doesn't motivate Philemon to welcome back Onesimus, even set him free, then Paul reminds Philemon that he owes much to Paul spiritually. So Paul encourages Philemon to help Paul by helping Onesimus. In point of fact, the apostle is confident that Philemon will not only welcome Onesimus back, but he will also set him free.

D. Vv. 22–25: Final Request, Greetings, and Benediction

In conclusion, Paul asks Philemon to prepare a room for him in the event Paul himself is set free by the Roman authorities. Paul then sends further greetings to Philemon and his house church and concludes by uttering a benediction on Philemon and the believers in the Lycus Valley.

CONCLUSION

We conclude this chapter on Philemon by making two remarks. First, Paul did not call slavery a sin or advocate rebellion against that hideous institution because he knew that the Roman Empire would destroy the Christian faith if he did so. So Paul did the next best thing; his message of equality in Christ sowed the seed for the eventual overthrow of slavery. Second, Paul's inaugurated eschatology stood behind his letter to Philemon: because the age to come has dawned, there is equality in Christ between slave and free, women and men, children and parents. But because the age to come is not complete awaiting the parousia, Christians should do their best in the present structures of society, however flawed they might be, to bring glory to God in it all.

Chapter 10

EPHESIANS

JUDAISM, THE IMPERIAL CULT, ARTEMIS,

AND THE BATTLE OF THE TWO AGES

A cts 19:1–41 records Paul's two- to three-year fruitful ministry in Ephesus on his third missionary trip. But such effective results did not come without a struggle: Paul met with fierce opposition from Judaism, Hellenistic religion, and the imperial cult. In what follows, we will look at that opposition through the lens of Ephesians and Acts 19.

Before proceeding ahead, however, we must address a key problem for interpreting Ephesians—does Paul[1] teach therein realized eschatology? Ephesians is

---

1   See Werner Georg Kümmel for an older survey of the issues regarding the Pauline authorship of Ephesians (*Introduction to the New Testament*. Rev. Eng. ed. Trs. Howard C. Kee [Nashville, TN: Abingdon, 1981], pp. 357–363). The following authors advocate Pauline authorship of the letter: Markus Barth, *Ephesians* AB, 2 vols., 34 (Garden City, NY: Doubleday and Co., 1974) 1:36–49; F. F. Bruce, *The Epistle to the Colossians, to Philemon and to the Ephesians*. New International Commentary on the New Testament (Grand Rapids, MI: Eerdmans, 1984) pp. 229–246; A. van Roon, *The Authenticity of Ephesians*, Supplement to Novum Testamentum 39 (Leiden: E. J. Brill, 1974); Clinton E. Arnold, *Ephesians: Power and Magic: The Concept of Power in Ephesians in Light of Its Historical Setting*, Society for New Testament Studies Monograph Series 63 (Cambridge: University Press, 1989), pp. 123–173. That the author was a later student of Paul's has more recently been restated by Andrew Lincoln (*Ephesians,* Word Biblical Commentary 42 [Waco, TX:

thought by some to offer a triumphalistic portrait of the church and a view of Christian existence which fails to embrace the dark side of life and therefore lacks the profundity of a theology of the cross with its note of God's identification with human suffering. The question is, has Ephesians replaced Paul's theology of suffering with a theology of glory? Is the latter a *fait accompli*? If so, the author will have deviated from the common pattern discovered in much of Jewish apocalypticism and in Paul which holds the two in dynamic tension. One can broach the issue by noting that the author of Ephesians does, in fact, associate the themes of glory and suffering; this is so for Christ, Paul and his audience. Our purpose at this particular juncture is to call attention to their association in the letter. "Glory" occurs five times in Ephesians, where it is predicated of God and mediated to believers through Christ. In Christ, believers share God's glorious inheritance (vv. 17–18) and such a heavenly possession will ultimately redound to God's glory (vv. 6, 12, 14). The basis for all of this is the blood of Christ (v. 7). This description, which is probably dependent on Colossians 1:13–14, 20, signifies the violent vicarious nature of Christ's death (cf. also Eph. 2:13, 16; 5:1, 25). In essence, then, according to Ephesians 1 the suffering of Christ secures for believers the glory of God. These two themes recur in Ephesians 3, where they are compressed into one sentence with reference to Paul's apostleship, "I beg you, therefore, not to become discouraged because of my sufferings on your behalf, which are for your glory" (v. 13). Scholars have been puzzled by the meaning of this statement, but Lincoln has argued that here the terms "suffering" and "glory" refer to that eschatological glory which belongs to Christians because of *Paul's* suffering. This concept is similar to, in fact draws its inspiration from, Colossians 1:24. One can basically agree with this perspective, except that in Ephesians, as was the case in Colossians, although the amount of suffering to be experienced by believers is reduced (because of Paul's absorption of persecution), it is not totally removed. Certainly believers are the recipients

---

Word Publishers, 1990], pp. lix–lxxiii) who, himself, is a "convert" to the Deutero-Pauline position. In light of current research on Pauline authorship, however, especially the work by Kenneth J. Neumann, this writer sees no inherent reason why Paul could not be the author of Ephesians (*The Authenticity of the Pauline Epistles in the Light of Stylostatistical Analysis,* Society of Biblical Literature Dissertation Series 120 [Atlanta, GA: Scholars Press, 1990]).

of divine glory (Eph. 1:6, 12–13, 17–18), but there are at least three passages in Ephesians which attest to the need for Christians to endure suffering: 4:17–24, with its ethical challenge to live righteously; 5:1, with its clarion call to believers to imitate God by sacrificially loving others, even as Christ loved them; and 6:10–18, with its appeal to the recipients to withstand their spiritual enemy. The presence of these two themes—glory and suffering—then, would seem to indicate that both realized and futurist eschatological elements are interwoven in the mind of the author. In other words, Ephesians espouses inaugurated eschatology.

We now look at the opposition Paul encountered at Ephesus as culled from his letter and Acts 19. After that, we survey the contents of Ephesians.

PAUL'S OPPOSITION AT EPHESUS

Three groups tried to stop Paul from preaching the gospel at Ephesus: non-Christian Jews; the Roman imperial cult; and Hellenistic religion, especially the worship of Artemis.

The Consistent Eschatology of Non-Christian Judaism

We know from Acts 19 that Jews in Ephesus strongly resisted Paul's apocalypse of Christ. Verses 8–9 of that chapter record that Paul preached in the synagogue in Ephesus for three months trying to persuade the Jews that the kingdom of God, the age to come, (cf. 8 with Eph. 1:21) had come in Jesus, Israel's Messiah (Acts 19:9). But the Jews rejected Paul's message, maligning the "way," that is, Jesus as the way to God, the distinctive message of early Christianity (see, for example, Acts 9:2; 18:25; 19:23; 22:4; 24:14, 22). No doubt the Jews abhorred the scandal of the cross (cf. Acts 28:23–28).

We find two other reactions to Paul's message by Jews in Ephesus. When the apostle first arrived in Ephesus, he encountered twelve Jews who still followed the baptism of John. That these Jews were not Christians is shown by the fact that they had not received the Holy Spirit and this was so because they had not yet received Christ. But thankfully these twelve accepted Christ and received the Spirit (Acts 19:1–7).

Another Jewish response to the gospel as Paul proclaimed it in Ephesus is almost funny; some Jewish exorcists tried to cast out demons in the name of

Jesus. But since these sons of Sceva, a Jewish chief priest, did not know Christ the demons bested them instead (Acts 19:13–16).

Ephesians 2:11–22 focuses on the Gentiles' conversion to Christ and incorporation into the people of God. But the flip side of this passage reveals the consistent eschatology of non-Christian Judaism. We now call attention to the five components of their eschatology as can be detected in Ephesians 2:11–22.

First, Jews expected that the Messiah would bring the age to come/ kingdom of God and, with it, peace (cf. Eph. 2:14–15, 17 with 1:21; Acts 19:8; 28:23–28).

Second, this age to come would be a new creation (Eph. 2:15), centered in the Jerusalem temple (cf. Eph. 2:21–22 with Ezek. 40–48).

Third, it would be God's Messiah who would bring the age to come; this was a covenant promise (cf. Eph. 2:12 and Rom. 9:1–5 with 2 Sam. 7:11–16).

Fourth, thus the Old Testament predicted the coming of the Messiah and the kingdom of God. By way of contrast, the Gentiles were outside the covenant with Israel and therefore were without God and hope (Eph. 2:11–12).

Fifth, the law of Moses—in particular, circumcision—was the only means to participate in God's covenant, something Jews embraced but Gentiles did not (Eph. 2:11, 14–15). Thus Jews celebrated their covenant with God and the hope for the restoration of Israel by submitting to circumcision and obeying the Torah. Indeed, because Jews practiced the Law they were confident that when the Messiah came they would enter his kingdom.

But in Ephesians 2:11–22 Paul proclaims his inaugurated eschatology in Christ:

First, Jesus has inaugurated the new covenant of peace with God, which pertains to both Jew and Gentile (Eph. 2:11, 14, 15).

Second, in Christ both Jew and Gentile are now the new creation, one new man in Christ the last Adam (Eph. 2:15). And in Christ, Gentiles are now members of the household of God (Eph. 2:19–20) and together with Christian Jews are the eschatological temple that the Messiah is building (cf. Eph. 2:21–22). It is interesting to compare Paul's concept here to the Dead Sea Scrolls which longed for the Messiah to come and build the end-time temple, a spiritual temple composed of the people of God not stone (4Q Flor. 1:1–12; 1QS 8:7–10).

Third, the cross of Jesus the Messiah (which so scandalized Jews) was precisely God's means of bringing the Torah, the barrier between Jew and Gentile, to an end (Eph. 2:14–16).[2]

Fourth, the Old Testament promises of a Messiah and the new covenant are now being fulfilled in Jesus (Eph. 2:11–13).

Fifth, not the Torah or circumcision, but faith in Christ as celebrated in baptism (cf. Eph. 2:1–10; 5:14) is the ritual of the new covenant.

Immediately following Ephesians 2:11–22 comes Paul's autobiographical piece in Ephesians 3:1–13 related to his conversion/call, which contains the apostle's fourfold eschatological message: (1) Jesus is the Christ, (2) who inaugurated the age to come, (3) which is entered into by faith, (4) including Gentiles. Recall our comments on this passage in Chapter 1.

The Realized Eschatology of the Imperial Cult

In Acts 19:40 the town clerk expressed concern that the riot in Ephesus caused by Paul's challenge to the Artemis cult (see below) might bring down the wrath of the Roman proconsul upon Ephesus. Paul Trebilco remarks on this:

> A city involved in riots could lose the respect of Roman officials (Dio, *Or.* 38.33–37), guilds which caused trouble could be disbanded, city officials could be punished, and a city could even lose its freedom (see for example Plutarch, *Praec. Ger. Reip.* 813F, 825C). In 20 BCE Cyzicus lost its freedom as a city after having permitted some Roman citizens to be put to death, apparently in connection with a riot (see Cassius Dio, 54.7.6; see also Magie 1950, p474. For another example see Tacitus *Ann.* 12.58; Suetonius, *Aug.* 47.) Further, Tacitus tells us of a situation that got out of control in Pompeii in 59 CE. During a gladiatorial show there was an "exchange of raillery" between local people and visitors from nearby Nuceria. This led to abuse, then to stone throwing and finally "to steel." Many of the Nucerians were killed or wounded. Tacitus (Tacitus, *Ann.* 14.17) notes that as a result "the Pompeians as a community were debarred from holding any

---

2   Paul may well be alluding to the Jewish warnings posted on the temple barricade forbidding Gentiles to proceed any further on pain of death. The notices were written in Greek and Latin, two of which have been discovered—one in 1871 (now in the Archaeological Museum in Istanbul) and one in 1934 (now in the Rockefeller Museum in Jerusalem).

similar assembly for ten years, and the associations (collegiaque) which that had formed illegally were dissolved."[3]

The city of Ephesus had much to fear because of the riot because the city was avidly devoted to the imperial cult: in 6 BC a temple to Augustus and Roma was built in Ephesus; the upper agora was redesigned during Augustus's rule resulting in architectural impact of the emperor which featured a statue to Augustus; by Domitian's rule (AD 81–96) Ephesus became a temple wonder of the emperor's cult, because he erected fifty-three statues to the Caesars and celebrated the imperial games. Thus in Ephesus the emperor's name or image met the eye at every turn.[4] Little wonder the Ephesians declared Caesar Hadrian (AD 117–138) their "savior." In the light of the strong presence of the imperial cult in Ephesus, we may safely assume its realized eschatology shaped the thinking of many Ephesians: Augustus the savior brought the golden age of peace, which had cosmic dimensions, was predicted of old and celebrated in the present.

We may also safely assume that what Paul said to non-Christian Jews would also apply to Caesar: Jesus is the inaugurator of the new age of peace (Eph. 2:11, 14, 15) whose ascension to heaven made him Lord over all, including Caesar (Eph. 1:19–23); about whom—the Messiah—the Old Testament witnessed (Eph. 2:11–13); whose reign is confessed in baptism (Eph. 5:14). Moreover, the household code of conduct approved by the emperor—with its demeaning of wives, abuse of children under the claim of *paterfamilias* (the father had all authority even being able to put to death his children), and violence to slaves—was transformed by the gospel such that husbands must love their wives, children, and slaves (Eph. 5:22–6:4). Furthermore, in Ephesians 6:10–18, using the imagery of the Roman soldier's armor, Paul details the ethical lifestyle of the victorious soldier of Christ in a spiritual warfare—one not withstood by even the might of Rome.

The Realized Eschatology of Hellenistic Religion

Acts 19 records the major opposition Paul faced in Ephesus—the Artemis cult. Antipater listed the temple of Artemis at Ephesus as one of the seven wonders of

3 Paul Trebilco, *The Early Christians in Ephesus from Paul to Ignatius* (Grand Rapids, MI/Cambridge: Eerdmans/Cambridge, 2007), pp. 161–62, footnote 27.
4 Ibid, pp. 35–37.

the world (Antipater of Sidon, *Anth. Paul.* 9:58). The grandeur and fame of the temple was only exceeded by the influence of the cult itself, not only in Ephesus but throughout all of Asia. We now summarize the presence of the Artemis cult in Ephesus, correlating Arnold's and Trebilco's data with the five components of the realized eschatology of Hellenistic religion. We are justified in calling the Artemis cult a Hellenistic religion because it was syncretistic, merging with the Greco-Roman pantheon Artemis (the huntress god of Greek mythology), and the mystery religions (perhaps the Cybele [Great Mother] mystery with its taurobolism).

First, the power of Artemis was thought to protect her devotees from ill fate. Clinton E. Arnold writes of this:

> The veneration of the Ephesian goddess did not come solely from her ability to be sympathetic and involved in human problems and predicaments of her worshippers. This aspect of her character was equally matched in the eyes of her suppliants by her transcendent power ... her ability to help her worshippers stemmed, in fact, from her awesome power. It was because of her supra-natural powers that she could intercede between her followers and the cruel fate which plagued them.[5]

Though debated, the egg-shaped objects on the front of the cult image may have been breasts, symbolizing that Artemis was the goddess of fertility.[6] Thus Artemis brought peace and perhaps fertility to her followers. Indeed, the *Ephesia Grammata* associated Artemis with magic.[7] The burning of books of magic and the decrease in sales of silver statues of Artemis in Acts 19 attest to that perception of Artemis.

Second, Artemis originated in heaven and came to earth (see Acts 19:35). And the devotee of Artemis was united with her through observance of the mystery. Arnold writes:

> There is a substantial amount of inscriptional evidence indicating the performance of certain mysteries in the cult of Artemis. On the basis of evidence

---

5   Clinton E. Arnold, *Ephesians: Power and Magic,* p. 21.
6   Trebilco, *The Early Christians in Ephesus from Paul to Ignatius,* pp. 22–23.
7   Arnold, *Ephesians: Power and Magic,* pp. 22–24.

from Strabo (14.1.20), Oster concludes that one of the occasions for the performance of the mystery was at the annual festival celebrating the birth of Artemis. Apart from this, there is virtually no other source giving us an insight into the nature of her mysteries. It could be assumed that her mysteries followed the general pattern of mystery rites, best known for their performance at Eleusis. This might partially be supported by Artemis' occasional identification with Persephone in the magical papyri. Further understanding of her mysteries might also be attained by observing what took place in the mysteries of Cybele, especially the Taurobolium. In this right the blood of a slaughtered bull was drained through the lattices of the altar onto the neophyte below, where the strength of the beast was allegedly transferred into the limbs of the devotee. The worship of Artemis is also thought to have been orgiastic in nature, with sacred prostitution as part of the ceremony.[8]

According to Acts 19:28, 34, the Ephesians felt a close bond with Artemis, even calling themselves the "temple warden (νεοκορος)" of Artemis (Acts 19:35).

Third, Artemis was thought to be divine. Oster has well summarized the inscriptional evidence extolling her transcendent power and supernatural character: "To those who called upon Artemis she was savior … Lord … and Queen of the Cosmos…. She was a heavenly goddess … whose being and character could only be described in superlatives."[9]

Fourth, Artemis' close association with the signs of the Zodiac might indicate the stars predicted her coming.

Fifth, Trebilco writes of two annual festivals that Ephesus celebrated in honor of Artemis:

We know of two major festivals held in honor of Artemis of Ephesus. The Artemisia was held annually in the month of Artemision (March-April), both names being derived from Artemis. The Artemisia probably included athletic, theatrical and musical competitions. One of the reasons for the popularity of the Artemisia may have been the custom described by Xenophon of Ephesus,

---

8 Ibid, pp. 26–27.
9 Quoted in Ibid, p. 21.

who said in his romance that it had become traditional for young women to select their fiancés, and young men their brides at this festival. As a result, according to Xenophon, at the time of the festival the city was full of local citizens as well as many visitors. A second festival was the celebration of the nativity of Artemis of Ephesus, held on the 6th of Thargelion (May-June). Oster notes: "Because of Artemis' close tie with the city of Ephesus, and because legend reported that it was the site of her nativity, we can be sure that this was one of the largest and most magnificent religious celebrations in Ephesus' liturgical calendar." The Salutaris inscriptions tells us that during this festival as on other occasions, a procession which included people who carried images of Artemis along with other images, departed from the Artemisium, entered the city at the Magnesian Gate, continued to the theater, left the city by the Koressos Gate and returned to the Artemisium. We also learn about some of the cultic acts performed during the nativity celebrations of Artemis from Strabo, who tells us something of what took place at Ortygia, the birth place of Artemis of Ephesus. Strabo writes: "A general festival is held there annually; and by a certain custom the youths vie for honour, particularly in the splendor of their banquets there. At that time, also, a special college of the Kouretes hold symposiums and perform certain mystic sacrifices. We can suggest that on the day of the festival "the whole city of Ephesus would have been decked out to celebrate the birthday party of Artemis …Visitors from around the whole Greek-speaking world [would have] come to see the annual re-enactment of Artemis' birth.[10]

These five points of the realized eschatology of the Artemis cult in Ephesus are tapped into by Acts 19, as we noted above.

But Paul opposed such fanciful thinking with his apocalypse of Christ. We may detect in Ephesians Paul's rebuttal of each of the preceding five points:

First, Christ, not Artemis, possesses supreme power (1:19–23; 2:6–7; 4:8–10; 6:10–18).

Second, Christ is the cosmic ruler (1:19–23; 4:8–10) whose death/resurrection has inaugurated the age to come (2:7, 13). And Christians are mystically

10 Trebilco, *The Early Christians in Ephesus from Paul to Ignatius*, pp.24–25.

united with him, not through the mystery religions, but through faith (2:6–8). Indeed the reconciliation of Jew and Gentile in Christ (2:11–22) is a foretaste of the coming reconciliation of the entire cosmos (1:9–10; 3:10–12).

Third, Jesus, not Artemis, is the Lord of all (1:3, 17; 3:11; 4:5; 5:19; 6:23–24).

Fourth, election in Christ from eternity past trumps any astrological soothsaying of Artemis. Arnold writes of this:

> We would safely say, however, that the author's concept of election in Christ would provide a comforting and instructive counter to the fears of Christians formerly under the influence of magic, the mysteries, and astrological beliefs. Christians who before their conversion received false comfort from Artemis by viewing the zodiacal signs so prominently depicted on her cultic image and assuming that their goddess held sway over the "powers" controlling fate would now experience true and profound comfort knowing that they had been chosen by God before the foundation of the world. There would be no reason for these converts to consult either Artemis or any other pagan deity for oracular advice. Their fate does not rest in the whims of hostile spiritual "powers." Their future is secure and blessed by virtue of their election in Christ.[11]

Fifth, Christians in Ephesus had their celebration too—baptism. Indeed, some interpreters have looked upon the letter of Ephesians itself as a baptismal homily.[12]

We may cite in this regard the baptismal context of the liturgical setting of Ephesians 1:1–14, the reception of the Spirit in 1:13–14, the mention of baptism in the creedal confession in 4:5, and the baptismal hymn of 5:14, to mention only a few references.

From Acts 19 and Ephesians, then, we see how Paul's apocalypse of Christ contradicted the eschatologies of non-Christian Judaism, the imperial cult, and Hellenistic syncretistic religion, especially the Artemis cult.

---

11 Arnold, *Ephesians: Power and Magic*, pp. 128–29.
12 Lincoln, *Paradise Now and Not Yet*, pp. 136–38.

Survey of Ephesians

We believe that Paul wrote Ephesians, as he did Philippians, Colossians, and Philemon, under house arrest in Rome ca. 60–62. The letter to Ephesians was most likely a circular letter written to not only Ephesus but other towns in the nearby area. The theme of the letter is "in Christ"; who Christians are in Christ (1:3–3:20) and how Christians in Christ should live (4:1–6:20). We may outline the book thusly:

A. 1:1–2: Greetings
B. 1:3–3:21: Christians Are in Christ
   - 1:3–14: Blessings in Christ
   - 1:15–23: Paul's prayer that Christians may realize their blessings in Christ
   - 2:1–10: Being in Christ is based on God's grace received through faith
   - 2:11–22: Being in Christ means one new man
   - 3:1–13: Paul the messenger of being in Christ
   - 3:14–21: Paul's second prayer that Christians may realize their blessings in Christ
C. 4:1–6:20: How Christians in Christ Should Live
   - 4:1–6: In unity
   - 4:7–16: In ministry and maturity
   - 4:17–5:21: In purity
   - 5:22–6:9: In harmony
   - 6:10–20: In victory
D. 6:21–24: Conclusion

Apparently, Christians in and around Ephesus were feeling inferior to Israel; they felt intimidated by the imperial cult; and they were enticed to go back to the Artemis cult. Paul counters such competition by reminding the Ephesian Christians (who were mostly Gentiles) to realize how exalted they were in Christ.

A. 1:1–2: Greetings

Paul begins the letter to Ephesians by identifying himself as an apostle of

Christ Jesus. Although it is debated, Paul may switch the order of "Jesus Christ" to "Christ Jesus" when he wants to emphasize his unique teaching on "in Christ" mysticism. Paul is an apostle of Christ by the will of God. He writes to the saints—Christians—in Ephesus. "In Ephesus" is not in the oldest Greek manuscripts, so the letter probably was circular, sent to Ephesus and the adjacent areas. "Saints" was a term for Israel now applied to the church, including Gentiles. Paul sends to them God's grace and peace.

B. 1:3–3:21: Christians Are in Christ

1:3–14: Blessings in Christ

Ephesians 1:3–14 is one long sentence in the Greek, declaring the blessings that belong to the Ephesian Christians. We may outline those blessings along the line of blessings from the Father (vv. 4–6), from the Son (vv. 7–12), and from the Spirit (vv. 13–14).

The blessing of the Father upon Christians is that they are predestined to be his sons (vv. 3–6). Interpreters debate whether Paul is speaking of God's election of individual Christians or the church. Either way, the message of vv. 3–6 is that Christians are secure in Christ. Not Judaism, the imperial cult, or Artemis can take that way away. For before the creation of the world, God determined that his people would persevere in faith and holiness until the parousia.

The blessing of Christ upon the believer is redemption based on the cross (vv. 7–12). And this redemption will one day include the entire cosmos. God has predestined this to be so. Thus God has already redeemed us in Christ but not yet has the cosmos been reconciled to God. This awaits the return of Christ. We see in this Paul's inaugurated eschatology.

The blessing of the Spirit is his indwelling in the believer, which is the promised Spirit of the new covenant (see Joel 2:28–29; Ezek. 36:25–28). This is the already aspect of eschatology—the Spirit indwells the believer. The not-yet aspect is that only at the parousia will believers receive their resurrection body.

1:15–23: Paul's prayer that Christians may realize their blessings in Christ

In Paul's first prayer for his audience, he prays that they may realize their blessings in Christ. His prayer consists of two parts in that regard. First, Paul prays that God will give the Ephesians the wisdom to see the hope of their calling (vv. 17–18). Second, the apostle prays that God will empower the Ephesians to reach that heavenly calling (vv. 19–23). Various terms for power are used here: "power," "working," "strength," "exertion." The net effect is that the Ephesians need to see that the power of God is at their disposal for overcoming any and all obstacles. The same power that raised Christ from the dead is at work in the Christian. Indeed God's resurrection power and the fullness of Christ are manifested through the church in this age and in the ages to come. These words tap into the Jewish two-age structure that early Christianity modified into inaugurated eschatology.

2:1–10: Being in Christ is based on God's grace received through faith

In 2:1–10, Paul paints a before and after picture. Before Christians were converted they, like the non-Christian world, were spiritually dead in their sins. They were under the sway of the devil (cf. 4:27; 6:11), the ruler of this world, the spirit behind all disobedience. Paul could be saying here that behind the stars of astrology, the imperial cult, the Artemis cult, is the devil, the god of this world (2 Cor. 4:4). This malevolent personage blinds people to the gospel and enchains them in fear.

But the Ephesians were converted to Christ by the grace of God through faith, and made alive spiritually. We see Paul's inaugurated eschatology in vv. 4–10. Christians have already been raised to heaven and seated with Christ (vv. 4–9) but they still live in this age and need to become what God created them to be (v. 10).

2:11–22: Being in Christ means one new man

As we noted in the first section of this chapter, Ephesians 2:11–22 strengthens the faith of the Gentile Christians by informing them that they are now a part of the people of God. Judaism has nothing over them. In Christ, Gentile believers participate in the new covenant (vv. 11–13). In Christ, the Gentile church is united to Jewish Christians to form the new creation of one man. This is because Jesus' death removed the Torah that had separated the two people groups (vv. 14–18). In Christ, Gentile and Jewish believers form the new temple of God, built on the foundation of the apostles and prophets with Jesus Christ as the cornerstone and indwelled by the Holy Spirit. Not a building, but the body of Christ is the true temple of God's residence (vv. 19–22).

Chapter 10

3:1–13: Paul the messenger of being in Christ
We recall Paul's fourfold eschatological message in 3:1–13. First, Jesus is the Christ (vs. 1). Second, the mystery that Paul preaches is that Old Testament prophecy is now being revealed through the apostle—Gentiles in Christ are now a part of the people of God (vv. 2–9). Another way to put it is that Christ has inaugurated the age to come, the time of fulfillment of Old Testament prophecy/mystery. Third, salvation is based on faith (v. 12), not works (2:8–9). Fourth, Paul's focus is on Gentiles. He is suffering the messianic woes on behalf of the Gentile church (vv. 11–13). This reconciliation of Jew and Gentile in Christ is an object lesson to the heavenly authorities, that they will one day bow before Christ. Thereby the cosmos will be reconciled to God, willingly or unwillingly (v. 10; cf. 1:9–10; 6:10–18).

3:14–21: Paul's second prayer that Christians may realize their blessings in Christ
Paul prays a second time for his readers. He prays that they will be divinely empowered to let Christ indwell them through faith (vv. 16–17). And he prays that God will empower them to know the unsurpassable love of Christ (vv. 17b–19). So the Ephesian believers are not the temple of Artemis but the Temple of God. And true love is to be found in Christ, not in some sexual encounter with the erotic rituals of Artemis and the mystery religions.

Paul concludes the first part of his letter with a benediction: to God be the glory whose power can give the victory to the Ephesian church (vv. 20–21). This is something it needed to hear in the face of non-Christian Judaism, the imperial cult, and the Artemis industry.

C. 4:1–6:20: How Christians in Christ Should Live
The first part of the letter to Ephesus is doctrine; who the believers are in Christ. The second part of the letter is duty; how believers in Christ should live.

4:1–6: In unity
The first mark of the Christian life Paul calls attention to here is unity. In 4:1–3, Paul talks about the attitude that produces the unity of the Spirit—humility. In vv. 4–6, Paul lists the basis of Christian unity; one body—the

body of Christ; one spirit—the Holy Spirit; one hope—the parousia; one Lord—Jesus Christ; one faith—the Christian faith; one baptism—water baptism as confessing one's faith in Christ and union with Christ; one God and Father—monotheism.

4:7–16: Ministry and maturity

Paul makes two points in 4:7–16. First, Christians are spiritually gifted, thanks to the victorious ascension of Christ. Christ is the one that descended to earth at his incarnation and ascended back to heaven at his resurrection. Now, by his Spirit, he endows church leaders to equip the saints to use their gifts in ministry (4:7–12). Second, as Christians grow in ministry they will grow into maturity in Christ. This will prevent the Ephesian believers from being deceived by doctrinal error found in non-Christian Judaism, the imperial cult, and the worship of Artemis. Rather, the believer will develop discernment in truth and love. Consequently the church will grow into the likeness of Christ (4:13–16).

4:17–5:21: In purity

This extensive section deals with Christian purity. In 4:17–19, Paul describes the past lives of the church. Before their conversion, the Gentile Christians (a hint that the Ephesian church and surrounding churches were predominately Gentiles) lived impure lives due to ignorance toward God (4:17–19). No doubt Paul has in mind the pagan lifestyle of the Artemis and imperial cults.

But that all changed with the Ephesians' conversion to Christ, for they have put off the old nature of sin and put on the new nature of righteousness (4:20–24).

Ephesians 4:25–32 amplifies the impure lifestyle that believers are to be done with: lying, anger, theft, unwholesome speech, grieving the Holy Spirit through bitterness, brawling, slander. Rather Christians should forgive others as Christ has forgiven them.

Ephesians 5:1–21 switches from the contrast of putting off/putting on to darkness/light in describing the purity of the Christian life. This section can be cared for by way of a chart:

DARKNESS: PAST PAGAN BEHAVIOR:	LIGHT: PRESENT CHRISTIAN BEHAVIOR:
5:3–7: immorality, greed, obscenity, idolatry	5:8–14: goodness, righteousness, truth
5:15–18a: drunkenness	5:18b–21: filled with the Spirit which results in joy, thankfulness, and submission

5:22–6:9: In harmony

Ephesians 5:22–6:9 speaks of Christian harmony in the household. The *Haustafeln* in Colossians 3:18–4:1 is here expanded. Even here there is a contrast before and after the Ephesians' conversion. In pagan Greco-Roman culture the familiar obligations looked like this:

- Wives—submit to your husbands (5:22–24)
- Children—obey your parents (6:1–3)
- Slaves—obey your masters (6:5–8)

But Christian conduct introduced the principle of reciprocity into the household:

- Husbands—love your wives (5:25–33)
- Fathers—nurture your children (6:4)
- Masters—respect your slaves (6:9)

The result of such reciprocity is harmony in the home.

6:10–20: In victory

Ephesians 6:10–20, along with 1:3–14, expresses Paul's inaugurated eschatology. Thus believers experience the age to come in that they have been raised to the heavenlies in Christ (13–14). But Christians are still in this present evil age and therefore must do battle with the devil (6:10–12). But victory belongs to the Christian in the form of the armor of God: the belt of truth, the breastplate of righteousness, the shoes of the gospel, the shield of faith, the helmet of salvation, and the sword of the Spirit, and prayer (6:13–18). One can detect in this description an irony: Paul compares each of the pieces of the armor of a Roman soldier to Christian character traits precisely to defeat the imperial cult. But the battle is not physical in nature but spiritual. And because the battle is the Lord's, victory belongs to the Christian.

D. 6:21–24: Conclusion

Paul will send Tychicus to deliver the letter of "Ephesians" and greet the believers there (vv. 21–22). Paul concludes his magnificent letter to the Ephesians by wishing them peace, love, faith, and grace (vv. 23–24).

CONCLUSION TO EPHESIANS

In concluding our study of Ephesians, we have argued that the Christians at Ephesus (mostly Gentiles) felt inferior to Israel; they were intimidated by the imperial cult; and they were enticed to go back to their former comfort zone with the Artemis cult. Paul, however, reminds the believers there that they were saved, raised, and exalted in Christ. To reign with him surpassed Judaism, Caesar, and Artemis combined. Therefore, the Ephesian Christians must put on the armor of God and boldly engage those hostile powers to the Gospel, knowing that the battle belonged to the Lord.

Chapter 11

THE PASTORALS

HELLENISTIC RELIGION, THE IMPERIAL CULT, PHILONIC MYSTICAL EXEGESIS, AND PAUL'S INAUGURATED ESCHATOLOGY

Those who assume Pauline authorship in some measure for the Pastoral Epistles (1, 2 Timothy and Titus) typically envision the following scenario: After Paul's house arrest in Rome (Acts 28), he was released (AD 62). After that, he most likely began a fourth missionary journey. That looked something like the following:

- Spain—62–64 (Rom. 15:24; 8; cf. Euseubius *Eclessiastical History* 2.22.2–3; Clement of Rome, *Epistle to the Corinthians*, chp. 5; *Muratorian Canon*, Lines 34–39).

- Crete—64–65 (Titus 1:5), where Paul had Titus to remain to be Paul's representative at the church
- Miletus—65 (2 Tim. 4:20).
- Colosse—66 (Philem. 22)

- Ephesus—66 (1 Tim. 1:3), where Paul left Timothy in charge of the church there
- Philippi—66 (Phil. 2:23–24; 1 Tim. 1:3), where Paul wrote 1 Timothy and Titus.
- Nicopolis—66–67 (Titus 3:12)
- Rome—67 and martyrdom in 67/68, before which he wrote 2 Timothy. Luke might have helped Paul to write 2 Timothy (2 Tim. 4:11), since the apostle was confined in prison.[1]

Key themes recur throughout the Pastoral Letters: God the Savior, sound doctrine, faith, teaching, godliness, controversies, and trustworthy sayings. As we say during the course of this chapter, all of these themes touch upon Paul's opposition in Ephesus. Such opposition was comprised of Hellenistic syncretistic religion, the imperial cult, and Philonic mystical exegesis—all of which contributed to the problem of realized eschatology in the Ephesian church and nearby congregations. We will cover these three opponents in the first part of our chapter, and then in the second part survey the contents of the Pastoral Epistles.

PAULINE OPPOSITION IN THE PASTORAL EPISTLES

Hellenistic Syncretistic Religion

The Artemis Connection
a. The Artemis Cult at Ephesus. In the last chapter we highlighted the influence of the Artemis cult and its integration with Greco-Roman worship and the mystery religions upon Ephesus and the churches nearby. Such realized eschatology continued to exert its influence on the Christians at Ephesus some five to ten years later at the time of the writing of the Pastorals, in at least three ways. First, some of the Ephesian Christian women were dressing in the immodest manner of Artemesian priestesses (1 Tim. 2:9–10). Those same Ephesian women had succumbed to false teaching to the effect that they were liberated from the authority of male leadership in the church (1 Tim. 2:11–14). And, third, young widows no longer were getting

---

1   The *New International Version* provides this typical scenario, p. 1872.

married to show their freedom from the authority of a husband (1 Tim. 2:15; cf. 4:3; 5:13–15). Although it is a second-century document, one can see how such a viewpoint is expressed in the *Acts of Paul and Thecla:*

The *Acts* seem to be an alternative interpretation of the Pauline tradition to that found in the Pastorals or the Acts of the Apostles, and a tradition which continues the traditions of women's leadership, celibacy, and greater social equality among Christians. It has been suggested that when the pastor argues against the teaching activity of women (1 Tim. 2:9–15) against celibacy (1 Tim. 4:3) and writes in 1 Tim 4:7 that his readers should "have nothing to do with godless myths and old wives' tales," the pastor is countering the sorts of traditions about Paul which are later found in the *Acts of Paul and Thecla,* in which Paul is an advocate that women should adopt traditional gender roles.[2]

Closer to home, the Kroegers[3] and Sharon Gritz[4] have argued that Paul's opponents in Ephesus taught the priority of Eve over Adam, and that Eve enlightened Adam with her teaching. Paul's restriction on women was therefore intended to counter some Christian women's devotion to Artemis, who was portrayed as the origin and illuminator of men.

b. Paul's Rebuttal. Paul offers three strictures in 1 Timothy 2:9–15 to such a perspective.[5] In this passage, Paul stresses three areas in which he believes Christian women should display an attitude of submission: (1) They are to show their compliant spirit by wearing modest adornment (1 Tim. 2:9–10), a standard apparently upheld by Gentiles (see Juvenal's *Satire* 6, Seneca, *To Helvia* 16:3–4), Jews (see Prov. 7:10–17; *T. Reu.* 5:1–5; *1 Enoch* 8:1–2), and Christians (1 Peter 3:1–6) alike. This deference in dress may well reflect Paul's abhorrence of the immodest attire that characterized the prostitute priestesses of the Artemis cult in Ephesus. (2) Christian women are to refrain from teaching or exercising authority over men (vv. 11–12). Recent exegetes of this text tend to mitigate the

---

2   Trebilco, *The Early Christians in Ephesus…*, p. 518.

3   R. C. Kroeger and C. C. Kroeger, *I Suffer Not a Woman: Rethinking 1 Timothy 2:11–15 in Light of Ancient Evidence* (Grand Rapids, MI: Baker. 1992).

4   Sharon H. Gritz, *Paul, Women Teachers, and the Mother Goddess at Ephesus: A Study of 1 Timothy 2:9–15 in Light of the Religious and Cultural Milieu of the First Century* (Lanham, MD: University Press, 1991).

5   Pate, *The End of the Age Has Come*, pp. 212–215.

stringency of these words by restricting their application to the subordination of wives to their husbands, or to the forbidding of interruptions of the worship services. These attempts are certainly understandable but they most probably involve reading modern sensibilities into the text, for a comprehensive prohibition of any leadership office seems clearly indicated by the words. In other words, 1 Timothy 2:1–12, like 1 Corinthians 14:33–35, seem to restrict women from uttering prophecies or authoritative teachings in the worship service in the presence of men, in keeping with the created order (Gen. 2–3). (3) Christian women will be saved by embracing the role of motherhood, especially the pain of childbirth (vv. 13–15). These words pose a hermeneutical thicket and have generated three basic interpretations. (a) "She will be *safely kept* through childbearing," with the term σωθησεται connoting physical preservation. But aside from the fact that the statement is simply not true (many Christian women have not survived childbirth), this rendering stumbles because σωζειν conveys a theological sense in the Pastorals (1 Tim. 1:15; 2:4; 4:16; 2 Tim. 1:9; 4:18; Titus 3:5), and because δια (through) is not taken in its normal instrumental sense. (b) "She will be saved through the childbearing," i.e., through the birth of Christ through Mary, the new Eve. While a messianic reading of Genesis 3:16 is possible in the context of 1 Timothy 2, nevertheless the word τεκνογονιας should be translated generically ("childbearing"), not specifically ("the childbearing"). (c) "She will be saved through childbearing." In other words the wife's path to salvation consists in accepting the role which was plainly laid down for her in Genesis 3:16 ("in pain you shall bring forth children").

Unpalatable as this may be to contemporary thought this third view seems to be the most natural reading of the text, both grammatically and contextually. Grammatically, this translation ascribes the customary theological sense to the word σωζειν and the normal instrumental rendering of δια ("through"). Moreover, it rightly translates τεκνογονιας in the generic sense—"childbearing." Contextually, this interpretation best takes into account the polemic of Paul, who undoubtedly aims his comments in 1 Timothy 2:15 and 4:3–4 at the false teachers who propagated disparaging views about marriage and sex. These people were not unlike the later Gnostics who, as Irenaeus described them , declared that marriage and the begetting of children are of Satan (*Heresies* 1.24.2). But according to 1 Timothy 2:13–15, Christian women rather express their faith, love, and holiness (v. 15b) through good works (v. 10), the most significant of which is submitting to the divine plan of bearing children, painful though it is (v. 15a). Such obedience transforms the curse of Genesis 3:16 into a blessing—it brings salvation (1 Tim. 2:15).

This subordinationist emphasis in 1 Timothy 2:9–15 bespeaks of the continuing presence of this age. But this does not mean that Paul overlooks the fact that the age to come has arrived. It is eminently possible, as recent authors have suggested (see the authors below), that the church at Ephesus, to whom Paul wrote 1 and 2 Timothy, had now come to believe that the age to come had fully arrived and therefore championed the casting off of all sexual distinctions. Paul thus used the submission principle to correct this emancipationist misconception. Probably three major strands of thought intersected to produce this rival message: (1) This group may well have appealed to the apostle's egalitarian attitude as identified in the tradition behind 1 Corinthians 12:13, Galatians 3:28, and Colossians 3:11. (2) The espousal of realized eschatology by these people, as William Lane, Gordon Fee, and Phillip H. Towner have shown, prompted them to proclaim the full arrival of the age to come and, with it, the new creation; hence the dissolution of all social distinctions and barriers.[6] (3) It may be that the Ephesian church took the contents of Paul's original letter to them too far, turning the apostle's inaugurated eschatology into realized eschatology.

Therefore, it can be proposed that Paul, in order to counteract this situation, responds in a twofold way here: (1) He introduces the principle of submission into the eschatological scheme of things to demonstrate that the age to come has already arrived but is not yet complete. Christians continue to live in this age. (2) More than that, Paul roots hierarchy and subordination in creation itself, before the Fall (1 Tim. 2:13), so that even though he believes the new creation has dawned in Christ, the apostle operates on the assumption that it, too, must follow the divinely prescribed chain of authority. On this reading, eschatological tension continues to characterize Paul's thoughts in 1 Timothy 2:9–15. This is his inaugurated eschatology.

---

6   William L. Lane, "1 Tim. Iv. 1–3. An Early Instance of Over-Realized Eschatology?" *New Testament Studies* 11 (1965), pp. 164–67; Gordon Fee, *1 and 2 Timothy, Titus* (Peabody, MA: Hendrickson Publishers, 1988); Philip Towner, *The Goal of Our Instructions. The Structure of Theology and Ethics in the Pastoral Epistles*, Journal for the Study of the New Testament Supplement Series 34 (Sheffield: JSOT Press, 1989).

The Imperial Cult

In the last chapter we discussed the importance of the imperial cult as a part of the background of Paul's letter to the Ephesians. Here we simply call attention to the language and ideology of the imperial cult as alluded to in the Pastoral Epistles. As Frances Young observes, "More than other New Testament texts the pastorals evidence the language that so intriguingly parallels the 'ruler-cult.'"[7] Some six points of contact with the worship of Caesar emerge in the Pastoral Epistles. Some of these were first pointed out by Adolf Deissmann in his monumental *Light from the Ancient East.*[8]

First, "gospel," "good news" (*evangelion)* was used in the Priene inscription regarding the *pax Romana* brought about by Augustus (cf. 1 Tim. 1:11; 2 Tim. 1:8, 10; 2:8).

Second, "appearance" (*epiphany*) as used in Greco-Roman literature for the appearance of the god to mortals was applied to the Caesars. Thus, for example, in an official inscription, the town council of Ephesus spoke of Julius Caesar as the "God made manifest (*epiphany*), offspring of Ares and Aphrodite, and common savior of human life" (cf. ἐπιφανεια in 1 Tim. 6:14; 2 Tim. 1:10; 4:1, 8; Titus 2:13, ἐπιφαινω in Titus 2:11; 3:4, and φανερω in I Tim. 3:16; 2 Tim. 1:10; Titus 1:3).[9]

Third, Caesar brought salvation (σωτερια) as a savior (σωτερ), as the above Ephesian inscription declares, along with other inscriptions (cf. 1 Tim. 6:14; 2 Tim. 1:10; Titus 2:13).[10] Indeed, the title "savior of the world" was applied to Julius Caesar, Augustus, Claudius, Vespasian, Titus, Hadrian and other emperors in Eastern inscriptions.[11]

Fourth, Caesar was proclaimed "Lord" (κυριος), especially in the Eastern Empire, as is evidenced from many inscriptions, ostraca, and papyri (cf. 1 Tim. 1:2, 12; 6:3, 14–15; 2 Tim. 1:2, 8; 4:8, 17–18, 22).[12]

---

7   Frances Young, *The Theology of the Pastoral Letters.* New Testament Theology (Cambridge: Cambridge University Press, 1994), p. 65.

8   Adolf Deissmann, *Light from the Ancient East: The New Testament Illustrated by Recently Discovered Texts of the Graeco-Roman World,* trans. by Lionel R. M. Strachan (Peabody, MA: Hendrickson, 1995; reprint from 1927), pp. 349–78.

9   Ibid, pp. 348–49.

10 Ibid, p. 369.

11 Young, *The Theology of the Pastoral Letters,* p. 64.

12 Deissmann, *Light from the Ancient East,* p. 357.

Fifth, "godliness" (ἐυσεβεια and cognates) are found thirteen times in the Pastorals (1 Tim. 2:2; 3:16; 4:7–8; 6:3, 5–6, 11; 2 Tim. 3:5; Titus 1:1 (ἐυσεβεια), 1 Tim. 5:4 (ἐυσεβειν), 2 Tim. 3:12; Titus 2:12 (*eusebos*). It will be recalled from an earlier chapter that Caesar Augustus's ἐυσεβεια/pietas was manifest in his respect for the Greco-Roman pantheon of deities. In the *Salutaris* inscription in Ephesus (ca. AD 103/4), the proconsul of Asia writes, "May I congratulate him that his piety (*eusebian*) toward the goddess [Artemis] and the Augusti [followers of Augustus] and his goodwill toward the city in the theatre now become clear to all.[13]

Sixth, Malcolm Gill argues that "mediator" (μεσιτης) in 1 Timothy 2:5 is a polemic against the claim of Roman emperors to be the mediator between the gods and the humans.[14]

Paul obviously will have none of the imperial cult. Francis Young summarizes Paul's polemic against it in the Pastorals:

> … this Saviour Christ is the true, universal Saviour, manifested according to the providential plan of the universal God who is Saviour of all, but this Lord demands exclusive loyalty, and is therefore not only the universal Saviour but the particular Saviour and Lord of those who entrust themselves to his plan. His "epiphany" as the man Jesus Christ, and his return as Lord and Judge, rival the claims of Lord Caesar, Saviour of the world; and Christ's slaves and servants should not be ashamed of the chains they may have to wear as subversives in the Caesar's empire.[15]

But has Paul in the Pastorals inadvertently acquiesced to Caesar by charging the Ephesian Christians to settle down and live in peace in Roman culture, since the parousia has been delayed? Philip H. Towner highlights this supposed shift in the Pastorals:

> Since Martin Dibelius first coined the term Christliche Bürgerlichkeit to express the goal of ethical instruction in the pastoral epistles, so many have followed suit

---

13 Ibid, pp. 361–62.
14 Malcolm Gill, *Jesus as Mediator: Politics and Polemics in 1 Timothy 2:1–7* (New York: Peter Lang, 2008).
15 Young, *The Theology of the Pastoral Letters*, p.65.

that one might almost conclude that this interpretation has become one of those unassailable "assured results of modern scholarship." By definition Christliche Bügerlichkeit, sometimes translated, "Christian good-citizenship," and sometimes "bourgeois Christianity," refers to a concept of Christian existence in which the primary goal is to achieve peaceful coexistence with the various orders of the world. Proponents are virtually unanimous in thinking that this concept marks a shift in thought within the NT caused by a transformed eschatological outlook....[16]

But Towner refutes such a notion, demonstrating that the past event of salvation creates an obligation to live out its consequences. The motive for ethical behavior is not a desire to avoid persecution and live peacefully, but it stems from the fact of salvation and a desire to proclaim the saving message. There is a strong forward look to the end of the age, the second epiphany, which will bring to completion that which was inaugurated at the first. Timothy and Titus are living in the last days, looking forward to the parousia. This emphasis, Towner argues, is intended to correct the opponents' overrealized eschatology. From the historical indicative of salvation comes the ethical imperative of response.[17]

In our work on the Pastorals we arrived at a similar conclusion as Towner, showing that those letters juxtapose suffering and glory such that the former in this age leads to the latter in the age to come.[18]

Mystical Exegesis of the Judaizers

a. The Evidence of the Pastorals. There is still a missing component in our identification of Paul's opponents as reflected in the Pastorals—the Jewish nature of the false teaching. Three characteristics surface in that regard: Jewish Christians, ascetic practice, and realized eschatology. We now discuss these in order. That Paul's opponents were Jewish is clear: they taught "Jewish myths" (Titus 1:14; 1 Tim. 1:3–4; 4:7; 2 Tim. 4:4) and speculative genealogies (1 Tim. 1:3–4; Titus 1:3–9); they were of the circumcision group (Titus 1:10); they promoted the Torah (1 Tim. 1:7–11; Titus

---

16 Towner, *The Goal of Our Instruction*, pp. 10–11.
17 Ibid, pp. 61–74.
18 Pate, *The Glory of Adam and the Afflictions of the Righteous*, pp. 313–337.

3:9), especially the dietary laws (1 Tim. 4:3; Titus 1:15). That the opponents were Jewish Christians from within the Ephesian congregations is also clear: Paul exhorts Timothy to warn the wayward members of the congregation (1 Tim. 1:3; 4:11; 2 Tim. 2:14); two of their names are mentioned because they were delivered to divine judgment—Hymenaeus and Alexander (1 Tim. 1:20; 2 Tim. 2:18); the church was mixed with orthodox and non-orthodox beliefs (2 Tim. 2:19–21).[19] Moreover, the opponents were leaders of the Ephesian congregation(s): the opponents portrayed themselves as teachers (1 Tim. 1:7); this explains Paul's extended discussion of the qualities expected of leaders (1 Tim. 3:1–13; 5:17–25; Titus 1:5–9); these were upsetting whole households (Titus 1:11), a possible reference to leaders of house churches, cf. Acts 20:28–31.[20]

The opposition was ascetic in practice. Thus, they forbade eating certain foods based on the Jewish dietary laws (see again 1 Tim. 4:3; Titus 1:15); they opposed marriage (1 Tim. 4:3; 5:14) and bearing children (1 Tim. 2:15); they saw the material world as evil in "good" Platonic style (1 Tim. 4:4; Titus 1:15).

The false teachers espoused realized eschatology. Thus, they claimed the resurrection had already happened (2 Tim. 2:18). Like the Corinthians, the Ephesians apparently thought they were raised in the Spirit at baptism. Therefore, they had no need for material things like food and marriage (see the references above). They encouraged emancipatory activism by women (cf. 1 Tim. 2:8–15; 5:3–16; 2 Tim. 3:6–7 with Gal. 3:28; 1 Cor. 11:2–16; 14:33b–35) and charged for their teaching (1 Tim. 6:3–21; cf. 1 Tim. 3:8; Titus 1:7).

Is there a way to integrate these three characteristics of Paul's opponents in Ephesus—Jewish Christians who emphasized the Torah and genealogies, were ascetic, and espoused realized eschatology? We believe there is. We suggest that the opponents embraced a mystical interpretation of the Torah, a type of charismatic exegesis—not of the *merkabah* variety, but rather of the Philonic kind. To that subject we now turn.

Philo was the Jewish philosopher (20 BC to AD 50) who wed Jewish faith with Greek philosophy, particularly Middle Platonism. We can identify

---

19 Trebilco, *The Early Christians at Ephesus*, p. 211.
20 Ibid, p. 212.

the above three components in Philo's writings: ecstatic exegesis, asceticism, myths, and genealogies.

b. Evidence of Ecstatic Exegesis in Philo's Writings. For Philo, in Platonic fashion the mind/reason taps into the invisible reality of the forms but the body corresponds to the inferior world of the shadows. According to Philo, the mind can contemplate God behind the forms/ideas. Indeed, when the mind fastens on the Torah/philosophy it enters into mystic communion with God:

> I am myself not ashamed to relate what has happened to me myself, which I know from having experienced it ten thousand times. Sometimes when I have desired to come to my usual employment of writing on the doctrines of philosophy though I have known accurately what it was proper to set down, I have found my mind barren and unproductive, and I have been completely unsuccessful in my object, being indignant at my mind for the uncertainty and vanity of its then existent opinions, and filled with amazement at the power of the living God, by whom the womb of the soul is at times opened and at times closed up; (35) and sometimes when I have come to my work empty I have suddenly become full, ideas being, in an invisible manner, showered upon me, and implanted in me from on high; so that, through the influence of divine inspiration, I have become greatly excited, and have known neither the place in which I was, nor those who were present, nor myself, nor what I was saying, nor what I was writing; for then I have been conscious of a richness of interpretation, an enjoyment of light, a most penetrating sight, a most manifest energy in all that was to be done, having such an effect on my mind as the clearest ocular demonstration would have on the eyes (*On the Migration of Abraham*, VII. 34–35)[21]

Similarly, Philo writes:

(68) Who, then, shall be the heir? Not that reasoning which remains in the prison of the body according to its own voluntary intentions, but

---

21 All quotes are taken from *The Works of Philo*, trans. by C. D. Yonge (Peabody, MA: Hendrickson, 1993).

that which is loosened from those bonds and emancipated, and which has advanced beyond the walls, and if it be possible to say so, has itself forsaken itself. "For he," says the scripture, "who shall come out from thee, he shall be thy heir." (69) Therefore if any desire comes upon the, O soul, to be the inheritor of the good things of God, leave not only thy country, the body and thy kindred, the outward senses, and thy father's house, that is speech; but also flee from thyself and depart out of thyself, like the Corybantes, or those possessed with demons, being driven to frenzy and inspired by some prophetic inspiration. (70) For while the mind is in a state of enthusiastic inspiration, and while it is no longer mistress of itself, but is agitated and drawn upwards to that object, truth removing all impediments out of its way, and making every thing before it plain, that so it may advance by a level and easy road, its destiny is to become and inheritor of the things of God (*Who Is the Heir of Divine Things*, XIV. 68–70).

Philo compares this mystical experience based on contemplating the Torah/philosophy to God "leading out" (*exegagen auton exō*) Abraham to see the stars in the heavens (Gen. 15:5). He says of this:

(81) And the statement, "He led him out"… has a bearing also on moral considerations, though some persons, through their want of instruction in moral philosophy, are accustomed to ridicule it saying, "For is any one every led out in , or led in out?" Certainly, I would reply, "you ridiculous and very foolish man; for you have never learnt how to trace the dispositions of the soul; but by this language of yours you only seek to understand those motions of the bodies which are exerted in change of place. On which account it seems paradoxical to you to speak of any one coming out into, or going in out; but to those acquainted with Moses none of these things seem inconsistent." Very correctly, therefore, it is said, he led him out of the prison according to the body, of the caves existing in the external senses, of the sophistries displayed in the deceitful speech; and beyond all this, out of himself and out of the idea that by his own self-exerted, self-implanted, and independent power he was able to conceive and comprehend (Ibid, XVI. 81, 85).

Thus contemplation on Torah/philosophy brings about ecstatic exegesis. In this trance, the philosopher sees the realities of existence. Such a mystical experience is not out of body but in the mind. Still, such mystic experience is realized eschatology in that the mind is united by contemplation with God and thereby delivered from the prison house of the body:

And this is naturally the case; for those who seek and desire to find God, love that solitude which is dearest to him, laboring for this as their dearest and primary object, to become like his blessed and happy nature. (88) Therefore, having now given both explanations, the literal one as concerning the man, and the allegorical one relating to the soul, we have shown that both the man and the mind are deserving of love; inasmuch as the one is obedient to the sacred oracles, and because of their influence submits to be torn away from things which it is hard to part; and the mind deserves to be loved because it has not submitted to be for ever deceived and to abide permanently by the outward senses, thinking the visible world the greatest and first of gods, but soaring upwards with its reason it has beheld another nature better than that which is visible, that, namely, which is appreciable only by the intellect; and also that being who is at the same time the Creator and ruler of both (*On Abraham*, XVIVI. 87–88).

Elsewhere Philo writes of this ecstatic exegesis of the Torah/philosophy:

(1) There was once a time when devoting my leisure to philosophy and to the contemplation of the world and the things in it, I reaped the fruit of excellent, and desirable, and blessed intellectual feelings, being always living among the divine oracles and doctrines, on which I fed incessantly and insatiably, to my great delight, never entertaining any low or groveling thoughts, nor ever wallowing in the pursuit of glory or wealth, or the delights of the body, but I appeared to be raised on high and borne aloft by certain inspiration of the soul, and to dwell in the regions of the sun and moon, and to associate with the whole heaven and the whole universal world. (2) At that time, therefore, looking down from above, from the air, and straining the eye of my mind as from a watch-tower, I surveyed the unspeakable contemplation of all the things

on the earth, and looked upon, myself as happy as having forcibly escaped from all the evil fates that can attack human life.... (5) And if at any time unexpectedly there shall arise a brief period of tranquility and short calm and respite from the trouble which arise from the state affairs, I then rise aloft and float above the troubled waves, soaring as it were in the air, and being, I may almost say, blown forward by the breezes of knowledge which often persuades me to flee away, and to pass all my days with her, escaping as it were from my pitiless masters, not men only but also affairs which pour upon me from all quarters and at all times like a torrent. (6) But even in these circumstances I ought to give thanks to God, than though I am so overwhelmed by this flood, I am not wholly sunk and swallowed up in the depths. But I open the eyes of my soul, which from an utter despair of any good hope had been believed to have been before now wholly darkened, and I am irradiated with the light of wisdom, since I am not given up for the whole of my life to darkness. Behold, therefore, I venture not only to study the sacred commands of Moses, but also with an ardent love of knowledge to investigate each separate one of them, and to endeavor to reveal and to explain to those who wish to understand them, things concerning them which are not known to the multitude (*The Special Laws* III, I. 1–2, 5–6).

Second, to prepare for ecstatic exegesis—mystical experience of the Torah/philosophy—the philosopher must submit to ascetic practice. Thus Moses purified himself before ascending the mount to receive the Torah:

(68) But, in the first place, before assuming that office, it was necessary for him to purify not only his soul but also his body, so that it should be connected with and defiled by no passion, but should be pure from everything which is of a mortal nature, from all meat and drink, and from all connection with women. (69) And this last thing, indeed, he had despised for a long time, and almost from the first moment that he began to prophesy and to feel a divine inspiration, thinking that it was proper that he should at all times be ready to give his whole attention to the commands of God. And how he neglected all meat and drink for forty days together, evidently because he had more excellent food in those contemplations with which he was inspired above from heaven,

by which also he was improved, in the first instance in his mind, and, secondly, in his body, through the soul, increasing in strength and health both of body and soul, so that those who saw him afterwards could not believe that he was the same person (*On the Life of Moses*, II, XIV 68–69).

Having done that Moses ascended the mount to receive the Torah. There he contemplated with his soul the incorporeal patterns of the heavenly tabernacle, the model from which the earthly tabernacle was built (Ibid, XV. 74–76). Speaking of purification before contemplating the first cause, Philo writes:

> XIV. (48) Now I bid ye, initiated men, who are purified, as to your ears, to receive these things, as mysteries which are really sacred, in your inmost soul; and reveal them not to any one who is of the number of the uninitiated, but guard them as a sacred treasure, laying them up in your own hearts, not in a storehouse in which are gold and silver, perishable substances, but in that treasure-house in which the most excellent of all the possessions in the world does lie, the knowledge namely of the great first Cause, and of virtue, and in the third place, of generation of them both. And if ever you meet with any one who has been properly initiated, cling to that man affectionately and adhere to him, that if he has learnt any more recent mystery he may not conceal it from you before you have learnt to comprehend it thoroughly (*On the Cherubim*—part 2, XIV, 48).

Third, there are remarkable parallels between Philo and the Pastorals in their treatments of "myth and genealogies" that Kroegers' have called attention to. They document that Philo embraces the Sophia myth, the idea that Eve preceded Adam and bequeathed to him life and wisdom. They write of this:

> Since sexual union was used in the pagan mysteries to heighten or portray religions experience, Philo draws on the same vein. For him, instruction in the mysteries was communicated by a feminine figure, whether a Bible character or an abstraction, such as Sophia (Wisdom). God, then, was the husband of Wisdom.[22]

---

22 Kroeger and Kroeger, *I Suffer Not a Woman*, p. 146.

They then quote Philo in this regard:

God, therefore, wishing to bestow upon him a grasp not only of immaterial but also of solid bodies, completed the whole soul, weaving together a second section which was fellow to that already crafted. To this he gave the generic name of "woman" and the personal name of "Eve," intimating perception. As soon as she was created, through each of her parts, as if through orifices, she directed massed light toward the mind and dispersed the mist. She rendered the mind capable of seeing distinctly and with the utmost clarity the nature of the bodies, as now being a master. Like one who is dazzled by a brilliant burst of sunshine, or rises up from a deep sleep, or like a blind man who suddenly recovers his sight, the spirit encountered all the entire assemblage of those things which comprised the creation: heaven, earth, water, air, plants, animals, along with their distinctive, qualities, faculties, habits, composition, movements, activities, actions, changes, degeneration. He saw them and heard them and tasted them and smelled them and touched them. He inclined toward those which worked pleasure and turned away from those that wrought pain (*On the Cherubim,* 59–62).

According to the Kroegers, Philo carried this Sophia myth a step further, by applying the image of enlightener to various biblical heroines.

He allegorized the marriages of Abraham, Isaac, and Jacob as being the beginning of their spiritual maturity. Their wives symbolized heavenly wisdom, and the consummation brought divine enlightenment. Sarah, for instance, represents "virtue made perfect through teaching." Rebecca's name is allegorized as Wisdom, the daughter of God, who is the first-born mother of all things. Her function as drawer and carrier of water symbolizes carrying eternal wisdom of knowledge from the divine spring. Philo conceived of Rebecca as instructor, "for the word was hes who was teaching, and the ears were his who received the teaching." Like Sarah, she is a teacher of a man, and her mother's house is called "the maternal household of wisdom." Rachel too brought enlightenment to her husband when he obeyed his father Isaac's command to take a wife who loved the wisdom of knowledge. "Where else except from the house of wisdom shall he find a partner, blameless in judgment, with whom to remain always?"

Zipporah, the bride of Moses, symbolized soaring virtue which contemplated the divine, and Eve illuminated Adam.[23]

The Kroegers conclude from their study that 1 Timothy 2:11–15 is a rebuttal to the very Sophia myth Philo parades—namely, Eve was not the source of life and wisdom because Adam came before her and it is the male who does the instructing, not the female. We agree and add the observation that the Philo teaching that Eve and the other biblical heroines above enlightened the leaders of Israel from Abraham to Moses lies behind Paul's words "genealogies" (1 Tim. 1:3–4; Titus 1:10) as well as "myth" (1 Tim. 1:3–4; 4:7; 2 Tim. 4:4; Titus 1:14). That is, the myth of the heroine enlightener intersects with the genealogies of the ancient leaders of Israel, from the patriarchs to Moses. Thus the Philonic background nicely explains the Pastoral Epistles' use of "myth" (the Eve/Sophia myth) and "genealogies" (Sophia myth as continuing through the matriarchs in their enlightenment of the patriarchs).

These remarkable parallels between myth and genealogies support our thesis that the Pastorals are rebutting teachings similar to Philo's.

These three characteristics are integrated in Philo's ecstatic exegesis: asceticism, mystical experience through contemplating the Torah/philosophy, and the Sophia myth and genealogies in the Old Testament.

c. The Apollos Connection. We are suggesting that Philonic ecstatic exegesis, which was precipitated by asceticism and contemplation and culminated in realized eschatology (a beatific vision in the soul/mind of God), also informed the false teaching censured in the Pastorals. But where would have such influence originated? Acts 18:24–28 supplies the answer: Apollos. Apollos was a Jewish Christian who came to Ephesus from Alexandria, Egypt. Alexandria, Egypt was the center of allegorical interpretation and the home of Philo. No wonder then that Acts 18:24–28 portrays Apollos as a learned man—a man of logos/reason. We learned earlier that this label conveyed a Hellenistic philosophical nuance. It seems quite plausible, then, that

---

23 Ibid., p. 146. The Kroegers supply documentation from Philo for their statements in this quote.

the false teachers in Ephesus took their point of departure from Apollos, though certainly in an unorthodox direction Apollos would not have condoned.

Paul's Refutation of the False Teachers

In the Pastoral Epistles, Paul rejects the threefold edifice of the false teachers. First, Paul rejects their Judaizing message of circumcision and the dietary laws along with their promotion of genealogies and myths. (1 Tim. 1:3–11; 4:7; 2 Tim. 4:4; Titus 1:10, 15; 3:9). Second, Paul rejects the asceticism of the false teachers born out of a Platonic/Philonic disparagement of the goodness of God's creation (1 Tim. 2:15; 4:4; Titus 1:15). Third, Paul counters his opponents' realized eschatology with his inaugurated eschatology. Thus resurrection is a future event (2 Tim. 2:11). Endurance is needed to complete salvation (2 Tim. 2:12). While salvation has been inaugurated because of the Christ event (1 Tim. 1:15–16; 2:3–6; 2 Tim. 1:9–10; 2:8–13; Titus 2:11–14; 3:4–7) there is an unfinished, future dimension to it (1 Tim. 4:16; 2 Tim. 4:18; Titus 1:2; 2:13; 3:7). Therefore, the Pastorals speak forcefully of the hope of Christ's return (1 Tim. 6:14; 2 Tim. 1:12, 18; 4:1, 8,18; Titus 2:13), when salvation will be complete and the age to come will be present in fullness (1 Tim. 4:8; 6:19; 2 Tim. 4:8, 18). Thus Paul uses "epiphany" of both the first coming of Christ (2 Tim. 1:10; cf. Titus 2:11; 3:4) and the second coming of Christ (1 Tim. 6:14; 2 Tim. 4:1, 8; Titus 2:13).[24]

SURVEY OF THE PASTORAL LETTERS

Before surveying the content of the Pastoral letters, it would be helpful to discuss the five faithful sayings in those letters, especially since they are intricately related to the ecstatic exegetes causing trouble in the Ephesian church.

Faithful Sayings

Our thesis: Each of the faithful sayings deal with some aspect of salvation Paul's opponents distorted:

- Faithful Saying: 1 Timothy 1:15–Christ came to save sinners:

---

24 See Trebilco's discussion, *The Early Christians in Ephesus*, pp. 219–20. I did not include this Philonic brand of opposition to Paul in my chart of apocalyptic scenarios in my introduction to this work because, so far as I can tell, it only occurs once in Paul's letters—in the Pastorals—whereas the other eschatological constructs occur more than once in Paul's writings.

- Contrary to Paul's opponents, 1:3–11 states that the Law was given to convict sinners and drive them to the gospel of grace — not to further obey the Law
- Paul—a sinner—1:12–15
- This counteracted the opponents' teaching that the right way to use the Law was to let it guide Christians into righteousness
- Faithful Saying: 1 Timothy 3:1—referring back to 2:15—childbearing saves women (spiritually):
    - Contrary to Paul's opponents, 1 Timothy 2:9–15 states that salvation comes *not through* Eve/women (contrast this to Philo's notion that Eve was the source of true knowledge not Adam) because Adam came before her and Eve was deceived, not Adam
    - Paul—So Eve/women are saved through submitting to the divine plan of childbearing
- Faithful Saying: 1 Timothy 4:9–10—God is the savior of all those who believe:
    - Contrasted to the opponents, 1 Timothy 4:1–10 asserts that God saves people *in* the world—all those who believe (in the present life and for the life to come)
    - But the opponents were ascetic, arguing that God saves people *out* of the material world
- Faithful Saying: 2 Timothy 2:11–13—believers need to persevere in salvation/faith:
    - Contrasted to the opponents, 2 Timothy 2:14–19 declares that the leaders of the heresy disrupting the church committed apostasy by saying that in baptism the resurrection had already happened (note that vv. 11–13 contains a baptismal hymn showing Paul's eschatological reservation—one must persevere in the confession of one's baptism if one is to raised with the Christ in the future)
    - Therefore 2 Timothy 2:11–13 teaches the antithesis of the heretics' claim—one must persevere in this age because the salvation of the age to come is not complete
- Faithful Saying: Titus 3:5–8a—one is saved by grace:
    - Contrary to the opponents, Titus 3:9–11 discounts the Law

(especially the Philonic emphasis on the Law's genealogies) as the means to salvation.

- Rather, according to vv. 3–5a one is saved by grace alone (note the synonyms—kindness/mercy/generously = grace)

1 Timothy
- A. 1:1–2: Salutation
- B. 1:3–11: Warning against False Teachers
  - 1:3–7: The Nature of the Heresy
  - 1:8–11: The Purpose of the Law
- C. 1:12–17: The Lord's Grace to Paul
- D. 1:18–20: The Purpose of Paul's Instructions to Timothy
- E. 2:1–3:16: Instructions concerning the Administration of the Church
  - 2:1–15: Public Worship
  - 3:1–13: Qualifications for Church Officers
  - 3:14–16: Purpose of These Instructions
- F. 4:1–16: Dealing with False Teaching
- G. 5:1–6:2: Methods of Dealing with Different Groups in the Church
  - 5:1–2: The Older and Younger
  - 5:3–16: Widows
  - 5:17–25: Elders
  - 6:1–2: Slaves
- H. 6:3–21: Miscellaneous Matters

1. 1:1–2: Salutation
The salutation broaches the subject of Pauline opposition in Ephesus. Paul reminds his audience that *he* is an apostle (not his opponents) of Christ Jesus by the command of God. The order "Christ Jesus" may reflect Paul's "in Christ" mysticism, which is the true mysticism, not the realized eschatology of Artemis, Caesar, or Philonic-style exegesis. Moreover, Paul calls Christ Jesus our "hope," which suggests that the age to come is not fully here. The age to come will only be complete at the return of Christ (cf. Titus 2:13). Paul calls God "Savior," a key title for God in the Pastorals. For Paul, God/Christ is Savior, not Artemis or Caesar. Paul addresses this letter to Timothy, Paul's spiritual son and pastor

of the church at Ephesus. Paul wishes God's grace, mercy, and peace upon Timothy, which come from God and Christ.

2. 1:3–11: Warning against False Teachers
a. 1:3–7: The Nature of the Heresy. Although the Artemis and the imperial cults loom large in the background of the Pastorals, the "ecstatic exegetes" are in the forefront of Paul's critique in these letters. As we saw above, these ecstatic exegetes promoted a mystical interpretation/experience based on the Torah in a manner similar to Philo. But for Paul, all such myths and genealogies concerning the Torah are false doctrines that promote salvation by work not by faith. "Faith" and "faithful" occur some thirty-three times in the Pastorals. The noun, πιστις, occurs both with and without the article. The former usually means "trust" while the latter usually means "the faith," as in the Christian faith versus the false teachings of the opponents. The adjective—πιστος—is associated with the five faithful sayings.[25]

b. 1:8–11: The Purpose of the Law. Rather than function as a positive guide for Christians, Paul asserts in vv. 8–11 that the law of Moses serves to convict sinners. His vice list here draws on the Decalogue, the ten commandments:

1 TIMOTHY 1:9B–10	EXODUS 20
1) lawless/rebellious	Need for the law (Ten Commandments)
2) godless	Ex. 20:3 (no other gods)
3) sinners (idolatry)	Ex. 20:4–5 (no graven images)
4) unholy	Ex. 20:8–11 sabbath is holy

---

25 William D. Mounce, *The Pastoral Epistles*, This one Word Biblical Commentary 46 (Nashville, TN: Thomas Nelson, 2000), pp. cxxx–cxxxii.

1 TIMOTHY 1:9B–10	EXODUS 20
5) profane	Ex. 20:7 not profane name of God
6) kill fathers/mothers	Ex. 20:12 positive (honor father/mother); Ex. 21:15 negative (strikes father/mother)
7) murderers	Ex. 20:13 not kill/murder; cf. Ex. 21:12
8) immorality and homosexuality	Ex. 20:14 no adultery Lev. 18:22/20:13 no homosexuality
9) kidnappers	Ex. 20:15 not steal (general) Ex. 21:16 kidnap (specific)
10) liars/perjurers	Ex. 20:16 not bear false witness; cf. Ex. 23:1–3, 6–8
11) not covet/not in 1 Tim. 1 but in 1 Tim. 6:9–10	Ex. 20:17 not covet

Here Paul argues that the moral law (the ten commandments) does not apply to the Christian but rather to non-Christians.[26] Elsewhere in the Pastorals, he will argue that neither do the dietary laws apply to the Christian.

3. 1:12–17: The Lord's Grace to Paul

Paul relates his conversion experience in vv. 12–17. Before he was a Christian, he persecuted the church (Acts 22:3, 4; 22:19; 26:9–11) and blasphemed God by abhorring his crucified son. But God's grace brought Paul to faith in Christ. Indeed Paul is a trophy of grace to others who need to be saved.

Paul concludes the paragraph with a doxology—God is king, who has inaugurated the age to come (v. 17) into this present age (1 Tim. 6:17; 2 Tim. 4:10; Titus 2:12) who is invisible, God alone, and glorious. Needless to say, Caesar is no match for God.

---

26 My chart is based on the discussion by George W. Knight III, *Commentary on the Pastoral Epistles,* New International Greek Testament Commentary (Grand Rapids, MI: Eerdmans, 1992), pp. 83–93.

4. 1:18–20: The Purpose of Paul's Instructions to Timothy
Paul instructs Timothy regarding two matters: his past calling and his present
conflict. Paul reminds Timothy of the past prophecies setting apart Timothy for
the gospel ministry (cf. 4:14; 2 Tim. 1:6). This will help Timothy in the spiritual
conflict facing him in the Ephesian church, concerning his opponents. Timothy
is to fight for the truth of the gospel, reinforced by obedience that leads to a
clear conscience. This is in contrast to the false teachers Hymenaeus and Alexander, who departed from the faith and caused others to do the same. The false
doctrine is that of the Philonic-like ecstatic exegesis. Paul has excommunicated
these two from the church.

5. 2:1–3:16: Instructions concerning the Administration of the Church
a. 2:1–15: Public Worship. Paul addresses two matters related to public worship in the Ephesian church. The first is prayer in public worship (2:1–8). Paul
urges Christians to pray for governmental officials, including Caesar. This indicates that neither Paul nor early Christianity desired to revolt against the Roman
Empire, this despite the apostle's polemic against the imperial cult. Paul believed
that prayer for Caesar leading to peace was the best environment for spreading
the gospel. Indeed, God desires for all to be saved and Christ the mediator (not
Caesar) is the means for accomplishing that goal. Paul was called as an apostle to
preach this gospel to the Gentiles. Paul reminds Timothy that prayer is effective
when God's people are holy.

The second matter Paul addresses regarding public worship is the role of women
in the service. We will let our earlier comments on this difficult passage suffice.

b. 3:1–13: Qualifications for Church Officers. In 3:1–13, Paul lists the qualifications for the two main offices in the early church—elders and deacons. The qualifications for elders are found in vv. 1–7. The general qualification is blameless
character. The specific qualifications are: the husband of one wife (though highly
debated, seems to mean that a man should not have been divorced), self-control,
wise, respectable, hospitable so the gospel could be advanced, a teacher, not addicted to wine, uncontentious, gentle, non-materialistic, a good manager of his

household, not a new convert, and possessing a good reputation. We note here that elder, bishop/overseer, and pastor seem to refer to the same person (cf. Acts 20:17, 28, 1 Peter 5:1–28, and Titus 1:5, 7).

The qualifications of deacons follow in vv. 8–13, which are similar to those of the elders: serious-minded, consistent in speech, not addicted to wine, not greedy, holds to the faith, is proven, has a godly wife (deaconess?), the husband of one wife (not divorced?), has a godly family.

Paul speaks of the rewards that await faithful elders and deacons in v. 13.

c. 3:14–16: Purpose of These Instructions. Verses 14–16 conclude the chapter with a description of the church and a hymn to Christ. The church is God's household, the depository of truth (the faith). The hymn to Christ in v. 16 seems to unfold in three stanzas, which we here supply:

- Work of Christ—revealed in the flesh (Christ's humanity: incarnation)/vindicated in the Spirit (Christ's deity: resurrection cf. Rom 1:4)
- Proclamation of Christ—seen by angels (resurrection [οφθη—used of Jesus' resurrection, cf. Luke 24:31; Acts 15:31; etc.])/preached among the nations
- Reception of Christ—believed on in the earth/received in heaven (ascension)

6. 4:1–16: Dealing with False Teaching

Chapter 4 deals with the false teaching of Paul's opponents in Ephesus, especially the ecstatic exegetes. In vv. 1–5 the apostle describes such teaching and in vv. 6–16 he offers his council for dealing with such teaching.

Regarding Paul's description of the false teachers, v. 1 makes it clear that Paul interprets their false doctrine as the end-time apostasy predicted by Jesus (cf. 1 Tim. 4:1–5; 2 Tim. 3:5–9 with Mark 13:22/Matt. 24:12/Luke 21:6). Indeed if we cast our net wider, we see that the signs of the times/messianic woes of the Olivet Discourse heralding the last days correspond with the Pastorals' situation:

OLIVET DISCOURSE AND THE MESSIANIC WOES	1 AND 2 TIMOTHY AND THE MESSIANIC WOES
1) Arrival of last days (Mark 13:19, 20/ Matt. 24:22, 29/Luke 21:6, 23)	1) Arrival of last days (2 Tim. 3:1/4:3; cf. 1 Tim. 4:1)
2) Persecution of believers (Mark 13:9–12/ Matt. 24:9/Luke 2: 1, 12, 13	2) Persecution of believers (2 Tim. 2:8–13; 3:10–12; 4:4–6)
3) False teachers of deception (Mark 13:5, 6, 21, 22/Matt. 24:11, 23, 24/ Luke 21:8)	3) False teachers of deception (2 Tim. 3:6; 4:3, 4; cf. 1 Tim. 4:1–5)
4) Apostasy (Mark 13:22a/Matt. 24:12/ Luke 21:6)	4) Apostasy (1 Tim. 4:1–5; 2 Tim. 1:10–16; 3:5–9; 1 Titus 3:9–11)
5) Parousia and judgment (Mark 13:26, 27/ Matt. 24:30; Luke 21:27)	5) Parousia and judgment (2 Tim. 4:1; Titus 2:13–14

The content of the false doctrine is asceticism, which we earlier correlated with Philonic type preparation for mystically experiencing the Torah (vv. 2–5). Paul refutes such a perspective by asserting the goodness of God's creation, including marriage.

In verses 6–16, Paul points out three ways Timothy can deal with the false teaching in his church. First, the young pastor should be sound in doctrine (vv. 6–7a). This means Timothy is to meditate on the truth of the gospel and alleviate the false teaching. Second, Timothy should conduct himself in a godly manner (vv. 7b–12). Timothy's life will then model the truth thereby dispelling the false doctrines. Third, Timothy should read and preach the Scriptures in the worship services (vv. 13–16). Not only will he grow spiritually thereby, but so will his congregation.

7. 5:1–6:2: Methods of Dealing with Different Groups in the Church
In 1 Timothy 5:1–6:2, Paul gives Timothy advice on how various members of the congregation should be treated.

a. 5:1–2: The Older and Younger. Like a family, pastor Timothy should gently treat the older man as if he were Timothy's father while he should treat the younger men as brothers. Timothy should treat the older women like mothers and the younger women like sisters.

b. 5:3–16: Widows. In verses 3–16, Paul offers Timothy instructions for caring for widows in the church. Verses 3–8 records the support of widows while vv. 9–15 provides the guidelines for selecting widows for that support. In vv. 3–8, Paul says that widows who have families should be cared for by those families. It is honoring to God when families care for themselves. A widow who has no family support, needs support from the church, and she should be devoted to a life of godliness.

In verses 9–15, Paul distinguishes older and young widows. The former, if she is to be supported by the church, should be sixty years old, was faithful to her deceased husband, is noted for good works (vv. 9–10). But the younger widows do not qualify to receive support from the church because they will be tempted to break their vow to serve Christ exclusively (like Paul?) and they will be vulnerable to become busybodies. Rather, the younger widows should marry and help to support older widows (vv. 11–16). No doubt, some of the widows in the Ephesian church (older and younger) were being drawn into the group of false teachers. We should also mention that, while the Pastorals do not seem to give evidence of an official order of widows in the early church, that development would occur in the second century (see *Didascalia Apostolorum*, chaps. 14–15).

c. 5:17–25: Elders. Verses 17–25 give guidelines for the treatment of spiritual elders in the church. Paul relates three points to Timothy in this regard. First, elders who serve the church faithfully should receive double honor—honor and honorarium (vv. 17, 18). Second, accusations of elders must be done carefully—two witnesses are needed. If the elder has sinned, his repentance should be done publicly in the church (vv. 19–22). Third, elders should be chosen carefully for their actions—good or bad—will affect the congregation (vv. 24–25).

d. 6:1–2: Slaves. Like Colossians 3:22–4:1 and Ephesians 6:5–9, 1 Timothy 6:1–2 exhorts slaves to honor their masters. This will honor God by communicating to the world that Christianity is not an insurrectionist movement.

8. 6:3–21: Miscellaneous Matters

Warnings about greed dominate 1 Timothy 6:3–21, in particular the greed of the false teachers. Verses 2–10 connect the false teachers (vv. 3–5a) with avarice (vv. 5b–10). It may be that, like ancient peripatetic philosophers, the Ephesian heretics were charging fees (exorbitant fees, at that) for their preaching/teaching sessions. Paul, however, did not charge for his preaching in order to show that the gospel is free (see 1 Cor. 9:12b, 15–18). Rather than money, it is godliness that brings true contentment. Juxtaposed to the ungodliness and greed of the false teachers (vv. 3–10) is Paul's challenge to Timothy to pursue godliness (vv. 11–16). In doing so, the young pastor will be true to his divine calling to imitate the obedience of Christ and bring glory to God.

Verses 17–19 resume Paul's polemic against the avarice of the false teachers. Those who are rich are to share that with others. In doing so, they will experience contentment in this age and approval in the age to come. Here we see Paul drawing upon the Jewish two age structure. The Pastorals, as we have seen, assume the age to come has broken into the present age through the first coming of Christ. Verses 20–21 conclude the letter by once again exhorting Timothy to be faithful to the gospel that has been entrusted to him (cf. 1:1–6).

Titus

Apparently Paul introduced Christianity in Crete when he and Titus visited the island, after which Paul left Titus there to organize the converts. Paul sent the letter with Zenas and Apollos (3:13) to instruct Titus in how to also deal with the same opposition that faced Ephesus. The fourth largest island in the Mediterranean Sea, the island of Crete lies directly south of the Aegean Sea, about two hundred fifty miles south of Ephesus. In New Testament times morality in Crete was virtually nonexistent (see 1:12; cf. Epimenides; Cicero [*Republic* 3.9.15]; Josephus, [*Ant.* 17.5.5/117,120]; Polybius [Hist. 6.46.3]). Titus may be outlined as follows:

    A. 1:1–4: Salutation
    B. 1:5–9: Concerning Elders
    C. 1:10–16: Concerning False Teachers
    D. 2:1–5: Concerning Various Groups in the Congregations
       - 2:1–10: The Instructions to Different Groups

1. 1:1–4: Salutation
The salutation confirms Paul's apostleship, a ministry of bringing the lost to faith and godliness (v. 1). Such salvation, or eternal life, was planned by God in the past and is now revealed through Paul (vv. 203). Titus is Paul's spiritual son in this endeavor (v. 4).

2. 1:5–9: Concerning Elders
In verses 5–9, Paul states that the reason he left Titus in Crete was to appoint elders in the church there (v. 5). Verses 6–9 list the qualifications for the elders to be chosen, traits that are similar to the list in 1 Timothy 3:2–7: blameless, not divorced, management of his family, patient, not given to drinking or violence, not greedy, hospitable and good, self-controlled, holy, disciplined, committed to the Christian faith so that he can teach others the same in the face of false doctrine.

3. 1:10–16: Concerning False Teachers
The false teachers that upset the churches in Crete matched the false teachers that infiltrated the church in Ephesus, they were: from the Jewish circumcision group (v. 10), greedy (v. 11), dishonest (vv. 12–13), enamored with Jewish myths (v. 14), ascetic (v. 15), and apostates (v. 16). Titus is to rebuke them in the hope that they will return to the faith (v. 13).

4. 2:1–5: Concerning Various Groups in the Congregations
a. 2:1–10: The Instructions to Different Groups. Like 1 Timothy 5:1–6:2, Titus 2:1–15 contains instructions on how Titus is to teach the various groups in the churches (minus any guidance for widows). Those older men should conduct

themselves with respect, in sound doctrine and with love (vv. 1–2). Older women are to be godly in word and conduct so that they can teach younger women to be godly, faithful wives and mothers (vv. 3–5). Titus, as a young pastor is to set an example to the young men in deed, teaching, and character (vv. 6–8). Slaves are to obey their masters so that the gospel will attract the lost (v. 9).

b. 2:11–14: The Foundation for Christian Living. Verses 11–14 provide a theological foundation for righteous behavior, which is the grace of God. The grace of God appeared with the first coming of Christ. It is that grace that transforms sinners into righteous people (vv. 11–12). That same grace will sustain Christians until the second coming of Christ. Such grace is rooted in Jesus' sacrificial death (vv. 13–14). One can see Paul's inaugurated eschatology in vv. 11–14:

- v. 11: age to come already dawned = grace of God appeared in Jesus' salvation
- vv. 12–13: age to complete not yet complete = that will happen at the return of Christ
- v. 14: age to come already dawned = grace of God in Jesus' sacrificial death. It may well be that v. 13 equates the great God with the Savior, Jesus Christ.[27]

Notice the chiastic structure here of those verses:

- age to come dawned—v.11
- age to come not yet complete—vv.12–13
- age to come dawned—v.14

c. 2:15: The Duty of Titus. Titus is to teach the true faith with authority from God.

5. 3:1–8: Concerning Believers in General
a. 3:1–2: Obligations as Citizens. Reminiscent of 1 Timothy 2:2 and Romans

---

27 See Mounce's defense of the Grandville Sharpe rule here, such that the one article refers to the same person—the great God who is Jesus Christ, *The Pastoral Epistles*, pp. 426–31.

13:1–7, Titus 3:1–2 exhorts believers to be subject to the governing authorities. Moreover, Christians should do good, not slander, be peaceable, considerate, and humble.

b. 3:3–8: Motives for Godly Conduct. The motive for godly conduct is God's grace. Such grace transformed Paul from being a self-righteous Pharisee whose inward passions drove him to persecute the church to becoming the apostle to the Gentiles (v. 3). God's grace appeared in Christ to save those whose faith is in him alone (vv. 5–8). That grace motivates believers to live good and godly lives (vv. 9–10).

6. 3:9–11: Concerning Response to Spiritual Error
In vv. 9–11, Paul returns to the theme of false teaching. Titus is to exhort the congregations to avoid the ecstatic exegetes (v. 9). More than that, if those Jewish Christians do not repent, they should be expelled from the churches (vv. 10–11).

7. 3:12–15: Conclusion, Final Greetings, and Benediction
Paul concludes his letter to Titus by encouraging him to try to visit Paul by winter (v. 12), by receiving the letter-bearers—Zenas and Apollos (v. 13), by challenging the churches in Crete to live godly and productive lives (v. 14), and by sending greetings to the churches in Crete (v. 15).

2 Timothy
Paul writes 2 Timothy—his swan song—from a Roman prison during Nero's reign (ca. 66–67). While his first imprisonment in Rome recorded in Acts 28 was under house arrest, now the apostle is sequestered away in a cold dungeon (1:17). He knows that he will be executed this time for the Christian faith. 2 Timothy interweaves three concerns of the Apostle—his desire to see his beloved Timothy before he is martyred, his warning about the persistence of the false teachers, and his update on his co-workers. The following outline will guide us through our survey of 2 Timothy:

A. 1:1–4: Introduction
B. 1:5–14: Paul's Concern for Timothy
C. 1:15–18: Paul's Situation

Chapter 11

D. 2:1–26: Special Instructions to Timothy
- 2:1–13: Call for Endurance
- 2:14–26: Warning about Foolish Controversies

E. 3:1–17: Warning about the Last Days
- 3:1–9: Terrible Times
- 3:10–17: Means of Combating Them

F. 4:1–8: Paul's Departing Remarks

G. 4:9–22: Final Requests, Greetings, and Benediction

1. 1:1–4: Introduction
In the introduction to 2 Timothy, Paul follows his customary pattern: He identifies himself as an apostle of Christ by the will of God; he names the recipient—in this case his beloved son, Timothy; and he sends greetings to the addressee—grace, mercy, and peace. Paul's reference to the promise of life in Christ conveys the apostle's hope in eternal life when he departs from this life (vv. 1–2). In vv. 3–4, Paul thanks God for the privilege of having served him; his conscience is clear. Now as his life draws to an end, he wants to see Timothy, whom he last saw in Macedonia (1 Tim. 1:3).

2. 1:5–14: Paul's Concern for Timothy
In vv. 5–10, Paul bolsters Timothy's faith by reminding him of his spiritual heritage (v. 5) and of his divine calling (v. 6). This will empower Timothy to be faithful to the gospel even in the midst of suffering (vv. 7–9). Indeed Timothy is called to suffer for his faith. Such afflictions are probably to be equated with the messianic woes (cf. 2 Tim. 3:1–5). But Timothy need not fear even death itself, because Christ has overcome that enemy by giving immortality to his own (v. 10).

3. 1:15–18: Paul's Situation
Paul too suffers for his faith having been imprisoned, but he unashamedly will continue to preach the gospel (vv. 11–12). Timothy also must be faithful to that gospel entrusted to him (vv. 13–14). Rather than being like the false teachers Phygelius and Hermogenes who departed from the faith, Timothy should remain true (v. 15). Onesiphorus also has been faithful to the gospel by continuing to support Paul, even in his chains (vv. 16–18).

280

4. 2:1–26: Special Instructions to Timothy
In 2:1–26, Paul sends special instructions to Timothy—first, a call for Timothy to endure (2:1–13); and second, a warning about the false doctrine that continued to wreak havoc among the Ephesian Christians (2:14–26).

a. 2:1–13: Call for Endurance. Timothy needs to pass on the gospel of grace to reliable Christian men to preserve the posterity of the Christian faith (vv. 1–2). To do that, the young pastor must be prepared to be focused like a soldier, disciplined as an athlete, and be diligent like a farmer (vv. 3–7). Timothy will be further motivated to endure for the faith by remembering Christ's endurance (v. 8), Paul's perseverance (vv. 9–10), and God's faithfulness (vv. 11a–13).

b. 2:14–26: Warning about Foolish Controversies. Paul presents three contrasts in vv. 14–26 that unmask the foolishness of the false teaching Timothy must squash:
- The false teaching is useless and destructive but God's word of truth is sure and eternal (vv. 14–19).
- The false teachers are vessels of dishonor but followers of truth are vessels of honor (vv. 20–21).
- The servant of the Lord leads a life approved by God but the false teachers are ensnared by the devil (vv. 22–26).

5. 3:1–17: Warning About the Last Days
2 Timothy 3:1–17 depict the last days as here. Verses 1–9 portray them as terrible times, while vv. 10–17 offer a strategy for combating them.

a. 3:1–9: Terrible Times. Like 1 Timothy 4, 2 Timothy 3:1–9 taps into the eschatological theme of the messianic woes, the transition period between this age and the age to come. Verses 1–9 use some eighteen characteristics to describe these signs of the times as present. And the false teachers are a large part of that problem that faced believers in Ephesus. The false teachers are now what the opponents of Moses—Jannas and Jambres—were in Israel's history.[28]

---

28 Neither of these men are mentioned in the Old Testament, but according to Jewish tradition they were the Egyptian court magicians that opposed Moses.

b. 3:10–17: Means of Combating Them. Paul provides a twofold strategy for Timothy to combat the evil of the messianic woes—endure persecution, even as Paul did (vv. 10–13), and embrace the Scripture (vv. 14–17).

6. 4:1–8: Paul's Departing Remarks
Paul has two parting words in vv. 1–8: The first is for Timothy to be faithful to preach the word of God (vv. 1–5); and the second is that Paul has been faithful to the gospel (vv. 6–8).

7. 4:9–22: Final Requests, Greetings, and Benediction
Paul concludes his swan song of 2 Timothy by requesting that Timothy come to him soon (vv. 9–13), issuing a warning about Alexander (vv. 14–15), praising God for Paul's past deliverances (vv. 16–18), and offering final greetings (vv. 19–22).

CONCLUSION TO THE PASTORALS

We conclude our discussion of the Pastoral letters by noting that therein one finds once again Paul's fourfold eschatological message, which we simply provide in chart form:

PAUL'S FOURFOLD ESCHATOLOGICAL MESSAGE:	THE PASTORAL EPISTLES PASSAGE:
1) Jesus is the Christ	1 Tim. 1:1(2x), 12, 14–16; 2:5; 5:21–6:3, 13–14; 2 Tim. 1:1 (2x), 9–10, 13; 2:1, 4, 8, 10; 3:12, 15; 4:1; Titus 1:1, 4; 2:13; 3:6
2) Whose death and resurrection inaugurated the age to come	1 Tim. 1:16; 4:8; 6:12, 19; 2 Tim. 1:10; 4:11, 18; Titus 1:1–3; 2:11, 14; 3:4–7
3) Entrance into the age to come is based on faith, not the Torah	1 Tim. 1:4–14, 16, 19 (2x); 3:13; 2 Tim. 1:5, 9–10; Titus 1:2, 13–14; 2:11; 3:5–7, 9
4) Paul is called to deliver that message, especially to the Gentiles	2 Tim. 4:17

Part Two

THE THEOLOGY
of
PAUL

In this second part of our work, which is briefer but tighter in argumentation, we examine the seven systematic categories into which Paul's theology is often classified: Theology proper, Christology, Pneumatology, Anthropology, Soteriology, Ecclesiology, and Eschatology. Our procedure for this part is to base our comments on the preceding categories by conducting key word counts related to the topic at hand, all the while taking note of the context of those relevant terms. The result is a rather thorough look at Paul's theology, one that happily coheres with the findings in Part I regarding Paul's life and letters.

THE THEOLOGY
OF PAUL

PAUL'S THEOLOGY PROPER

Paul uses θεος (God) some 387 times, if my count is correct. I chose not to include Paul's usage of κυριοςs (Lord) in that number because that term is ambiguous—sometimes it means God the Father while other times it means God the Son. But counting only θεος still demonstrates that God is central to Paul's thought. Thus we properly begin to highlight the theology of Paul by examining his employment of the term "God." What one discovers in doing that is that Paul views God through an apocalyptic lens. Not that we are the first to notice that. Sometime ago, J. Christiaan Beker devoted an entire book to recovering Paul's apocalyptic understanding of God.[1] I tried to do the same in a chapter in one of my earlier books,[2] but here I attempt to be more thorough in investigating Paul's apocalyptic perspective of God by taking into consideration every usage of the term "God" in Paul's writings. The result is that those some 387 references to God by Paul cluster into eleven categories, each of which relates to some aspect of the age to come: the preparation for the age to come, the

---

1   J. Christiaan Beker, *Paul the Apostle: The Triumph of God in Life and Thought* (Philadelphia: Fortress, 1980).
2   Pate, *The End of the Age Has Come*, ch. 1.

inauguration of the age to come, divine judgment on this age, the sign of the age to come, Paul the messenger of the age to come, entrance into the age to come, participants in the age to come (that is, the people of God), blessings of the age to come, perseverance in the age to come, revelation of the age to come, and the completion of the age to come. We now discuss the preceding categories.

A Preparation for the Age to Come

The Pauline writings describe God in numerous ways. He is truthful (e.g. Gal. 1:20; Rom. 3:4; 15:8; Titus 1:2); all wise (e.g. 1 Cor. 1:19–25, 30; Rom. 11:33–36); all powerful (e.g. Eph. 1:19–23); everywhere present (e.g. Rom. 10:6–8, 18 as referring to God's word in Christ); eternal, immortal, invisible (see 1 Tim. 1:17); one God (e.g. Rom. 3:29–30; 1 Cor. 8:4; 1 Tim. 1:17; 2:5) yet three persons (e.g. 1 Cor. 8:4–6; 1 Tim. 2:5–6; 2 Cor. 13:14; Eph. 1:3–14). But the two clusters of characteristics of God that stand out in Paul's letters are his holiness/righteousness (e.g. Gal. 5:21; 6:7; 1 Thess. 2:12; 3:12; 4:1, 3; 4:7–8; 5:23; 2 Thess. 1:5–6, 8; 2:13; Rom. 3:5, 25) and his love/mercy/grace (e.g. 1 Thess. 1:2; 2 Thess. 1:12; 1 Cor. 1:3–4; 2 Cor. 1:2; Rom. 1:7; 5:2; Eph. 2:8–9; Titus 3:4–5). And it is these two clusters of attributes that prepared the way for the arrival of the age to come. Galatians 3:6–25 juxtaposes the preceding two clusters of the divine character. Thus God's promise of the gospel of love/mercy grace through Abraham to all the nations is the point of departure for salvation history. As such, Abraham became the model of faith to all who would later believe the promises of God. The law of Moses later entered into the picture, for the express purpose of convicting humanity of its sin and thereby moving along salvation history to the coming of Christ, especially his death and resurrection. So like Luther's law/gospel hermeneutic, the law of Moses convicts all people in this evil age in order to drive them to the gospel of the age to come that has broken into the present. According to Romans 3:26, at the cross the holiness and mercy of God were reconciled. Through the death of Jesus, God could be both just and justifier. The cross of Christ was the hinge of salvation history, transitioning this age into the age to come.

The Inauguration of the Age to Come

With the last statement we reach a second apocalyptic perspective of Paul toward

God—Jesus is God's Messiah, and through him God inaugurated the age to come. More particularly, through the cross/resurrection of Jesus Christ the age to come broke into this present age (e.g. Gal. 1:1, 3–5; 1 Thess. 2:12; 2 Thess. 1:5; 1 Cor. 7:17–31; 15:20–28; 2 Cor. 5:11–6:2; Phil. 2:6–11; Col. 1:12–20; 3:1–4; Eph. 1:20–23; 2:4–10; Titus 2:11–14; 3:3–8; 2 Tim. 1:8–12).

Yet, Jesus as the Messiah of Israel, the Savior of the world, and the Lord of the universe is nevertheless subordinate to the Father according to Paul (so 1 Cor. 15:24–28; cf. the numerous times Paul juxtaposes God the father with Christ or Christ the son [e.g. Gal. 1:1; 1 Thess. 1:1, 3; 3:11; 2 Thess. 1:1; 2:16; 1 Cor. 1:3; 2 Cor. 1:2; Rom. 1:7; Phil. 1:2; Philem. 1:3; Eph. 1:2; 1 Tim. 1:2; 2 Tim. 1:2; Titus 1:4]). Another way to say this relative to 1 Corinthians 15:24–28, a key passage in the discussion, is that Jesus' death and resurrection inaugurated the temporary messianic kingdom, which will give way to the eternal kingdom of God. The notion that the temporary messianic kingdom was the transition between this evil age and the eternal kingdom of God was known in Second Temple Judaism; see *1 Enoch* 93:3–17 (ca. 150 BC); *4 Ezra* 7:26–44/12:31–34 (AD 90); *Apocalypse of Baruch* 29:3–30:1/40:1–4/72:2–74:3 (ca. AD 100), as well as by some ancient rabbis (Akiba, AD 135; Eliezer b. Hurcanus, ca. AD 90; Jehoshua, ca. 90), and probably the apostle John (Rev. 20; ca. 95 AD).

Divine Judgment on This Age

Paul says that this present age is passing away (1 Cor. 7:31) which, for him, is because the age to come has dawned in Christ. The most vivid way that Paul depicts the passing away of this age is by his application of the wrath of God to unbelievers in this world. There are two aspects of divine wrath according to Paul. First, God's wrath rests now upon nonbelievers in Jesus (1 Thess. 4:5, 6; Rom. 1:21, 23–24, 28, 30, 32; 9:21, 27; 12:18; Col. 3:6). This is so also for Jews (1 Thess. 2:15–16). The language here is that of divine wrath in the form of the continuing exile of Israel due to her unbelief in their Messiah. Second, God's wrath on the unbelieving world is still future, awaiting the parousia and judgment day: 2 Thessalonians 1:6–8; 2:4, 6 (on the man of lawlessness and his followers); Romans 2:2, 3, 5–6, 11, 13, 17, 23, 27; 3:6; 14:7, 11–12; 16:17 (on Satan himself). These present and future aspects of divine wrath are related: The judgment of the end time has already appeared in this age for those who reject Jesus as the Messiah, and that wrath will be made visible for all to see at the parousia on the day of the Lord/God. Of course, Paul hopes that those presently under divine judgment will repent and believe in Jesus, and thereby be spared end-time judgment.

The Sign of the Age to Come

The sign of the presence of the age to come *par excellence* is the presence of the Holy Spirit in the individual believer (1 Cor. 6:19–20) and in the church (1 Cor. 3:16–17; 2 Cor. 6:14–7:1; Eph. 2:19–22). Moreover, the indwelling of the Spirit is the earnest of the believer's future resurrection body (2 Cor. 5:5; Eph. 1:13–14). And the spiritual gifts of the believer due to the resident Spirit (1 Cor. 12–14) along with the character he produces (Gal. 5:22–23) continue the life of Jesus through his church. All of this is in accord with the prophecy of Joel 2:28–32, that God will pour out his Spirit upon the people of God in the latter days.

The Messenger of the Age to Come

We learned earlier that Paul identified himself as an apostle of God in Christ who preached a fourfold apocalyptic message: Jesus is the Christ, whose death and resurrection initiated the age to come, which is entered into by faith not the works of the Torah, including Gentiles. There are multitudinous statements by Paul in his letters connecting his apostleship with God's call upon his life: e.g. Galatians 1:15, 24; 1 Thessalonians 2:2, 4–5, 8–11, 13; 1 Corinthians. 1:1; 2:1, 5, 7; 3:6–7, 19; 4:1, 4–5, 9; 7:40; 9:9, 21; 15:9–10; 2 Corinthians 1:1; 2:12–15; 3:4–5; 4:7, 15; 6:1–2; Romans 1:1, 10; 15:6; Philippians. 1:1; Colossians 1:1, 25; 4:2; Ephesians 1:1; 3:2, 5, 7–8; 1 Timothy 1:1; 5:12; 2 Timothy 1:1, 3; Titus 1:1. Several remarks can be made based on these references. First, Paul viewed his apostolic authority as originating in God. Second, Paul understood his apostolic ministry as apocalyptic in orientation. More particularly, Paul believed that he was divinely commissioned to win the Gentiles to Christ—which was the fulfillment of the Old Testament prophecies of the end-time conversion of the nations—and that this conversion would hopefully spark the turning of Israel to Jesus the true Messiah. Third, another key apocalyptic aspect of Paul's apostleship was the juxtaposition of his constant suffering and God's continual deliverance of Paul from his trials. We have argued elsewhere that the afflictions Paul encountered were none other than the messianic woes, which Jesus himself experienced on the cross, and that God's deliverance of Paul from those hardships "re-presented" Christ's resurrection. In other words, Paul's suffering and deliverance re-presented the death and resurrection of Jesus to the Gentile world. Palestinian Jews had had the opportunity to witness the death of Jesus and to hear the news of his resurrection, but the majority of them rejected that message. However, the Gentiles were not privy to that information, so God reenacted the death and resurrection of Christ through his servant Paul to visualize that message to Gentiles. This in no way detracted from the sufficiency of Christ's atonement. It was rather a divine object lesson for the nations.[3]

Entrance into the Age to Come

The Pauline references that connect "God" with entrance into the age to come can be reduced to two interrelated statements. First, entrance into the age to come/kingdom of God is based solely on the grace of God offered through the atoning death of Jesus Christ (e.g. Gal. 1:3–4; Rom. 3:24–26; Eph. 1:7–8; 2:4–9; Col. 1:6–14; Titus 3:4–7). Second, God's gift of grace is received by faith, not by the works of the Torah (e.g. Gal. 2:19, 21; 3:5–6, 8, 11, 17–18; 4:4; Rom. 3:21–26; Col. 2:5–23).

The Participants in the Age to Come

Three key Pauline texts connect God with the participants in the age to come: Galatians 3:15–24; Romans 3:29–4:17; 11:17–24. What emerges from these important passages is the following theological axiom: The one God has one people, who are the children of Abraham (believing Jews and Gentiles), and these are saved by faith in Christ, not the works of the Law. According to this scenario, the Torah is a later addition in the plan of God to prepare humanity for the gospel, not the means of salvation.

---

3   See Pate and Kennard, *Deliverance Now and Not Yet: The New Testament and the Great Tribulation.*

The Blessings of the Age to Come

Paul speaks of numerous blessings from God to the believer who belongs to the age to come but during this present age: (1) God enclothed the Christian with his (God's) righteousness in Christ (2 Cor. 5:21). (2) God reconciled the believer to himself through Christ (2 Cor. 5:18–20). This is a remarkable statement given the fact that the Greek term καταλλασσω (reconcile) is not even used in classical Greek for humanity's relationship with the pagan gods and when it is used in the LXX, the term is employed of Israel's attempt to initiate reconciliation with God. For the first time in the history of religion, however, καταλλασσω is used in 2 Corinthians 5:18–20 in the sense that God is the one who seeks humankind through Christ. (3) God restored the image and glory Adam lost because of sin to the believer in Jesus (see especially 2 Cor. 4:4–6). In other words, God in Christ is recovering for the Christian the original divine plan for humankind. (4) God has delivered the believer in Christ from divine wrath, both now and in the future (1 Thess. 1:9–10; 5:9; Rom. 5:9). (5) God has given the Christian hope now in this age, of the future resurrection body of the age to come (1 Thess. 4:13; 2 Cor. 5:1–10). This is so because the resurrection of Christ was nothing less than the inbreaking into this age of the general resurrection of the age to come (1 Cor. 15:20–28). (6) God's grace in Christ has already saved the Christian, though its completion is not yet realized (see particularly Phil. 2:12–13; 3:12–14). (7) So also is the Christian justified already in this age, but the final realization is not yet, awaiting the full arrival of the age to come at the parousia (Rom. 5:1–5; cf. 6:1–14).

The Completion of the Age to Come

God will complete the age to come at the parousia of his son (e.g. 1 Thess. 1:10; 4:13–18; 2 Thess. 1:7–8; 1 Cor. 15:20–28). Until then the believer must live a worthy life before God, which means they should be holy and endure the messianic woes as their Lord Jesus did (1 Thess. 2:12; 2 Thess. 1:5, 11).

The Revelation of the Age to Come via the Cross

One of the amazing connections between Paul's references to God and the age to come is the apostle's perspective that the cross is the means of true divine revelation. This is especially prominent in 1 Corinthians 1:18–2:16. Gordon Fee captures the meaning of this text:

> The crucifixion and resurrection of Jesus for Paul marked the "turning of the ages," whereby God decisively judged and condemned the present age and is in process of bringing it to an end. Those who still belong to it, therefore, are in process of "perishing" with it. From this "old age" point of view the message of the cross is foolishness. On the other hand, those "who are being saved"… come to see their present existence as the result of God's power, which was also effected by God through the cross and resurrection of Jesus.[4]

We noted in an earlier chapter that the cross is the true means for accessing the age to come, not the Torah, as Paul's opponents had claimed. Moreover only the Holy Spirit can open those enslaved to this age to the wisdom, power, and salvation of the cross and the new age in Christ it signals (1 Cor. 2:1–16).

Christology

Christ receives pride of place in Paul's theology; he uses the term "Christ" or "Lord" some 514 times. We will now trace the various associations that Paul makes between Christ and the age to come. Some of these connections overlap with what Paul says about God that we noted above.

The Promise of the Age to Come

According to Galatians 3:6–18 and Romans 4:1–17, God's promise to Abraham included a people that shared in Abraham's faith, both Jew and Gentile. This promise is seen by Paul as anticipating the coming of Christ and the advent of the age to come. Indeed, from those two passages, especially Romans 4, one can see that the apostle actually pitted the Abrahamic covenant against the Mosaic covenant. Thus:

---

4   Gordon D. Fee, *The First Epistle to the Corinthians* (Grand Rapids, MI: Eerdmans, 1987), p. 69.

ABRAHAMIC COVENANT	MOSAIC COVENANT
vv. 1–5: Abraham was justified by faith	The individual is saved by the works of the Torah
vv. 6–8: Paul separates Genesis 15 from Genesis 17 and/or 22	The Pentateuch and Second Temple Judaism combine Genesis 15 and Genesis 17 and/or 22
vv. 9–12: Paul (like the Old Testament prophets before him) maintains that there is discontinuity between the divine promise to Abraham that he will be the father of many nations and the divine command to Abraham to be circumcised	The Pentateuch and Second Temple Judaism maintained that there is continuity between the divine promise to Abraham that he will be the father of many nations and the divine command to Abraham to be circumcised
vv. 13–25: According to Paul, the law of Moses stirs up disobedience (vv. 13–17a) whereas the promise engenders faith and obedience (vv. 17b–25)	The Law engenders obedience to God, the basis of the divine promise to Abraham

The Preparation for the Age to Come

What then is the purpose of the law of Moses if it is at odds with the covenant of Abraham? Paul's answer in Galatians 3:19–25, as we noted above, is that the Torah convicts humanity of its sin and thereby drives people to the gospel of Christ. We will reserve further comment on the Law for later in this point on Christology.

The Messiah of the Age to Come

Jesus is the Messiah/Christ who inaugurated the age to come. Paul describes Jesus Christ in several ways. (1) Jesus is God (see, for example, Rom. 1:3–4; 10:9; Phil. 2:9–11; Titus 2:13 [based on Granville Sharp's rule that the one article governs the two genitive nouns—God and Savior—thus equating those two nouns]). (2) Jesus is human (see Rom. 1:3–4; Phil. 2:6–8; 1 Tim. 2:5; 3:16). (3) Jesus is the last Adam (1 Cor. 15:20–28, 45–49; Rom. 5:12–21; Phil. 2:6–11). As such, Jesus is the true image and glory of God (2 Cor. 4:4–6). (4) Jesus is the wisdom of God (1 Cor. 1:30; 8:4–6; Col. 1:15–20; 2:2–3). (5) Yet still Jesus is the son who is subordinate to God the Father (1 Cor. 15:24–28). This preserves the monotheistic faith of Christianity.

The Inauguration of the Age to Come

While the four gospels indicate that the age to come or the kingdom of God was inaugurated in Jesus' life, Paul pinpoints the "already" aspect of the age to come in the death and resurrection of Jesus (see for example: Gal. 1:1–3; 6:14; 1 Thess. 4:14; 1 Cor. 2:8; 15; 2 Cor. 5:14–15; Rom. 1:3–4; 3:21–25; 4:24–25; Eph. 1:20–22; 1 Tim. 3:16; 2 Tim. 1:10; 2:8; Titus 2:11–14). It is clear that Paul viewed the cross and resurrection of Jesus as the turning point of the ages—the hinge of history.

Entrance into the Age to Come

Two significant observations may be made regarding Paul's understanding of how the sinner enters into the age to come/kingdom of God. First, entrance into the age to come is by faith in Jesus Christ, not by observing the works of the Torah (Gal. 2:16; 3:13–14; Rom. 3:9–20; 4:1–25; 7:4, 25; Eph. 2:1–10; Col. 2:6–23; Titus 3:4–7). Second, the believer's faith in Jesus mystically unites them with his death and resurrection (Gal. 2:20; Rom. 6:3–5; Phil. 3:10–11; Col. 3:1–4; 2 Tim. 2:11–13). That is, the sinner at the moment of belief in Jesus becomes a participant in the cross/resurrection and the turning of the ages.

The Messenger of the Age to Come

Culling together Paul's many references to himself as a special messenger of Christ and the age to come, we may categorize them into four remarkable statements. First, Paul is an apostle of Christ (Gal. 1:1; 1 Cor.1:1; 2 Cor. 1:1; Rom. 1:1–7; Eph. 1:1; etc.) through whom (Paul) Christ is revealed (Gal. 1:12, 16; 1 Cor. 9:1–2). Second, more specifically, Christ's death and resurrection are manifested through Paul's afflictions and divine deliverance, respectively. The former consists of the messianic woes, and the latter is a display of the resurrection of Jesus (Gal. 3:1; 4:14, 19; 6:17; 1 Thess. 2:6; 1 Cor. 2:2; 4:4, 10; 2 Cor. 1:5; 2:14–15; 4:5, 10–11; 5:16, 20; Phil. 3:10–11; Eph. 3:1–13; Col. 1:24). Third, Paul's representation of Christ's death and resurrection is aimed at winning Gentiles to Christ (see e.g. Eph. 3:1–13; Col. 1:24–28). Therefore, to embrace Paul was to embrace Jesus and the gospel (2 Cor. 5:20–6:13). Fourth, Paul interprets his role to the Gentiles as bringing about the end-time conversion of the nations, as we have noted before (see especially Romans 1:1–16; 15:14–32; 16:25–27).

Blessings of the Age to Come

We list here in no particular order some of the numerous blessings that belong to those who through Christ are participants in the age to come, including the following: They are sons of God (Gal. 3:26); equal in Christ (Gal. 3:28); free from the condemnation of the Law (Gal. 5:1; Rom. 8:1–4; 10:4); have faith, hope and love (1 Thess. 1:3); are saved from divine wrath (1 Thess. 5:9); are justified and sanctified (1 Cor. 1:2; 6:11; Rom. 5:1); possess the Spirit (Rom. 8:9–10), who is the earnest of their resurrection body (Rom. 8:11; Eph. 1:11–14); possess eternal glory (2 Cor. 3:18; Rom. 8:16–17, 30); are reconciled to God (2 Cor. 5:18–21; Rom. 5:11); participate in the new creation (2 Cor. 5:17); have eschatological joy (Rom. 14:17; Phil. 3:1; 4:4–7); constitute the elect of God (Eph. 1:3–6); are beloved by God (Eph. 3:18); belong to the kingdom of God in Christ (Col. 1:13); are regenerated (Titus 3:4–6); and are secure (Rom. 8:35, 39).

Perseverance in the Age to Come

The blessings of the age to come are not guaranteed without further ado; Christians must persevere in their faith, according to Paul. At least four aspects of persevering in the faith are touched upon by the apostle. First, Christians must stand firm in the gospel (1 Thess. 3:8; 1 Cor. 15:1–3; Col. 1:23). Second, believers should live lives of holiness (1 Thess. 4:1; Rom. 13:14). Third, Christians persevere in the faith by serving fellow believers (Rom. 14:15, 18; 15:5; 1 Cor. 1:10). Fourth, believers persevere by imitating Paul who imitates Christ's suffering (Gal. 4:12; 1 Cor. 4:15–16; 11:1).

The People of God and the Age to Come

Paul employs a number of metaphors for the people of God in Christ, including the "tree" of God's people by faith (Rom. 11:17–24); the temple of God (1 Cor. 3:16–17; 2 Cor. 6:14–18; Eph. 2:19–22), and the household of faith (1 Tim. 3:15). But the most important metaphor for the people of God that Paul uses is the church as the body of Christ (1 Cor. 12; Rom. 12; Eph. 4). Here we must pause and consider the origin of such a metaphor for Paul. Some seven theories have been proposed in the history of the debate.

(1) Eduard Schweizer called attention to the political view, which compared the body of Christ with the Greek idea that a gathered political group of people is to be associated with a human body (Livy, *Hist.* 2:32).[5] But while this view explained the parallel (community = body), it left unanswered the question of why Paul speaks of the "body *of Christ*" (e.g., 1 Cor. 12:27).[6]

(2) Similarly, W. L. Knox argued that the notion of the body of Christ originated in Stoicism, "The church as a body, of which the individuals were members, was derived from the Stoic commonplace of the state as a body in which each member had his part to play."[7] But like the political theory, this suggestion cannot explain why Paul calls it the "body *of Christ*." Ernst Best points out in this regard that the comparison is not between the body and its members, but between the members as members of the body of a person. He also notes that Stoicism never expressly called the cosmos the body of God.[8]

(3) L. Cerfaux claimed that the idea of the body of Christ originated in the church's celebration of the Lord's Supper.[9] But the theory that the body of Christ is equivalent to the bread of Christ is based on the assumption that Paul's teaching on the Eucharist is borrowed from the mystery religions' belief that partaking of the meal of the deity was tantamount to being united with the god—a hypothesis now discarded by most scholars.[10]

---

5 Eduard Schweizer, "*sōma*," *Theological Dictionary of the New Testament*, ed. by Gerhard Kittel and Gerhard Fridrich; trans. by Geoffrey W. Bromiley (Grand Rapids, MI: Eerdmans, reprint 1999), pp. 1038–39.

6 Dunn, *Romans 9–16*, p. 723.

7 Wilfred L. Knox, *St. Paul and the Church of the Gentiles* (Cambridge: University Press, 1939), p. 161.

8 Ernst Best, *One Body in Christ: A Study in the Relationship of the Church to Christ in the Epistles of the Apostle Paul* (London: Society for the Promotion of Christian Knowledge, 1955), p. 83.

9 L. Cerfaux, *The Church in the Theology of St. Paul*, trans. by Geoffrey Webb and Adrian Walker (New York: Herder and Herder, 1959), pp. 263–265.

10 See Best's critique of the influence of the mystery religions on Paul, *One Body in Christ*, 87–89. See also the criticisms of Gunter Wagner, *Pauline Baptism and the Pagan Mysteries: The Problem of the Pauline Doctrine of Baptism in Romans VI. 1–11, in the Light of its Religio-Historical Parallels*, trans. by J. P. Smith (Edinburgh and London: Oliver & Boyd, 1967). The most recent work is by A. J. M. Wedderburn, *Baptism and Resurrection: Studies in Pauline Theology Against Its Greco-Roman Background*, Wissenschaftliche Untersuchungen zum Neuen Testament 44 (Tübingen: J. C. B. Mohr [Paul Siebeck], 1987), who provides a devastating critique of the purported impact of the mystery religions on Paul.

(4) Rudolf Bultmann popularized the position that Gnosticism informed the Pauline concept of the body of Christ. That view promoted the primal man myth, a teaching identifying individuals as pieces of an original cosmic, heavenly man who, upon his fall to earth, disintegrated into myriads of human bodies. On recollecting their original spiritual state, however, those individual pieces are ultimately regathered into the one primal man.[11] Few scholars today, however, date that myth to the first century AD. Furthermore, the myth never was monolithic in structure, contrary to the protests of Bultmann.

(5) James D. G. Dunn roots the body of Christ concept in the charismatic worship setting of the early church. As believers gathered for worship and as God manifested himself through the *charismata* (spiritual gifts), the people sensed themselves to be a corporate body, unified in Christ.[12] There is an element of truth in this suggestion, but it is too generic, especially since two other ideas are more available to explain the phrase.

(6) W. D. Davies insightfully argued that the Jewish apocalyptic/rabbinic concept of the corporate body of Adam is the best antecedent to the notion of the universal body of Christ. He writes:

> Paul accepted the traditional Rabbinic doctrine of the unity of mankind in Adam. That doctrine implied that the very constitution of the physical body of Adam and the method of its formation was symbolic of the real oneness of mankind. In that one body of Adam east and west, north and south, were brought together male and female.... The "body" of Adam included all mankind. Was it not natural, then, that Paul should have conceived of it [the church] as the "body" of the second Adam, where there was neither Jew nor Greek, male nor female, bond nor free.[13]

There is much to commend this point of view, especially since many interpreters see the person of Adam behind the Pauline passages on the body

11 Rudolf Bultmann, *Theology of the New Testament*, trans. by Kendrick Grobel (New York: Charles Scribner's, 1951), 1:178–79.
12 Dunn, *Romans 9–16*, pp. 723–24.
13 W. D. Davies, *Paul and Rabbinic Judaism: Some Rabbinic Elements in Pauline Theology* (New York: Harper & Row, 1948), p. 57; cf. pp. 53–57.

of Christ (cf. 1 Cor. 12 with 1 Cor. 15:44–49; Rom. 12: 4–5 with vv. 1–2; 5:12–21; 7:7–13; 8:17–25; Col. 1:18 with v. 15; Eph. 4:7–16 with 1:15–23; 5:22–33). The major objection to this argument is that there is no explicit mention of the "body of Adam" in the Jewish literature contemporaneous with Paul. But this objection can be adequately met by the next theory, which fits nicely with the Adamic hypothesis.

(7) A. J. M. Wedderburn[14] proposes that the roots of the idea of the body of Christ stem from the ancient Hebrew mentality of corporate personality, the belief that one person represents many and many are incorporated in the one (Gen. 12:1–3; cf. Gen. 14:17–20 with Heb. 7:4–10; Josh. 7:16–26). This reciprocal relationship takes one a long way toward understanding the body of Christ, and it is commensurate with the Adamic theory that the first man is the representative of the fallen human race (Rom. 5:12–21). If so, then we see that the church, the corporate body of Christ, is none other than the eschatological Adam (1 Cor. 15:45), the new humanity of the end time, which has now appeared in human history.

Apostasy and the Age to Come

Regrettably, believers can depart from the gospel and thereby be disqualified from the age to come. This was especially the situation that faced the Galatian church (Gal. 1:6–10; 5:4; 6:12), the Corinthian church (1 Cor. 10:14; 11:2–4), the Colossian church (Col. 2:1–23) and the Ephesian church (1 Tim. 4:1–5; 6:3–5; 2 Tim. 3:1–4:5; Titus 1:10–16). Paul himself feared that he might fall to such a fate (1 Cor. 9:24–27), but God is faithful to keep his own (1 Cor. 10:13).

Divine Wrath in This Age and the Age to Come

There are two aspects to Paul's comments about wrath. First, for those who have rejected Christ already in this age divine wrath rests upon them (1 Thess. 2:16; Rom. 1:18; 3:5; 4:15; Eph. 2:3; 5:6). Second, such people will still have

---

14 Wedderburn, *Baptism and Resurrection*, 350–56. Wedderburn also convincingly responds to criticisms of the Hebrew corporate personality theory. For more discussion, see Pate, *The End of the Age*, pp. 170–72.

to face divine judgment on the last day; this is the not-yet aspect of God's wrath (Rom. 2:5, 8; Col. 3:6).

The Parousia as the Completion of the Age to Come

The second coming of Jesus will be the completion of the age to come, according to Paul (1 Thess. 2:15; 4:13–18; 5:1–11;2 Thess. 2:1, 8, 14, 16; 1 Cor. 15; 2 Cor. 5:1–10; Phil. 3:19–20; 4:4; 1 Tim. 4:1; Titus 2:11–14). From these references we may deduce three disclaimers. First, Paul does not seem to distinguish a secret rapture from the second coming of Christ. Thus 1 Thessalonians 4:13–18; 5:1–11 appear to be the same event Jesus predicted in the Olivet Discourse, namely, the parousia. Therefore the church presently experiences the messianic woes and the kingdom of God. But when Christ returns in power and glory, his kingdom will prevail over the enemies of God. Second, the overlapping of the two ages for Paul—Christ inaugurated the kingdom of God at his first coming and will complete that kingdom at his return—governs Paul's eschatology. We therefore do not need to propose major development in Paul's thinking on the subject, other than the possibility that Paul became aware that he might not be alive at the parousia. Third, Paul does not explicitly posit a temporary reign of Christ on earth after his return, though 1 Corinthians 15:20–28 is interpreted by some to mean that. In other words Paul does not come out and identify himself as a "premillennialist" (though I think 1 Cor. 15:20–28 should be read that way, and I think Rev. 20 should definitely be interpreted along that line).

Pneumatology

Paul uses the name "Holy Spirit" or "Spirit" some 82 times. The vast majority of these references associate the third member of the Trinity with the age to come. Another way to put the matter would be to say that many of the blessings that Judaism reserved for the age to come the apostle Paul declares have arrived with the advent of the Holy Spirit. That should not be surprising because the Old Testament prophesied that the latter days would witness the arrival of the Spirit (see, for example, Joel 2:28–32). For Paul and early Christianity, Pentecost marked the fulfillment of Old Testament prophecy in that regard (Acts 2). We now highlight some ten aspects of the end-time associations with the Spirit that Paul makes.

Justification

In Second Temple Judaism the common conviction was that not until judgment day would one know whether or not he or she was justified by God, since such acceptance depended on a life-time of obedience to the Torah. But Paul asserts that God justifies now the believer in Jesus. In other words, the justification of the age to come is a present reality for the Christian because the Spirit has placed the believer in Christ (Rom. 8:1).

The New Covenant of Obedience

The Old Testament prophesied that in the latter days God would establish his new covenant with Israel, one that would be characterized by obedience from the heart generated by the indwelling of God's Spirit (Ezek. 36:24–32; cf. Jer. 31:31–34). According to Paul, that promise is now being fulfilled by the indwelling Spirit within the church and its members (2 Cor. 3:1–4:6). It is interesting that the apostle juxtaposes the Spirit and the new covenant to the old covenant, the law of Moses, and the flesh. Thus Paul opposes the Spirit and the new covenant with the old covenant (see again 2 Cor. 3:1–4:6; Rom. 7:1–6). Related to this, Paul pits the Spirit and the new covenant against the law of Moses (Gal. 3:2–4; 4:6; Rom. 2:28–29; 8:2–4; Phil. 3:1–3). Moreover, it is clear from Galatians 5:16–23, 25; 6:8 that Paul believes that the Law stirs up the flesh to disobey God, and that only faith in Christ and the Spirit can defeat the flesh.

The Spirit and the End-Time Temple

There was a strong expectation in Second Temple Judaism that God or his Messiah would build an end-time temple which would be indwelled by the Holy Spirit (see especially Ezek. 40–48 and the DSS [4 Q Flor.; 4 Q Test.). The Dead Sea Scrolls went even further and declared that the end-time temple would consist, not of a building, but of the people of God (1 QS 8; cf. Rev. 21–22). For Paul the end-time temple is none other than the church, which is indwelled by the Spirit (1 Cor. 3:16–17; Eph. 2:22; 3:17), which includes the individual Christian (1 Cor. 6:19; Rom.8: 9–10).

The Spirit and the Resurrection of the Age to Come

Ezekiel 37 envisions the future restoration of Israel as a resurrection accomplished by the power of God's Spirit (cf. Dan. 12:1–3). In Second Temple Judaism, the conviction cemented that there would be an end-time resurrection activated by the Holy Spirit. Paul believed that the Spirit's resurrection of Jesus begins that general end-time resurrection (1 Cor. 15:35–49; Rom. 1:4; 8:11). Furthermore, the Spirit's presence within the believer is the earnest of the future resurrection body of Christians (2 Cor. 1:22; 5:5; Rom. 8:11, 23–25; Eph. 1:13–14).

The Spirit and the End-Time Children of God

Hosea 2:4, 23 forecasts that Israel, whom God no longer called his children and people during the exile, would be restored to God in the future restoration by being renamed the children and people of God. In Romans 9:25, Paul applies that prophecy to Jewish and Gentile Christians, who by the indwelling of the Spirit are now known as the eschatological children of God. Indeed, believers may now address God as their Abba (Rom. 8:15–16). Moreover, the Spirit intercedes to God on behalf of his children (Rom. 8:26–27).

The Spirit and the Gifts of the Age to Come

Joel 2:29–32 predicts that when God pours out his Spirit on his people of God in the latter days that they will dream dreams, see visions, and perform miraculous wonders. Acts 2 records the fulfillment of that promise on the day of Pentecost. The rest of Acts documents how the Spirit did indeed work through the church mightily even as he worked through Christ. Paul taps into that tradition in his lists of the gifts of the Spirit (1 Cor. 12–14; Rom. 12:3–8; Eph. 4)—gifts that included special revelation and miracles. Truly, the prophecy of Joel had been fulfilled.

The Spirit and the End-Time Revival of Prophecy

Ancient Judaism felt devoid of the Spirit and prophecy (*Sir.* 49:10; 1 Macc. 4:46; 9:27; 14:41; *Sib. Or.* 1:386). Only at the end of history was God expected to restore his Spirit and the prophetic word to Israel (see again Joel 2:28–32). Like the early church (refer to Acts 2 again), Paul believed that the pouring out of the Spirit in the last days was accompanied with the renewal of prophecy (1 Thess. 5:19–21; 1 Cor. 14; 1 Tim. 4:1). Related to this, the Spirit was revealing eschatological mysteries to Paul regarding the church (Eph. 3:5). The greatest mystery was the cross of Christ, the meaning of which could only be ascertained by the illumination of the Spirit (1 Cor. 2:10–14).

God's end-time revelation was now being inscripturated by the Spirit (2 Tim. 3:16). More than that, the Spirit and the word of God are available to the Christian who fights the end-time holy war against the devil and his forces (Eph. 6:17).

The Spirit and the Kingdom of God

Jesus proclaimed that only through the new birth of the Holy Spirit could one enter the kingdom of God (John 3:3, 5). The apostle Paul echoes Jesus' sentiments in Galatians 5:19–26 and Romans 14:17; 15:13. The first passage states the matter negatively: those who follow the works of the flesh (stimulated by the Law) will not enter the kingdom of God but those who display the fruit of the Spirit show that they have entered that spiritual realm. The second text states the principle positively: The Spirit is associated with the righteousness, joy, peace, and the power of the kingdom of God. All of this to say that Paul agrees with his Lord Jesus that it is through the new birth of the Spirit that one enters the end-time kingdom of God.

Paul, the Messenger of the Spirit

It is obvious that Paul believed that he was the messenger of the Spirit in these last days (1 Thess. 1:5; 4:8; 1 Cor. 2:4; 7:40).

The Spirit and the Eschatological People of God

In Romans 15:8–13, Paul quotes Old Testament promises that one day God will unite Jew and Gentile together in true worship of God (2 Sam. 22:50; Ps. 18:49; Deut. 32:43; Isa. 66:10; Ps. 11:10; 117:1). For Paul, the coming of Jesus the Messiah and the power of the Spirit are bringing those end-time predictions to pass. Because of that the people of God—Christian Jew and Christian Gentile—should be unified in practice (cf. Eph. 3:1–11 with 4:3–4) and loving to one another (cf. Rom. 5:5 with 15:30). Both of these characteristics come from the Holy Spirit.

ANTHROPOLOGY

Paul uses the term "man" ($\dot{\alpha}\nu\theta\rho\omega\pi\text{os}$) some 134 times. Bracketing out the some 20 generic usages of the term, we are left with a decidedly clear portrait of humanity in the Pauline literature, namely, humanity divides into two categories: the first Adam and the old humanity and the last Adam and the new humanity. Moreover, these two representative personages have subsumed under them the two ages:

The First Adam	Christ, the Last Adam
This Age	The Age to Come

In this section we will survey the seven topics that fall under the above two categories: the constitution of man, the depravity of humanity, Christ as the last Adam and the creator of the new humanity, the salvation of humankind through faith in Christ apart from the Torah, Paul the messenger of Christ and the new humanity, the temporary institutions of man, and the man of lawlessness in this age. After summarizing these categories regarding Paul's anthropology, we will offer a chart that classifies Paul's anthropology into the two Adams/ages.

The Constitution of Man

Two key passages communicate Paul's understanding of the constitution of humanity: 1 Thessalonians 5:23 and 2 Corinthians 4:16–5:10. The first seems to say that the human consists of body, soul, and spirit; that is, the trichotomist viewpoint. This may be, but one could just as well read that text as a dichotomist: humans are a combination of body and soul/spirit, with no distinction between the latter two. 2 Corinthians 4:16–5:10 clearly divides man into an outer body and an inner soul/spirit. At death, the latter goes immediately into the presence of the Lord awaiting the parousia and the resurrection of the body. The commentators on 2 Corinthians 4:16–5:10 rightly note that the "outer man" is the body bequeathed to us by the first Adam, one in constant decay, while the "inner man" is the soul/spirit renewed in the Christian by Christ the last Adam. Moreover, the outer/inner man corresponds to the overlapping of the two ages for the believer: The renewed image and glory of God in Christ is not only the internal presence of the age to come in the believer, but within this present age in which the outer body decays and dies.

The Depravity of Mankind

Here we make four points about Paul's understanding of the sinfulness of humankind. First, we find the best explanation in Paul regarding total depravity in Romans 3:9–20. According to these verses, the totality of man is infected by sin: deeds, words, and thoughts. Thus sin has impacted every aspect of man's relationship with God. Second, the extent of depravity includes all people, Jew and Gentile (Rom. 1:18–3:8), and it involves both the erosion of morality (see again Rom. 1:18–3:8) and the mortality of the human body (1 Cor. 15:21, 47). Third, Paul attributes the origin of depravity to Adam and Eve, especially the former (Rom. 5:12, 15, 17–19; 1 Cor. 15:21, 47). Fourth, Adam's sin and this age still inflict even the Christian, because he lives between the two ages (Rom. 7:13–25; Eph. 4:22, 24). This will be so until the parousia.

Christ the Last Adam and the New Humanity

Paul's point here is as simple as it is powerful: Jesus Christ became human and in doing so obeyed God where Adam failed and thereby as the last Adam has inaugurated the age to come and the new humanity: Philippians 2:7–8; compare Romans 1:3–4; 5:7, 15, 17, 18, 19; 6:6; 8:4; Ephesians 2:15; 1 Timothy 2:5.

Humans Are Saved by Grace, Not by the Torah

There are three tenses to salvation regarding humanity that trusts in Christ. There is the past tense of salvation, by which the sinner was delivered from Adam's sin and this age (Rom. 5:15–21). There is the present tense of salvation, in which the believer still struggles with the old nature of the first Adam that characterizes this evil age but overcomes that by aligning himself/herself with the new nature of the true Adam that has initiated the age to come (Rom. 6:1–21; 7:1–25). And then there will be the day when the believer is totally in sync with the age to come at the parousia of Jesus Christ, the new Adam (Rom. 8:17–30).

These three tenses of salvation also correspond with the Torah. (1) Sinners were driven to Christ when they realized that they could not keep the law of Moses. Indeed, the Torah stirred up disobedience to God. Trying to be justified by good works only lead to a dead-end street (Gal. 2:4, 17; 3:12, 28;

4:4–6; Rom. 5:17–19; 8:4; 10:5; 2 Cor. 5:11, 19; 1 Tim. 4:10; Titus 2:11). (2) The law of God continues to convict the believer showing them their sins and driving them further to the grace of God. This creates internal struggle for the believer (Rom. 7:1–25). (3) However, when the age to come is fully realized at the return of Christ, the struggle with the Torah will be over (cf. Rom. 5:20–21 with 6:23; 1 Cor. 15:56–57).

Paul the Messenger of Christ and the New Humanity
As we observed earlier, Paul considered himself the messenger of the new covenant *par excellence* (2 Cor. 3:1–4:6). This new covenant is nothing less than a new creation in Christ, a new humanity (2 Cor. 5:17). But it is interesting in this regard that Paul consistently uses "man" (ἄνθρωπος) in a negative way, namely, to state that the authority behind his message is not of human origin (Gal. 1:1, 10, 17, 23; 2:7; 1 Thess. 2:4, 6, 13, 15; Eph. 3:5; etc.). So Paul bases his apostolic calling in God through Christ, not in man.

The Temporary Human Institutions
First Corinthians 7 is a key passage in which Paul speaks of the institutions of his day: marriage, celibacy, slavery, circumcision, etc. His point there is that this age of human institutions is already passing away since the advent of Jesus Christ. Soon Jesus will come again and demolish those institutions created by humans (see especially 1 Cor. 7:17–31). Paul would have no doubt agreed with the apostle John in this matter who writes, "The world and its desires pass away, but the man who does the will of God lives forever" (1 John 2:17).

The Man of Lawlessness
In 2 Thessalonians 2:3 Paul refers to the coming man of lawlessness—no doubt the Antichrist—who will try to woo humanity, believers included, into worshipping him instead of the one true God. But Jesus will return and destroy the man of lawlessness along with his devotees. Here we see an implied Adamic contrast: The man of lawlessness will be the culmination of the idolatry of the first Adam, but Christ the last Adam will destroy the final rebellion of the Antichrist at the parousia.

The following chart summarizes the preceding topics according to the two Adams/ages construct:

OLD ADAM/THIS AGE	NEW ADAM/AGE TO COME
Constitution of man: outer man/old Adam/ this age	Constitution of Christian: inner man/new Adam/age to come/resurrected body like Christ
Depravity of man due to the sin of first Adam, which created this present evil age	New humanity in second Adam, which already participates in the age to come. Paul is the messenger who proclaims the presence of this new creation.
Adam's fall instigated sin and the law of Moses stirs up disobedience	Faith in Christ the obedient Adam places one in the age to come, yet within the context of this age, the result of which is struggle. But that struggle will be resolved at the parousia.
Human/Adamic institutions are passing away along with this age	because Christ the last Adam has arrived and inaugurated the age to come
The man of lawlessness will arise at the end of this age	but he will be destroyed by Christ the obedient Adam at his return

SOTERIOLOGY

"Salvation" (σωτηριας) occurs some twenty times in the writings of Paul, but the idea is broader than the term, as we will see in this section. According to Paul, salvation and related ideas cluster around what is often called the three tenses of salvation: past tense = justification; present = sanctification; future = glorification. Moreover, these tenses of salvation are intimately connected to the overlapping of the two ages. Thus, believers have already been saved in that they are justified before God and this attests to the dawning of the age to come. But Christians are still in the process of being saved in the sense that they are being sanctified. This is evidence that the age to come is not yet complete. The present age continues. Finally, believers will be saved at the return of Christ when they will experience glorification. At that time the age to come will be complete. Our procedure in this section will therefore be to list the associations of these three tenses of salvation.

The Past Tense of Salvation: Justification and the Dawning of the Age to Come
At least twelve items fall into this category in Paul's letters, which we do little more than list here: (1) Christians have been delivered from this present age (Gal. 1:4), which involves being saved from the wrath to come (1 Thess. 1:10; Rom. 5:9). This is another way of saying that the age to come has dawned in Christ and for his followers. (2) This also means that believers have entered the kingdom of God (1 Thess. 2:12; 1 Cor. 6:11; Col. 1:12–13). More specifically, Christians at the moment of conversion are raised to heaven and enthroned with Christ in the glory of his heavenly kingdom (Eph. 2:6–7; Col. 3:1–4). But that glory will not be manifested until the parousia. (3) All of this is based on the atoning death and resurrection of Christ (Rom. 3:21–31; 1 Cor. 1:18–31). (4) This salvation is received by faith in Christ alone and not by the works of the Torah (Gal. 2:16; 3:6, 9; 3:10, 12–13; 4:8; Eph. 2:8–9; Phil. 3:1–11). (5) Indeed, the divine purpose of the Law was to drive the sinner to the gospel of grace (Gal. 3:21–25). (6) Because of this, Christians are now free from the Law (Rom. 7:1–8; Col. 2:14, 16–23). (7) Since salvation is by faith in Christ apart from the Torah, Gentiles too can be saved (Rom. 1:6; 11:11–27; Eph. 2:11–21; Col. 1:24–29). (8) Salvation in Christ is nothing less than participating in the new covenant of the Spirit (2 Cor. 3:1–4:6) and (9) in the new creation (2 Cor. 5:17). (10) Salvation is by the power of God (Rom. 1:16); the same power that raised Christ from the dead and inaugurated the age to come (Eph. 1:20–2:7). (11) This salvation of God involves deliverance from Satan and the demons (Col. 2:15), who somehow adversely influenced the Torah (Gal. 4:9; Col. 2:8). (12) Salvation involves a cluster of related ideas: justification (Rom. 5:1; 8:1); life (Rom. 5:15–20); righteousness (Rom. 1:16–17; 2 Cor. 5:21); and reconciliation (Rom. 5:11; 2 Cor. 5:18–21).

The Present Tense of Salvation:
Sanctification and the Continued Presence of This Age
But, according to Paul, salvation is not fully here for the believer. Christians have to work out their salvation (Phil. 2:12–13) and, while it is nearer than when Christians first believed, salvation is still forthcoming (Rom. 13:11–14). These verses and others in Paul have to do with sanctification and the present aspect of salvation. Some twenty-one items can be included in this aspect of

salvation: (1) Even though the believer has been raised to the heavenlies with Christ they still live on earth and must develop in sanctification (cf. Col. 3:1–4 with vv. 5–17). (2) Therefore Christians have not yet arrived at spiritual perfection (Rom. 13:11–14; 3:12–16). (3) They have to work out their salvation (Phil. 2:12–13) by being obedient children of God, not like ancient Israel (Phil. 2:14–18). (4) Christians are in union with Christ by faith and therefore his life flows through them (Rom. 6:1–23; cf, the many times Paul says that believers are "in Christ"). (5) Because Christians are in the new covenant of the Spirit they now have the power to live holy lives (Rom. 8:2–8). (6) Christians should produce good works as they serve the Lord and others (1 Cor. 15:58; Eph. 2:10; 4:7–12). (7) Loving others is a significant part of sanctification (1 Cor. 13; Rom. 12:9–21). Indeed love fulfills the Law (Gal. 6:2; Rom. 13:8–10). (8) Sanctification also involves being at one with other Christians (Eph. 4:1–6), (9) being like Christ (Eph. 4:13–16), (10) walking worthy before the Lord (Eph. 4:1; Col. 1:10), and (11) growing in the knowledge of Christ (Phil. 1:9–11; Col. 1:9–10). (12) A part of living for the Lord in this present age means to love one's family by performing God-given roles assigned to them therein—that is, the *Haustafeln* (Col. 3:18–4:1; Eph. 5:22–6:9).(13) Sanctification obviously includes living a holy lifestyle (1 Thess. 4:3–8; 5:4–8; 2 Thess. 1:3–4; 1 Cor. 1:30; 2 Cor. 6:14–7:1; Phil. 4:8–9) and (14) striving to be blameless until the return of Christ (1 Thess. 3:13; 1 Cor. 1:2; Phil. 1:6; 2 Tim. 2:3–13). (15) Sanctification also entails imitating Paul who imitates Christ (1 Cor. 4:16; 11:1; Phil. 2:5). (16) Because believers continue to live in the world they should expect to suffer for the cause of Christ; suffering which is mostly likely to be equated with the messianic woes (1 Thess. 2:14–16; 3:3; 2 Thess. 1:5, 11; Rom. 5:2–4; 8:16, 17; 2 Cor. 1:3–11; Phil 1:29; 2 Tim. 1:8, 12; 2:3–13). (17) Sometimes such affliction is internal, as in the Christian's struggle with the old nature (Rom. 7:13–25), (18) which is also the spiritual end-time holy war internalized (2 Cor. 10:3–6; Rom. 6: 11–14; Eph. 6:10–18). (19) But believers can be assured that God will deliver them from their trials and temptations, because the age to come has broken into this evil age (1 Cor. 10:11–13). (20) Such encouragement is needed because there is always the danger of end-time apostasy (1 Cor. 11:13–15; 1 Tim. 4:1–5; 6:3–10; 2 Tim. 3:1–9; Titus 1:10–16), which can apparently forfeit one's salvation (1 Cor. 9:24–27; 11:27–31; 2 Cor. 13:5; Col. 1:23; 2 Tim. 2:17–18). (21) But the glory of the age to come and the new covenant in the heart of the follower of Jesus will sustain the believer during this age (2 Cor. 3:1–4:6 with 4:7–5:21).

The Future Tense of Salvation and the Completion of the Age to Come

At the parousia the age to come will be complete. Eight items fall under this category in Paul's writings. (1) The return of the Lord is near (Phil. 4:5). (2) But if the Christian dies before the parousia, then his or her soul goes immediately to be with the Lord as a disembodied soul (2 Cor. 5:8; cf. Phil. 1:21). There they await the return of the Lord (2 Cor. 5:10). (3) In God's timing, Christ will return in glory and power (Col. 3:4; Titus 2:11–14). (4) Coinciding with the parousia will be the conversion of Israel to Christ (Rom. 11:25–27). (5) The return of Christ will mean glory for the believer (2 Thess. 2:14; Rom. 5:2; Rom. 8:17–30), which (6) is associated with the resurrection of the body (1 Cor. 15:42–44; cf. Rom. 8:11) as it is reunited with the departed soul. (7) At that time, believers will be vindicated before the world (2 Thess. 1:10). (8) And they will be found blameless in Christ (1 Thess. 2:13).

ECCLESIOLOGY

The New Testament word for "church" is ἐκκλησια, which means "the called out ones." In classical Greek, the term was used almost exclusively for political gatherings. In particular, in Athens the word signified the assembling of the citizens for the purpose of conducting the affairs of the city. Moreover, ἐκκλησια referred only to the actual meeting, not to the citizens themselves. When the people were not assembled, they were not considered to be the ἐκκλησια. The New Testament records three instances of this secular usage of the term (Acts 19:32, 41).

The most important background of the term ἐκκλησια is the Septuagint (the Greek translation of the Hebrew Old Testament produced in approximately 250 BC), which uses the word in a religious sense about one hundred times, almost always as a translation of the Hebrew word *qahal*. While *qahal* does not indicate a secular gathering (in contrast to *eda*, the typical Hebrew word for Israel's religious gathering, translated by the Greek, συναγωγη), it does denote Israel's sacred meetings. This is especially the case in Deuteronomy, where *qahal* is linked with the covenant.

In the New Testament, ἐκκλησια is used to refer to the community of God's people 109 times (out of 114 occurrences of the term). Although the word only occurs in two Gospel passages (Matt. 16:18; 18:17), it is of special importance in Acts (23 times) and the Pauline writings (46 times). It is found twenty times in Revelation and in isolated instances in James and Hebrews. Three general conclusions can be drawn from this usage. First, ἐκκλησια (both in the singular and plural) applies predominantly to a local assembly of those who profess faith in and allegiance to Christ. Second, ἐκκλησια designates the universal church (Acts 8:3; 9:31; 1 Cor. 12:28; 15:9; especially in the later Pauline letters, Eph. 1:22–23; Col. 1:18). Third, the ἐκκλησια is *God's* congregation (1 Cor. 1:2; 2 Cor. 1:1; etc.).

The predominate nuance of Paul's usage of "church" or related ideas is that it is composed of the eschatological people of God. The following points will demonstrate this to be the case as we note from Paul's writings at least eight apocalyptic images for the church.

The Church Is the Body of Christ

We begin this discussion by observing in a little more detail that Paul refers to the church at the local level (1 Cor. 1:2; 4:17; 6:4; 16:19; 2 Cor. 1:1; Rom. 16:1, 5, 23; Phil. 4:15; Col. 4:15–16; 1 Thess. 1:1; 2 Thess. 1:1; Philem. 1:2) and as the church universal (e.g., 1 Cor. 5:12; 10:32; 11:22; 12:28; 14:4–5, 12, 19, 26, 28, 35; Col. 1:18, 24; Eph. 1:22; 3:10, 21). It can be deduced from this that Paul believed that the church universal manifested itself at the local level of the particular congregation. What emerges especially from the above Corinthian, Colossian, and Ephesian references is that the church is the body of Christ, Paul's main contribution to ecclesiology. We remember from an earlier point that the origin of Paul's metaphor of the church as the body of Christ most likely proceeded from his Adam theology: The church is the cosmic body of Christ, the last (eschatological, 1 Cor. 15:45) Adam who is the head of the people of God. In other words, the church is the new humanity in Christ of the last days.

The Church Is the Bride of Christ

We also learn from some of the Ephesian passages above that the church is the bride of Christ, the new Eve (Eph. 5:22, 24, 25, 27, 29, 32). The idea that the church is the bride of Christ is an adaptation of the pervasive Old Testament notion that Israel was the wife of Yahweh (Isa. 54:5–6; 62:5; Hos. 2:7; etc.). Moreover, Revelation 21–22 provides the eschatological background for the idea that the church is the eschatological Eve in the way it presents the church as the new Eve/new Jerusalem descending to earth at the end of time. That Paul was familiar with such a concept can be seen in his allegory in Galatians 4:21–31. According to Paul, Christ, the bridegroom, has sacrificially and lovingly chosen the church to be his bride (Eph. 5:25–27). Her responsibility during the betrothal period is to be faithful to him (2 Cor. 11:2; Eph. 5:24). At the parousia the official wedding ceremony will take place and, with it, the eternal union of Christ and his wife will be actualized (Rev. 19:7–9; 21:1–2).

The Church Is the Restored Israel of the End Times

Paul joins other New Testament authors who portray the church as the new, restored Israel. The many Old Testament names for Israel applied to the church in the New Testament establish that fact. Some of those are: "Israel" (Gal. 6:15–16; Eph. 2:12; Heb. 8:8–10; Rev. 2:14; etc.); "a chosen people" (1 Peter 2:9); "the true circumcision" (Rom. 2:28–29; Phil. 3:3; Col. 2:11; etc.); "Abraham's seed" (Rom. 4:16; Gal. 3:29); "the remnant" (Rom. 9:27; 11:5–7); "the elect" (Rom. 11:28; Eph. 1:4); "the flock" (Acts 20:28; Heb. 13:20; 1 Peter 5:2); "priesthood" (1 Peter 2:9; Rev. 1:6; 5:10). Indeed, a significant aspect of Paul's calling as an apostle to the Gentiles was to reveal the mystery that Christian Gentiles now constitute the true Israel (Col. 1:24–27; Eph. 3:1–13); so also do Christian Jews (Rom. 11:1–10). Furthermore, that mystery reverses the Old Testament prophecy that in the end of time first Israel will be restored to God and then the nations will be converted to God, such that Gentiles are now being converted before Israel's restoration. Indeed, the Gentiles' conversion to Christ is the beginning of the restoration of Israel.

The Church Is the Beginning of the New Creation of the Age to Come

We learn this truth from a passage like 2 Corinthians 5:17. Ephesians 1:7–10 and 3:10 fill out this detail by noting that the reconciliation of Jew and Gentile in Christ is a divine object lesson to creation that God will one day reconcile the cosmos to himself through Christ. So the church is the avant-garde of both the kingdom of God and the new creation of the age to come.

The Church Is Comprised of the People of the New Covenant

Second Corinthians 6:16 applies the covenant formula to the church; compare 1 Corinthians 11:23–26. Indeed, as noted above, *qahal*/ἐκκλησια are rooted in God's covenant, as spelled out in Deuteronomy.

The Church Is the Eschatological Temple of God

Both the Old Testament and Judaism anticipated the rebuilding of the temple in the future kingdom of God (Ezek. 40–48; Hag. 2:1–9; *1 Enoch* 90:29; 91:3; *Jub.* 1:17, 29; etc.). Jesus hinted that he was going to build such a structure (Matt. 16:18; Mark 14:58; John 2:19–22). Pentecost witnessed to the beginning of the fulfillment of that dream in that when the Spirit inhabited the church, the eschatological temple was formed (Acts 2:16–36). Paul especially perceived that the presence of the Spirit in the Christian community constituted the new temple of God (see 1 Cor. 3:16–17; 2 Cor. 6:14–7:1; Eph. 2:19–22; cf. also Gal. 4:21–31; 1 Peter 2:4–10). However, that the eschatological temple is not yet complete is evident in the preceding passages, especially in their emphasis on the need for the church to grow toward maturity in Christ, which will only be fully accomplished at the parousia. In the meantime, Christians, as priests of God, are to perform their sacrificial service to the glory of God (Rom. 12:1–2; cf. Heb. 13:15; 1 Peter 2:4–10).

The Church Is the Eschatological Flock of God and Her Elders Are Their Shepherds

New Testament scholars have noted for some time now the connection between Mark 14:27 ("I will strike the shepherd, and the sheep will be scattered") and Zechariah 13:7–14:5—a prophecy of the tribulations that are to precede the Day of the Lord. Thus Mark portrays Jesus as the true shepherd of Israel whose death is stamped by the messianic woes. First Peter 5:2–4 applies that imagery to the church—the flock of God that Peter and other elders are to shepherd in the last days of the great tribulation. Paul does the same in Acts 20:25–30. Notice the connections between the kingdom of God, the elders, and their opposition to false teachings and trials (according to Acts 14:22 these trials are the messianic woes):

> Now I know that none of you among whom I have gone about preaching the kingdom of God will ever see me again. Therefore, I declare to you today that I an innocent of the blood of all men. For I have not hesitated to proclaim to you the whole will of God. Keep watch over yourselves and all the flock of which the Holy Spirit has made you overseers. Be shepherds of the church of God, which he bought with his own blood. I know that after I leave, savage wolves will come in among you and will not spare the flock. Even from your own number men will arise and distort the truth in order to draw away disciples after them.

The point we wish to make from this is that Paul's instructions to elders in the churches he wrote to are informed by the theme that the eschatological flock of God—the church—needed the guidance of its elders in order to navigate through the false doctrine and persecutions that were unleashed upon them (1 Tim. 3:5, 15; 5:16–17; etc.). It is interesting in this regard to observe that the Dead Sea Scroll community, which considered itself to be the new covenant community of the last days, also elected elders to preserve true doctrine and guide believers through the tribulation period (see, for example, CD 13:9–19).

The Church and the Messianic Woes
Continuing the previous point, Acts 14:22 records Paul as saying that the people of God must endure the tribulation of the last days—a conviction that is pervasive in the apostle's writings, as we have repeatedly mentioned in earlier chapters of this work.

Three Other Issues
There are three other issues that have to do with the church and eschatology in Paul's letters. These topics are not pervasive in Paul's correspondences but they are nonetheless important. We simply state those concerns here and mention their eschatological associations. First, the sacraments or ordinances of the church—baptism and the Lord's Supper—are important to Paul's understanding in that the

former symbolizes entrance into the kingdom of God/age to come based on the believer's union with Christ's death and resurrection (Rom. 6:1–14) and the second both commemorates Jesus' death and the institution of the new covenant as well as anticipates his return (1 Cor. 11:23–26). Second, Paul never states it, but it does seem that he differentiates the church from the kingdom of God. This can be deducted from Paul's statements acknowledging that Christians and churches sin, something he would never say of the kingdom of God. Perhaps the better way to put the matter would be to say that the church is the beachhead, the invasion point in this evil age for the advancement of the kingdom of God and the age to come. Third, the overlapping of the two ages seems to account for Paul's understanding of the relationship between the church and the state. Thus the Christian is a citizen of the kingdom of God because the age to come has dawned in his or her heart, but they still live in this age of accountability to government (see Rom. 13:1–7). Of course, Paul's own apostolic afflictions showed that when the two clashed—church and state—he chose to suffer for righteousness's sake even if it meant being imprisoned and beheaded for the sake of the gospel.

So we see that the church for Paul is thoroughly eschatological in nature.

ESCHATOLOGY

It is only fitting that we bring this overview of Paul's thought to a close by examining the doctrine of Pauline eschatology, especially in light of apocalyptic Jewish expectation that certain signs of the times would occur before the advent of the Messiah. These signs signaled the transition between this age and the age to come. But for Paul and the other New Testament authors the life, death, and resurrection of Jesus the Christ initiated the age to come within history. There the messianic woes/great tribulation/signs of the times (all the same) would intensify and culminate in the parousia. Thus, believers live in between the times. The Old Testament and Second Temple Judaism associated the coming age to come with a number of events: the rise of the antichrist, the messianic woes, wide-scale apostasy of the people of God, the advent of the kingdom of Messiah and God, the resurrection of the body of the righteous by the Spirit, the judgment of the righteous and the wicked, the new creation, a new temple, Israel's restoration and the conversion of the Gentiles. We will now summarize how Paul viewed each of these events through the lens of the overlapping of the two ages.

Chapter 12

The Rise of the Antichrist

Judaism and early Christianity expected that at the end of time all evil and rebellion against God would combine together in the antichrist. According to 2 Thessalonians 2:3–6, 8–12, while that person has not yet appeared on the human scene, the spirit of lawlessness that will drive that individual is already at work in the world (cf. Matt. 24:23–24/Mark 13:21–22; 1 John 4:3).

The Messianic Woes

The messianic woes or the great tribulation are the signs of the times that will be unleashed on the people of God before the advent of the Messiah. Paul draws often on this topic, claiming that Christians continue to experience such affliction in union with Christ's suffering, death, and resurrection (Rom. 5:1–11; 1 Cor. 15: 2 Cor. 4:7–5:21; 12:1–10; Gal. 3:26–29; 4:26; 6:17; Eph. 1:15–23; 3:13; 2 Thess. 2:1–12; 1 Tim. 2:1–15; 2 Tim. 2:10–12). Three facts emerge from these passages. First, each one juxtaposes the themes of suffering and glory. Second, such a twofold combination stems from Paul's belief that the two ages overlap for the Christian. Thus, on the one hand, because believers share an intimate union with the cross of Christ, the suffering and death he experienced now characterize their suffering. This is the not-yet side of Paul's eschatology. On the other hand, because believers also share an intimate union with the resurrection of Christ, the heavenly glory he now possesses belongs to them as well. This is the "already" side of Paul's eschatology. Yet that glory is invisible, being perceptible only to the eye of faith (see Rom. 8:24–25; 1 Cor. 2:8–16; 2 Cor. 4:17–18). Only at the parousia will that glory be publicly manifested (cf. Phil. 3:20–21; Col. 3:1–4). Third, even though Paul expects that all Christians should expect to suffer the messianic woes he does hope that he can absorb as much of that affliction as possible so that he can spare the church some measure of tribulation (Col. 1:24; Eph. 3:13; etc.).[15]

Apostasy

Jewish and Christian apocalypticism maintained that the end of time would witness a large scale falling away from the faith by the people of God because

---

15 See my *The Glory of Adam and the Afflictions of the Righteous: Pauline Suffering in Context* for documentation of this overall point.

of persecution of their faith (*Jub.* 23:14–23; *4 Ezra* 5:1–13; *1 Enoch* 91:3–10; 93:8–10; Dead Sea Scrolls [1Qp Hab. 2:1]; Matt. 24:12/Mark 13:5, 22a/Luke 21:6; Rev. 2–3; 6–19). Paul affirmed this conviction in 1 Thessalonians 2:14–17; 2 Thessalonians 2:3–12; Galatians 1:6–19; 1 Timothy 4:1–5; 2 Timothy 3:1–5 with regard to non-Christian Jews who killed Jesus and persecuted Christians, the followers of the man of lawlessness (the Roman emperor?), the Judaizers, and the false teachers in Ephesus, respectively.

Kingdom of Messiah and God

Paul's usage of the terms "kingdom of Messiah" and "kingdom of God" also reflect his belief that Christians live in the overlapping of the two ages. That is to say, the messianic kingdom was established at Jesus' resurrection but which anticipates the forthcoming kingdom of God. A glance at the occurrences of those two terms confirms our claim.

The term "kingdom of God" and/or "kingdom of Christ" occurs twelve times in Paul's writings. These are listed below:

TEXT	KINGDOM DESCRIPTION	VERB TENSE
Rom. 14:17	Kingdom of God	Present tense
1 Cor. 4:20	Kingdom of God	Present tense
1 Cor. 6:9–10	Kingdom of God (twice)	Future tense
1 Cor. 15:24	Kingdom of Christ/God	Present/ future tenses
1 Cor. 15:50	Kingdom of God	Future tense
Gal. 5:21	Kingdom of God	Future tense
Eph. 5:5	Kingdom of Christ/God	Future tense
Col. 1:13	Kingdom of Christ	Present tense
Col. 4:11	Kingdom of God	Present tense
1 Thess. 2:12	Kingdom of God	Future tense
2 Thess. 1:5	Kingdom of God	Future tense

Three observations emerge from this chart: (1) The kingdom of Christ/God is both present and future, already here and not yet complete. (2) Christ and God are, in at least two instances, interchanged, suggesting equality of status between them (cf. Eph. 5:5; Rev. 11:15; 12:10). (3) 1 Corinthians 15:24 gives the most precise description of the exact relationship between the kingdoms of Christ and God—the interim messianic kingdom begun at the resurrection of Christ will one day give way to the eternal kingdom of God. Such a temporary kingdom is attested to in apocalyptic Judaism and may be behind Revelation 20:1–6. For Paul, then, the order of history would be as follows:

This Age ⊠	Temporary Messianic Kingdom ⊠	The Age to Come (Kingdom of God)

Christians therefore live in between the two ages, in the Messianic kingdom.

Resurrection of the Body by the Spirit

Judaism, as noted early on in this study, assigned the resurrection of the body and the coming of the Spirit to the end of time (Ezek. 37; Dan. 12:1–3; *1 Enoch* 62:15; *2 Enoch* 22:8; *4 Ezra* 2:39, 45). According to Paul, those realities are both present and future. A believer's present spiritual resurrection will culminate in a future physical resurrection, both based on the resurrection of Jesus Messiah (Rom. 8:9–11; 1 Cor. 15; Eph. 1–2).

Judgment of the Righteous and the Wicked

The overlapping of the two ages informs Paul's teaching on the justification of the saved and the divine wrath on the lost. Thus the saved have already been declared righteous in Christ and found to be not guilty (Rom. 3:21–26; 5:1; 8:1, 33–34; 2 Cor. 5:21; 1 Thess. 1:10; 5:9). Yet they still must appear before the judgment seat of Christ/God to have their works evaluated for rewards or lack thereof (Rom. 14:10; 1 Cor. 3:12–15; 2 Cor. 5:10; Gal. 5:5; cf. Rom. 2:7, 10). This combination of already/not yet also impacts the lost, in that they will appear one day before God as recipients of divine wrath (Rom. 2:5, 8, 19; 9:22), which has already begun to impinge upon their lives because they have not accepted Christ (Eph. 2:3).

New Creation

The aspiration for a new creation runs deep in Judaism (Isa. 11:6–8; 65:17, 22; Ezek. 34:25–27; *Jub.* 1:29; *1 Enoch* 91:16; *4 Ezra* 6:1–6; cf. 2 Pet. 3:10–13; cf. Rev. 21–22 with Gen. 1–3). For Paul, the new creation has already broken into this present age through Christ (2 Cor. 5:17), but its consummation awaits the parousia (Rom. 8:19–23; cf. Eph. 1:10; Phil. 2:9–11; Col. 1:20).

New Temple

We noted above that Jewish apocalyptic circles longed for the Messiah to come and build a new temple. Paul claims that both the Christian and the church comprise the eschatological temple (1 Cor. 3:16; 6:19–20; 2 Cor. 6:14–7:1; Eph. 2:11–22), but that temple still needs to grow until the parousia (Eph. 2:21; cf. 2 Cor. 5:1–2).

The Restoration of Israel and the Conversion of the Gentiles

As we have seen throughout this work, another event associated with the signs of the times in Judaism was the re-gathering or restoration of Israel to final salvation (Isa. 51:5; 60:11; Dan. 7:27; Zech. 8:23). For Paul, the current Jewish Christian remnant indicates that the restoration of Israel has already begun (Rom. 11:1–6) but the restoration of the nation awaits Jesus' return (Rom. 11:25–27). Moreover, the conversion of the nations that the Old Testament predicted has already begun in Christ, as we have mentioned numerous times in this study.

CONCLUSION TO THE THEOLOGY OF PAUL

We conclude this section of our work by encapsulating in seven statements how apocalypticism influenced Paul's major categories of theology: (1) Regarding theology proper, Paul viewed God through an apocalyptic lens: This age is evil and in these last days is getting worse; the signs of the times are upon Christians and Christ will return at any moment; as a matter of fact, the only hope the church has is the parousia. This is the unfolding of the plan of God. (2) Concerning Paul's Christology, Jesus' death and resurrection inaugurated the age to come; Jesus' death and resurrection is being "re-presented" through Paul; and those who believe Paul's message are united to Christ's death and resurrection. Consequently, the Christian lives in the intersection of the two ages— deliverance now but not yet. (3) Paul's pneumatology is straightforward: The presence of the Holy Spirit in the believer and in the church is a key sign that the age to come has dawned; and the Spirit is received by faith in Christ alone, not by the works of the Torah. In point of fact, the Law stirs up the flesh. Only the Spirit can subdue the old nature with the obedience of the heart that comes from participating in the new covenant. (4) Regarding Paul's anthropology, the two Adams represent the two ages: the first Adam is the head of this age and the old humanity while Christ the last Adam is the head of the age to come and the new humanity. (5) Paul's soteriology unfolds in three tenses, which is governed by the overlapping of the two ages. The Christian was justified before God at the moment of faith and now participates in the age to come. But the believer continues to live in this present age, which calls for daily sanctification. When Christ returns the believer will experience the full scope of salvation on resurrection day. (6) Paul's ecclesiology is simple—the church is the eschatological people of God in Christ. Yet, no one metaphor is sufficient to capture the full-orbed picture of the church, for it ranges from the body of Christ to the bride of Christ to the restored Israel. Still, the multi-images of the church are rooted in eschatology. (7) Paul's eschatology attests to the overlapping of the ages, in that the signs of the end times began with the first coming of Christ but they will not be complete until his return. The Christian therefore must endure the great tribulation until the consummation.

Conclusion

We conclude this work on Paul, apostle of the end times, by attempting to answer the question: Why the opposing reactions of the various religious perspectives we have identified that were contemporaries with Paul? I think there are two answers to that question: one spiritual, the other political. We have already spelled out the first answer during the course of this study—Paul's apocalyptic gospel of the cross did not sit well with the other religious constructs examined in this work. Jews were scandalized by a crucified messiah; Greeks abhorred the idea that God could take on flesh, and die; Romans ridiculed the notion of an executed king.

But when we turn to the political answer of why Paul's gospel was at odds with the other dominant religious groups of the day, we need to reconfigure the situation by acknowledging that those various eschatological theories were also reactions to Roman realized eschatology. Rome had ruled the world since 63 BC but had undergone civil wars and chaos since. However, with the advent of Augustus, the Roman Empire regained its footing; indeed, Augustus brought a new day to Rome. And the benefits of his reign were portrayed as nothing less than realized eschatology—heaven on earth, at least for Romans.

But it was a different matter for the other religions in town, and this dynamic helps to explain why certain apocalyptic scenarios were embraced. Thus Hellenistic religion, though amalgamated into the Roman pantheon of gods including Caesar, still was a conquered people group. Greeks no longer ruled the day, and their religion showed it. Thus it was that utopia could only be obtained for these people through mystic union with the deity. Only in the spirit could eschatology be realized, certainly not on earth while mighty Rome ruled it.

The Jews fared no better in their relationship with Rome. Oh, they may have been exempt from worshipping Caesar, but the kingdom of God Judaism longed for had not yet arrived on earth. The Jews' repeated skirmishes with Roman rule convinced them of that. So for non-Christian Jews, the hope of the imminent kingdom of God to be brought by the messiah lay consistently in the future. For the non-*merkabah* Judaizers, Jesus was indeed the hoped-for messiah, whose Spirit empowered the people of God to obey the Torah. This would bring the divine kingdom to earth—to Jerusalem, no less. Nevertheless, the visible, earthly arrival of that kingdom was forthcoming, as evidenced by the grim reality that Rome still ruled over Israel. And the *merkabizers'* mystical union with God in Christ in heaven would have to suffice until Jesus returned to put the world to rights, especially Rome. These Jewish responses, though different from each other, tragically shared the same fate of defeat and destruction at the hands of Rome in the Jewish revolt of AD 66–73.

On the surface, Paul and his inaugurated apocalyptic gospel met with the same response as his Jewish kinsmen received. After all, Paul too was executed by Rome, probably because his gospel was branded as insurrectionist, like his master's. Yet Paul's gospel survived his death, eventually defeating Rome itself without raising a sword, becoming the standard for defining Christianity. Why? Because Paul's apocalyptic construct of Christianity involved removing geographical and ethnic barriers to the gospel. Not Jerusalem, but the world, is God's kingdom, and not just Jews but all people groups are its recipients.

This "democratization" of the gospel could not be stopped in Paul's day, or beyond. Its message that the kingdom of God dawned in the person of Jesus Christ and is entered into by faith not by works is a message that appeals to many, and its hope for the full and final manifestation of that kingdom on earth at the parousia has sustained millions through the trials and tribulations of this age. Paul's eschatological dynamic of the already/not yet helps the church maintain a balanced perspective, as it continues to live between the two ages.